WORKING FOR THE RAILROAD

WALTER LICHT

WORKING FOR THE
RAILROAD

≡

The Organization of
Work in the Nineteenth
Century

PRINCETON UNIVERSITY PRESS
PRINCETON, NEW JERSEY

Copyright © 1983 by Princeton University Press
Published by Princeton University Press, 41 William Street, Princeton, New Jersey
In the United Kingdom: Princeton University Press, Guildford, Surrey

All Rights Reserved

Library of Congress Cataloging in Publication Data will be found on the last
printed page of this book

ISBN 0-691-04700-6

Publication of this book has been aided by a grant from The Andrew
W. Mellon Foundation

This book has been composed in Linotron Sabon

Clothbound editions of Princeton University Press books are printed on
acid-free paper, and binding materials are chosen for strength and durability.
Paperbacks, although satisfactory for personal collections, are not usually
suitable for library rebinding.

Printed in the United States of America by Princeton University Press,
Princeton, New Jersey

*Dedicated to My Mother
and the Memory of My Father*

CONTENTS

≡

LIST OF TABLES

≡

LIST OF ILLUSTRATIONS

≡

PREFACE

≡

A CONFESSION at the outset. I am not a railroad buff. My father never drove a locomotive; my uncle was not a conductor. I rarely played with the model trains my parents obligingly provided. To this very day, I have yet to take a long-distance train trip. Born and bred a big-city kid, I grew up with subways and commuter lines; they represent the extent of my rail transport experience. I thus came to this study of the working and personal lives of the first two generations of American railwaymen without any inherent interest or expertise in American railroads or American railwaymen.

Three distinct but converging paths led me here. First, I had a long-standing interest in labor history and affairs and a more recently acquired concern for the history and sociology of work. The latter evolved through graduate study in sociology and history, the influence of a new generation of labor historians, exposure to a growing popular literature and public dialogue concerned with the quality of the working life, and through the impact of my own work experiences.

A reading of a remarkable but rarely read or cited social history provided the second impetus: Peter Kingsford's *Victorian Railwaymen: The Emergence and Growth of Railroad Labour, 1830–1870*. In his study of pioneer British railway workers, Kingsford raised and answered questions about changes in various aspects of the job experience in a way that intrigued me. His book encouraged a search for comparable studies of American railroad laborers, and the discovery of an almost complete vacuum of scholarship first put the idea into my mind. Readers familiar with Kingsford's work will undoubtedly recognize my debt; his book and other European monographs on the subject have also allowed me to draw a variety of cross-national comparisons throughout this study.

The third, and most important, stimulus came from my reading of works on American railroads by business historians such as Thomas Cochran and Alfred Chandler. In a number of studies, Cochran and Chandler have highlighted the trailblazing role that American railroads played in introducing modern forms of corporate ownership and bureaucratic principles and techniques of management. Farsighted railway executives, as both historians have shown, shaped and structured mammoth business enterprises over a century ago that became models for the giant firms that are a natural and easily taken-for-granted part of the economic landscape of our own day. Neither Cochran nor Chandler, however, devoted much attention to the question of what it must have been like for pre- and early industrial workers to enter and be employed in these new kinds of work institutions.

Three paths converged into one, and this intellectual odyssey brought me to a project: to examine the work experiences of the first two generations of American railwaymen as a case study of the first American workers in large-scale, corporately owned, bureaucratically managed work organizations. Following Kingsford's lead, I decided to focus on the intricate informal and formal arrangements by which men were hired, trained, disciplined, paid, promoted, fired, and retired, and on changes in the intrinsic and extrinsic meaning, rewards, and perils of their labor.

In its initial conception, the topic had great appeal. Work was a subject either ignored by historians or dealt with abstractly, schematically, or indirectly. Most studies in the field, especially those inspired by Max Weber's seminal essay on the Protestant work ethic and the development of capitalism, have been concerned more with the idea than the reality of work, more with evolving attitudes and intellectual conceptions than with basic actualities. Business historians, in documenting shifts in the organization and management of enterprises, have been more concrete and have pointed to transformations in the structure of work. However, in concentrating on decision making from the top down and on formal relations and agreements, they have rarely delved beneath the level of organizational charts and managerial pronouncements to study work in its daily manifestations. Social historians likewise have used occupational titles to trace patterns of intra- and intergenerational social mobility, yet they have not for the most part inquired into the nature and content of the work behind the titles. A history of occupations is necessary before meaningful judgments on status distinctions and mobility can be drawn. Finally, even labor historians, in emphasizing strikes, workingmen's culture and politics, and the growth of the trade union movement, have treated the realities of work as a matter of tangential interest. Working conditions and wages are mentioned, to be sure, but usually in passing and often only in terms of their role in precipitating worker actions. Historians, in general, have made few efforts to penetrate beyond publicized facts and figures and objective situations to study personal aspects of work. Informal relations among peers and between workingmen and their supervisors, the intangible rewards and satisfactions of workmanship, conscious and often accepted disregard for rules and authority, promotions, job security, sabotage, thefts, boredom, fatigue, unauthorized efforts to humanize working conditions and create areas of autonomy—these are a few of the subjects that seldom find their way into historical studies. An examination of railroad work and railwaymen offered an opportunity to right the balance.

The study of the first generations of American railroad workers also afforded a chance to deal with certain aspects of industrialization that have not traditionally been stressed. The industrial revolution was a complex process, the causes and effects of which can easily be obscured by generalizations. The term itself is highly misleading, implying radical transformation when in fact industrial expansion was gradual and developmental. Countless case studies have revealed that the course of industrialization in the Western world was uneven and irregular, occurring with varying intensity in different countries, regions within countries, and trades and sectors of the economy.

There are other points where generalizations lead to confusion.

The causes, preconditions, and consequences of industrial development are still matters of considerable debate. The tendency to correlate industrialization with the wholesale changeover to the factory system overlooks the role that industrial growth played in creating new forms of service employment, stimulating agricultural production, and spawning small and medium-size work places as well as factories. Finally, and most important for this study, the process of industrialization is obscured profoundly by associating change solely with the introduction of machinery and inanimate sources of energy. Mechanization was important, but it was only one factor in a whole complex of change. The spread of the market economy, the rising demand for cheap standardized goods and services, and the extension of capitalist relations of production and the wage labor system were as critical in producing changes in work as the adoption of machinery and were historically antecedent incentives to mechanical innovation. In many trades—like textiles and shoemaking—radical transformations in work structures and relationships were effected decades before machines were even introduced.

The railroad industry provides a focus on changes in the organization of work, an aspect of industrialization which has received less emphasis than mechanization. The typical study on work and the industrial revolution asks: What was it like for laboring people, accustomed to working with their own hands at their own pace and with their own tools, to become appendages of capital-owned machinery? This study will measure the impact of new forms of work organization and ask a different question: What was it like for working people, who had labored in small, owner-managed, functionally specific units where the pace of work was discretionary and relations with superiors informal, customary, and face-to-face, to enter into employment in large, complex, bureaucratically managed corporate enterprises?

Finally, the topic had great appeal because its limits were easily and well-defined. For instance, the study would not deal with the construction crews who built the railroads, but rather focus on the men who ran them—the engineers, firemen, brakemen, conductors, clerks, agents, station, yard and track laborers, and the unskilled and skilled mechanics in the shops. Railroad companies rarely employed construction workers directly. Since they were hired, managed, and paid by local, small-scale builders who contracted with the companies to build portions of the line, construction laborers technically do not belong in a study of employees of large-scale organizations. For the same reasons, Pullman porters are excluded as well. Both deserve full-length treatment in their own right.

The study also had an easily conceived temporal and spatial focus. The time period would be 1830 to 1877, the preunion period of railroad development. The study would end with the railroad strikes of 1877, when most discussions of railroad labor begin. This would permit concentration on the first two generations of railroad workers, make the issue of strikes and unions a lesser concern, and fill in a gap about the early period for which little scholarship on railroad employees exists. The specific time frame would also limit by necessity the geographical range of the study to the eastern third of the country. While rail lines were penetrating the West by 1877, the bulk of traffic and operations was still east of the Mississippi.

The topic as conceived further provided a means to deal with railway shopmen, who presented a number of methodological and conceptual problems. Although they were employed directly by railroad companies, the nature of their work was so different from other railroad employees, that they, too, warrant separate treatment (or consideration at least within studies of the machine industry). Shop workers also tended to live in exclusive railroad shop communities. To study them accurately required a community study approach. Since this was an inquiry into work, an industry-wide purview was in order, one grounded in no single location. Shop workers would be dealt with, but not in great detail.

The fruits of my initial reflections and subsequent research appear in the following pages. Three points before embarking. First, I have tried to create a complete portrait of the work experiences of America's first operating railwaymen, as well as to sketch in many details about their personal lives. At every stage, an attempt has also been made to probe beneath the surface to investigate day-in and day-out realities of work. There were obvious limits to this endeavor. Unlike the contemporary sociologist or student of industrial relations, I could not study informal relations and arrangements first-hand, nor could I interview workers to ferret out subjective feelings. What was available were fragments of information gathered from railroad corporation papers, government reports, trade journals, union newspapers, and published reminiscences. Care has been taken to note when the surviving evidence warrants either partial or general conclusions.

Second, this study began as an investigation of anonymous Americans in faceless institutions. After just a few months of research, I had assembled sufficient information to challenge a number of my initial conceptions and assumptions. A new understanding gradually emerged, and that understanding forms an overarching argument that unifies the various parts of this study. Pioneer railway workers entered work organizations bureaucratically shaped and structured by innovative businessmen. Yet in the early period, the work experience for the average railwayman remained a function of his personal relations with local foremen and supervisors, men who ruled in arbitrary and discretionary ways. After 1877, American railway workers organized to demand stricter bureaucratic standards and procedures to control as much of the work experience as possible. Pioneer railway executives imposed bureaucratic structures from on high, but bureaucratization was a process resulting in large measure from pressure from below.

Third, and finally, the subtitle of this study best describes what is to follow. This is an investigation into the organization of work. Topics of interest to traditional labor historians—unionization and strikes—are treated, but not as a primary focus. Matters of concern to so-called "new" labor historians—working-class consciousness and culture—are examined similarly but in an ancillary fashion. The book has been written with a wide audience in mind, from labor economists to general readers. And if there are any railroad buffs in that audience who derive some knowledge and pleasure from the pages that follow, then the work of this historian and fledgling railroad buff is done.

I HAVE INCURRED a number of debts in preparing this study. I would first like to thank librarians at the following archives for their assistance: The Newberry Library, Chicago, Illinois; Baker Library, Harvard University; Maryland Historical Society, Baltimore, Maryland; The American Antiquarian Society, Worcester, Massachusetts; The Eleutherian Mills Historical Library, Wilmington, Delaware; Syracuse University Library; Bowdoin College Library; Cornell University Library; The Historical Society of Pennsylvania, Philadelphia, Pennsylvania; The Historical Society of Delaware, Wilmington, Delaware; The New York Public Library; University of Vermont Library, Burlington, Vermont; The Historical Society of Wisconsin, Madison, Wisconsin; and the Library of the Bureau of Railway Economics, Washington, D.C.

Special research and computer funds were granted by Princeton University, The Newberry Library, The Shelby Cullom Davis Center, and the University of Pennsylvania, and I am appreciative of the support of these institutions.

I also received valuable advice at the outset of my research from Thomas Cochran, Alfred Chandler, Jr., and Paul Black, and they have followed and encouraged my progress. The manuscript was read at various stages by the following scholars, and I am grateful for their comments and suggestions: James Obelkevich, James McPherson, James Banner, Gerald Grob, Thomas Dublin, Charles Rosenberg, David Hogan, and James Ducker. I would also like to thank Theodore Hershberg, director of the Philadelphia Social History Project, for allowing me access to the Project's vast historical data bank; my editors at Princeton University Press, Gail Filion and Alice Calaprice, for their support and assistance; and Ronald Shumate of the Association of American Railroads for facilitating the collection of photographs and illustrations.

My greatest debt is owed to Professor Arthur Link of Princeton University, who has given generously of his time, advice, and expertise to me and this book. Under his tutelage I began to learn the art of historical research and writing. I am privileged to have been an apprentice to this master craftsman.

Finally, to my wife Lois, who through more better than worse, listened, edited, badgered, and humored—to her go incalculable thanks. The humanity that lies in the following scholarly pages is greatly attributable to the sensibility and sensitivity that she demands and encourages.

Philadelphia, Pennsylvania   WALTER LICHT
June 1982

WORKING FOR THE RAILROAD

1

THE VIEW FROM THE TOP

≡

No written history of nineteenth-century America is complete without a due account of railroads. Cliometricians may attempt to persuade with counterfactual arguments and extended calculations that the railroads' contribution to economic growth was less than indispensable; that, in effect, if the railroads had not been built, the graph of American economic progress would have assumed a shape similar to its realized pattern.[1] While the iconoclastic contentions and methods of the "new" economic historians certainly dazzle the mind, no amount of inverted logic, fanciful model building, or simultaneous equations can obliterate the reality that the railroads *were* built and that they had in fact an enormous economic, social, and political impact on American history.

The railroads significantly lowered transportation costs, insured regular, year-round, relatively safe carriage of goods and passengers, quickly and efficiently extended the scope of the market economy, linked agriculture and industry in an interdependent network, and were important consumers of basic products like iron, steel, coal, lumber, machinery, and machine

[1] The railroads' contribution to American economic development during the nineteenth century remains a significant issue of debate among economic historians. The traditional view holds that the railroads were prime movers in this country's drive toward sustained economic growth. See Leland Jenks, "Railroads as an Economic Force in American Development," *Journal of Economic History* 4: 1–20 and Walt Whitman Rostow, *The Stages of Economic Growth*. Robert Fogel has challenged this view in *Railroads and American Economic Growth*. For a balanced assessment see Albert Fishlow, *American Railroads and the Transformation of the Ante-Bellum Economy*.

tools. The railroads also stimulated and benefited from western urban and frontier settlement and were agents of immigration, population dispersion, and real estate development. They pioneered in the introduction of corporate forms of ownership and bureaucratic principles of management, and were instrumental in the creation of new techniques and institutions for capital formation.

Less directly, the railroads served to create and heighten political tensions in the late nineteenth century, forcing government-business relations and the problem of concentrated political and economic power into the limelight. The railroads similarly provided the setting for several crucial incidents of nineteenth-century labor violence. At the same time, they comprised the first enterprises in America to undergo full-scale unionization and to develop institutionalized means for arbitrating employee-management disputes. As vivid examples of the power of American know-how and energy, the railroads also had important symbolic value, serving to engender optimism and belief in the potentialities of life in the young republic. Finally, in supplying the inspiration for numerous tales of mighty machines, daring enginemen, and ruthless promoters, the railroads contributed much that is rich in American folklore and song.

It is not the intention of this study, however, to add or subtract to lingering debates over the railroads' contribution to American history. The railroads' impact on the nation's economic, political, and cultural development will be taken for granted. What is of concern is to treat the railroads in a different way from those mentioned above—as places of work. The railroads will appear here not as agents of economic growth or political controversy, but rather as organizations employing and managing labor, organizations which mid-nineteenth-century American laboring people entered to earn their daily keep and in which they subsequently had work experiences.

The railroads did not provide a new kind of employment. For centuries, laborers had been occupied both in the overland and water transport of goods and people. It has been estimated that by 1830, when rail transport was in its infancy, 70,000 American workers, or approximately 2 percent of the labor force, were engaged in the carrying trades.[2] While the numbers seem small, concentrations of transport workers did exist. In the burgeoning commercial cities of the East, hauling, carting, and general dock work were major sources of employment for the preindustrial urban laboring classes.[3] On the high seas, a cadre of men formed an active merchant marine. Along the length and breadth of the nation's canals and turnpikes lived men who either worked full time or combined agricultural pursuits with work as boatmen, lightermen, loaders, and wagon and stagecoach drivers and conductors.

The railroads offered a new type of work experience. The rail companies that had emerged in America by mid-nineteenth century were vastly different kinds of business enterprises and employers than had ever existed. In terms purely of size—of initial capitalization, operating expenses, revenues, and number of laborers engaged—the railroads were comparable to no other concerns. In terms, too, of the complexity, diversity, and geographical range of operations, the railroads were rivaled perhaps only by earlier military organizations and campaigns. Finally, in the way in which work was structured and managed, the railroads introduced principles and techniques which were unique for their day. For men who had worked on farms, in homes, small workshops, or even textile mills, to enter into hire in a railroad company was to encounter an entirely new kind of work situation.

ON FEBRUARY 12, 1827, twenty-five prominent citizens of the city of Baltimore gathered at the home of George Brown, a banker and member of a famous family of Baltimore merchants, to discuss the city's future commercial fortunes. The group included men whose very success in business affairs had enabled Baltimore to emerge as a leading shipping, trading, financial, and food-processing center for commerce passing to and from the trans-Appalachian West. However, the planning and completion of internal transportation improvement projects in Pennsylvania

[2] Stanley Lebergott, *Manpower in Economic Growth*, p. 510.
[3] David Montgomery, "The Working Class of Pre-Industrial American Cities, 1780–1830," *Labor History*, 9: 14-15; George Rogers Taylor, *The Transportation Revolution, 1815–1860*, chaps. 2–4, 6–8.

and New York and the potential diversion of trade to Philadelphia and New York City had begun seriously to jeopardize Baltimore's position and prosperity. Loss of western markets accordingly increased as a matter of concern and debate within the city during the 1820s. Among the men who assembled at George Brown's home, a number had closely followed experiments in England with steam locomotives and rail transport, and had become convinced of the advisability and necessity of building a railroad connecting Baltimore with points along the Ohio River.

During the course of their meeting, the group decided to appoint a committee to investigate various transportation alternatives. A week later they reconvened to hear a report strongly advocating the construction of a railroad linking Baltimore with the West. The report received unanimous approval, and the meeting adjourned with the group resolving to apply to the state legislature of Maryland for a charter of incorporation. Just nine days later, on February 28, 1827, an act establishing the Baltimore & Ohio Railroad Company passed the legislature. The state's charter provided for a capital stock of $3 million, to consist of thirty thousand $100 shares. Ten thousand shares were reserved for subscription by the state of Maryland, five thousand for the city of Baltimore. Once $1 million were raised through private stock purchases, the company could organize officially with an elected board of directors and a president. The state charter further stipulated that construction had to be completed within ten years, that the legislature reserved the right to fix passenger and freight rates, and that the line would be exempt from state taxation.

Investors responded to the offering of company stock with enthusiasm. By April 23, 1827, sufficient funds had been raised to allow for the formal organization of the B. & O. Elected company officials then authorized the surveying of the line and the purchase of property. Planning proceeded apace and one year later, on Independence Day, 1828, amidst citywide parades and speeches, ground was broken in Baltimore to begin construction of the nation's first railroad. The initial stretch of line—13¾ miles of roadbed and track reaching from Baltimore to Ellicott's Mills, Maryland—took two years to build. On May 22, 1830, the Baltimore & Ohio Railroad commenced operations with a team of horses drawing a train of passenger carriages and freight wagons along the track. Steam locomotive power did not come into regular service until two years later; the dream of building a railroad linking Baltimore and the Ohio River did not become a reality until the 1850s.[4]

The men who had assembled in George Brown's home in February of 1827 underestimated the dimensions of the task they initiated and the project's ultimate returns. The committee appointed to draft a report on the feasibility of building a railroad calculated that 290 miles of track had to be constructed to reach the Ohio River; the length of the road when actually completed to the river was 379 miles. Similarly, they figured the costs of construction at $5 million. By the time the line reached the Ohio, close to $16 million had been spent. Finally, the architects of the road estimated revenues per annum at $750,000. In 1853, the board of directors of the B. & O. proudly reported that the company had earned more than $2 million during the fiscal year.[5] With concern for their city's and their own financial futures, twenty-five prominent citizens of Baltimore thus launched a venture which would become one of the nation's major rail trunk lines and one of the country's largest and most important corporate enterprises.

Similar scenes, occurrences, facts, and figures can be cited for other towns and cities in the United States during the second and third quarters of the nineteenth century when railroad fever gripped the nation.[6] Events unfolded in a fairly regular pattern. In community after community, local newspaper editorialists, politicians, bankers, merchants, manufacturers, and farmers first

[4] Details on the formation of the Baltimore & Ohio Railroad are provided in Edward Hungerford, *The Story of the Baltimore and Ohio Railroad, 1827–1927*; Milton Reizenstein, *The Economic History of the Baltimore and Ohio Railroad, 1827–1853*; Julius Rubin, "Canal or Railroad? Imitation and Innovation in the Response to the Erie Canal in Philadelphia, Baltimore, and Boston," *Transactions of the American Philosophical Society* 51: 69–72.

[5] Reizenstein, *Economic History*, p. 86.

[6] On the circumstances surrounding the formation of America's first railroads see Taylor, *Transportation Revolution*, chap. 5; Rubin, "Canal or Railroad," pp. 5–103; John Stover, *American Railroads*; Stephen Salsbury, *The State, the Investor and the Railroad*.

expressed concern for the loss of markets, the need to seize new commercial oppportunities, and the importance of transportation linkages. Discussions took place in public forums, newspaper columns, private offices and homes, as well as in municipal, state, and eventually federal legislative bodies. Debate centered not only on the necessity of internal transportation improvements, but also on the respective merits of natural waterway, turnpike, canal, and railroad systems.

Support for internal transportation projects issued from various quarters and with a mixture of motives. Some promoters of improvements acted out of civic pride or from ideological commitments to economic expansion, while others clearly became involved to protect or boost their own business interests. Similarly, the stocks and bonds of transportation companies represented an attractive long-term outlet for surplus capital for some purchasers, while other investors had purely speculative ends in mind. Conversely, opposition generally surfaced in communities not served or favored by particular plans and in neighborhoods disrupted by construction and operation; among farmers and manufacturers threatened by competition from hinterland areas and individuals set against the increased taxation needed to pay for state-supported improvements; and finally, from groups who feared that government charters would aid only the privileged few and generate monopolies that could endanger republican ideals and institutions.

The early acceptance in this country of the legal principle of limited liability, liberal state incorporation procedures and laws, and the very decentralized structure of American government assisted the initiatives of those men of wealth and influence who attempted to translate concern into action. The state legislature of Maryland ruled favorably on the petition to charter the Baltimore & Ohio Railroad Company within a few days of application. The relative ease of incorporation proceedings contributed to the unprecedented pace of railroad company formation and construction in nineteenth-century America.

The original charter of the B. & O. also served as a model for subsequent initiatives. With the exception of a few states that established for brief periods of time rail lines completely government owned and operated, state legislatures generally entertained petitions from private citizens for incorporation rights, but treated the chartered firms as quasi-public agencies. Early railroad charters included stipulations regulating the organization, capitalization, construction, administration, and prospective services of the carriers. In return, state governments extended various franchise and incorporation privileges to petitioners, and frequently established provisions for public financial assistance.

The securing of capital for the construction of railroads took several forms. Chartered companies first sold stocks and bonds to private citizens locally and in financial centers in the United States and Europe. The growing circulation of railroad securities, in fact, served to hasten the creation of formal exchanges and investment institutions in the 1830s and 1840s.[7] Government also played an important, if not indispensable role. Municipal, state, and federal legislative bodies purchased sizable blocks of company stocks and bonds, and provided both direct donations of money and various indirect subsidies, including tax exemptions and land grants. The sale of government-offered land represented a major source of capital for road construction, especially for rail lines built in the Midwest and in western states. A hazy line thus existed between private and public initiatives in the building of the American railway network.

The legal formation of companies and the raising of adequate capital allowed railroad promoters to forge ahead with construction plans. To that task came a pioneer corps of civil engineers hired by boards of directors to survey and plot rights of way, and to supervise the construction and grading of roadbeds, the laying of track, the building of bridges, tunnels, stations, and shops, and the purchase of rolling stock. In the early years, rail companies normally contracted with local builders to construct portions of the road; later, lines either assumed direct charge of construction or established separate joint stock companies to perform the work. The latter course produced some of the more notorious boondoggles and scandals of the railway age.

[7] Arthur M. Johnson and Barry E. Supple, *Boston Capitalists and Western Railroads*.

The building of the American railroad system during the second and third quarters of the nineteenth century constituted a massive and historically momentous undertaking. By the end of 1830, the year the B. & O. inaugurated operations, twenty-three miles of track had been built in the country. Just ten years later close to three thousand miles had been constructed, largely within the Atlantic coast states, at an estimated cost of $75 million.[8] The United States by that early date already surpassed Great Britain in railroad construction.

By 1850, nine thousand miles of track had been completed at a cost of $310 million, and rail lines now stretched to and beyond the Appalachian range. The decade of the 1850s then witnessed an unprecedented boom. By 1860, 350 American railroad companies had invested close to $1.2 billion in the construction of thirty-one thousand miles of operating line. Most areas east of the Mississippi River already had convenient access to rail transportation facilities.

The Civil War failed to halt development. While the sectional crisis raged, plans were adopted to build a transcontinental road, and by war's end construction had nearly been completed. By 1870, rail lines had penetrated the Far West with track construction totaling fifty-three thousand miles. Another great building period ensued. Ten years later, the country had been linked by ninety-three thousand miles of operating line at the cost of $5.4 billion.

The return on the investment matched hopes and expectations. In 1880, American rail carriers reported total revenues of $613 million; in that year, purchasers of railroad stock received $77 million in dividends, while bond holders earned $107 million in interest payments. The benefits of railroad building, of course, filtered far beyond company investors to commercial interests in the country at large. Five decades after plans had been laid for the nation's first railroad line, a profitable and impressive intercontinental railway transportation system had been fashioned.

[8] Figures on track construction, costs, and returns can be found in U.S. Department of Commerce, Bureau of the Census, *Historical Statistics of the United States, Colonial Times to 1970*, pt. 2 (Washington, D.C., 1975), pp. 727, 731, 734; Stover, *American Railroads*, pp. 20, 29, 38, 175.

THE PROMINENT stockholders who served as directors of America's first railroad companies confronted entirely new sets of problems when their lines commenced operations. The management of business enterprises as large, complex, and geographically dispersed as railroads had few precedents. Rapid expansion and various exigencies forced early railroad managers to promptly devise administrative structures that were revolutionary for their day.

The earliest glimpse of the management of America's pioneer railroads is available in a report prepared in 1838 by Jonathan Knight and Benjamin Latrobe, two civil engineers in the employ of the Baltimore & Ohio Railroad. At the behest of the B. & O.'s board of directors, Knight and Latrobe surveyed the administration of nine operating carriers, and in their published study, *The Locomotive Engines and the Police and Management of Several of the Principal Rail Roads in the Northern and Middle States*, they rendered details on the organization of four. In each case, the primitive administrative arrangements they delineated reflected the small-scale nature of operations at the time.

One manager, for instance, supervised the twenty-seven-mile long, two-engine, three-trips-per-day Long Island Railroad. The directors of the company had authorized their elected vice president to oversee operations. The vice president in turn appointed a resident engineer who single-handedly administered the activities of the company's fifty-odd-men task force of ticket masters, conductors, enginemen, firemen, brakemen, machinists, carpenters, and track, yard, and station laborers.[9]

On the larger Boston & Worcester Railroad, Knight and Latrobe noted that authority was slightly more decentralized. The directors appointed a superintendent who delegated power to two depot masters at the ends of the line. These two officials directly supervised all employees. Similarly, the Boston & Providence and the Boston & Lowell Railroads adopted primitive decentralized structures, with the stationmasters of the large depots delegated managerial responsibilities. These two companies,

[9] Jonathan Knight and Benjamin Latrobe, *Report Upon the Locomotive Engines and the Police and Management of Several of the Principal Rail Roads in the Northern and Middle States*, p. 3.

however, added a new wrinkle. The superintendents of each appointed master enginemen to oversee the machine shops and the activities of the locomotive drivers and firemen.[10] The Boston & Providence and Boston & Lowell Railroads thus created early simple examples of administrative structures in which authority was decentralized not only geographically but also departmentally by function.

As the operation of rail companies expanded in size and complexity in the 1840s and 1850s, the problem of managing large numbers of employees became more pressing. The first road seriously to be affected was the Western of Massachusetts. When that line had opened in 1839, the company had adopted a loose regionalized and departmentalized structure.[11] A general superintendent appointed two masters of transportation to supervise activities at the major depots in Springfield and Worcester. Under the master of transportation at Springfield was a master mechanic who had immediate charge of the shops and control over the enginemen and firemen. A separate department directly under the superintendent was also created, headed by a road master who received responsibility for the maintenance of the road along the entire length of the line.

In 1841, after a series of accidents, including a spectacular head-on collision near Westfield, Massachusetts and a resulting state investigation of the line's management, the board of directors of the Western was forced to reorganize the company's operating procedures.[12] After due consideration, the directors adopted a regional approach and divided the line into three sections.[13] A general superintendent appointed road masters for each division to oversee repairs of the track, and three masters of transportation were made responsible for managing all business within each region. A master mechanic in charge of shop work was also appointed and placed under the authority of the master of transportation based at Springfield. This divisional ap-

---

[10] Ibid., pp. 7–18.

[11] Report on the Running of the Road, June 12, 1838, Western Railroad Papers, case 1, Baker Library, Harvard University.

[12] Salsbury, *State, Investor and Railroad*, pp. 185–186.

[13] *Regulations for the Transportation Department of the Western Rail Road* (Springfield, Mass., 1842).

proach thus localized authority and served to create in effect three small operating units within the one company. In addition to the structural changes, the board of directors issued a regulations manual strictly delineating the tasks and responsibilities of each manager and operating employee. The regulations established a clear chain of command with rules to guide the actions of each link in the network.

The managers of the Baltimore & Ohio Railroad assumed the next initiatives in developing new administrative structures and procedures. In 1846, Louis McLane, second president of the B. & O., anticipating the completion of the road to Wheeling, Virginia and seeking to enhance the line's financial position by increasing efficiency and cutting costs, ordered a reevaluation of the company's management.[14] A year later Benjamin Latrobe, now chief engineer of the firm and assisted by a committee of board members, devised a new plan embodied in a report entitled *Organization of the Services of the Baltimore and Ohio R. Road under the Proposed New System of Management*. This was a unique document. As business historian Alfred Chandler has noted, the B. & O. report of 1847 represented one of the first efforts of an American concern to thoroughly systematize its operations.[15]

The plan for reorganization divided the operation of the road under two main headings: "The Working of the Road" and "The Collection and Disbursement of the Revenue."[16] As to the latter, the new proposal established an office of treasurer, who was to be the road's senior financial officer. In addition to handling all external financial matters, he also assumed responsibility for supervision of the secretary and chief clerk of the company, who were placed in charge of controlling and checking the internal flow of revenues. The report further stipulated in great detail new procedures for collecting fares, receiving and receipting freight, and transmitting funds.

---

[14] Hank Bowman, *Pioneer Railroads*, p. 66.

[15] Alfred D. Chandler, Jr., "The Railroads: Pioneers in Modern Corporate Management," *Business History Review* 39:23.

[16] *Organization of the Service of the Baltimore & Ohio R. Road under the Proposed New System of Management* (Baltimore, 1847).

Under the heading of operations, the plan established a general superintendent. Directly responsible to him were his three chief lieutenants. The master of the road was responsible for the maintenance of the roadbed, bridges, depots, water stations, and other structures not connected with the machine shops. He appointed local supervisors who had direct charge of this work. The master of machinery had command of the machine and car repair shops and the shop foremen. The third and most important official in the operating department was the master of transportation, whose duties "embrace[d] all such as belong specially to the forewarding of passengers and tonnage over the road."[17] In his charge were engineers, firemen, conductors, and fuel, lumber, and depot agents and stationmasters. The latter, in turn, supervised station employees—clerks, weight masters, car regulators, watchmen, switchmen, porters, and general station hands.

The B. & O.'s plan not only clearly detailed the tasks and responsiblities of both managers and managed, it also provided for monthly reports which each level of management was expected to present to those immediately above. The great innovation of the B. & O. plan was its establishment, in Professor Chandler's words, of "one of the very first functionally departmentalized, administrative structures for an American business enterprise."[18] It served as an important model for other railroads and other concerns.

A crucial modification of the B. & O. structure was effected in the 1850s on the New York & Erie Railroad. Of all the American railroads built in the nineteenth century, the Erie probably had the most curious history. Conceived, built, operated, bankrupted, and reorganized with a good deal of financial skullduggery, and faced with constant popular opposition from people living along the line, the Erie was also the only American railroad company to adopt the inordinate six-foot gauge track. In fact, everything about the Erie was extravagant.[19] When the line's operations began in 1851, it was by far the largest railroad

[17] Ibid., p. 20.

[18] Chandler, "Railroads," pp. 26–27.

[19] The two standard histories of the Erie Railroad are Edward Mott, *Between the Ocean and the Lakes*, and Edward Hungerford, *Men of the Erie*.

in the country; by the mid-1850s, it employed more than four thousand men. Needless to say, the administrative problems of managing such an early giant were enormous. High costs, great inefficiencies, and waste plagued the Erie in its early years. A pressing need for systematized management existed.

Daniel McCallum, general superintendent of the Erie, seized the opportunity. In a report to stockholders in 1855, McCallum analyzed the company's problems. "A Superintendent of a road fifty miles in length," he first noted, "can give its business his personal attention. . . . Each person is personally known to him . . . and any system however imperfect may under such circumstances prove comparatively successful." On a road as large as the Erie, however, McCallum continued, "a very different state exists. Any system which might be applicable to the business and extent of a short road would be found entirely inadequate to the wants of a long one." McCallum then concluded that "I am fully convinced that in the want of a system perfect in its details, properly adapted and vigilantly enforced, lies the true secret of their [the large roads] failure; and that the disparity of cost per mile in operating long and short roads, is not produced by *a difference in length*, but is in proportion to the perfection of the system adopted."[20]

Over a number of years, McCallum and the directors of the Erie moved to develop that perfect system. They first divided the line into four geographical regions, each with a divisional superintendent.[21] These officers were placed under the direct authority of the general superintendent of the road and were responsible for the day-to-day movement of trains and traffic and the upkeep of the track within their domains. In addition, McCallum established department offices to conduct functional activities such as the purchase of fuel, the general handling of freight and passenger business, the building and repair of machinery, and the operations of the telegraph system. The heads of these departments reported directly to the general superin-

[20] Quoted in Chandler, "Railroads," p. 21.
[21] New York & Erie Railroad Company, *Organization and General Regulations for Working and Conducting the Business of the Railroad & Its Branches* (New York, 1852).

tendent and were considered superior to divisional superintendents, although the precise relationship between functional and
regional officers was never clear. Whether a stationmaster, for
instance, was directly subordinate to the general freight agent,
the general ticket agent, or his divisional superintendent remained uncertain.

While serving as general manager of the road, McCallum honed
and refined the Erie's mixed departmental-divisional approach
to railroad management.[22] Where ambiguities existed, Mc-
Callum made certain that well-understood lines of authority were
drawn. To increase control over subordinates, he stressed the
importance of local command and gave the powers of hiring,
disciplining, and firing of officers and employees to immediate
superiors. He also instituted a system of detailed hourly, daily,
and monthly reports, which became a model for other railroads.
The notion of systemized administrative hierarchy was so important to McCallum that he drew up and had lithographed for
public distribution a detailed organizational chart of the Erie's
operations, probably the first of its kind for an American enterprise. Finally, in keeping with his organizational theories,
McCallum also ordered Erie employees to wear prescribed grade-
specific uniforms.

McCallum, however, never solved a critical problem on the
Erie—the unclear relationship between departmental and divisional officers—and it remained for executives on the Pennsylvania Railroad to fully develop and realize his innovations. In
the 1880s the Pennsylvania Railroad emerged as the nation's
largest rail carrier, with over five thousand miles of track and
fifty thousand employees. The company's basic administrative
structure, which improved on McCallum's work, actually had
been conceived in the 1850s when the line was half the size of
the Erie.[23]

The Pennsylvania plan, devised by J. Edgar Thomson, president of the road during its formative years, appeared in a manual
published in 1858. Like the B. & O. and Erie schemes, the plan
drew a sharp distinction between financial and operational ac-

[22] Chandler, "Railroads," pp. 28–33.
[23] Ibid., p. 33.

tivities of the firm. As to the latter, Thomson followed the Erie model. A general superintendent oversaw the performance of functional department heads and divisional officials. The crucial innovation, however, involved the delegation to regional officers of direct and definitive charge of all operations within their domains, including the daily movement of traffic, maintenance of the roadbed, and the work of the shops. The plan specified that "The Division Superintendents shall on their respective divisions . . . exercise all the powers delegated by the organization to the General Superintendent for the control and use of the road, its branches and connections."[24] Department heads at central headquarters, on the other hand, under Thomson's scheme received authority to develop plans and overall strategies, set standards and procedures, make inspections, and advise divisional officers. They were afforded no direct role in the daily supervision of operations and employees.

The Pennsylvania plan thus established a clear differentiation between the functions of line and staff officers, a distinction between what students of management would call the functions of operating and entrepreneurial decision makers. In its unique combination of the divisional and departmental approaches of the Western and B. & O. plans, the Pennsylvania scheme eliminated the ambiguities of the Erie's system. In decentralizing authority and the supervision of activities, the Pennsylvania design also served to create small, relatively independent units, in effect local fiefdoms, within the one mammoth enterprise. As Alfred Chandler and Stephen Salsbury have noted, "The division superintendents [on the Pennsylvania] . . . though their actions were in harmony with the railroad as a whole, had much of the autonomy and authority characteristic of the manager of a small railroad in the 1830's."[25]

With minor variations, other major trunk lines in the United States during the last half of the nineteenth century adopted the Pennsylvania's line and staff-differentiated administrative plan.

[24] Quoted in ibid., p. 35.
[25] Alfred D. Chandler, Jr. and Stephen Salsbury, "The Railroads: Innovators in Modern Business Administration," in Bruce Mazlich, ed., *The Railroad and the Space Program*, pp. 153–154.

The organizational charts of the Illinois Central, Michigan Southern, and Chicago, Burlington & Quincy roads conceived in the
1860s bear great resemblance.[26] While other lines leaned more
in favor of the Baltimore & Ohio or Erie models, the basic
formats were there to be applied and modified as local circumstances warranted. The New York Central Railroad represents
a major exception. A systematized plan of management did not
evolve there. For a variety of reasons, including the manner in
which the company was formed and the individuals who were
involved, the senior executives of the railroad paid little attention
to administrative problems.[27] The railroad ran in an ad hoc
fashion with a general superintendent and a few immediate officers supervising practically all aspects of the line's operations.
A vague centralized, departmental structure emerged from this
situation, with top executives assuming responsibility over specific functions. When Cornelius Vanderbilt and later his son
William assumed charge, they attempted to standardize and rationalize procedures; however, authority remained fairly centralized in their hands.[28]

The first two generations of American railroad workers thus
entered work situations bureaucratically shaped and fashioned
by a pioneer corps of business managers. Mid-nineteenth-century
railwaymen worked in enterprises where ownership and management evolved as separate domains; where chains of salaried
officials, whose sole function was that of managing, supervised
tasks; where a multiplicity of assignments existed, each defined
specifically; where authority was delegated and functions performed according to stated guidelines; and where the work was
compartmentalized into separate, often geographically dispersed
units—work situations, in other words, in which each person
occupied a small place in a large complex setting. The railroads
comprised the first American enterprises to introduce bureau-

---

[26] Chandler, "Railroads," p. 36; Paul Black, "The Development of Management Personnel Policies on the Burlington Railroad, 1860–1900" (Ph.D. dissertation, Univ. of Wisconsin, 1972), pp. 60–64; David Lightner, "Labor on the
Illinois Central Railroad, 1852–1900" (Ph.D. dissertation, Cornell Univ., 1969),
pp. 67–69.

[27] Chandler and Salsbury, "The Railroads," pp. 141–142.

[28] Chandler, "Railroads," p. 39.

cratic principles and techniques of management, and their laboring forces represented the first American workers to enter such kinds of employment structures.

BUREAUCRATIZATION is easily viewed and presented as a naturally emergent process, an inevitable step forward in civilization's march toward greater degrees of organization and rationality. The bureaucratic principles and structures introduced by American railroad companies did not materialize spontaneously, nor were they the work of some invisible hand. The installation of bureaucratic administrative procedures progressed in stages and involved a good deal of trial and error and variation. It was also a process consciously and deliberately initiated and enacted by men—an attempt by this nation's pioneer railroad executives to systematize the operations of the growing complex, large-scale organizations over which they presided. Corporate profits, the need to create and shape as well as respond to new market opportunities, and the desire to enhance their own careers, salaries, status, and investment holdings, motivated their efforts.

In the process of developing new techniques and principles of management, a small group of early railroad executives also experimented with nonbureaucratic forms of administration. The most widely discussed and important alternative considered was the contract system, a business technique commonly employed by nineteenth-century American enterprises. Under this system, companies arranged with other, usually smaller, firms or individuals to have articles manufactured or services rendered. In addition to paying for the work performed, the firms letting the contracts often agreed to supply space, machinery, raw materials, and working capital. The contractors, in turn, had sole discretion over the hiring, management, and reimbursement of their labor forces and were responsible for purchasing materials or tools not provided for in the original agreements.

Contracting in nineteenth-century America was practiced mainly in the building and construction industries, the machine and tool trades, and garment making. Such major manufacturers as Eli Whitney, Robbins and Lawrence, Brown and Sharp, Colt, Remington, Singer, Pratt and Whitney, and Winchester also operated under the contract system.[29] In all of these firms, every aspect of production, from parts manufacture to assembly, was conducted inside the walls of company-owned buildings on the basis of contracts. The owners of these enterprises set production quotas and supplied the plant, machinery, raw materials, and working capital. However, they left actual production and the supervision and payment of labor completely in the hands of independent contractors who occupied rooms within the factory structure.

In the American railroad industry, the chief advocate of contracting was Henry Varnum Poor, an important railroad booster and editor of the influential *American Railroad Journal*.[30] In 1849, Poor began reporting on successful experiments in England and on the Continent with the use of the contract system in the running of trains. In these experiments, locomotive drivers agreed to drive company-owned engines for a given number of trips for a set fee. The drivers assumed responsibility for keeping the engines in good working order and for making necessary repairs. They also had to supply their own fuel, water, tallow for oiling, tools, and labor. Poor reported that the savings to the companies under this system were substantial. Contractors used fuel more efficiently, maintained the machinery more carefully, and hired cheaper labor than company managers had. Poor also saw the system providing work incentives and engendering discipline needed among railroad workers.

Poor pursued his campaign in favor of contracting throughout the early 1850s. Other journals, like the *American Railway Times* and *Holley's Railroad Advocate*, supported his contentions and called for extension of the system to all aspects of railroad operations.[31] Earnest attempts were made to introduce the practice. As early as 1840, the board of directors of the Boston & Worcester Railroad announced a decision to contract out the lading of merchandise at depots.[32] In 1850, following Poor's original articles, the Philadelphia & Reading Railroad similarly informed

[29] John Buttrick, "The Inside Contract System," *Journal of Economic History* 12:206.

[30] Alfred D. Chandler, Jr., *Henry Varnum Poor*, p. 165.

[31] *American Railway Times*, May 3, 1866, p. 2; *Holley's Railroad Advocate*, March 14, 1857, p. 8.

[32] Report, June 18, 1840, Boston & Worcester Railroad Papers, case 6, Baker Library.

its stockholders that contracting had been adopted in the company's stations and shops with satisfactory results.[33]

Another company to experiment with contracting was the Fitchburg Railroad. In 1856 the carrier introduced the practice at major depots along the line. In a report to stockholders, company officials justified the move by stressing the merits of contracting over bureaucratized management. Under the old system of managerial rule, they noted, "service, if performed at all, was rendered grudgingly." By "combining individual interest with direct responsibility," the contracting "mode of transacting the business of the company" had improved performance with "savings of expense" to the line. The directors of the Fitchburg concluded that continued success with the system warranted possible extension of the practice to other branches of the company's operations.[34]

From the letterbooks of Herman Haupt, superintendent of the Pennsylvania Railroad, we learn that the Pennsylvania contracted conductors. Although no mention of the practice is made in official company reports, Haupt wrote President Thomson in June 1852 that an injured brakeman who had applied for compensation was not legally an employee of the company since he had been hired by and been under the direct charge of a conductor contracted to run trains.[35] A similar system apparently was practiced before the Civil War on the Nashville, Chattanooga & St. Louis Railroad.[36] On another southern line, the Wilmington & Raleigh, engineers ran trains under contracts and bought or hired their own slave labor. One enterprising locomotiveman even made a substantial profit by leasing slave firemen he had purchased and trained to other drivers and companies.[37]

By far the most watched and discussed experiment with the

---

[33] *Report of the President and Managers of the Philadelphia & Reading Rail Road Company to the Stockholders, January 14, 1856* (Philadelphia, 1850), p. 9.

[34] *Report of the Committee of Investigation Appointed at Annual Meeting of the Fitchburg Railroad Company, January 29, 1856* (Boston, 1857), pp. 31–32.

[35] Herman Haupt to J. E. Thomson, June 29, 1852, Herman Haupt Letterbook, Historical Society of Pennsylvania.

[36] Jesse C. Burt, Jr., "The Savor of Old-Time Southern Railroading," *Railway and Locomotive Historical Society Bulletin*, no. 84, p. 38.

[37] Howard Dozier, *A History of the Atlantic Coast Line Railroad*, p. 38.

contract system was that of the Philadelphia, Wilmington &
Baltimore Railroad Company. The top officers of that line informed their stockholders in 1855 that they had been looking
with interest at the results that other companies had achieved
with contracting.[38] A year later, shareholders learned that steps
were being taken for the general adoption of the system.[39] In
1857 the line announced that the company had become the first
railroad to institute contracting in every phase of its operations.[40]

The wholesale adoption of the contract system by the Philadelphia, Wilmington & Baltimore Railroad can be attributed to
the resolve and initiative of its president, Samuel Morse Felton.
Felton had commenced his career in railroading as a civil engineer
and quickly advanced to top echelon positions through his vast
managerial acumen. His experiences on a number of lines had
convinced him of the potential of contracting, and he viewed the
system as a critical innovation for the industry.[41] For the first
six years of its application, the profit reports of the P.W. & B.
warranted Felton's faith and the continued interest in his efforts.[42]

In 1863, at a time of severe wartime inflation, however, the
directors of the Philadelphia, Wilmington & Baltimore abruptly
announced the abandonment of the system. As explained to
stockholders, "This system [contracting], which has been in operation on this road for several years, and resulted in great saving
in expenses, has been given up for the coming year in most of
the departments, because the prices of principal articles used in
operating the road has so rapidly increased and were so uncertain
in the future, that it was deemed more for the interest of the
Company to take the risk of future prices, than to pay an amount

[38] *Seventeenth Annual Report of the Philadelphia, Wilmington and Baltimore
Rail Road Company* (Philadelphia, 1855), p. 5.
[39] *Eighteenth Annual Report of the Philadelphia, Wilmington and Baltimore
Rail Road Company* (Philadelphia, 1856), p. 11.
[40] *Nineteenth Annual Report of the Philadelphia, Wilmington and Baltimore
Rail Road Company* (Philadelphia, 1857), p. 15.
[41] S. M. Felton to General Columbus O'Donnell, April 6, 1858, Felton Papers,
box 1, file 2, Historical Society of Pennsylvania.
[42] *Twenty-Third Annual Report of the Philadelphia, Wilmington and Baltimore Rail Road Company* (Philadelphia, 1861), p. 18.

for service which would cover all the risk that the contractors would be liable to." The directors noted, however, that they had "lost none of our confidence in the system" and "when the prices of material and labor again assume a permanent shape, the contract system should again be resorted to."[43]

The following year, the managers of the Philadelphia, Wilmington & Baltimore Railroad informed their stockholders that, despite enormous difficulties, contracting was in fact being reintroduced partially in track maintenance. "We hope," they added, "that the time may soon come, when prices for labor and materials will assume such certain and fixed value as to enable us again to resort to the contract system, which we still believe to be, under ordinary circumstances the best system, both for building and operating railroads."[44] That is the last mention of contracting in published reports of the Philadelphia, Wilmington & Baltimore Railroad Company. It is also one of the last references to the system found in any railroad trade journal or corporate document. The Civil War seems effectively to have diminished interest and discussion in what was considered for a brief period of time a serious alternative to bureaucratic management. Surveying the wreckage of the railroad strikes of 1877, the railroad commissioners of Maine harkened back to earlier experiments on the P.W. & B. to argue in favor of contracting as a means of engendering urgently needed worker loyalty to railroad companies.[45] There is no evidence, however, to indicate, that their proposal was ever considered or discussed, much less adopted.

The railroad industry's brief affair with the contract system is an interesting chapter in the history of American management, one usually bypassed by students of American business history. While some nineteenth-century railroad executives carefully and meticulously built bureaucratically structured enterprises, other administrators searched for nonbureaucratic solutions. Propo-

[43] *Twenty-Fifth Annual Report of the Philadelphia, Wilmington and Baltimore Rail Road Company* (Philadelphia, 1863), p. 15.

[44] *Twenty-Sixth Annual Report of the Philadelphia, Wilmington and Baltimore Rail Road Company* (Philadelphia, 1864), p. 16.

[45] *Report of the Railroad Commission of the State of Maine, For the Year 1877* (Augusta, Me., 1878), pp. 6–8.

nents of contracting generally questioned whether the managers of large-scale enterprises could adequately and effectively supervise the diverse activities their companies had assumed. Rather than rely on complex administrative structures and managerial authority, they favored parceling tasks to independent suppliers of goods and services and encouraging self-engendered discipline and diligence.[46] Embodied in their proposals was a noncorporatist or Jeffersonian vision of an American nation of autonomous producers and citizens.

Unfortunately, there are many questions about contracting on American railroads during the nineteenth century that cannot be answered. It is practically impossible, for instance, to learn about the independent contractors and their experiences as management-sponsored, small-time operators. It is equally difficult to discover what it was like for workers to labor under contractors whose personal income was derived from their high productivity and low wages. Contrasting the experiences of railroad workers under contractors and appointed, salaried officials would have been a valuable exercise, had it been possible. Finally, whether the effects of spiraling, unstable prices during the Civil War spelled a premature deathknell to experiments with the contract system is a question only open to speculation. The eventual jettisoning of the system in the railroad industry might serve to buttress an argument in support of the inevitability of bureaucratic controls. That this option was conceived, advanced, and effected does weaken the contention somewhat. In any event, the contract system appeared and served as an administrative alternative and ultimately was abandoned.

[46] Business historians tend to emphasize and celebrate the work of those innovative corporate managers who first expanded and then coordinated the activities of the firms over which they presided. The term "managerial revolution" is a catchword to describe this process. Such an emphasis normally neglects the important role of letting, contracting, and brokering—the parceling of operations to independent producers and servicers. While Alfred Chandler, Jr. has aptly highlighted the importance of decentralized managerial control, he has stressed how this process unfolded and was accomplished within single business enterprises. His work misses the above described parceling process and the adoption of nonbureaucratic strategies and innovations. See Alfred Chandler, Jr., *Strategy and Structure* and *The Visible Hand*.

THE AMERICAN railroad executives who introduced bureaucratic principles and techniques of management devised innovative administrative schemes to coordinate the work of the men and the machines in their employ. Before 1877, however, they did not act as a cohesive class to lend a definitive character to the work institutions they established and directed. The letters and memoranda of the first two generations of American railroad managers reveal that they devoted little formal attention to labor-related matters and held few views in common on the subject.[47] Labor loomed as an area of interest inasmuch as labor costs represented a major component of railway operating expenses.[48] Early nineteenth-century railroad executives forged prototypic business bureaucracies, but personnel problems and industrial relations did not impend as a singular or conscious concern.

The social composition of the men who oversaw the operations of the country's first railroads changed over the course of the nineteenth century. The general entrepreneurs who created and later became the principal stockholders of the nation's original lines formed the initial management core. Most of these men had outside business interests and entered railroading through experience in banking, manufacturing, and dry goods merchandising.[49] According to Thomas Cochran, the foremost student of nineteenth-century railway executives, this early group shared similar social backgrounds. They were of native-born parentage, northeastern and urban in origin, from families of high standing, and well educated.[50]

As railroad operations increased in size and complexity, the general entrepreneurs gradually and often reluctantly relinquished their supervisory roles to professional managers. These new men generally were recruited from the construction, machine, and civil engineering trades, and were largely responsible

---

[47] Thomas Cochran, *Railroad Leaders, 1845–1890*, p. 174.

[48] Most studies indicate that on nineteenth-century American railroads, employees' wages amounted to about 60 percent of operating costs and 40 percent of revenues. See Marshall Kirkman, *Railway Expenditures*, vol. I, p. 97; Paul Black, "Development of Management Personnel Policies," pp. 12, 549; Fishlow, *American Railroads*, p. 123.

[49] Stuart Morris, "Stalled Professionalism," *Business History Review* 47:320.

[50] Cochran, *Railroad Leaders*, pp. 52–53.

for the administrative innovations introduced by the railroads.[51] They came from less wealthy backgrounds than the original group of officials and were typically self-made individuals, although most had had the benefit of some formal education. By the latter part of the nineteenth century, however, recruitment into managerial positions increasingly became a matter of inbreeding, with men promoted from within their respective companies. By 1885, the largest percentage of railway managers actually had begun their careers as station clerks.[52]

In their leadership capacity, America's pioneer railway managers acted in varied ways. One breed of railroad executive consciously assumed the role of strict disciplinarians. George Burrow, superintendent of the New York Central, wore a silk hat and ruled autocratically.[53] He based his reputation on the fact that he was known impulsively to discharge locomotivemen who drove sixteen miles an hour when he had stipulated fifteen as the rule. James Clarke came to the Illinois Central first as a division superintendent; later, as master of transportation, he ushered in a period of tight control.[54] He quickly fired employees for the slightest infractions of his orders and instituted a system whereby each man's presence was recorded three times daily. As a result of his new regimen, many enginemen and shop mechanics left the I.C. to find employment elsewhere. Charles Eliot Perkins, who occupied various top posts on the Chicago, Burlington & Quincy, similarly had a particularly pessimistic view of human nature and believed that men would work effectively only under extremely firm supervision.[55] Perkins often likened the organization of a railroad to a "machine" and argued that the army provided the most appropriate model of administration for railroad managers.[56]

There were others, however, such as Herman Haupt, superintendent of the Pennsylvania Railroad in the 1850s, William

[51] Ibid., pp. 28–29.
[52] Morris, "Stalled Professionalism," pp. 323, 326.
[53] Stewart Holbrook, *The Story of American Railroads*, p. 91.
[54] Lightner, "Labor on the Illinois Central," pp. 109–110.
[55] C. E. Perkins, Memoranda on the Relation of the Corporation to the Employee, 1883, Chicago, Burlington & Quincy Railroad Papers, Newberry Library.
[56] Quoted in Cochran, *Railroad Leaders*, pp. 429–430.

Ackerman, president of the Illinois Central, and Robert Harris, general superintendent of the Chicago, Burlington & Quincy, who believed that strong discipline destroyed work incentives and morale and did not ultimately benefit efficient operations.[57] They counseled their managerial staffs to practice leniency and discretion in dealing with employees. Harris, among all the figures, was the most outspoken on this point. In a typical letter to a division superintendent in 1869, he cautioned: "Of course I recognize that this matter of discipline if properly looked at is a delicate and complicated thing—as to which no rules can be laid down but each case treated from the common sense standpoint and with a blending of firmness and kindness."[58]

Nineteenth-century railroad managers also acted within the context of a prevailing laissez faire ideology. Not all of the executives, however, worshipped blindly at the altar of the free-market economy. Most early railroad managers did vigorously oppose all attempts at unionization in the name of free-market principles, yet there were exceptions like William Vanderbilt, who signed the first contract with the Brotherhood of Locomotive Engineers, and Frederick Kimball of the Norfolk and Western, who accepted the organization of his employees by the Knights of Labor.[59] The great majority similarly took the position most eloquently and persistently stated by Perkins that the "solid bed rock of supply and demand" should be the criterion by which wages were to be fixed and the men to be treated in general.[60] Yet, once again, there were dissenters. George D. Phelps, president of the Delaware, Lackawanna & Western Railroad, for

[57] Cochran, *Railroad Leaders*, pp. 174–177; Paul Black, "Robert Harris and the Problems of Railway Labor Management: 1867–1870" (unpublished manuscript in author's possession); Herman Haupt to J. E. Thomson, June 21, 1852, Herman Haupt Letterbook.

[58] Robert Harris to H. Hitchcock, February 8, 1869, Chicago, Burlington & Quincy Railroad Papers, 3H4.1. Henry Varnum Poor also warned railroad managers against treating railwaymen as "mere machine[s]." See Chandler, *Henry Varnum Poor*, p. 155.

[59] Cochran, *Railroad Leaders*, p. 33; Dan Mater, "The Development and Operation of the Railroad Seniority System," *Journal of Business of the Univ. of Chicago* 13:396.

[60] Charles E. Perkins, Memorandum on Wages and Sentiment, October 30, 1877, Chicago, Burlington & Quincy Railroad Papers.

one, as early as 1856 advocated high wage incentive policies and cautioned against "the payment of small and inadequate salaries."[61] John Brooks of the Michigan Central similarly advised local officials of the line that, in times of depression, single young men should be dropped before older married employees.[62] Harris was also a strong proponent of offering "reasonable" rather than market-dictated compensation to railroad laborers. "If we try to obtain labor at the lowest price at which it can be got and thus help to pauperize it," he wrote, "we should expect and most certainly shall get the results of pauperized labor."[63]

Pioneer railway executives similarly disagreed about the corporation's potential role in enhancing the general material and spiritual well-being of their employees. Perkins in typical fashion strongly opposed the railroad's assuming any paternal function. In a memorandum circulated throughout the C.B. & Q.'s management in 1877, he wrote: "That it is the moral duty of the fortunate to help the unfortunate may be conceded. But that is not business; it is philanthropy, or charity. Charity and philanthropy are precisely outside the business of corporations, because corporations are made up of individuals each of whom is doing what of charity and philanthropy he thinks proper in his own town or neighborhood, as an individual member of society."[64]

Clarke of the Illinois Central similarly warned all supervisors against allowing personal feelings to intrude. In a letter to his divisional superintendents and department heads he ordered: "No officer controlling men should have any favorites or permit his personal feelings to enter his official duties."[65] Similarly, Henry Brockholst Ledyard, general superintendent of the Michigan Central in the 1870s, and William Davis Bishop, president of New York, New Haven & Hartford Railroad, firmly rejected any programs or practices on behalf of their employees which hinted at charity.[66]

[61] Quoted in Cochran, *Railroad Leaders*, pp. 449–450.
[62] Ibid., p. 274.
[63] Ibid., p. 352. Also see quote on p. 354.
[64] Charles E. Perkins, Memoranda on Supply and Demand, August 6, 1877, Chicago, Burlington & Quincy Railroad Papers.
[65] Quoted in Cochran, *Railroad Leaders*, p. 295.
[66] Cochran, *Railroad Leaders*, pp. 174, 261.

Herman Haupt, in contrast, took pride in his close rapport with Pennsylvania Railroad workers and made it a practice to visit injured men and widows.[67] Edwin Denison Morgan, president of the Hudson River Railroad, and William Osborn, president of the Chicago, St. Louis & New Orleans, both worried about the education and "moral status" of the men under their charge and recommended that their companies pay greater attention to these matters.[68] Robert Harris was known to act as an arbiter in personal disputes among workers and was an early advocate of such company-sponsored welfare measures as group health and life insurance and profit sharing.[69]

Mid-nineteenth-century railroad leaders thus behaved in varied ways and held diverse opinions and sentiments. Although they occupied a common position in the productive process, they did not forge a common or coherent philosophy of labor relations; in fact, labor-related matters occupied little of their attention. With the possible exception of a few strong figures, like the paternal Harris and that quintessential laissez-fairist Perkins, early railroad managers did not consciously attempt to impart particular tones to the organizations over which they presided. They carefully and deliberately devised bureaucratic structures to manage the performance of work, yet once the organizational charts were drawn and in place, the manner and spirit in which the work was supervised was left to individuals and circumstance. Their successors would not be as fortunate; violent confrontations between railroad management and labor late in the century would force industry executives to treat industrial relations with all due care. A view from the top thus offers a critical

---

[67] Herman Haupt to J. E. Thomson, June 21, 1852, Herman Haupt Letterbook.
[68] Cochran, *Railroad Leaders*, pp. 408, 427.
[69] Robert Harris to W. H. Hawkins, May 17, 1867, Chicago, Burlington & Quincy Railroad Papers, 3H4.1. Harris's welfare programs will be treated in greater detail in chapters 5 and 7. Even though a good number of examples can be cited to indicate paternal sentiments, it should be emphasized that nineteenth-century railroad managerial ideology was noteworthy for its absence of paternalism. Railroad executives for the most part viewed their respective companies, to use Thomas Cochran's words, as "financial entit[ies] belonging to the stockholders, rather than as . . . service structure[s] composed of . . . employees." See Cochran, *Railroad Leaders*, p. 92.

but only partial insight into the new world that the first two generations of American railway workers entered.[70] To fully comprehend the nature of their work experience, it is necessary to delve below and beyond formal structures and pronouncements. An appropriate start will be at the point of hire.

[70] The world "made" by pioneer railway executives thus differed from the environment created and structured by southern plantation owners as depicted by Eugene Genovese. See Eugene Genovese, *The World the Slaveholders Made*, and also his *Roll, Jordan, Roll*.

2

THE SUPPLY OF LABOR

ENTERPRISES thrive on adequate supplies of capital, land, and labor. The labor component in the productive process has an absolute and qualitative dimension. The sheer existence of sufficient numbers of workers is one requisite; of equal importance is the skill and ability of the available labor pool. Industrializing nations in general, and industrial firms in particular, face the double-edged problem of recruiting both ample and competent work forces.

The process of recruitment is also an important part of the work experience. Who is recruited into different occupations and the formal and informal arrangements by which men initially are employed have great impact on subsequent work situations for managers and managed alike. Enterprises can seek to develop job placement techniques to insure the loyalty and diligence of their laboring people. The peculiarities of the hiring process can in turn determine the actual job experiences of individual workers. The concern in this chapter will be to chart evolving recruitment practices and procedures on the nation's pioneer railroads and to examine the larger problems these companies faced in terms of labor supply and retention.

In 1880 the Census Bureau reported that American rail lines employed a total of 418,956 workers.[1] That is the earliest reliable aggregate figure available for the industry. Before 1880 federal census enumerators counted only engineers, firemen, conductors,

---

[1] John L. Ringwalt, *Development of Transportation Systems in the United States*, p. 361.

and brakemen as "railroad men."[2] Federal returns as a result greatly underestimate the number engaged in railway work in the early years. For example, in 1860, 6,272 railway workers were officially listed as residing in the state of New York, at a time when the New York & Erie Railroad alone employed more than 5,000 men.[3] The railroad commissioners of the state in fact reported in 1855 that 18,012 workers were engaged by roads operating in New York, which the commissioners duly noted represented 1/36 of the state's voting population.[4]

Contemporary estimates of railway employment are as problematic as official government counts. In 1859 the *Railroad Record* figured total employees in the industry at 70,000 men. A year later the *Record* offered 80,000 as a projected estimate, which represents a fairly unrealistic increase for one year's time.[5] To add to the confusion, *Hillyer's American Railway Magazine* in 1860 reported that the New York Chamber of Commerce estimated total railroad employment at 100,000.[6]

Recent projections by labor economists provide accurate approximations of the number of men working in the industry in the pre-1880 period (Table 2.1).[7] The estimates of Stanley Lebergott and Albert Fishlow indicate that railway employment, hovering in the low thousands by 1840, basically tripled in every decade thereafter, with the greatest surge occurring in the 1850s.[8]

[2] George Rogers Taylor, *The Transportation Revolution, 1815-1860*, p. 291; Albert Fishlow, *American Railroads*, p. 402.

[3] Ringwalt, *Development of Transportation Systems*, p. 140; *Holley's Railroad Advocate*, October 11, 1856, p. 1.

[4] *Annual Report of the Railroad Commissioners of the State of New York, 1855* (Albany, 1856), p. lii.

[5] *Railroad Record*, June 30, 1859, p. 219; Fishlow, *American Railroads*, p. 408.

[6] Fishlow, *American Railroads*, p. 408.

[7] Stanley Lebergott, "Labor Force and Employment, 1800–1960," in *Output, Employment, and Productivity in the United States after 1800*, p. 191; Fishlow, *American Railroads*, pp. 405–408.

[8] Lebergott and Fishlow used simple linear regression techniques to produce their estimates of railway employment before 1880, which appear in table 2.1. Both cliometricians took known, partial data, constructed equations which best fit these data, and then projected overall employment figures on the basis of these formulas. Lebergott gathered information from individual companies on track mileage and numbers of workers employed. For each decade between 1840 and 1880 he then calculated average employee per mile ratios based on these limited

Table 2.1. Estimates of Total Railway Employment, 1840–80

Year	Estimates of		Total labor force	Railroad workers as a percentage of the total
	Lebergott	Fishlow		
1840	7,000	2,200– 5,300	5,660,000	.09–.1
1850	20,000	15,000–20,000	8,250,000	.18–.2
1860	80,000	75,000–90,000	11,250,000	.7–.8
1870	160,000	—	12,930,000	1.2
1880	416,000	—	17,390,000	2.4

By 1880, with more than 400,000 men engaged in the industry, railway workers comprised roughly 2.5 percent of the nation's total work force.

The employees of the nation's pioneer railroads shared the title of railroad worker, but in reality they comprised an extremely diverse occupational group. The variety of skills involved in the smooth operation of railroads is noteworthy and it is difficult to cite another industry with such a variegated work force. An accurate breakdown of railway employment by grade of employ is again only first available for the year 1880. The figures provided by the U.S. Census of Occupations for 1880, which appear in table 2.2, do conform, however, to breakdowns calculated from surviving payroll records for the earlier period.[9] These figures indicate that trackmen engaged in the construction and maintenance of roadbeds represented the largest single group of employees, close to 30 percent of the total. Shopmen, involved in the building and repair of the rolling stock, comprised one-

---

cases. He multiplied these ratios by known total track mileage to arrive at his projected total employment counts. Fishlow, on the other hand, constructed relationships between employment and ton and passenger miles, total receipts, and operating expenses. He then established three different equations for estimating total employment and used these formulas to provide minimum and maximum estimates. Total employment figures for the labor force which are reported in table 2.1 are derived from Stanley Lebergott, *Manpower in Economic Growth*, p. 510.

[9] The figures presented in table 2.2 are derived from Ringwalt, *Development of Transportation Systems*, pp. 361–362. The figures include only general office executives and do not give an accurate picture of manager/employee ratios. Actual payroll analyses reported later in the chapter indicate that upper and lower level managers represented about 5 percent of the total work force, so that there was approximately one supervisor for every twenty railwaymen.

Table 2.2. Total Railway Employment by Grade, 1880

Category	Number	Percentage
White-collar	12,030	2.9
General officers	3,375	.8
General office clerks	8,655	2.1
Stationmen	63,380	15.1
Trainmen	79,650	19.0
Engineers	18,977	4.5
Conductors	12,419	3.0
Brakemen, etc.	48,254	11.5
Shopmen	89,714	21.4
Machinists	22,766	5.4
Carpenters	23,202	5.5
Others	43,746	10.5
Trackmen	122,489	29.2
Others	51,694	12.3
Total	418,957	99.9

fifth of all employees, while another 20 percent of the work force included trainmen responsible for the movement of traffic. Fifteen percent of the task force worked in and around stations and yards facilitating the transfer of freight and passengers, while slightly more than 2 percent were engaged in clerical pursuits. Approximately 1 percent of the force were high officials involved in supervising the activities of the other 99 percent.

Mid-nineteenth-century railwaymen also worked in companies of varying size. Even today, after one hundred years of consolidations, it is still possible to find small, twenty-mile-long roads with less than fifty workers. Before 1880, the size of companies as defined by number of men employed varied significantly, and variation was not simply a matter of track mileage. The length of a line certainly influenced the number of workers on a company's payroll, but the availability of labor and the complexity and nature of the line's operations were important factors, too. In 1850 a committee of stockholders investigating the management of the Northern Railroad in New England issued a report showing that while the Northern was the longest of the five major railroads in the section, it employed the fewest number of men.[10]

[10] Report of the Investigating Committee of the Northern Railroad, May 1850, foldout (Concord, N.H., 1850).

Table 2.3. Size of Work Place by Number Employed, 1880

Firm size	Number of firms	Percentage of firms	Number of employees	Percentage of employees
1000 +	84	12	311,955 (exact figure)	74
500–999	60	9	42,300 (estimate)	10
100–499	185	27	47,150 (estimate)	11
0–99	354	52	17,700 (estimate)	4

The line stretched through expanses of unsettled territory and had relatively few stations; the company's shop facilities were also of a less substantial nature. Lines running through densely populated, highly commercial areas generally engaged larger numbers of workers. With a smaller volume of business, the average southern railroad accordingly had a small roster of employees. Although a third of the nation's track mileage in 1860 was in the South, the section actually employed only one-fifth of the nation's total railway labor force.[11]

Industry-wide statistics for firm size are unavailable before 1880. Again the occupational census of 1880 provides the only reliable source of information. Table 2.3, drawn from the census, lists numbers and percentages of companies and employees for four different categories of firm size.[12] The figures reveal that by far the greatest number of railway companies employed fewer than one hundred men. On the other hand, they also show that the great majority of railway workers were employed in companies of more than one thousand employees. In fact, the figures clearly indicate that three out of four mid-nineteenth-century railwaymen worked in truly large work organizations.

[11] John Stover, *The Railroads of the South, 1865–1900*, p. 13.
[12] The figures in table 2.3 are derived from Ringwalt's analysis of the 1880 Census returns. See Ringwalt, *Development of Transportation Systems*, pp. 361–362. Unfortunately, while Ringwalt presents an exact figure for the number of employees enrolled in companies of more than 1,000 men, he gives only cumulative data for small firms based on categories of a hundred (e.g., "Seven companies employed between 800 and 900 men"). To arrive at the estimates given in column four of table 2.3, halfway averages for each 100 category were assumed and multiplied by the number of firms in that category (e.g., 850 was taken as the average number employed in the 800–900 category and this was multiplied by seven to get an estimate of 5,950 workers in this firm size group). Figures were then totaled into the firm size categories listed in the table.

A final caution about total employment figures is in order. Employment rosters of individual companies fluctuated substantially even within short periods of time. Growth was one important factor. For instance, the Baltimore & Ohio Railroad listed 516 employees on the company's payroll in 1852. Three years later, with the extension of the line into Ohio, the B. & O.'s roster mushroomed to 4,259 men.[13] Seasonal fluctuations and emergency situations were other important factors. Extra men would be hired in the early spring to make repairs on the winter-torn roadbed. In September and October temporary hands would be employed to handle heavy harvest shipments. A snowstorm in January might add hundreds of men to clear the tracks. On the Hartford & New Haven Railroad, surviving payroll records indicate that between 1845 and 1847 monthly totals ranged from a low of 82 to a high of 233 men; between 1850 and 1853 the monthly figures ranged from 316 to 575; and between 1868 and 1870 from 765 to 965.[14]

THE AMERICAN railway industry went through two different phases of development in the matter of recruitment. In the first twenty to thirty years, pioneer companies faced the problem of recruiting both a new and a complete task force into every branch of the trade. Engineers, firemen, conductors, brakemen, agents, machinists, clerks, and trackwalkers had to be enlisted en masse at once. After this period, recruitment practices were combined with promotional policies to facilitate supply problems. Men would enter the trade at early ages in low-grade positions and gradually work their way through the ranks. The question of promotions both as a form of recruitment and as an instrument of work incentive will be treated in chapter 4. Here the concern will be to outline the sources of recruitment of the original task force.

Given the diversity of skills required for the successful oper-

[13] List of Officers and Employees in the Service of the Baltimore R. Road Company with their Salaries, Duties, & c., September, 1852, February, 1855 (Baltimore, 1852, 1855).

[14] Hartford & New Haven Railroad Payroll Records, New York, New Haven & Hartford Railroad Papers, vols. 89–91, Baker Library, Harvard University.

ation of a railroad, it is not surprising that pioneer railroad managers recruited different classes of railway labor from occupations where skills were roughly analogous and transferable. The small but growing iron, machine, and building trades served as obvious sources of supply for the blacksmiths, machinists, and carpenters who worked in railway company shops. The world of merchandising and commerce similarly offered a pool of potential agents and clerks. The construction crews of general day laborers likewise represented a readily accessible source for track repairmen. For every function, in other words, there existed a possible reservoir.

The first conductors, for example, were usually drawn from existing transportation concerns and were familiar with the needs and demands of the traveling public. P. C. Hale and James Potter, the first conductors on the Eastern Railroad, and S. A. Lawrence and Humphrey Cozzens, pioneer conductors on the Atlantic & St. Lawrence, were former stagecoach drivers.[15] One of the first conductors on the Western, whose name is not given in a report detailing his responsibility for an accident, came highly recommended to the company as an agent from a steamship firm.[16] Nathaniel Williams, who operated a wagon freight business, was hired by the Auburn & Syracuse Railroad in the early 1830s to be a conductor on the line's freight train runs.[17] Moving further westward, the first group of conductors on the Chicago & Rock Island Railroad in the 1850s were former captains of packet ships on the Great Lakes.[18]

Station agents and depot masters similarly were drawn from commercial enterprises. In sparsely populated areas, proprietors of crossroad stores often ran stations on a commission basis.[19]

[15] Francis Bradlee, *The Eastern Road*, p. 18; petition to the directors of the Atlantic & St. Lawrence Railroad, March 6, 1848, Atlantic & St. Lawrence Railroad Papers, Correspondence, 1845–1848, Bowdoin College Library; Henry Carter, L. M. Goodwin, John Dow, and George F. Emery to the president of the Atlantic & St. Lawrence Railroad Company, July 10, 1849, ibid., Correspondence, 1849–1855.

[16] Report on the collision of trains, near Chester, October 16, 1841, Western Railroad Papers, case 1, Baker Library.

[17] Charles F. Carter, *When Railroads Were New*, p. 163.

[18] *Rock Island Magazine* 17 (October 1922): 12.

[19] Paul Black, "The Development of Management Personnel Policies on the

Judging from applications for agency positions, station officials were also drawn from mercantile firms, overseas shipping companies, and stagecoach and freight wagon businesses.[20] The clerks who assisted the agents in receipting and bookkeeping tasks, in turn, were recruited from business and governmental offices where they had developed what one early applicant for a railroad clerkship called "a handsome hand" and an ability to keep ordered ledger books.[21] Agencies and particularly clerkships in this early period were also noted sinecures for the younger relatives of major stockholders and officers of the roads.[22]

The recruitment of the first generation of engine drivers is especially interesting to the modern historian, because engine drivers were unique among railwaymen. Like airplane pilots in our own century, the enginemen were products of swift and dramatic developments in technology. The skills required by their job were new and had few antecedents.

The honor of running the first steam locomotive in the United States on an actual operating railroad belongs to Horatio Allen, a young civil engineer assisting in the construction of the Delaware & Hudson Railroad in the late 1820s.[23] When the track was finished he volunteered to run the company's newly purchased engine. He was totally unprepared for the experience. As he explained fifty years later in an interview: "I had never run a locomotive or any other engine before; I have never run one since; but on that eighth of August 1829, I was the first loco-

---

Burlington Railroad, 1860–1900" (Ph.D. dissertation, Univ. of Wisconsin, 1972), p. 206.

[20] The following correspondence in the archives of the Atlantic & St. Lawrence Railroad in the Bowdoin College Library will illustrate this: Samuel McCobb and C. Barnes to the directors of the Atlantic & St. Lawrence Railroad, December 6, 1848; S. J. Corser to same, April 3, 1848; John M. Adams to same, August 9, 1849; H. B. Hitchcock to same, December 25, 1848. Similar letters of application can be found in the Baltimore & Ohio Railroad Papers in the Maryland Historical Society, the Nashua & Lowell Railroad and Boston & Lowell Railroad Papers in Baker Library, Harvard University, and the Illinois Central Railroad and Chicago, Burlington & Quincy Railroad Papers in the Newberry Library.

[21] James Harmer to I. S. Little, n.d., Atlantic & St. Lawrence Railroad Papers, Correspondence, 1849–1855.

[22] Thomas Cochran, *Railroad Leaders, 1815–1890*, p. 90.

[23] Ringwalt, *Development of Transportation Systems*, p. 72.

An engine driver and fireman on the Philadelphia & Reading Railroad. The engine "Ontalaunee" was built in 1843. (Courtesy of Smithsonian Institution.)

motive engineer on this continent—and not only engineer, but fireman, brakeman, conductor and passenger."[24]

The first man to operate an engine during a regular passenger run fortunately was better equipped than Allen. In 1831 the South Carolina Canal & Rail Road Company became the first line to commence scheduled steam locomotive service. At the throttle of the company's engine, "The Best Friend of Charleston," was Nicholas W. Darrell. He had been a machinist's ap-

[24] Quoted in Richard Reinhardt, ed., *Workin' On The Railroad*, p. 24.

prentice in the West Point Foundry in New York where the engine parts were forged. He traveled south with the finished components of the engine and directed its assemblage. The South Carolina company then hired him as the line's lone locomotive driver. Darrell presided at the company's celebrated first run, was its regular engineer for several years, and later became the firm's first superintendent of machinery.[25]

This pattern was repeated by other lines in the 1830s and '40s. When rail transport began in New York State in 1831 on the Mohawk & Hudson Railroad, at the throttle of the company's engine was David Matthew, who had supervised its construction.[26] In 1832, the Baltimore & Ohio accepted for use a steam locomotive built by Phineas Davis of Grafton County, New Hampshire. Davis brought his machine to Maryland, drove for the B. & O., and later became the manager of the company's shop where he served until 1835, when he was crushed to death in a derailment of a new locomotive he had designed.[27] Engineers in this early period thus were recruited from the machine shops where the pioneer locomotives were built. They generally were machinists or machinists' apprentices by training and trade and in most cases actually had been involved in the construction of the engines they eventually drove. As a result they came to the railroads with a good deal of mechanical expertise.[28]

The railroads also recruited enginemen from locomotive machine shops when engines were not being purchased directly. W. D. Lewis, presiding officer of the New Castle & Frenchtown Railroad in Delaware, wrote Matthias Baldwin of the Baldwin Locomotive Works in 1832 asking him to supply an engineer to operate the line's single locomotive. Baldwin not only engaged

[25] *Railroad Record*, December 23, 1869, p. 450.

[26] Alvin Harlow, *The Road of the Century*, p. 12.

[27] Stewart Holbrook, *The Story of American Railroads*, p. 22.

[28] The locomotive machine shops were not only a source of supply of enginemen for the early railroads. The shops were an obvious training ground for new recruits and also served as agencies for the retraining of veteran drivers. When the Norris Locomotive Works sold engines to a rail company, arrangements were made to have the line's drivers assist in assembling the new engines that they would man. See Dionysus Lardner, *Investigation of the Causes of the Explosion of the Locomotive Engine, "Richmond," near Reading, Pa., on the 2nd Sept. 1844*, p. 5.

a machinist, Edward Young, for the railroad, but also suggested that the company pay the new recruit sixty dollars a month since engineers on steamboats at the time were making between forty and eighty dollars.[29] Baldwin personally supplied many of the early railroads with engine drivers and apparently was able to set conditions of employment on behalf of the men he engaged. This is illustrated in the following two letters of introduction written by Baldwin in 1836 and 1842.

Mr. L. Foster the bearer of this, is the Engineer we have engaged to take charge of your engine.

The time you specified for his entering his duties has arrived, and he leaves tomorrow for Lexington. Mr. F has made a conditional engagement with an assistant to go out as soon as you may require.

Mr. Foster's salary is fixed at 1000 dollars per year, and he expects to occupy all his time in the service of the state, either to run an Engine, or repair, or any other work connected with his department. You will find him a steady industrious man, and understands his machines well and will carry on the operations of the Road with economy.

It is usual in cases where men have their business here, and go and journey so far, that they should be paid the expense in going. This may be asked by Mr. F, but we have not stipulated for it. This is left for you to decide.

The bearer of this Mr. David Cockley is the person I send to run the Engine. There will accompany him two young men by the name of Fleming. One of them will act as fireman during Mr. Cockley's stay (which will be about a month). He will then take charge of the engine. In the mean time the brother of Mr. Fleming may be employed as fireman or in any way at fireman's wages and take his brother's place as fireman when he takes charge of the Engine. All of these men are from the Columbia Road and are considered the best Engineers on that Road.[30]

These letters also show that the early machine shops supplied the pioneer railroads with firemen to assist the engine drivers. Ross Winan's firm of Baltimore, Maryland, a major competitor

[29] Diary of W. D. Lewis, Thursday, March 15, 1832 entry, Newcastle & Frenchtown Railroad Company Papers, Historical Society of Delaware.

[30] Baldwin and Whitney to William McKee, November 15, 1842, Baldwin Locomotive Papers, Outgoing Letters, Historical Society of Pennsylvania; M. W. Baldwin to William Woolsey, May 4, 1836, ibid., Letterpress Book No. 1.

of Baldwin's, furnished enginemen and firemen with every locomotive sold, and, like Baldwin, was able to stipulate the terms
of employment for the men recruited.[31] The South provides the
only notable exception to this pattern. There the ranks of firemen
on the early roads were generally comprised either of hired or
company-owned slaves. When Nicholas Darrell drove the "Best
Friend of Charleston" in the nation's first scheduled passenger
run, a black fireman assisted him at the boiler.[32]

Not all of the early enginemen were recruited from American
machine shops. Imported English locomotives, for instance, arrived with English engineers who came with newly ordered machines.[33] The first engineer on the Boston & Lowell Railroad
was an Englishman named Robinson, who legend tells us wore
kid gloves and began and completed his runs at his own pleasure.[34] Since most American rail companies in this early period
imported machinery from England, it can be assumed that a
significant percentage of the original task force of engine drivers
were recent British arrivals.

Finally, in terms of early labor recruitment, the pioneer railroads also had on hand a general pool of casual day labor to fill
unskilled positions. Young men in their late teens would leave
family farms to seek adventure as railroad brakemen. Construction workers at the end of their stints would sign on as track
repairmen.[35] Common day laborers would be hired to load merchandise at depots. In emergency situations, casual laborers could
be enlisted to put out fires caused by sparks from engines, clear

[31] George D. Phelps to D. H. Dotterer, October 18, 1854, Delaware, Lackawanna & Western Railroad Papers, Letterbooks of George D. Phelps, 1854–
1856, Syracuse University Library.

[32] *American Engineer*, July 11, 1857, p. 6; Reinhardt, *Workin' On The Railroad*, p. 107.

[33] "Report of the Committee on Cars to the Directors of the South Carolina
Canal & Railroad Company, 1833," in *Railway and Locomotive Historical
Bulletin*, no. 7 (1924), p. 14.

[34] Francis Bradlee, *The Boston and Lowell Railroad, the Nashua and Lowell
Railroad, and the Salem and Lowell Railroad*, pp. 9–10. There are many amusing
tales about early English locomotivemen. The English recruits, for instance,
apparently were noted for their secretiveness, having been instructed not to tell
the Americans about the intricacies of the engines. See Holbrook, *Story of American Railraods*, p. 30.

[35] Lightner, "Labor on the Illinois Central Railroad," p. 50.

snow from the tracks and rescue snowbound trains, and help with unusual repairs to the roadbed.[36] In the North, the growing immigrant population served as an important source of unskilled labor. In the South, the early railroads relied heavily on readily available supplies of slave labor.[37]

The factor of skill levels, then, did not prove to be an impediment to the development of rail transport in this country. For each grade of service there were sources of supply to be drawn on. Skills from existing pursuits could be transferred and adapted to the needs of railway operations. If the recruitment of labor is seen as a problem with qualitative and quantitative dimensions, in terms purely of competency and not necessarily of numbers, the American railway industry in its initial period of development faced no formidable obstacles.

BEFORE THE 1880s, there were few formal requirements for entrance into service in American railway companies. Two states did enact laws establishing certain qualifications. In New York, a statute of 1870 forbade railroads to employ as engineers applicants who could not read printed timetables or ordinary handwriting.[38] In Tennessee, a postbellum code expressly outlawed the employment of blacks as engineers.[39] No other state or municipality, and certainly not the federal government, passed similar restrictive legislation in the period under study. This is quite different from Europe, where in France, for example, national laws required rail companies to leave open half of all positions to discharged sailors and soldiers and where the employment of convicted persons was also prohibited.[40]

American railroads usually established their own formal or informal requirements. Most companies demanded performance

---

[36] Ibid., p. 77; Account for Service, 1843, Western Railroad Papers, case 4, Baker Library.

[37] Lightner, "Labor on the Illinois Central," p. 63. The question of slave labor will be treated later in this chapter and again in chapter 6.

[38] *Annual Report of the State Engineer and Surveyor on the Railroads of the State of New York* (Albany, 1880), p. 1142.

[39] *Articles and Charters of Incorporation of the Chesapeake, Ohio & Southern R.R. Co.* (Louisville, n.d.), p. 75.

[40] F. Jacqmin, *Railroad Employes in France*, pp. 7–8.

bonds from employees handling fares and receipts. Conductors, cashiers, and station agents, in particular during the 1850s and '60s, were required to sign bonds of from one to five thousand dollars before they secured employment. Companies often contracted with bonding agencies to handle the underwriting of their employees' performance.[41] Some railroads also demanded as requisites for employment written pledges from recruits promising abstention from the use of hard liquors and involvement in labor organizations.[42] In most cases, written affidavits were not required, it being assumed or announced company policy not to hire either known union activists or men who drank. Presence on circulating blacklists, of course, was a cause for immediate rejection.[43]

A few railroads set age qualifications. Suits brought by parents of minors injured and killed while in the employ of the Baltimore & Ohio and the Chicago, Burlington & Quincy Railroads forced these two companies to adopt policies of not hiring trainmen below the age of twenty-one and shop mechanics below eighteen.[44] The C.B. & Q., in addition, in 1870 instituted the formal practice of refusing employment to enginemen and firemen who could not read and write and began hiring only single men for rural agency positions, since the line could not provide proper facilities or salaries to keep whole families stationed at out-of-the-way places.[45]

By and large, though, employment requirements were loosely defined and enforced during the first fifty years. When railway officers or editors of railway trade journals considered the ques-

[41] Bonds for cashiers, conductors, station agents, 1857–1871, Boston & Lowell and Nashua & Lowell Railroad Papers, vol. 181, Baker Library; Paul Black, "Development of Management Personnel Policies," p. 470.

[42] Robert Bruce, *1877: Year of Violence*, pp. 57–58; *Valedictory Address of the General Superintendent of the Pennsylvania Railroad to the Officers and Employees of the Company* (Philadelphia, 1859), pp. 6–7.

[43] The issue of blacklisting will be discussed in chapter 3.

[44] Paul Black, "Development of Management Personnel Policies," pp. 206–207; J. W. Garrett to John Wilson, August 21, 1866, Baltimore & Ohio Railroad Letterbooks, Maryland Historical Society.

[45] Paul Black, "Development of Management Personnel Policies," p. 206; Robert Harris to C. F. Jauriet, April 1, 1870, Chicago, Burlington & Quincy Railroad Papers, 3H4.1.

tion of qualifications, they usually spoke in vague moralistic terms and phrases. Conductors should be "sober," "prompt," and "honest" and "exhibit gentlemanly behavior towards passengers." Agents should show an "aptness in getting along with men." Railway employees in general were to be hired on the basis of their "honesty," "faithfulness," "intelligence," "moral character," and "temperance."[46] Even when more specific guidelines were formulated, compliance was minimal. Known alcoholics, minors, and labor activists officially may have been excluded from railway employment, yet heavy drinkers, young workers, and union organizers worked on many if not all railroads.[47]

Notably absent from discussions before 1880 was a concern for educational credentials or health standards. In 1853, the *Railroad Record* recommended a requisite of a "good common school education" for railroad workers.[48] Four years later, it supported a petition before the General Assembly of Maryland that would have established statewide, formal licensing procedures for engineers.[49] The *American Railway Review* in 1859 similarly proposed the idea of a board of examiners established by railroad companies to pass on the qualifications of locomotivemen.[50] This, however, was the extent of discussion and action before 1880 on implementing formal educational or technical prerequisites.[51]

[46] Paul Black, "Development of Management Personnel Policies," p. 203; Cochran, *Railroad Leaders*, p. 229; *Colburn's Railroad Advocate*, June 9, 1855, p. 1.

[47] The question of intemperance, child labor, and unionism will be treated in chapters 3, 6, and 7, respectively.

[48] *Railroad Record*, June 2, 1853, p. 216.

[49] Ibid., August 20, 1857, p. 414.

[50] *American Railway Review*, September 29, 1859, p. 4.

[51] Many rail companies did establish formal apprenticeship programs in the repair shops during the 1870s, and passage through these programs was a requirement for promotion to journeyman mechanic status or other higher grades of railway work. There were no official requirements, however, for entrance into apprenticeship. It should be noted also that shop apprentices do appear in the earliest payroll records available. These young men were actually glorified shop hands since structured apprenticeship programs generally were not introduced until the late 1870s. It was really in the 1880s, moreover, that the technical education of railway workers became an important topic of concern among railway executives. The often cited example of Baltimore & Ohio Railroad's

The question of health requirements also received little attention. The Massachusetts Board of Railroad Commissioners in
1879 suggested the idea of giving visual acuity and color blind-
ness tests.[52] A year later the railroad commissioners of Connecticut seconded the motion; as a result, Connecticut became
the first state to pass legislation requiring eye examinations for
railroad workers. The measure was so unpopular among trainmen, because of the unreliable and discretionary nature of existing testing procedures, that the issue successfully served as
grist for insurgent political candidates, and the law was almost
immediately repealed.[53] During the 1880s, many railroad companies voluntarily instituted physical examinations.[54]

IN THE EARLY years, then, there were few formal restrictions or
requisites for entrance to the trade. By and large, any white male
roughly above the age of sixteen could become a railwayman.
Winning a job, however, was another matter. Recruitment procedures, of course, varied from firm to firm, but certain general
patterns are discernible. As the industry developed and railway
operations increased in size and complexity, recruitment became
a less formalized process and one characterized by arbitrariness
and individual discretion. The reasons for this are not difficult
to find. With growth and the introduction of bureaucratic principles of management came the decentralization of decision making on many labor-related matters. Hiring, in particular, became
the concern of local officials. As a result, an individual recruit's
prospects for employment often became a function of his personal association or rapport with regional, line supervisors.

In the very early years, boards of directors of railroad com-

---

Technical School was established in 1885. Albert Fishlow's contention that the
"railroads were quite interested in industrial education" is unsubstantiated for
the pre-1880 period. See Lightner, "Labor on the Illinois Central," p. 162; W. T.
Barnard, *Service Report on Technical Education*; and Albert Fishlow, "Productivity and Technological Change in the Railroad Sector, 1840–1910," in *Output,
Employment, and Productivity in the United States after 1800*, p. 634.

[52] *Eleventh Annual Report of the Board of Railroad Commissioners, January
1880* (Boston, 1880), pp. 65–66.

[53] Marshall Kirkman, *Railway Train and Station Service*, pp. 85–88.

[54] Lightner, "Labor on the Illinois Central," p. 242; Paul Black, "Development
of Management Personnel Policies," pp. 235–238.

panies actually elected railwaymen to their posts. Committees of presiding officers would be delegated to consider letters of application for employment and lists of recommendations submitted by appointed superintendents. Entire boards would then vote on the committees' endorsements. In the minute books of the Schenectady & Troy Railroad, one of the original small lines which was later absorbed into the New York Central system, entries like the following were common during the 1830s: "On motion, Resolved that this Board now proceed to the electing by ballot of a Ticket Agent & Clerk for Troy."[55] The minutes show that a discussion then ensued, with the board eventually voting unanimously to elect one N. S. Hollister as an agent at a salary of $450 a year. In the same session a clerk, conductor, and baggage master were elected to office.

The well-preserved minute books of the Boston & Worcester Railroad provide additional evidence of the formal nature of the recruitment process in the early period. In 1834 the board of directors of the B. & W. voted "That J. Leach be employed by the superintendent as Engineer to take charge of the Locomotive, called the Meteor, at the rate of two dollars per day."[56] In 1837 similar entries indicate that the appointment of individual shop carpenters and machinists was considered in committee and then approved by formal vote of the directors.[57] The minutes of a year later show the board also rejecting the superintendent's nomination of Daniel D. Fuller to be an engineman.[58]

Until 1842 recruitment on the Boston & Worcester was handled through such formal channels. In that year a change was effected when the directors voted on February 21 to accept a report "revising the orders of the Board in relation to the appointment and discharge of certain agents and officers of the corporation."[59] The specific details of the report were not outlined in the minutes, nor was a copy saved for the corporation's

[55] B. A. Botkin and Alvin Harlow, eds., *A Treasury of Railroad Folklore*, p. 158.

[56] Minutes of directors' meetings, vol. 1, Boston & Worcester Rail Road Papers, Baker Library, pp. 215–216.

[57] Ibid., vol. 2, p. 20.

[58] Ibid., vol. 3, pp. 45–46.

[59] Ibid., vol. 4, p. 143.

files. It is evident, though, that the report officially delegated complete recruitment authority to the superintendent and other appointed officials of the line, because after the date of the passage of this resolution the minutes of the board contain no reference to either the election or selection of employees.

In the large, bureaucratically structured railroad companies that emerged in the late 1840s and '50s, recruitment was completely a managerial prerogative. More important, the effect of ordering authority hierarchically and creating separate functional and geographical jurisdictions of command was to dispense and disperse hiring powers to local officials. On the Erie Railroad, General Superintendent Daniel McCallum explicitly delegated the recruitment function to immediate superiors. Local hiring, McCallum argued, would be more efficient because it would eliminate lengthy and involved approval procedures. Decentralized control of recruitment would also serve to engender discipline since workers would recognize that their very employment was contingent on the authority and discretion of their immediate supervisors.[60] The Erie plan of organization did make provision for all appointments to be subject to the approval or disapproval of higher authorities, but in practice, recruitment generally was local.

The Erie model served as the basis for other large roads, and where theory did not guide actions, practical concerns dictated the necessity of decentralized recruitment methods. Rapid growth in size and complexity and the fluctuating manpower needs of different departments and divisions precluded in most cases either centrally directed or standardized hiring practices. Track foremen employed maintenance-of-way workers. Trainmasters or divisional masters of transportation engaged station agents, dispatchers, conductors, brakemen, and switchmen. Agents, in turn, hired their own station help. Masters of machinery recruited enginemen and firemen, while shop foremen were authorized to employ skilled and unskilled shop mechanics. There are exceptions, but the general pattern was one of local hiring.[61]

[60] Alfred D. Chandler, Jr., "The Railroads," *Business History Review* 39:29; *Holley's Railroad Advocate*, p. 8.
[61] Paul Black, "Development of Management Personnel Policies," p. 191.

The growing decentralization and informality of recruitment procedures opened the hiring process to various forms of discretionary favoritism. Family and personal connections, extortion, and political affiliations were important factors in determining the success of individual applicants. Enough evidence exists to say that such subjective criteria played a signficant role in the recruitment of mid-nineteenth-century American railwaymen.

Family connection represented probably the most important asset in securing employment for all grades of railway workers. A common theme running through published reminiscences of mid-nineteenth-century railwaymen is the way in which either fathers or older brothers helped the narrators obtain their first positions. In *Railroadman*, Harry French notes how his brother, a telegraph operator, used his influence with a local supervisor to get the younger Harry a spot as a depot messenger when he was just fourteen years of age.[62] Harry, in turn, learned to operate a telegraph in his own right, then worked as a switchman and a brakeman, and at the age of twenty-one was promoted to freight conductor. The cycle of family connections was continued when Harry later secured for his younger brother a job as brakeman on the same line. In a similar fashion, Otis Kirkpatrick relates how he began his career as a depot laborer working directly under his father, who was a station agent.[63] Charles George, Harvey Reed, and Gilbert Lathrop further elucidate the role that relatives played in securing positions.[64]

Additional evidence can be found in corporate documents. In nineteenth-century railroad company payroll accounts, for instance, groups of similarly surnamed employees with names of both the common and uncommon variety abound. In the Hartford & New Haven's payroll for the years 1851–53 are listed James Shirrell and William Shirrell, machinists, and Thomas Shirrell, machinist's apprentice; Edward Wandless and Thomas Wandless, brakemen; Owen McColliff, Jeremiah McColliff, and

[62] Chauncey Del French, *Railroadman*, p. 32.
[63] Otis H. Kirkpatrick, *Working On The Railroad*.
[64] Charles George, *Forty Years On The Rail*; Harvey Reed, *Forty Years A Locomotive Engineer*; Gilbert Lathrop, *Little Engines and Big Men*.

John McColliff, laborers; and Francis Ford, engineer, and Humphrey Ford, fireman. In the same company's payroll account for the years 1868–70 can be found Henry Stowell and Bishop Stowell, conductors; W. E. Goodnough and G. A. Goodnough, brakemen; Edwin Sawtell, engineman, Edwin M. Sawtell, fireman, and Edwin A. Sawtell, machinist's apprentice; James Waters, Sr., boilermaker, and James Waters, Jr., machinist's apprentice; Francis Brassill, Sr., stationary engineer in the machine shop, Francis Brassill, Jr., tinsmith shop hand, and Michael Brassill, tinsmith shop foreman. Further examples using such uncommon names from these and other payroll records also can be cited, along with a host of cases of pairs and groups of Adamses, Clarks, Farrells, Kelleys, Murphys, Reeds, and Sullivans. Unfortunately, no payroll record discovered includes addresses of employees, so that it is not possible to give a precise indication of the percentage of railwaymen working alongside family members in particular firms. On a more grisly note, corporate records also reveal the existence of family-based teams of workers in published summaries of accidents resulting in the death or injury of company employees. A report prepared by the Old Colony Railroad, for instance, noted that on "December 15, 1849, David Long of Boston broke his leg while volunteering without the knowledge of the Superintendent to help his brother, a brakeman on the road, couple cars."[65] Stockholders of the Philadelphia, Wilmington & Baltimore Railroad were similarly informed in 1879 that, during a particularly disastrous collision, "The engineman, who had been long in the service of this company, and his son, the fireman, were killed."[66]

Letters of application for employment also reveal the significance of family connections. When F. I. Kimpton wrote to the Nashua & Lowell Railroad in 1858 asking for a position, he emphasized that his father was a veteran employee of the line.[67] J. C. Proctor, a freight agent with the same company, wrote the

[65] *Seventh Annual Report of the Old Colony Railroad Corporation of the State of Massachusetts* (Boston, 1851), p. 163.

[66] *Forty-First Annual Report of the Philadelphia, Wilmington & Baltimore Railroad Company* (Philadelphia, 1879), p. 14.

[67] F. I. Kempton to George Stark, January 1, 1858, Nashua & Lowell Railroad Papers, vol. 203.

road's officials recommending his younger brother for employ-ment.[68] George L. Button, a telegraph operator for the Delaware, Lackawanna & Western Railroad, even wrote the president of that company requesting permission to license his two sisters as operators so that they could be employed by the road.[69] Letters of introduction found in company archives also indicate that it was a common practice for young men from high standing and influential families to receive low echelon managerial posts or clerkships after relatives connected with the line in executive positions intervened on their behalf.[70] This form of nepotism, prevalent in the early years of American railroading, is recalled in an article in the *Railway Clerk*, a union journal:

In the old days it was not an infrequent occurrence to see inexperienced men brought into an office and put to work at wages higher than men received who had spent years in the service. Many times have we seen it happen, that when a job that paid a top wage became vacant a greenhorn would be brought in to do the work! Nepotism was a curse in the clerical service before we organized. A clerical job could always be found for the nephew, niece, cousin or neighbor of a chief clerk or official, even if it meant getting rid of an old employee to make a place for him.[71]

Mid-nineteenth-century railway companies often encouraged the informal practice of permitting family connections to influence hiring. In agreements with local building contractors, companies frequently promised to employ the relatives and friends of contractors once construction was completed and the lines were opened for operation.[72] James Rutter, who rose to the presidency of the New York Central, began his railroad career

[68] J. C. Proctor to Bernard Stearns, January 8, 1847, ibid., vol. 191.
[69] George L. Button to John Brisbin, February 13, 1865, Delaware, Lacka-wanna & Western Railroad Papers, Counsel's Letters, box 1, Syracuse University Library.
[70] Cochran, *Railroad Leaders*, p. 90. Charles Eliot Perkins, the foremost ad-vocate of employing strict supply and demand criteria in all dealings with railroad employees, actually began his career as a station clerk—a position he secured after marrying the niece of John Murray Forbes, an important railroad promoter and member of the board of directors of the Chicago, Burlington & Quincy Railroad. See Paul Black, "Development of Management Personnel Policies," p. 44.
[71] *Railway Clerk*, January, 1929, p. 7.
[72] Edward Mott, *Between the Ocean and the Lakes*, p. 399.

as a freight clerk on the Erie Railroad, a job he received as part of an agreement between his father, a building contractor, and the line.[73] Companies often proudly pointed to the fact that successive generations of families had worked for the road. The directors of the Mine Hill & Schuylkill Haven Railroad, in their annual report of 1864, commended company workers for their diligent performances and noted that "many of [them], natives of the districts bordering upon the Company's road, entered its service in boyhood and youth, succeeding in some instances to positions held by their parents."[74] On the Connecticut & Passumpsic Rivers Railroad, it became the deliberate policy of the line's superintendent, Colonel Harley E. Folsom, to hire sons of employees. Folsom believed that transient railroad laborers, or "boomers," were unreliable and undisciplined and that family-based teams of workers constituted a potentially industrious and loyal work force.[75]

How influential family connections were is difficult to ascertain. One quantitative indication comes from the biographical sketches of representative employees compiled by the Illinois Central Railroad in 1900. Of the 155 workers born before the year 1850 (they were among the first men to be employed on the line), 50 percent reported having at least one close relative in the trade.[76] Of these, 21 percent had fathers, 60 percent sons, and 16 percent brothers in the industry. Practically all the relatives of these pioneer railwaymen worked for the Illinois Central. Whether it was a result of nepotism or of workers hearing of vacancies and beseeching local foremen to hire their brothers and sons, the available evidence indicates that direct family connections played a significant role in nineteenth-century recruitment practices.[77]

[73] Cochran, *Railroad Leaders*, p. 29.

[74] *Report of the Board of Managers to the Stockholders of the Mine Hill and Schuylkill Haven Railroad Company, 1864* (Philadelphia, 1864), p. 7.

[75] John S. Kendall, "The Connecticut and Passumpsic Rivers R.R.," *Railway and Locomotive Historical Society Bulletin*, no. 49, p. 31.

[76] Illinois Central Railroad, *History of The Illinois Central Railroad Company and Representative Employees* (Chicago, 1900).

[77] Unless the railroads themselves kept records of family connection, it is impossible to establish with precision the number of railwaymen who had kin in the trade. No nineteenth-century payroll record located included addresses; link-

Personal and nonfamilial associations also represented valuable assets in securing railway employment. Close friends, of
course, could be as helpful as relatives in intervening to secure
positions. Letters of recommendation from clergymen, former
employers, railroad company stockholders, and prominent men
of the community served to enhance an applicant's chances. For
example, in 1848 thirty-five citizens of Danville, Maine, signed
a petition lauding the achievements and virtues of Cyrus Green
and sent it to the directors of the Atlantic & St. Lawrence Railroad. He was recommended for the position of depot master at
Danville.[78] Joel Prince, applying for a station agency at Cumberland, Maine, similarly presented a letter of testimony signed
by fifteen fellow townspeople.[79] George H. Cushman even so-
licited petitions of recommendation from community members
to further his application for a refreshment concession in his
town's local depot.[80]

Letters of reference from stockholders and high officials of the
lines carried particular weight. Herbert Hamblen related the experiences of a veteran engineer named Pop, who was a machinist
by trade. Pop apparently never fired an engine a day in his life

---

ing individuals to the manuscript census was thus impossible. Using the census
itself proved problematic. One can establish how many railwaymen resided in
homes with other relatives in the trade, but kin relationships across addresses
cannot be ascertained. In Philadelphia, for example, analysis of the manuscript
census revealed that in the period 1860 to 1880 between 2 and 4 percent of the
railwaymen listed lived with relatives who were railroad workers—a small number to be sure. The number of men who had kin in the industry who lived at
different addresses cannot be established. The above aggregate figures also obscure significant distinctions. Between 1860 and 1880, 13 to 18 percent of all
Philadelphia Irish-born railwaymen lived in homes with other relatives in the
trade (the figure for native-born workers is less than 1 percent). Family connection
then apparently played a greater role for the Irish-born railwaymen. These figures
have been accessed from the data bank of the Philadelphia Social History Project.
Finally, a recently completed study of recruitment patterns on the Atchison,
Topeka & Santa Fe Railroad in the late nineteenth century indicates that upwards
of half the men employed on that line may have had relatives working for the
company. See James Ducker, "Men of the Steel Rails: Workers on the Atchison,
Topeka, and Santa Fe" (Ph.D. dissertation, Univ. of Illinois at Urbana-Cham-
paign, 1980), p. 52.

[78] Petition of Recommendation, September 20, 1848, Atlantic & St. Lawrence
Railroad Papers, Correspondence, 1845–1848.

[79] Petition of Recommendation, n.d., ibid.

[80] Recommendation for Refreshment Concession, n.d., ibid.

and stepped right into a locomotiveman's position. As he explained, "When this road opened, I had a letter from a big man. I asked for a job and was given an engine at once."[81] Neal and Josiah Dow, directors of the Atlantic & St. Lawrence Railroad, regularly submitted names of young men of humble backgrounds from Portland, Maine, for consideration as brakemen and firemen.[82] Alvah Hersey and Ozene Spaulding, seeking employment in the same company as a depot master and a baggageman, respectively, were able to include in their applications petitions of recommendation signed by stockholders of the road. They attested to the applicants' moral worth and general abilities and added that their approval would be welcomed by the upstanding men of the communities served by the railroad.[83]

Close associations with certain officials and foremen also enhanced the chances of a railwayman, once hired, for future employment. Letters of recommendation and introduction from former supervisors were a necessity for migrating workers.[84] In his "boomer" days, Harry French frequently relied on his past associations and an informal network of friendships between local officials of different lines to secure new positions.[85] Evidence also indicates that superintendents and foremen practiced what amounted to a "spoils" system. In their own frequent moves between companies, they often took their favorite employees and gave them choice jobs after displacing other workers.[86] When Superintendent Charles Minot of the Boston & Maine left to take the superintendency of the Erie Railroad in the 1850s, he brought with him a good number of his immediate assistants plus many engineers and conductors.[87] Charles George relates

---

[81] Quoted in Reinhardt, *Workin' On The Railroad*, p. 120.

[82] Neal Dow to the President and Directors of the Atlantic & St. Lawrence Railroad, n.d., Atlantic & St. Lawrence Railroad Papers, Correspondence, 1849–1855.

[83] George F. Emery to the President and Directors of the Atlantic & St. Lawrence Railroad, August 9, 1849, ibid.; Recommendation from Seven Stockholders on Behalf of Ozene Spaulding, n.d., ibid.

[84] Lathrop, *Little Engines and Big Men*, p. 60.

[85] French, *Railroadman*, p. 118.

[86] Dan Mater, "The Development and Operation of the Railroad Seniority System," *Journal of Business of the Univ. of Chicago* 13:400.

[87] George, *Forty Years on The Rail*, p. 60.

in his reminiscences how he left his home in Vermont and his job as a conductor on the Vermont Central to move to Illinois at the behest of his local supervisor who was transferring to another line. George was lured by an offer of a station agency.[88] This form of favoritism apparently was prevalent enough to warrant comment in a report prepared by a federal commission investigating the railroad industry in the early twentieth century. Commenting on past recruitment procedures, the report briefly noted that "Superintendents and others in authority were continually shifting from road to road, and they naturally liked to bring with them friends and trusted subordinates."[89]

If direct family or personal, nonfamilial connections failed as means of obtaining employment, bribery offered a third alternative. Again, documentation for this kind of activity is scanty, but enough evidence exists to indicate that the outright selling and purchasing of jobs was frequently practiced. In 1847, for instance, E. M. Webber, writing to Superintendent Charles Gore of the Nashua & Lowell Railroad requesting employment, offered Gore fifty dollars if his application were accepted.[90] In 1868 John Garrett, president of the Baltimore & Ohio Railroad, was informed that William Shipley, foreman of the blacksmith shop at Mount Clare, was demanding and receiving money from men taken on at the shop. Shipley, Garrett learned, also was taking a percentage of the earnings of new recruits amounting to an average of five dollars per month and was encouraging these workers "voluntarily" to offer gifts to his son.[91]

The letterbooks of officials of the Chicago, Burlington & Quincy Railroad reveal that extortion was a persistent problem on that line. In 1868 General Superintendent Robert Harris was notified that one of his divisional superintendents was requiring the men under his command to buy accident policies from an insurance company for which he worked as a part-time agent. Purchasing

[88] Ibid., p. 75.

[89] U. S. Eight Hour Commmission, *Report of the Eight Hour Commission* (Washington, D.C., 1918), p. 307.

[90] E. M. Weber to Charles Gore, December 15, 1847, Nashua & Lowell and Boston & Lowell Railroad Papers, vol. 191.

[91] James Sullivan to J. W. Garrett, May 2, 1868, Baltimore & Ohio Railroad Papers, file 3089.

these policies was not only a prerequisite for employment in this division, but also a requirement for continued service.[92] Three years later, Harris learned that the practice of offering gifts and money as payment for jobs and continued employment was still rampant throughout the line's extensive system. This time Harris ordered an investigtion and issued a strongly worded memorandum prohibiting such activities. "Let us keep Satan out as much as possible," he beseeched.[93] Harris's efforts were to little or no avail, for seven years later, in 1878, President Perkins again was forced to warn company officers against the practice of demanding or accepting gifts.[94] The problem obviously was deeply rooted and not easily solved by managerial edict. Few railroad companies escaped from such practices. As Dan Mater, a student of railway union contracts, has indicated, evidence from arbitration proceedings in the early twentieth century reveals that the custom of divisional officials and local foremen accepting a steady stream of little tokens of esteem from recruits and admiring subordinates at Christmas time, birthdays, and on other occasions was fairly widespread throughout the industry during the nineteenth century.[95]

Finally, political affiliations also at times played a part. On the state-owned Western & Atlantic Railroad in Georgia, for instance, old employees were dismissed after the Civil War to make way for political "patriots," with the well-paying conductors' jobs being reserved for the sons of legislators.[96] Politicians, such as James Kelley, Commissioner of Immigration in New York during the 1850s, used their influence to secure railroad positions for their relatives and friends.[97] The political problems of the unpopular railroads sometimes even influenced employment choices. I. F. Babcock wrote to officials of the Hartford &

[92] Robert Harris to H. Hitchcock, May 6, 1868, Chicago, Burlington & Quincy Railroad Papers, 3H4.1.

[93] Robert Harris to H. Hitchcock, July 24, 1871, Chicago, Burlington & Quincy Railroad Papers, 3H4.1.

[94] C. E. Perkins's memorandum of July 10, 1878, Chicago, Burlington & Quincy Railroad Papers, 3P4.92.

[95] Mater, "The Development and Operation," pp. 400–401.

[96] John Stover, *American Railroads*, p. 109.

[97] Cochran, *Railroad Leaders*, p. 407.

New Haven Railroad in 1851 recommending a relative for a position as conductor and gave political expediency as a prime justification for the railroad to hire him. Given "bitter feelings in the city [of New Haven] towards the Hartford Company," Babcock argued, "it would not be amiss to appoint a New Haven man for conductor."[98] Often applicants would cite their political persuasions as part of their credentials. Writing to top officials in New York, A. G. Henry in his application for a position as a station agent on the Illinois Central stressed that he held no grudges against eastern men or eastern capital and gave Senator Stephen Douglas as a reference. Henry also felt moved to state firmly his political biases:

I am a Western Man in feeling and interest. I have been actively identified with the interests of the State [Illinois] for the last twenty years and having been a prominent and active *Whig* (being Chairman of the Whig State General Committee for the past two years) I am well and favorably known to all the leading Whigs of the State and not obnoxious to the Democrats.[99]

Political affiliations certainly played a much less substantial role in recruitment practices than family or other personal connections, yet the presence of political statements in many letters of application suggests that some recruits thought political affairs important enough to mention.

A few final comments concerning recruitment patterns are worthy of emphasis. First, the informal and subjective nature of recruitment procedures and practices on the nation's pioneer railroads served indirectly as a means of engendering loyalty and disciplined behavior. Since purely objective, market-oriented criteria did not always dictate employment decisions, the attachments formed between employees and railroad companies generally were of a personal character. Many mid-nineteenth-century railwaymen were, in fact, directly beholden for private reasons to line officials for their initial engagement and continued job

[98] I. F. Babcock to E. C. Read, October 23, 1851, New York, New Haven & Hartford Railroad Papers, vol. 398.

[99] A. G. Henry to William Ward, January 2, 1852, Illinois Central Railroad Papers, 3P4.92, Newberry Library.

security. Patronage, favoritism, nepotism, and extortion served in this way to bind workers and managers in a manner which would not have been duplicated had hiring been solely a function of idealized labor market conditions. Many railroads recognized this reality and deliberately sought to utilize recruitment practices as a means of molding diligent work forces by encouraging the employment of family-based groups of workers.

Second, in the available reminiscences, biographical sketches, and tales of railwaymen, one is struck by the relative ease with which men secured their first and subsequent positions in the industry. Railroad workers like Harry French, Charles George, Harvey Reed, and the 155 representative employees of the Illinois Central Railroad previously mentioned were constantly changing jobs and employers. What is noteworthy about this process is that, whenever and wherever these men migrated, contacts existed to aid them in obtaining new employment. A veritable nationwide network of friends, relatives, fellow employees, and former supervisors appears to have emerged in the nineteenth century to facilitate individual railway labor recruitment.[100]

Of related and equal importance is the fact that every crossroads depot served as an informal clearinghouse for the exchange of information concerning job possibilities. A common scene depicted in railroad reminiscences is of different grades of workers gathered together in rail shops, stations, or roundhouses trading rumors about employment openings on new lines.[101] Railwaymen thus were one of the first groups of industrial workers to benefit from technological advances in transportation and communications. The very trains they worked on or near not only facilitated the flow of goods and people, but also the flow of ideas and information. Direct and easy access to reports on the growing job market within their trade often aided and pro-

---

[100] French, *Railroadman*, p. 118; Inglis Stuart, "George Althouse," *The Railway and Locomotive Historical Society Bulletin*, no. 11, pp. 1–12. The ease by which men secured new positions is illustrated in a story told by Harvey Reed. When a new, stern master mechanic replaced a well-liked supervisor, Reed and seventeen of his fellow locomotive drivers just left their company and found work elsewhere. See Reed, *Forty Years a Locomotive Engineer*, p. 33.

[101] George, *Forty Years on The Rail*, p. 70.

moted their own and their friends' and relatives' railroading careers.

Finally, the evidence pointing to the importance of personal and family connections in employment decisions suggests the necessity of reassessing the significance of recent findings on nineteenth-century patterns of residential mobility. Following the pioneer efforts of Stephen Thernstrom, a good number of scholars working at the community level have established that massive, continual migration was a basic phenomenon of life in nineteenth-century America.[102] In any given community in any given decade, upwards of 60 percent of the inhabitants moved. The picture in these studies is one of a wandering people— rootless, atomized, and disassociated.

The study of recruitment patterns of mid-nineteenth-century railwaymen suggests that despite geographical mobility, interpersonal associations of both the familial and nonfamilial kind still loomed large in work situations and work experiences. A free-floating market of anonymous applicants who would be judged purely on merit and achievement-oriented priorities did not exist. Railwaymen moved frequently but often only to reestablish contacts with relatives, friends, fellow employees, and former supervisors. Family and personal connections remained important factors in securing jobs, and their influence within the industry quite often transcended geographical distances.

IF EXTERNAL and internal sources of supply were discovered and developed to meet the various skill needs of the railroad industry both in its very early and later periods of growth, and if formal restrictions or informal procedures and practices did not impede the recruitment of workers into the trade, the question still remains whether American railroad companies faced any significant problem in attracting adequate supplies of labor purely in terms of numbers. The industry grew dramatically throughout the century, and its manpower requirements were sizable. The issue of labor supply in the railroad industry during the nineteenth century is not an idle one, since the general question has

[102] Stephen Thernstrom, *Poverty and Progress* and also his *The Other Bostonians*, especially chap. 9.

emerged as a topic of controversy among economic historians. It has been argued, for instance, and most forcefully by H. J. Habbakuk, that a relative scarcity of labor in the United States during the early stages of the nation's industrial development proved an unusual incentive for American entrepreneurs to quickly and extensively adopt labor-saving, capital-intensive techniques of production; further, that American workers, in relatively high demand, possesᵣed the means to bid their wages up effectively, thereby easing the dislocations of industrialization and creating a healthy home market for the standardized goods rolling off American assembly lines.[103] The scarcity-of-labor argument is both intriguing and provocative and replete with broad implications for American economic, political, and social history. It is a thesis, however, which has also generated much skepticism and dissent.[104]

The labor supply question on the nation's pioneer operating railroads provides further interest because during periods of construction, nineteenth-century American rail carriers experienced severe difficulties in recruiting adequate numbers of workers. The massive importation of cheap, unskilled Oriental labor to build the rail lines of the West is now a familiar chapter in the country's history. The original eastern railroads faced similiar problems. In the early period companies encountered frequent construction delays induced by labor shortages. Construction was "unexpectedly retarded by the great scarcity of labor," the directors of the Baltimore & Susquehanna Railroad sadly announced to stockholders in 1836. Public works projects throughout the country, they explained, meant that "the demand for hands was greater than could be supplied."[105] Progress on the extension of the B. & O. into Ohio was similarly impeded by labor supply problems. "Deficiency of hands" and resulting high

---

[103] H. J. Habakkuk, *American and British Technology in the Nineteenth Century.*

[104] Peter Temin, "Labor Scarcity and the Problems of American Industrial Efficiency," *Journal of Economic History,* 26; Paul David, *Technical Choice, Innovation and Economic Growth,* chap. 1.

[105] *Ninth Annual Report of the President & Directors to the Stockholders of the Baltimore and Susquehanna Rail Road Company* (Baltimore, 1836), p. 5.

labor costs, complained the directors, necessitated the delays.[106] The problem was so severe during the construction of the Illinois Central in the early 1850s that company officials were compelled to establish a recruiting organization in the East to attract immigrant labor. Private contractors of the road, forced to compete with each other for the limited numbers of workers, actually bid up the wages of unskilled workers to $1.25 a day, equivalent to what skilled mechanics and artisans were earning in Chicago at the same time.[107]

Once construction was completed and operations commenced, the problem of labor supply appears to have abated. There were still isolated complaints. When the Baltimore & Ohio Railroad extended passenger and freight service into Ohio in the mid-1850s, there occurred an immediate manpower crisis as the company's operating labor supply needs multiplied tenfold.[108] Throughout its early years the Illinois Central also faced competition from local farmers along the line who outbid the company for hired, unskilled labor. In 1857, when a depression forced the I.C. to discharge men and cut wages, a general scarcity of common laborers still pressured divisional road masters into raising the pay rates of track repair hands from $1.00 to $1.12 a day.[109] Other specific incidents like these can be cited, but the overall pattern is one of adequacy and even surplus of labor.

One indication that labor shortage did not plague the operating railroads is provided by the general absence of recruitment advertisements. While printed circulars publicizing openings for construction workers can be found in company archives, similar notices enticing operating railwaymen cannot be located. In labor journals and railway trade papers, as well, recruitment advertisements are searched for in vain. In the *American Railway Journal*, the most prominent publication of its kind during the early period of rail transport, only one notice announcing op-

---

[106] *Twenty-Seventh Annual Report of the President and Directors to the Stockholders of the Baltimore & Ohio Railroad Company* (Baltimore, 1853), app., p. 5.

[107] Lightner, "Labor on the Illinois Central," pp. 16–28.

[108] *Twenty-Seventh Annual Report of the President & Directors to the Stockholders of the Baltimore & Ohio Railroad Company* (Baltimore, 1853), p. 32.

[109] Lightner, "Labor on the Illinois Central," p. 83.

erating positions appeared during the first forty years of the paper's existence. This was an advertisement placed by the Mobile & Ohio Railroad in 1856 seeking fifteen to twenty experienced locomotive drivers and machinists.[110] The railroads apparently did not have to rely on the formal broadcasting of openings to fill their respective manpower needs. Nor does it appear that they resorted to recruitment agencies to help secure their operating labor, as was done for construction workers. A memorandum in the archives of the Chicago, Burlington & Quincy Railroad does refer to the line's contracting with the Northwestern Employment Agency of Chicago to supply track repairmen, but that is the lone reference to such a practice.[111]

More definitive evidence can be found in managerial letterbooks. For example, Herman Haupt, superintendent of the Pennsylvania Railroad, wrote to a newly appointed division official in 1852, outlining his duties and advising him on procedures and standards for recruiting new men. Haupt noted that local officials could afford to be deliberate in their selection of recruits since "the list of applicants is always very large."[112]

The Baltimore & Ohio Railroad, after some immediate problems following the line's extension, experienced no later difficulties in attracting adequate supplies of workers. In 1864, when the road was particularly strained on account of its key role in troop, supply, and merchandise movements during the Civil War, President Garrett asked his master of transportation, William Smith, to advertise in newspapers in New York and New England for freight conductors and brakemen.[113] A month later, Garrett summarily ordered Smith to terminate the recruitment campaign since the line was being deluged with applicants.[114] So ample were the supplies of even skilled labor that a year after this incident Garrett was told by a department head that the company could proceed with a plan to institute a fifty-cent reduction in

[110] *American Railway Journal*, January 12, 1856, p. 30.

[111] Paul Black, "Development of Management Personnel Policies," p. 201.

[112] Herman Haupt to General A. L. Rumfort, June 23, 1852, Herman Haupt Letterbook, Historical Society of Pennsylvania.

[113] J. W. Garrett to W. P. Smith, November 18, 1864, Baltimore & Ohio Railroad Letterbooks.

[114] J. W. Garrett to W. P. Smith, December 20, 1864, ibid.

daily pay to machinists. Even if some men objected and quit, their places could be filled almost immediately.[115] Requests for employment continued to come into the offices of the B. & O. in such numbers after the war that answering the applicants occupied much of the time and attention of the clerical staff. The following form letter of rejection, with Garrett's secretary's signature, was used: "From the numerous applications for employment recently received by this office, the President is under the impression that his corps is now entirely full."[116]

Other railroads experienced similar conditions. When the Reading Railroad was faced with wage demands in 1868, the general superintendent advised the president that there was no reason to grant increases, since there were enough applicants to fill the positions of dissatisfied workers.[117] The Chicago, Burlington & Quincy in the late 1860s was so inundated with employment requests that General Superintendent Harris initiated a policy of drawing up lists of candidates' names and circulating them among other midwestern roads.[118] Few letters in the C.B. & Q.'s extensive archives, moreover, reflect any great concern for labor shortage problems. Most items dealing with the issue, in fact, note a glut rather than a scarcity of available workers.[119] Railroad work as a source of employment apparently was so much in demand, finally, that when the New York, Chicago & St. Louis Railroad commenced operations in 1882 the company received over six thousand applications for various positions on the line.[120]

Quantitative evidence confirms the literary record. One means of measuring whether labor scarcity was a pressing condition of

[115] J. C. Davis to J. W. Garrett, July 17, 1865, Baltimore & Ohio Railroad Papers, file 6837.

[116] Andrew Anderson to James Hamilton, February 22, 1866, Baltimore & Ohio Railroad Letterbooks.

[117] Copy of letter to President Smith about increases of wages, March 29, 1868, Reading Railroad Papers, Eleutherian Mills Historical Society Library.

[118] Paul Black, "Robert Harris and the Problem of Railway Labor Management: 1867–1870" (unpublished manuscript in author's possession), pp. 10–11.

[119] Paul Black, "Development of Management Personnel Policies," p. 194; Robert Harris to George McKay, October 7, 1869, Chicago, Burlington & Quincy Railroad Papers, 3H4.1.

[120] Taylor Hampton, *The Nickel Plate Road*, p. 138.

Table 2.4. Wage Averages and Differentials, 1838–73

	Average daily wages (in dollars)			Wage differentials		
	Railroad track & station laborers	Railroad locomotive engineers	Common laborers	Railroad engineers/ Railroad laborers	Railroad laborers/ Common laborers	Railroad engineers/ Common laborers
1838–47	.92	2.03	.95	2.21	.97	2.14
1848–57	1.04	2.26	.96	2.17	1.08	2.35
1858–67	1.37	2.57	1.27	1.87	1.08	2.02
1868–73	1.55	3.19	1.66	2.06	.93	1.92

the industry is to contrast various wage differentials. If the demand for workers increased this should be reflected in comparative wage statistics. What is of interest in this kind of analysis is not just changes in average earnings, but, more important, changes in differentials over time.

To measure statistically the phenomenon of labor scarcity in the nineteenth-century railroad industry, daily wage rate information was gathered from seventy-eight separate payroll records during the period 1838–73. Average earnings were then calculated for general station workers and locomotive drivers. These figures were compared with the daily rates for common laborers during the same time span. The averages and differentials resulting from this investigation are reported in table 2.4.[121]

The differential figures in table 2.4 reveal that, relative to common labor, no great increase in demand emerged for either unskilled or skilled railroad workers during the period under study. During the 1850s and '60s there was a slight rise in the comparative price of general railroad labor, but this appears to have leveled off after 1868. The demand for locomotive drivers, moreover, actually fell relative to the cost of hiring common workers. Of equal significance is the fact that demand for railroad engineers declined also in relation to demand for unskilled railwaymen. This corresponds to the literary findings which indicated that when railway managers complained of labor scarcity

[121] Complete figures and information concerning the data sources for table 2.4 are contained in a methodological note in appendix A.

they spoke mainly in terms of their problem of recruiting track repairmen and station workers and not of the need for skilled, upper-grade railwaymen.

Literary and statistical evidence then points to a general pattern of labor adequacy and even surplus. There are two exceptions to this finding, however, and they deserve mention. The average earnings and wage differentials reported above are composite figures, which necessarily hide important regional and temporal differences. Southern railroad companies throughout the early years of rail transport development faced severe difficulties meeting both their unskilled and skilled manpower needs. During the Civil War, moreover, railroads both in the Confederacy and the Union were hard pressed on account of the drafting of railway workers.

The South experienced particular problems in attracting skilled engineers and machinists. When J. Edgar Thomson was superintendent of the Georgia Railroad in the 1830s, for instance, he wrote Matthias Baldwin requesting his assistance in recruiting locomotivemen and mechanics. Baldwin replied that he was having little success convincing potential recruits of the merits of taking employment on that railroad. As he noted, "It is out of the question to get good sober industrious Men to go to the South for anything like the sum they work for here." Baldwin further warned Thomson that he should exercise great caution in hiring poorly trained southern machinists to tend the machines. "I hope you will be very cautious about who the Company employs for if they [Baldwin's engines] should fall into the hands of some machinists they can make it cost them more than three times the salary each year and all under the guise of advancing the interests of the Company. This was the case on the Charleston Road and has been on others."[122]

Baldwin's difficulties in convincing enginemen to transfer to southern railroads is further revealed in the following letter, written in 1836 to David Deshla, an official of an Alabama company:

[122] M. W. Baldwin to J. E. Thomson, May 24, 1836, Baldwin Locomotive Papers, Letter Copy Book, no. 1, Historical Society of Pennsylvania.

Yours of January 18th duly rec'd. Immediately after the recpt. of your letter I made an effort to obtain such a man as you wanted and after some delay I found one who I thought would answer. I applied to him and after much conversation, I succeeded in getting his promise to go on the following terms. His salary is to be 1100 dollars per year and found and his expenses paid to your place. I was induced to offer this because of the difficulty of prevailing on any good man to go to the South at any rate. And he is a man who now is filling a situation similar to the one you want him for and is sober, steady and industrious man. Previous to making this assignment I consulted Mr. Ferguson, who opposed the measure. After all was settled as I supposed, he set about making inquiry of the expense of taking his family on and he found it would cost about $300, which was more than he had. He wrote me a note stating his situation and said, unless that sum was advanced as a loan he could not go. I did not think it advisable to proceed any further in the matter without your advise. Thomas Riley is his name and is now on the Philadelphia & Trenton R.R. If you please you can confer with him direct. I don't know how long he will be willing to wait as nothing has been said to him on the subject.[123]

The South Carolina Railroad in the same period encountered such difficulties in finding locomotive drivers that the directors of the line seriously considered employing company-owned slaves. The minutes of a meeting of the board on September 20, 1836, include the following reference: "The expediency of running freight trains with black engineers under the management and control of a white conductor was suggested by the president—when on motion, the expediency was approved, and the measure ordered to be adopted as soon as practicable."[124] It is unclear whether the company ever implemented this motion.

The absence of adequate local sources of supply for enginemen meant that southern railroads had to look to the North for these workers and lure them with high wages. As a result, southern locomotive drivers in the antebellum period were able to draw from between twenty-five and thirty dollars more in monthly salaries than their northern counterparts. The preponderance of northern engineers also had later political ramifications. As John Stover in his history of the railroads of the South notes, "The

[123] M. W. Baldwin to David Deshla, March 10, 1836, ibid.
[124] Samuel Derrick, *Centennial History of the South Carolina Railroad*, p. 124.

southerner's traditional dislike for mechanical pursuits left much of the actual railroad operation in the hands of northern trainmen in 1861. Some of these returned home with the outbreak of war. Those that remained on the job were viewed with suspicion, and sometimes rightly so."[125] After the war all indications are that the problem of scarcity of skilled laborers did not abate for the southern railroads.[126]

The supply of unskilled labor also proved to be a source of trouble for the early southern rail lines. In the antebellum period, hired slaves formed the backbone of the South's railway labor force of track repairmen, station helpers, brakemen, firemen, and sometimes even enginemen. The southern railroads, however, faced strong competition for slave labor from the agricultural sector. As a result, southern rail companies were forced in many cases to purchase slaves directly and provide for their upkeep. The process is well described in the following passage from Howard Dozier's A History of the Atlantic Coast Line Railroad:

For the rough work of operating and loading trains, negroes were hired directly by the railroad company. The contracts or bonds were signed on the first of January. The usual price for the ordinary unskilled laborer was from $75 to $100 and his "find"; that of the skilled laborer, such as the fireman or brakeman, was often as high as $250 per year. . . . For a number of years the system of using hired slaves was employed with success, but as agriculture became more profitable, it was increasingly difficult to secure them and resort was had to hiring white men for the work. This proved unsuccessful as the class of white men secured was less reliable than the slaves. As the price of slave labor advanced the roads began to buy slaves of their own. In 1857 the Wilmington & Weldon owned 13, valued at $15,000, and the Report of 1860 advises the purchase of twenty more for use on trains and at warehouses.[127]

Increased pressure from agriculture and rising hiring prices during the 1850s forced the southern railroads to resort more and more to slave purchasing as a means of meeting their man-

---

[125] Stover, Railroads of the South, p. 18.

[126] Proceedings of the Sixteenth Annual Meeting of the Stockholders of the North Carolina Railroad Company, July 13, 1865, pp. 26–27; Derrick, Centennial History, pp. 223, 236.

[127] Howard Dozier, A History of the Atlantic Coast Line Railroad, p. 90.

A re-creation of a scene on the Natchez & Hamburg Railroad. The engine "Mississippi" was built in 1834. (Courtesy of Illinois Central Railroad.)

power supply needs. In 1856 the president of the North Carolina Rail Company recommended to his directors the acquisition of one hundred hands "as a measure of economy and good policy." Ownership of slaves would entail new costs and responsibilities, he admitted, but ultimately the company would profit by reducing yearly hiring expenditures.[128] By 1860 the Nashville & Chattanooga had expended no less than $128,773.29 on the purchase of slaves; the Raleigh & Gaston, $125,000. At the end of 1859 the South Carolina Company owned ninety slaves with a book value of more than $80,000, while the Montgomery & West Point had purchased sixty slaves and the miniscule Baton Rouge, Opelousas & Gross Tete Railroad had invested $115,000

[128] *Report on the North Carolina Rail Road, January 20, 1859* (Salisbury, N.C., 1859), pp. 18–19.

in bonded labor.[129] Slave purchasing as a source of labor supply continued and increased during the Civil War as the southern railroads became more hard pressed to meet their general manpower requirements.

The war, however, brought the issue of labor scarcity to the fore in the North as well as the South. On the Western Railroad in Massachusetts, for instance, local foremen complained in 1863 that they could not recruit enough common labor to unload coal trains.[130] Officials of the Pennsylvania similarly noted that the company was experiencing great difficulty in finding a sufficient number of men even to run trains.[131] A dearth of skilled mechanics forced the Chicago & Alton Railroad to suspend service temporarily as all the company's engines were in need of repair.[132] The Baltimore & Ohio lost most of its labor force through conscription, while enlistments cut the number of men employed on the Illinois Central by one third.[133] Throughout the North, labor scarcity functioned effectively to drive up daily wages. On the Western Railroad, station laborers were making as much as $2.50 a day during the war while locomotive drivers were making $5.65 on the Illinois Central.[134] In few cases, however, did increases in wages translate into gains in real income as war-induced inflation also drove up the prices of food, housing, and clothing.

Northern railroads attempted to deal with the problem by redoubling efforts to recruit men. In some instances, like on the Baltimore & Ohio, advertising and other campaigns met with a modicum of success.[135] Other railroads endeavored to keep their labor forces intact by arranging to pay their employees' con-

[129] Robert C. Black III, *The Railroads of the Confederacy*, pp. 29–30.

[130] H. Chapin to G. H. Powers, April 21, 1863, Western Railroad Papers, case 5.

[131] Thomas Weber, *The Northern Railroads in the Civil War, 1861–1865*, p. 63.

[132] *Second Annual Report of the President and Directors of the Chicago and Alton Railroad Company* (Chicago, 1865), p. 11.

[133] Weber, *Northern Railroads*, p. 18; Lightner, "Labor on the Illinois Central," p. 93.

[134] Lightner, "Labor on the Illinois Central," pp. 97–99.

[135] See notes 115 and 116.

scription bounties and finding men to volunteer in their stead. As the crisis continued and deepened, though, railway managers were forced to redirect their energies solely toward convincing the War Department of the necessity of exempting railwaymen from military service. Secretary of War Edwin Stanton had decreed that only locomotive engineers who were employed when the draft was enacted would be deferred. Led by Thomas Scott of the Pennsylvania, railroad executives lobbied to have this exemption extended to other grades of workers. Various schemes were devised and offered to lessen the effects of conscription, and much pressure was brought to bear upon Stanton. Finally, in August 1862, he ruled that exemptions would not be extended beyond those applying to locomotive drivers, but that in certain circumstances the War Department would discharge drafted railway employees "on the ground that their mechanical service is more valuable than service in the field."[136] Railroad companies did of course petition for the release of specific workers, but labor scarcity continued to plague the northern part of the industry throughout the war.

In the South, the war only exacerbated an already serious labor shortage. Many companies complained that the high wages offered by the Confederate government to carpenters and machinists were hampering their efforts to find men to rebuild bridges and keep locomotives and cars in repair.[137] In Georgia the state assembly was forced to vote a 50 percent increase in pay to skilled workers on the state-owned Western & Atlantic Railroad in order to keep them from leaving.[138] Demand and inflation in other areas boosted railroad mechanics' wages from $2.50 to as high as $20.00 a day.[139] The draft in addition depleted the lines of available trainmen. Train service, as a result, was maintained with a dangerously low number of crew members. A veteran conductor on the Nashville, Chattanooga & St. Louis Railroad, J. H. Latimer, thus recalled in 1907 what it was like to be in charge of a train during the war when labor was scarce:

[136] Weber, *Northern Railroads*, pp. 130–133.
[137] Angus James Johnston II, *Virginia Railroads in the Civil War*, p. 286.
[138] Robert C. Black III, *The Railroads of the Confederacy*, pp. 128–129.
[139] Stover, *American Railroads*, p. 57.

After the beginning of the Civil War we had a great deal of trouble in securing trainmen. On one occasion I left Nashville with a full train [sixteen freight cars] and had one trainman and a pouring rain. When I arrived at Murfreesboro, he played out and left me—I went to work, switched all my good brakes together and lit out alone, thinking I would be sure to pick up someone at Decherd—I arrived at Decherd all wet and cold, and to my astonishment the next morning I left for Chattanooga without a man, and had the assistance of the fireman down the mountain [setting brakes]; half my cars stopped at Stevenson. The acting agent at Stevenson gave me a lot of cars there for Chattanooga. I asked him if he was going to play brakeman on those cars to Chattanooga. He replied "not much". . . . I felt the effects of this trip for two weeks.[140]

A growing shortage of slave labor also proved a problem for the southern railroads during the Civil War. A number of factors were at work. Slave captures by the Union armies and an increase in slave runaways diminished the available supply pool. Agricultural production and wartime manufacturing increasingly became strong competitors with the railroads for bonded labor. Slaves now were also needed to replace white, drafted railwaymen who occupied high-grade positions. Southern railroads thus were faced with a new and greater common labor supply problem and their troubles were further complicated by the war-inflated prices of hired slaves. As a result, many southern railroads were forced to resort exclusively to slave purchasing to an even greater extent than before the outbreak of hostilities.[141] In Virginia the price of both hired and purchased slave labor loomed so dear that the directors of the Virginia Central sought a third solution by petitioning the state assembly for legislation empowering the governor to impress slaves for use on the road. The legislation was enacted but disgruntled owners effectively blocked its enforcement.[142]

Finally, it should be noted that the Confederate government

---

[140] Quoted from Jesse C. Burt, Jr., "The Savor of Old-Time Southern Railroading," *Railway and Locomotive Historical Society Bulletin*, no. 84, pp. 39–40.

[141] Johnston, *Virginia Railroads*, pp. 70, 225; Robert C. Black III, *Railroads of the Confederacy*, p. 130.

[142] Charles Turner, "The Richmond, Fredericksburg and Potomac, 1861–1865," *Civil War History* 7:256–257.

A train crew of the Orange & Alexandria Railroad stopped en route. The photograph was taken during the Civil War. (Courtesy of The National Archives.)

developed slightly more liberal policies for exempting railwaymen from military service than its northern counterpart. The
southern conscription law of April 1862 provided for deferments
for all railway employees at the option of the Secretary of War.
By August of that year, 5,718 railwaymen had received official
exemptions along 6,222 miles of operating track. In April 1863
the government, however, reduced deferments to include only
specific categories of railway personnel. Those now exempted
included the president, superintendents, conductors, treasurer,
chief clerk, engineers, managers, station agents, section masters,
two expert track hands for every section of eight miles, and shop
mechanics. Laborers, porters, and messengers were not exempt.
In 1864 the exemption codes were revised to stipulate that a
maximum of one man per mile of railroad in use could be deferred on any given line. Since four or five men per mile were
considered the minimum number of workers needed to operate
a line safely, it is apparent that the southern roads were kept in
service during the war with an absolutely subsistence level of
manpower.[143]

ONE LAST issue remains to be considered on the topic of labor
supply and that is the question of turnover or labor retention.
In the historical literature, supply usually is treated solely as a
problem of the recruitment of adequate numbers of competent
workers. For individual firms, however, the question of supply
goes beyond the mere existence of an available labor pool. Once
labor is mobilized, there persists the problem of maintaining
stability of employment. High productivity and efficiency, in
particular, are difficult to achieve in the context of high turnover
and labor mobility.

Surviving payrolls indicate that turnover on the nation's pioneer railroads reached staggering proportions. On the Hartford
& New Haven Railroad in the 1840s, 1850s, and 1860s, upwards of 50 percent of the men engaged by the line remained
with the company for a maximum of six months. Conversely,
slightly more than a quarter of the work force stayed with the

[143] Robert C. Black III, *Railroads of the Confederacy*, pp. 129–130; Johnston,
Virginia Railroads, p. 225.

firm for two years or more (Table 2.5). Figures for the Boston & Worcester at midcentury and the Cleveland & Toledo Railroad in the 1860s are almost identical.[144] Partial returns available for the Western, Eastern, Boston & Maine, and Chicago, Burlington & Quincy Railroads in the period under study repeat the pattern; with a few minor exceptions, at any given moment in time, one-half of the men listed on the rolls of a particular company would not be with that line six months later.[145] Only one-quarter remained with their respective firms for a sufficient time to be characterized as long-term employees. Though the specific figures for the Hartford & New Haven Railroad, which stretch over three decades, indicate that turnover may have subsided during the course of the century and that employment patterns stabilized, the improvement was slight and the overriding impression is one of intense labor mobility.

Tracing employees through surviving payrolls to measure mobility also reveals that turnover was a grade-specific phenomenon. A strong, statistically significant correlation emerged between length of service and position in the railway occupational hierarchy.[146] While 57 percent of the managers of the New Haven & Hartford Railroad remained with the line for more than two

[144] Turnover figures for the Boston & Worcester Railroad for the years 1849–51 can be found on table B.1, which appears in appendix B; for the Cleveland & Toledo Railroad in the period 1864–66 see table B.2, also in appendix B. A methodological note in the appendix describes the sources and methods employed in constructing these tables.

[145] Statistics on turnover of blacksmiths, carpenters, machinists, engineers, and firemen employed by the Western Railroad between January and December 1842 can be found in table B.3 in appendix B; average number of years served by top officers, locomotive drivers and conductors on the Eastern Railroad between 1836 and 1847 appears in table B.4 in appendix B. Similar averages for officials, office workers, agents, conductors, and enginemen on the Boston & Maine Railroad between 1849 and 1868 are contained in table B.5 in appendix B; a two-year breakdown of turnover by grade for workers employed in the Car and Locomotive Department of the Chicago, Burlington & Quincy Railroad in 1861 and 1862 appears in table B.6 in appendix B; table B.7 in appendix B lists figures for length of service of C.B. & Q. enginemen who were present on the payroll in 1877. A methodological note in appendix B describes the sources and methods employed in constructing the above-mentioned tables. Identical figures on turnover have also recently been calculated for the Atchison, Topeka & Santa Fe Railroad in the late nineteenth century. See Ducker, "Men of the Steel Rails," pp. 132–142.

[146] Statistics are provided in appendix B.

Table 2.5. Turnover Analysis for the Hartford & New Haven Railroad, 1845–47, 1851–53, 1868–70

Time period and grade level	Total number employed	Number employed, by months				Percentage employed, by months			
		1–6	7–12	13–18	19–24	1–6	7–12	13–18	19–24
1845–47									
Total force	465	269	69	38	89	58	15	8	19
1851–53									
Upper-level management	3	1	0	0	2	33	0	0	67
Lower-level management	41	10	6	6	19	24	15	15	46
White-collar	33	13	8	4	8	40	24	12	24
Conductors	14	4	2	0	8	29	14	0	57
Baggagemen	12	1	0	6	5	8	0	50	42
Brakemen	21	9	3	3	6	43	14	14	28
Enginemen	19	1	5	5	8	6	26	26	42
Firemen	30	15	3	3	9	50	10	10	30
Skilled shop mechanics	99	44	15	11	29	45	15	11	29
Unskilled shop mechanics	29	8	8	4	9	28	28	13	31
Station and track labor	568	333	64	58	113	59	11	10	20
Total force	869	439	114	100	216	51	13	12	25
1868–70									
Lower-level management	77	13	15	5	44	17	19	7	57
White-collar	93	20	24	14	35	21	26	15	38
Conductors	24	2	4	1	17	8	17	4	71
Baggagemen	21	4	5	2	10	19	24	9	48
Brakemen	158	92	29	12	25	58	18	8	16
Enginemen	52	13	9	5	25	25	17	18	48
Firemen	60	24	13	9	14	40	22	15	23
Skilled shop mechanics	272	116	51	21	84	42	19	8	31
Unskilled shop mechanics	110	33	19	12	46	30	17	11	42
Station and track labor	944	517	134	68	225	55	14	7	24
Total force	1811	834	303	149	525	46	17	8	29

years, only 24 percent of the company's station and track labor
force persisted in service to the firm as long. In general, high-
level officials stayed longer than lower-management figures, and
both groups served for greater periods of time than their white-
collar clerical assistants. Conductors and enginemen similarly
remained on specific company payrolls for longer durations than
baggagemen and firemen. Skilled mechanics, too, were more permanent than their shop hands and apprentices, and, not surprisingly, general station and track laborers were the most transient of all railwaymen. The finding of a clear-cut relationship
between grade stratum and length of service should not, however,
obscure the reality that turnover was a significant occurrence at
all levels of the railway occupational scale.

It should also be emphasized that the statistics reported above,
while indicating the presence of substantial turnover, in and of
themselves offer no explanations for the high degree of mobility.
The dynamics of turnover actually are more complex than may
appear. Seasonality and the irregular demand for common labor
were two important factors that tended to increase rates of turnover. Yet, as will be shown in the next chapter, official disciplinary discharges also represented an important cause of changes
in the labor force. Nor should the fact that railwaymen frequently
left companies to take higher-grade positions with other firms
be overlooked. The 155 representative employees of the Illinois
Central Railroad mentioned previously, for example, worked for
an average of close to three different companies during their
careers. Movement between firms for them represented a step
upward on the railway grade ladder. The whole question of inter-
and intracompany promotion-based moves will be treated in
greater detail in chapter 4. What should be clear here, however,
is that turnover was a multifaceted problem and that disciplinary
discharges and voluntary career decisions as well as obvious
seasonal factors functioned to heighten employee transiency.

It is also difficult to ascertain whether the figures cited above
on turnover are unusual. Recent studies have shown that residential mobility was a basic reality of life in nineteenth-century
America, and one safely can assume that job mobility was also
generally high during this period. The question remains, though,

whether the railroad industry experienced the phenomenon of turnover to a greater extent than other trades and whether railwaymen were particularly more transient than other workers. Unfortunately, there are very few studies on nineteenth-century patterns of employment stability; in addition, the techniques adopted to measure turnover vary so in the existing literature that direct comparisons are difficult to establish. The earliest Department of Labor statistics, moreover, were first compiled in the second decade of the twentieth century. Though they indicate that employment stability was generally 10 to 15 percent greater in the 1910s than existed in the railroad industry in the mid-nineteenth century, an accurate assessment of the significance of nineteenth-century employee-turnover figures awaits further study.[147]

Two comments concerning labor turnover can serve as concluding remarks for this chapter. First, the figures on labor mobility suggest that for American railroad companies the real question of labor supply was not whether an adequately large and competent pool of workers existed to staff the industry, but whether railway labor once mobilized could be retained. Thus retention, and not surplus, scarcity, or adequacy was the salient problem. Whether this applies to other industries or trades in nineteenth-century America remains an open issue. What is suggested here is that the whole question of labor supply, as raised by economic historians, is greatly in need of redefinition and refocus.

Second, the existence of high turnover figures also raises the important issue of labor control. If both nineteenth-century American railroad managers and railroad employees constituted a highly mobile and transient work force, how could industrial efficiency and discipline have first been achieved and then maintained? Recent studies documenting the intensity of geographical mobility in the nineteenth century have hinted at some of the political ramifications of this phenomenon for American history, but they generally have overlooked the problems that labor in-

---

[147] Paul Brissenden and Emil Frankel, *Labor Turnover in Industry*, chaps. 8 and 9.

stability must have presented to American business enterprises a century ago.[148] America's pioneer railroads thus emerged under conditions of labor surplus and not scarcity, but more important, within the context of high employee turnover. This introduces the question of industrial discipline, the next topic of concern.

[148] See, for example, Stephen Thernstrom, "Urbanization, Migration, and Social Mobility in Late Nineteenth-Century America," in Barton Bernstein, ed., *Towards a New Past*, pp. 158–175.

3

WORKING TO RULE

≡

THE IRON HORSE was an apt symbol of the new age
of mechanical energy, speed, and expanded commerce. The railroads provided other, more subtle testimonials to the changes
wrought by industrial capitalism. The printed train schedule and
the conductor's gold timepiece were also emblems. The pace of
life had quickened and become more ordered. Thoreau noted
the difference. The railroads, he wrote:

> They come and go with such regularity and precision, and their whistles
> can be heard so far, that the farmers set their clocks by them, and thus
> one well-regulated institution regulates a whole country. Have not men
> improved somewhat in punctuality since the railroad was invented? Do
> they not talk and think faster in the depot than they did in the stage-
> office?[1]

Industrial capitalism demanded the synchronization of labor.
The pace of work in preindustrial agrarian and craft pursuits
had been discretionary and spasmodic. The profit motive, the
expanding market for standardized goods, and the introduction
of machinery required greater routinization and labor discipline.
Attitudes and behavior had to be changed accordingly. As the
English social historian, E. P. Thompson, has written, "The tran-
sition to mature industrial society entailed a severe restructuring
of working habits—new discipline, new incentives, and a new
nature upon which these incentives could bite effectively."[2]

[1] Quoted in Stewart Holbrook, *The Story of American Railroads*, p. 15.
[2] E. P. Thompson, "Time, Work-Discipline, and Industrial Capitalism," *Past
and Present* 38:57.

Railroad managers were especially attuned to the problem of industrial discipline. Public safety and convenience, the importance of keeping to schedules, competition and the pressure to reduce expenditures, the geographic range of operations, and the very nature and multiplicity of skills and tasks found in railroading—all these made the synchronization of labor an imperative. Railroad executives developed bureaucratic principles and techniques of management, experimented with the contract system, and divided work into well-defined, limited spheres to deal with the problem. Informal and formal recruitment procedures and practices served as other means of establishing loyalty and diligence. America's pioneer railroad managers also attempted to restructure the working behavior of their recruits and employees in a more direct and deliberate fashion, namely, through the expedients of rule books and disciplinary proceedings.

ALTHOUGH the railroads were not the first business enterprises to utilize rule books—apprentices, journeymen, and mill workers in eighteenth-century England commonly received impersonal written codes to guide their actions—rail companies did greatly expand their application and importance.[3] In the first two decades of rail transport development, workers entering railway employ normally were handed single sheets of paper, with timetables listed on the front and a relatively small number of company regulations on the back.[4] By the 1870s, rules governing the performance of duties had multiplied in scope and scale. Railroad companies now distributed rule books to their employees which frequently extended to a hundred pages and were often leatherbound.[5] Upon receipt, workers were expected to sign pledges to read the rules thoroughly and to carry them on the job at all times. These pledges were either pasted or printed on the back of the front cover of the books. Management then informed

[3] Sidney Pollard, "Factory Discipline in the Industrial Revolution," *Economic History Review* 16:258.

[4] David Lightner, "Labor on the Illinois Central Railroad, 1852–1900" (Ph.D. dissertation, Cornell Univ., 1969), pp. 102–103.

[5] Warren Jacobs, "Early Rules and the Standard Code," *Railway and Locomotive Historical Society Bulletin*, no. 50, p. 38. A large collection of early railroad rule books can be found in Baker Library, Harvard University.

workers of additions or amendments to existing procedures through a steady stream of printed circulars.

Railroad company rule books imparted three kinds of information. The rules demarcated lines of authority, established standards for personal behavior, and gave precise instructions for the exercise of tasks. On the latter point, details were essential. Each grade of employ received minutely drawn directives.

Railroad rule books, for example, generally delegated a multitude of responsibilities to conductors. The rules formally placed conductors in direct charge of the running of trains and prescribed strict guidelines for the collecting and recording of fares. Printed regulations further required conductors to attend to the brakes of the first cars and to supervise the loading of freight and the boarding of passengers; instructed them "to allow no riotous or unruly conduct on the trains"; authorized them to remove travelers refusing to pay their way; and made them responsible for the general appearance of the coaches and the comfort of passengers.[6] Other rules stipulated exact procedures for reporting on delays and accidents. Few particulars were overlooked. The rule book of the Michigan Central Railroad in the 1850s even included the instruction that conductors "in addition to their care and courteous treatment of all passengers on their respective trains, [should] see that the passengers are well provided with good and cold ice water on every trip."[7]

Enginemen also received precise directives. They were made responsible for the care and management of their engines and were ordered to assist in the machine shops when not on running duty. On the Western Railroad in Massachusetts, locomotive drivers were further forbidden by fiat to "leave the depot without a full tender of water, a sufficiency of oil in the can, six water buckets suspended to the tender, two jack screws, axe, crowbar, shovel, and a full complement of other tools."[8] Once on the line, the speeds at which they drove were carefully defined and reg-

---

[6] *Rules of the Boston & Lowell and Nashua & Lowell Railroad Companies* (Nashua, 1857), p. 7.

[7] Quoted in Alvin Harlow, *The Road of the Century*, p. 87.

[8] *Regulations for the Transportation Department of the Western Railroad* (Springfield, Mass., 1842), p. 9.

ulated as well. Locomotive drivers on the Boston & Worcester were prohibited "from passing over the whole road in a shorter time than three hours under any circumstances."[9] The regulations of the Western Railroad stated that "in descending grades higher than 60 feet per mile passenger trains [were] not to exceed 18 miles per hour and merchandise trains not over 10 miles per hour."[10] The use of road signals and switches, and procedures to be followed at stations, bridges, and crossings were covered by other rules.

Firemen and brakemen received their own printed orders. Firemen were placed under the absolute authority of enginemen. According to one set of instructions, they had to "see that the boilers are properly filled before firing up, that the fires are kindled in proper time, that all the working joints of the engine are kept well oiled, that the signal cord is attached to the cab bell and kept clear from obstruction, together with such other duty as the Enginemen may require of them."[11] They were also to "assist in wooding and watering" and to man the tender brakes.[12] Firemen were instructed to work in the shops when not on running duty and were expressly forbidden to operate engines except in cases when locomotivemen were disabled.

Brakemen were delegated a variety of tasks. On the Boston & Lowell Railroad in the 1850s, printed rules instructed them to arrive at least fifteen minutes before the departure of their trains and see that the brakes, stove fires, and lamps in their assigned cars were in proper condition. They were to assist in the handling of baggage and to make sure that the conductor's cord was properly connected between the engine and the coaches. During the run they were responsible for twisting brakes on at least two cars and for any other work that their immediate superiors, the conductors, might require. Afterwards they were to help unload baggage, inspect the cars, and collect any articles left by passengers.[13]

[9] Minutes of directors' meetings, vol. 2, pp. 207–208, Boston & Worcester Railroad Papers, Baker Library.

[10] Quoted in Stephen Salsbury, *The State, the Investor and the Railroad*, p. 188.

[11] *Rules of the Boston & Lowell*, pp. 13–14.

[12] Ibid., p. 13.

[13] Ibid., p. 14.

On the New York Central in the 1850s, the rules specified even more involved tasks for brakemen. They were instructed to sweep the cars and mop them, wash windows, fill wood boxes, help load the tender with wood and water, and assist in the making up of trains.[14] On the Western Railroad, brakemen, in addition to their normal assignments, received formal orders to examine wheel bearings and brakes at each stop and to act as flagmen at turn-outs when their trains were stalled. In cases of emergency, the brakemen were required to assist in a way which seems almost comic in our age of electronic communications. The regulations of the Western Railroad issued in 1842 state:

If a train be detained on the road from any causes, and is unable to proceed, the Conductor will send a Brakeman to the nearest point for assistance, with instructions to procure a horse if possible, to enable him to proceed without unnecessary delay. And if he is expecting to meet a train on the road he will send another Brakeman forward with his signal, who will proceed with all possible dispatch till he reaches the train expected, with which he will return to the train. If another train is following he will send another Brakeman to meet it with a signal.[15]

Other grades of railwaymen were issued rules pertaining to their tasks. Station agents received directives on the selling and receipting of tickets, the maintenance of company buildings and furniture, and the supervision of switchmen and porters. Clerks, way-billers, tallymen, and baggage masters were given explicit instructions on keeping ledgers, billing, filing, weighing, preparing vouchers, and forwarding freight. Supervisors and dispatchers had their guidelines, while shop foremen, mechanics, and apprentices worked according to their separate rule books. In 1875 the Pennsylvania Railroad printed a lengthy set of 410 regulations for employees in the company's transportation department, which in minute detail outlined the expected activities of every grade of operative from foremen to road repairmen.[16]

In addition to imparting technical knowledge, rule books also

[14] Harlow, *Road of the Century*, pp. 87–88.

[15] *Regulations for the Transportation Department of the Western Railroad*, pp. 7–8.

[16] A copy can be found in William Sipes, *Pennsylvania Railroad*, pp. 255–271.

aimed at establishing general standards of behavior. An attitude of compliance and diligence was first demanded. "A prompt and cheerful obedience therefore, with a zealous, honest and conscientious performance of duty will be required of all," stated the rule book of the North Pennsylvania Railroad. "The acceptance of service is a pledge to fulfill these requirements."[17] Rule No. 1 of the 1852 regulations of the Central Ohio Railroad made the same point, but in more negative terms. "All persons in the employ of the Company disapproving of these or other Regulations of the Road, or not disposed to aid in carrying them out, are requested not to remain in the service thereof."[18] James Clarke, President of the Illinois Central, in a memorandum on regulations sent to division superintendents, similarly stressed the importance of employees' attitudes. "Let it be distinctly understood we don't want discontented men to work for this company, but request them if any to quit our service."[19]

Propriety and manners were also a subject of regulations. The rule book of the Boston & Lowell Railroad informed employees that "civility to passengers and freighters, is a *duty* on the part of every person employed by the company, and any well founded complaint for violation of this duty will be followed by dismissal."[20] Railwaymen on the Pennsylvania were instructed that "strict propriety of conduct, and the avoidance of profane or indecent language in the presence of passengers, and the transaction of business with others, and with one another is required."[21] The rule book of the Central Ohio Railroad put it simply: "Rudeness or incivility to passengers will, in all cases, meet with immediate punishment."[22]

Appearance went hand in hand with proper manners. Employees were ordered to dress neatly and in specific uniforms if required. Badges were to be worn by men in the passenger de-

---

[17] Quoted in Charles Clark, "The Railroad Safety Movement in the United States" (Ph.D. dissertation, Univ. of Illinois at Urbana, 1966), p. 11.

[18] Central Ohio Rail Road, *Instructions for the Running of Trains* (Zanesville, Ohio, 1852), p. 1.

[19] Quoted in Thomas Cochran, *Railroad Leaders, 1845–1890*, p. 295.

[20] *Rules of the Boston & Lowell*, p. 20.

[21] Quoted in Sipes, *Pennsylvania Railroad*, p. 256.

[22] *Instructions for Running of Trains*, p. 2.

partment, especially those handling fares and baggage. The question of appearance was deemed so important by top officers of
the Chicago, Burlington & Quincy Railroad that special circulars
on the subject were issued:

The attention of employees, more especially those engaged in train and
station service, is called to the importance of neatness in their personal
appearance, of orderly and manly deportment whether on or off duty,
and further to the desirability of neatness in the care of the Company's
property in their charge.

This recommendation is as much for the advantage of the employees
as for the credit of the Company. It will suggest itself to everyone, that,
other things being equal, the man who presents a neat appearance,
whose conduct is at all times gentlemanly, and who keeps his cars and
station clean and orderly, is the one most likely to attract the favorable
attention of the public and officers of the Company, and is remembered
as opportunity offers for promotion.[23]

Proper behavior naturally precluded indulgences in such habits
as smoking or drinking, activities sternly prohibited by railroad
companies. The rule book of the Central Ohio Railroad thus
warned employees: "No Smoking will be allowed in any of the
Freight Houses, or on the Engines or Tenders, or Passenger or
Freight Trains, excepting by Passengers in places where allowed."[24] Pennsylvania Railroad workers were similarly instructed that "smoking in or about the shops, or while on duty
at the depots, or on the passenger engines and trains is prohibited."[25]

The use of alcohol was even more firmly proscribed. At the
first meeting of the board of directors of the Boston & Worcester
Railroad after the road was opened in April 1834, the initial
matter of business was the adoption of a resolution "that no
person be employed to take charge of the Engines, or the cars
or to act in any other situation in the service of this corporation,

[23] Quoted in Paul Black, "The Development of Management Personnel Policies
on the Burlington Railroad, 1860–1900" (Ph.D. dissertation, Univ. of Wisconsin,
1972), p. 400.
[24] *Instructions for Running of Trains*, p. 12.
[25] Quoted in Sipes, *Pennsylvania Railroad*, p. 256.

who shall not wholly abstain from the use of ardent spirits."[26]
When the directors of the twelve small lines of the Mohawk
Valley, which were to become the New York Central, first met
in 1843 to coordinate their affairs, the only subject they agreed
on was the wording of the following proclamation: "Resolved,
that the several companies upon the Rail Road line will not
employ persons in the business of transportation, who ever drink
intoxicating liquors."[27] The gravity of management's concern is
reflected in a circular issued to officers and employees of the
Baltimore & Ohio Railroad in 1850:

No man who uses intoxicating drinks at all can thus rely upon himself,
or be relied upon, and it is intended as far as possible to deny employment to all who use them. It is hoped, therefore, that those who desire
to remain in the service will avail themselves of this notice and abstain
entirely from a habit which is full of evil to themselves as well as their
employers, and is now acknowledged to do no one any good.[28]

Printed rule books were emphatic on the issue of drinking.
Boston & Lowell railwaymen were warned: "The use of ardent
spirits on the road or about the premises of the company, except
for mechanical purposes, is strictly forbidden. No one will be
employed or continued in employment, who is known to be in
the habit of drinking ardent spirits. The sale of liquors of any
sort at the Refreshment Rooms at the Station House, is strictly
prohibited."[29] Rule No. 2 of the Central Ohio Railroad stated:
"All persons in employ of the Company and known to be in the
habit of using Spiritous Liquors while on duty, or of being in-
toxicated therewith, will be immediately discharged."[30] Rule books
varied in function and format, but a standard clause was an
antidrinking injunction. The regulations of the Central Railroad
of Georgia even added an amusing twist to its rules. Not only
were employees counseled against the use of ardent spirits, but

[26] Minutes of director's meetings, vol. 1, pp. 190–191, Boston & Worcester
Railroad Papers.
[27] Quoted in Harlow, *Road of the Century*, p. 55.
[28] Quoted in Edward Hungerford, *The Story of the Baltimore & Ohio Railroad, 1827-1927*, vol. 1, p. 273.
[29] *Rules of the Boston & Lowell*, p. 20.
[30] *Instructions for Running of Trains*, p. 1.

also against influencing the drinking habits of passengers. Rule No. 12 thus declared: "Conductors and other trainmen must not attempt to influence passengers in favor of or against certain saloons, but must act impartially in this respect."[31]

To uphold general discipline, railroad company rule books also encouraged workers to spy on each other. Rule No. 10 of the Central Ohio Railroad put the issue bluntly: "All persons in places of trust in the service of the Company, must report any misconduct or negligence affecting the safety of the Road, which may become within their knowledge, and their withholding any such information, to the detriment of the Company's interest, will be considered a proof of neglect and indifference on their part."[32] The regulations of the Baltimore & Ohio Railroad treated the matter in a slightly more discreet fashion. A B. & O. conductor was "expected to keep up a friendly and a harmonious intercourse with the enginemen; but should occasion require it, no false delicacy is to intimidate him from reporting any want of cooperation on the part of that or any other individual to the master of transportation."[33] The rule book of the Pennsylvania Railroad assumed a rather democratic posture; lower grade workers were encouraged not to feel indisposed to informing on their superiors. "Agents, watchmen and track repairers must not fail to report engineers who run beyond the speed allowed, or leave any station ahead of time. . . . Any employee noticing a disobedience or neglect of rule is required to report it to the proper officer."[34]

Rule books placed other personal demands on employees. By edict they were told that they were "beholden to change their work at any time, or to do extra work if required."[35] Employment, moreover, represented a full-time commitment, and railwaymen were informed that even their places of residence could be dictated by company officials. "Each person in the employ of the company," noted Rule No. 3 of the Central Ohio Railroad,

[31] Quoted in *Railway Age*, July 2, 1932, p. 24.
[32] *Instructions for Running of Trains*, p. 2.
[33] Quoted in Hungerford, *Story of the Baltimore & Ohio*, vol. 1, p. 278.
[34] Quoted in Sipes, *Pennsylvania Railroad*, p. 256.
[35] *Rules of the Boston & Lowell*, p. 20.

"is to devote himself exclusively to its service, attending during the prescribed hours of day or night, and residing wherever he may be required."[36] The regulations of the Utica and Schenectady Railroad in the 1840s instructed station agents in capital letters that they "MUST LODGE AND BOARD IMMEDIATELY ADJOINING THEIR RESPECTIVE RAILROAD STATIONS."[37] Railwaymen were also directed to wear badges, to carry "good watches and correct them daily," to dress in proper attire, and if need be supply their own lanterns and tools.[38] They were not to leave work without permission; nor were they "allowed to quit the Company's service, without giving ten days notice."[39] The rules also forewarned workers that their "regular compensation . . . covers all risk or liability to accident," and that "if an employee is disabled by sickness or other cause, the right to claim compensation is not recognized."[40]

The rule books of antebellum southern railroads generally followed the same format and served the same function as those issued on northern lines. The one difference was the addition of directives pertaining to slave labor, especially hired slaves. Slave hiring was an extremely formal process. Contracts between railroad companies and slaveholders set forth in detail responsibilities of lessees as to food, shelter, clothing, and medical care. Copies of contracts were deposited with state boards of public works or transportation, and owners were assured of indemnification in cases of injury or death of their slaves. In 1859 the Richmond & Danville Railroad paid no less than $1,379.44 to a master whose hireling had been accidentally killed while in service to the company.[41]

Since the railroad companies held and managed other men's property, strict rules were issued to supervisors on the treatment

[36] *Instructions for Running of Trains*, p. 1.
[37] Quoted in Harlow, *Road of the Century*, p. 32.
[38] Hungerford, *Story of the Baltimore & Ohio*, vol. 1, p. 274; Lightner, "Labor on the Illinois Central," p. 102; "Special Order, Engineers, Conductors and Employees Eastern Division. Pittsburgh, Ft. Wayne & Chicago Rail Co., on and after November 1st, 1861," printed circular, American Antiquarian Society, Railroad Pamphlet Collections, case PFTW & CR.
[39] *Instructions for Running of Trains*, p. 2.
[40] Quoted in Sipes, *Pennsylvania Railroad*, p. 255.
[41] Robert C. Black III, *The Railroads of the Confederacy*, p. 30.

of hired slaves. Section foremen on the Memphis & Ohio Railroad before the Civil War, for instance, were formally admonished to give "particular attention to the condition and health of Negroes under their charge." They were to deal with them in a firm, resolute, but temperate manner. "Chastisement if required," the rules noted, "must be administered in moderation, and within the bounds of the law, which is not to exceed thirty-nine lashes."[42]

The same rule book specifically forbade section bosses from striking a hireling with a fist, club, stick, or any other heavy instrument. "Should a Negro run away," the book continued, "notice of the fact must be immediately given to both the road master and the assistant superintendent, stating the name of the Negro, date and causes of his running away, together with all attending circumstances." Limited punishments were prescribed for runaway hirelings. The hiring system and rule books thus allowed for a modicum of decency in the treatment of bonded blacks—a point echoed in many recent studies of industrial slavery.[43]

RAILROAD rule books provide a partial, surface view of work—of the behavior expected of railway employees by their employers. An effort at labor control, rules often are presented as descriptions of the normal working day. The true picture—of what actually occurred on the job on a daily basis—was more complicated. No matter how detailed and precise the regulations, a good deal of contingency and indeterminacy remained in railroad work in the early years of rail transport development. Rules, not surprisingly, were also constantly violated and ignored by the men for whom they were written.

[42] Quoted in Richard Reinhardt, ed., *Workin' on the Railroad*, p. 231. While thirty-nine lashes were both a legal and customary punishment, the rule book of the Tallahassee, Pensacola & Gorger Railroad of 1858 set thirty-nine lashes at one time and sixty during the course of a day as a limit for any one offense. The same rule book also included the injunction that "No negroes must be allowed to bring or have at the shanty any fresh meat or poultry, unless the overseer is satisfied he or she came by it honestly." Quoted in Willard Hertel, *History of the Brotherhood of Maintenance of Way Employees*, p. 70.

[43] See Charles B. Dew, "Disciplining Slave Ironworkers in the Antebellum South," *American Historical Review* 79.

Pioneer railwaymen faced countless impromptu assignments. Engine drivers often had to complete and submit lengthy reports on mileage rates, fuel consumption, and accidents. When water ran low in boilers during trips, they joined bucket brigades of trainmen to fetch water from local streams.[44] One dedicated engineman on the Boston & Albany in 1835 trudged several miles through a raging snowstorm to find a team of horses to help free his locomotive.[45] If switching, doubling hills, waiting time, or even repairing engines on the road was required, drivers assumed these additional functions without expecting extra compensation. Unusual, unanticipated tasks were always arising, and they took time and required attention. An article in the *Locomotive Engineer's Journal* in 1880 spoke to this issue:

On nearly all roads, the engineer is required to carefully inspect the machinery under his charge, to report all defects and breakages, and indicate the repairs necessary to be made; clean, trim and fill the headlight, and do all hemp packing, together with such odd jobs as are necessary to keep the machinery in such condition as will enable him to make his trips without unneccessary detention, and in doing so from two to five hours are readily taken up.[46]

The brakeman's workday was also never fixed and never ending. In his reminiscence, Herbert Hamblen describes how, in addition to his normal responsibilities as brakeman, he served as the engineer's flagman, opened and closed switches, cut off and coupled cars, watched for the caboose on curves and over hills, took water into the tender, shoveled coal down to the fireman, rang the bell at crossings, turned on the blower, oiled the valves, and lit the driver's cigar.[47] In *Railroadman*, Harry French similarly relates how he received telegraph messages and delivered them to the conductor and engineer while attending to his regular duties.[48] Brakemen were also known to fill in at a moment's notice for absent or disabled firemen and assumed through custom the chore of keeping the caboose neat and tidy.

[44] Reed Richardson, *The Locomotive Engineer*, p. 94.
[45] Salsbury, *State, Investor and Railroad*, p. 116.
[46] Quoted in Richardson, *Locomotive Engineer*, p. 225.
[47] Clark, "Railroad Safety Movement," p. 17.
[48] Reinhardt, *Workin' on the Railroad*, pp. 90–102.

On the Erie Railroad they fed and cared for livestock on openbed freight cars.[49] Prior to the adoption of a device to eject sand ahead of the drive wheels to facilitate traction, brakemen were called upon to sit on the front of engines to sweep snow off the rails and to sprinkle sand.[50] Finally, while officially delegated the task of twisting brakes on from two to five cars, brakemen frequently found themselves responsible for braking on as many as ten coaches.[51]

The flexibility of assignments affected other grades of railwaymen. Shop machinists were often pressed into service on an emergency basis as engine drivers.[52] When men were in short supply, baggage masters assumed the role of brakemen.[53] Maintenance-of-the-way crews similarly could be transferred to construction work.[54] Firemen on the Michigan Central in the 1850s had to gather fallen limbs on the tracks to use for firewood and shoveled snow to add water to boilers when they ran low in wintertime.[55] A veteran fireman, James Chadbourne, reveals in his recollections that, in addition to his normal tasks, he helped make up his train each morning and did switching in the yards.[56]

Depot agents, especially at small stations, were jacks-of-all-trades. If assistance was wanting, they would attend to switching, pumping, wooding, telegraphing, and to the rough work of hauling baggage and freight.[57] Soliciting business, paying local taxes, and dealing with the inevitable deluge of complaints on lost or damaged items were added chores not usually mentioned in the rule books. Agents were also called upon to provide reports to central offices on local agricultural and manufacturing conditions.[58]

---

[49] Hank Bowman, *Pioneer Railroads*, p. 70.

[50] Richardson, *Locomotive Engineer*, p. 95.

[51] Clark, "Railroad Safety Movement," pp. 14–15.

[52] Bowman, *Pioneer Railroads*, p. 95.

[53] Lightner, "Labor on the Illinois Central," pp. 79–80.

[54] *Second Annual Report of the Directors of the New Hampshire Central Rail Road, October, 1850* (Manchester, N. H., 1850), p. 8.

[55] Bowman, *Pioneer Railroads*, p. 77.

[56] James Chadbourne, "Recollections," *The Railway and Locomotive Historical Society Bulletin*, no. 4, pp. 15–16.

[57] Lightner, "Labor on the Illinois Central," p. 71.

[58] Paul Black, "Development of Management Personnel Policies," pp. 201–203.

Equally diffuse were the actual tasks of conductors. Rule books placed them in charge of trains and defined their functions, yet their work was never clear or simple. Brakemen had to be given instructions and assigned positions, car doors and seals had to be inspected, couplings had to be tested, and emergency equipment checked. The lost child, the motion-sick passenger, the inebriated lout, the boxcar tramp, and the hold-up gang also demanded their attention. For the conductor, a normal day's work rarely proceeded according to official guidelines. Rules

Snowstorms added duties to the work of train crews and trackmen. The photograph depicts a scene on the Milwaukee Railroad in the winter of 1868-69. (Courtesy of Milwaukee Railroad.)

A Currier & Ives rendition of a snowbound train scene. (Courtesy of Association of American Railroads.)

were thus formulated to facilitate the division and control of labor. In reality, however, work for all grades of pioneer railwaymen was characterized by contingency and an absence of specification.

Official regulations were also forgotten, ignored, and consciously defied. Pioneer railroad managers were bedeviled by constant disciplinary problems, for their bureaucratic structures proved weak as instruments of labor control. As a result, they were forced to develop a series of disciplinary tactics which ranged from reprimands and warnings to fines, demotions, suspensions, probations, and outright dismissals, along with the use of blacklists and spies.

Railroad worker intractability took many forms. The theft of company property and revenues was one manifestation. On the Erie Railroad in 1864, Thaddeus Ward was hired to investigate the loss of goods in and around the Susquehanna Station. During a five-day period he noted more than ten incidents of local women, children, and Erie employees taking wood and stones from company storage places. Ward reported that townspeople stole in sight of workers who did nothing to stop them.[59]

The corporate records of the Erie reveal other examples of expropriation. Sworn testimony of shop foremen and mechanics gathered in 1864 indicates that the stealing of iron and tools was common and that company facilities were used to make items for sale and personal use.[60] One shop supervisor supplemented his income by fixing carriages during working hours with the aid of company mechanics, tools, and materials. A group of shop workers built a machine to saw wood which they eventually sold for $1,500. A printed order issued in 1875 reveals that Erie telegraph operators were also not above temptation. The circular expressly warned them against the practice of "stringing . . . private wires from company batteries to private homes."[61]

Pilferage was rampant on other lines. G. Clinton Gardner, general superintendent of the Pennsylvania Railroad, complained that the company shops never had enough brass on hand. "I have no doubt," he wrote, "that most of the brass is carried off and taken by workmen in their dinner buckets or else wrapped up in their overalls."[62] Robert Harris of the Chicago, Burlington & Quincy was repeatedly informed by his personal investigators that work was being done in company shops for private parties and that local foremen were using laborers on company time to help build their homes with lumber taken from the C.B. & Q.'s warehouse.[63] On the Baltimore & Ohio, President John W. Gar-

[59] Report of Thaddeus Ward, July 30, 1864, Alexander S. Diven Collection, Erie Railway Company Papers, box 3, Cornell University Library.

[60] Statement of C. S. Bennete, August 8, 1864, ibid.; statement of Dr. Smith, August 6, 1864, ibid.; statement of Mark S. Barnwell, August 6, 1864, ibid.

[61] "To All Operators and Repairers, April 6, 1875," Erie Railroad Company Papers, Letterbook of Incoming Correspondence and Miscellaneous, Syracuse University Library.

[62] G. Clinton Gardner to Theo. W. Ely, November 22, 1876, G. Clinton Gardner Letterbook, G. Clinton Gardner Letters, Eleutherian Mills Historical Library.

[63] Robert Harris to W. E. Hoyte, May 21, 1868, Chicago, Burlington & Quincy Railroad Papers, Robert Harris Out-Letters, CBQ-3H4.1, Newberry Library; Robert Harris to J. M. Horton, April 4, 1873, ibid.

rett in 1864 ordered an investigation of allegations that shop employees at Wheeling were using company time, materials, and space to repair their own machines and manufacture implements for personal profit.[64] A year later an incident involving boiler-makers and the theft of copper occupied his attention, as well as charges that trainmen were throwing coal off of trains as they passed near their homes.[65] The coal, Garrett was told, was taken both for private use and for sale. Finally, one example of em-ployee theft on the Illinois Central is of more than anecdotal interest. In April 1857 a group of workers heisted $600 worth of company equipment and disappeared. Marshals were sent out after them, but to no avail. Their local foreman then suggested a novel solution—incarcerating the culprits' wives. Unfortu-nately, letters in company archives do not reveal how the matter was eventually prosecuted.[66]

Embezzlement of revenues was another constant worry. Most incidents involved conductors and the handling of fares. A case that achieved notoriety in the 1860s was that of George Clough, a veteran conductor of twenty-four years on the Concord Rail-road in New Hampshire. In October 1865, after an investigation disclosed gross mishandling of tickets and fares, the Concord discharged its whole corps of conductors.[67] Most were eventually rehired, but George Clough was brought to court by the line, charged with giving a merchant hundreds of tickets in return for household wares. The case dragged on for three years and re-ceived widespread press coverage. The testimony of the trial was printed and circulated. Eventually the court awarded in favor of the Concord for the amount of $5,635.[68]

The sums of money embezzled by conductors were not trivial.

[64] J. W. Garrett to W. P. Smith, February 9, 1864, Baltimore & Ohio Railroad Papers, file 3089, Maryland Historical Society.

[65] J. W. Garrett to W. P. Smith, February 9, 1865, Baltimore & Ohio Railroad Letterbooks; J. W. Garrett to J. C. Davis, July 25, 1865, ibid.

[66] M. M. Bayes to J. C. Jacobs, April 22, 1857, Illinois Central Railroad Papers, J. C. Jacob In-Letters, IC-1J2.1, Newberry Library.

[67] State of New Hampshire, *Hearing in the Matter of Concord Railroad Cor-poration vs. George Clough and Trustees* (Concord, New Hampshire, 1869), pp. i–iii.

[68] *Twenty-Eighth Annual Report of the Directors of The Concord R.R. Cor-poration* (Concord, N. H., 1869), p. 12.

Agents of Allan Pinkerton's National Detective Agency, hired by
the Philadelphia & Reading Railroad in 1862 to investigate employee thefts, discovered that the company's conductors embezzled 32 percent of their collections, or eighteen cents per mile.[69]
A conductor on the Chicago, Burlington & Quincy allegedly
kept from $65 to $200 per trip and over a five-year period
accumulated $17,000 in extra income.[70] The Massachusetts Board
of Railroad Commissioners in 1869, after investigating the problem, concluded that conductor dishonesty was widespread and
"a serious cause of loss to railroads" within the state.[71]

Railroad companies were hard pressed to deal with conductor
thefts of revenue. To locate offenders, many lines resorted to
employing spotters directly or to contracting with detective agencies. Various proposals were offered and experiments tried: ro-
tating train assignments to compare average receipts on specific
runs, higher salaries to encourage greater allegiance, bonding,
intricately numbered ticket systems, frequent settlement of accounts, extensive character investigations of applicants, and the
raising of the cost of fares purchased on trains.[72] The Massachusetts Board of Railroad Commissioners even recommended
an end to the collection of fares by conductors. To facilitate the
purchase of tickets, they suggested the building of more depots,
adding "that the expense of employing ticketmasters in such
stations could be mainly obviated by selecting females for such
duties."[73]

Most plans proved impractical or ineffective. The managers
of the Illinois Central in the 1850s thought that bonding would
solve the problem, only to find that many men holding conduc-

[69] Allen Pinkerton, *Tests on Passenger Conductors Made by the National
Detective Agency*, p. 4.

[70] Paul Black, "Development of Management Personnel Policies," pp. 455–
456.

[71] *First Annual Report of the Board of Railroad Commissioners, January, 1870*
(Boston, 1870), p. 64.

[72] *Report of the Directors of the Boston & Providence Railroad* (Boston,
1849), p. 19; Lightner, "Labor on the Illinois Central," pp. 104–105; *Twentieth
Annual Report of the Philadelphia, Wilmington and Baltimore Rail Road Company* (Philadelphia, 1858), pp. 14–15; J. W. Garrett to W. P. Smith, November
11, 1864, Baltimore & Ohio Railroad Letterbooks.

[73] *First Annual Report of the Board of Railroad Commissioners, January, 1870*
(Boston, 1870), p. 64.

tors' positions were young and new to their communities and unable to furnish the required security.[74] Even with seemingly foolproof ticket systems, nothing prevented conductors from allowing passengers to travel free or from pocketing fares without recording the rider's presence. Beefed-up surveillance and well-publicized discharges and legal suits did act as deterrents.

Station, ticket, and freight agents also frequently absconded with company funds. Flyers circulated among rail lines giving descriptions of employees guilty of such misdeeds.[75] Padding payrolls proved another form of embezzlement in which various grades of workers indulged. In 1866, John Garrett of the B. & O. was informed that a timekeeper in collusion with several trainmen had recorded their time in excess of actual hours worked. The men had been paid for time not served and were summarily discharged when the conspiracy was uncovered.[76] A similar incident on the Atchison, Topeka & Santa Fe Railroad in 1881 led to the arrest of eighteen section men.[77]

Insubordination was a third kind of discipline problem. Nineteenth-century railwaymen were a headstrong lot. The English driver Robinson, who began and completed his runs at his own pleasure, was not an anomaly. Herbert Hamblen described a line of which he was put in charge as a general manager. "The conductors," he wrote, "had been running the trains to suit themselves, and as the conductor and the engineman of each train lived near each other, their principal efforts had always been to get home at night, where they could lay over, train and all, until the next morning."[78] Railroad employees, the *American Railroad Journal* bemoaned in 1858, lack "the right kind of sentiment." They established their own "rules for the regulation of their own conduct."[79]

[74] Lightner, "Labor on the Illinois Central," pp. 104–105.

[75] File 76, Baltimore & Ohio Railroad Papers; "Information, November 22, 1876," Erie Railroad Company Papers, Letterbook on Incoming Correspondence and Miscellaneous, Syracuse University Library.

[76] W. P. Smith to J. W. Garrett, June 7, 1866, Baltimore & Ohio Railroad Papers, file 3089.

[77] Keith Bryant, Jr., *History of the Atchison, Topeka and Santa Fe Railway*, p. 57.

[78] Herbert Hamblen, *The General Manager's Story*, p. 301.

[79] *American Railroad Journal*, March 13, 1858, p. 168.

When it came to the manner in which they thought the work should be performed, railwaymen could be openly and deliberately defiant. Firemen on the Western Railroad in the 1840s refused to work on a new engine which required tremendous stoking effort. The line offered them extra compensation, but to no avail. Attempts to lure new men also failed. The firemen preferred the old engine, and eventually the Western's management relented, admitting that the seemingly more powerful locomotives were actually quite inefficient.[80] Similarly, in the 1870s, when most companies adopted the coupling stick and insisted that brakemen use it, few did. The stick was an awkward device which added to the hazards involved in coupling cars. Its use was written into rule books, but since there was so little compliance, companies rarely tried to enforce the regulation.[81] Another device similarly resented was the Dutch Clock, an instrument which recorded the speed of trains over time. Conductors and enginemen were given orders, accompanied by the threat of discharge, not to exceed or go below specific speed limits—in the 1870s usually eighteen miles per hour on the open road.[82] Accordingly, they were not allowed to make up for lost time due to breakdowns or other delays (time they would not be paid for). Train crews quickly learned how to undo the Dutch Clock system. The caboose, where the clock was kept, was uncoupled. The engineer would then ram into the car exactly at eighteen miles per hour. This affected the internal mechanism of the clock, and it continued to record eighteen miles per hour regardless of the speed achieved.[83]

Sometimes outright defiance could be foolhardy. Legend has it that when Charles Minot, general superintendent of the Erie Railroad, introduced the use of telegraphs in dispatching trains, a locomotive driver refused to run his engine by telegraphic order. In 1851, Minot apparently was traveling eastbound on the then single-track Erie road. Upon reaching Monroe, where his train was to meet the opposing train and go off on a siding, Minot

[80] Salsbury, *State, Investor and Railroad*, p. 191.
[81] Clark, "Railroad Safety Movement," pp. 25–26.
[82] Holbrook, *Story of American Railroads*, p. 269.
[83] Ibid., p. 269.

An engine crew stops to chat with friends at a woodlot on the Chicago & Eastern Illinois Railroad. The engine was a wood-burner of the 1850s. (Courtesy of Chicago & Eastern Illinois Railroad.)

telegraphed ahead to order that a new meeting place be established further east. When he attempted to get the driver of his train to move, the engineer refused, insisting on adhering strictly to prior instructions. Minot then took over and drove the engine himself.[84] Unfortunately, the engineer's thoughts on this incident are lost to history. Was he merely a traditionalist who would have nothing to do with newfangled inventions? Was he appre-

[84] Richardson, *Locomotive Engineer*, p. 98.

hensive about disobeying his initial order? Or did Minot and the telegraph represent a serious threat to his authority? Whatever the answers, this erstwhile Erie engineer exhibited the kind of stubbornness which plagued nineteenth-century railroad managers.

When railwaymen were not deliberately defying orders and rules, they often just ignored them. Firemen ran trains while enginemen relaxed. Nonpaying travelers and unauthorized personnel rode in the cab. Track crews frequently reported late to work. Brakemen played cards and smoked in baggage cars. Shopmen were found asleep on the job. And, as will be shown in this and later chapters, the use of so-called ardent spirits was pandemic.

The general unruly habits of railwaymen presented problems to discipline-minded managers. The implications of chronic alcoholism are obvious. Fighting and quarreling also caused frequent disruptions. In 1859 a fracas that started in the Mount Clare machine shops of the Baltimore & Ohio Railroad threatened to escalate and impede operations along the entire line. Top executives were called on to intervene and to quell the disturbances.[85] On the Illinois Central, which ran north and south of the Mason-Dixon line, heightened sectional tensions during the late 1850s were the frequent cause of worker donnybrooks. James Clarke, master of transportation, advised local foremen to instruct employees that their primary allegiance was to the corporation, to "the whole Road both North and South," and that there were to be "no party feelings."[86]

The letterbooks of Robert Harris of the Chicago, Burlington & Quincy reveal that employee fighting was constantly being brought to his attention and occupying his time. Harris believed that quarrels squandered precious energies that were better directed at work and carefully advised foremen on how to settle personal disagreements. When an employee named Ducelle was

[85] R. S. Woodside to H. Tyson, January 18, 1859, Baltimore & Ohio Letterbooks.

[86] J.C. Clarke to Phineas Pease, March 20, 1857, Illinois Central Railroad Papers, J. C. Clarke Out-Letters, IC-1C5.1.

discharged for "being in a row in a saloon," he approved it as a necessary example to other workers.[87]

Other habits were frowned upon. A conductor named Hooker on the Illinois Central was discharged for gambling. He had lost a considerable sum of money and was told by company officials that his employment had been terminated for fear that he would resort to embezzling fares.[88] Harris initiated a campaign against pool halls. Such places, he explained, "generally had corner bars and too often had their walls decorated with bar pictures—and were frequented too largely by those with whom we did not wish to see the men associate—as we were fully persuaded one cannot touch filth without being defiled." Harris rescinded his order against frequenting pool halls when it was pointed out that he regularly played billiards with the chief attorney of the road.[89]

Concern for the moral deportment of railway employees even extended to their sexual behavior. Tyler Davis, a conductor on the Baltimore & Ohio, was discharged in 1865 for "accompanying a lady to a hotel."[90] A depot agent on the Illinois Central lost his job for what were termed "immoral habits." It turned out that he was living with his mistress at the stationhouse.[91] On the Chicago, Burlington & Quincy, an assistant to the chief engineer was dismissed when it was learned that he "was in rather a dirty scrape with a woman."[92] Disciplinary actions were also initiated against William Collins, a station policeman on the same line, when it was brought to the knowledge of company

[87] Robert Harris to C. F. Jaurret, January 14, 1869, Chicago, Burlington & Quincy Railroad Papers, Robert Harris Out-Letters, CBQ-3H4.1; Robert Harris to C. F. Jaurret, March 1871, ibid. In the early years fights also often broke out between locomotive drivers on single track lines. Disputes over the right of way and which train was supposed to pull off at sidings were frequently settled by resorting to fisticuffs. See Bowman, *Pioneer Railroads*, p. 51.

[88] J. C. Clarke to James Hooker, April 29, 1858, Illinois Central Railroad Papers, J. C. Clarke Out-Letters, IC-1C5.1.

[89] Paul Black, "Robert Harris and the Problem of Railway Labor Management" (unpublished manuscript in author's possession), pp. 18–19.

[90] Tyler Davis to J. W. Garrett, November 11, 1865, Baltimore & Ohio Railroad Papers, file 3089.

[91] Lightner, "Labor on the Illinois Central," pp. 111–112.

[92] Paul Black, "Development of Management Personnel Policies," p. 483.

officers that he, to use Robert Harris's words, "made a mistake in offering his amorous attentions to the wrong woman" and "use[d] the convenience at the depot in a manner not at all creditable to him or the R. R. Co."[93] Drake Mills, president of the Delaware, Lackawanna & Western Railroad spoke to this issue in 1857, when he was informed that an employee had acted in an indiscreet manner. Mills noted that the company had a position to maintain in the community. It could not be indifferent to the "conduct and moral development of men." He thus instructed the superintendent of the line "to see to it that we admit into our employ none but men whose examples and influence will be on the side of virtue and good order."[94]

From the employers' perspective, Mills had a point. Railroad companies were public conveniences. They were chartered publicly and their construction was often publicly subsidized. Their relationship with passengers, shippers, and the communities they served was a delicate one. Business could easily be affected by the personal behavior of employees, and this posed additional burdens for railway officials. Company presidents, like John Garrett and Robert Harris, each year were deluged with letters lodging complaints against workers. Passengers complained about the "impertinency," "discourteousness," "toughness of manners," "incivility," and "abusiveness" of railwaymen. Shippers complained about fraudulent invoicing and damaged and lost freight. Merchants and others wrote about debts incurred by employees, often demanding compensation from the companies. Anonymous letters further told of the immoral and criminal acts of various workers, of drunken "randies" and defiled daughters.[95] These letters of complaint had to be answered and the serious charges investigated. Cases involving the garnishing of wages were especially time-consuming. Writs had to be processed, letters sent to employees informing them of actions to be

[93] Robert Harris to H. W. Mead, July 1, 1870, Chicago, Burlington & Quincy Railroad Papers, Robert Harris Out-Letters, CBQ-3H4.1.

[94] Drake Mills to John Brisbane, July 18, 1857, Delaware, Lackawanna & Western Railroad Papers, Letterbooks of Drake Mills, 1856–1858, Syracuse University Library.

[95] File 3089, Baltimore & Ohio Railroad Papers.

taken, and payroll department officials notified. Such activities kept the clerical staff busy.[96]

Negligence, carelessness, and incompetence were other forms and manifestations of labor indiscipline. While the technology was primitive and unsafe, and employees were often overworked and wrongly blamed for mishaps, accidents were frequently caused by neglect of duty, inattention, and ineptness. Companies assumed a strict posture on the subject. As the directors of the Boston, Concord & Montreal Railroad explained to stockholders in 1853:

> The discipline of the road had been as rigid, it is believed, as can possibly be carried into effect. Under our system an employee is uniformly discharged for negligence, or neglect of orders which might possibly cause an accident, even if none should occur. Instances of neglect or disobedience have been rare, but, when they have occurred, the discipline has been strictly enforced, even in one instance to the removal of a valuable man, whose duties were governed by *time* for allowing his watch to stop.[97]

Finally, there were troublemakers. Union leaders, union sympathizers, and strikers in general were obvious disruptive influences and candidates for disciplinary actions. During a work stoppage of station laborers in 1864, John Woods Brooks, president of the Michigan Central, instructed the line's superintendent in no uncertain terms: "I hope you will find out who the leaders are or were and weed out all such from the lot as rapidly as you can consistent with safety but be sure to do it unforgettingly."[98] "I would proceed to discharge every man on the Buffalo Division who continued to foment, and cause a disturbance as had been carried on the last six weeks," advised John Devereaux, general manager of the Lake Shore & Michigan Southern, referring to a job action of locomotive engineers in 1872.[99] Yet,

[96] Writs of Attachment of Wages of Employees of R. R. for Debts Incurred, Boston & Lowell and Nashua & Lowell Railroad Company Collection, vol. 181, Baker Library.

[97] *Seventh Annual Report of the Directors of the Boston, Concord, & Montreal Railroad, May 1853* (Concord, N. H., 1853), p. 9.

[98] Quoted in Cochran, *Railroad Leaders*, p. 277.

[99] Ibid., p. 314.

less obvious kinds of troublemakers also presented problems to order-conscious railway executives. Herbert Hamblen recalled that his first discharge as a railway employee came as a result of refusing to give testimony at a trial which would have absolved his employers from responsibility in a train wreck.[100] James Clarke of the Illinois Central ordered a division superintendent in 1857 to dismiss a ticket agent, who, it was charged, "makes general practice of speaking of the present administration of the Illinois Central R.R. in very denunciary terms."[101] A similar fate befell Charles P. Sales, an employee of the Baltimore & Ohio Railroad. In 1869 Sales was dismissed for "speaking of the company in an improper manner." Apparently he had told two farmers, whose cows had been killed by a B. & O. train, that they could recover damages on account of the excessive speed of the engine.[102]

THE INTRACTABILITY of mid-nineteenth-century railroad workers can be described and categorized but not easily or accurately measured. Disciplinary matters were generally handled informally at the local level, and records were seldom kept. The pervasiveness of the problem, the prevalence of different forms of indiscipline, and the specific grades of workers most often involved are questions without precise answers.

Two surviving documents offer some clues. The first is a printed circular issued by the president's office of the Erie Railroad, listing men discharged from service on the line in the first three months of 1873.[103] The second is a handwritten ledger of discharges kept by the management of the Chicago, Burlington &

[100] Hamblen, *General Manager's Story*, p. 67.

[101] J. C. Clarke to John Jacobs, April 11, 1857, Illinois Central Railroad Papers, J. C. Jacobs In-Letters, IC-1J2.1.

[102] C. P. Sales to J. W. Garrett, May 17, 1869, Baltimore & Ohio Railroad Papers, file 1573.

[103] Circular Notice, March 31, 1873, Erie Railway Company Papers, Letterbook of Incoming Correspondence and Miscellaneous, Syracuse University Library. The notice lists the names of 157 employees, representing twenty-six positions on the road, and gives thirty-six different reasons for their dismissal. The circular heading simply announces "that the following Discharges have been made from the service of the Erie Railroad Company to March 31st, 1873." Dates are not given, and without additional information one can only assume that the notice includes men discharged in the first three months of the year 1873.

Quincy Railroad during the period between 1877 and 1892.[104]
Information from these two primary sources has been compiled
in tables 3.1 and 3.2. Table 3.1 reports the numbers and percentages of men dismissed on the two roads by the reasons given
for their discharge. The variety and range of indiscretions is truly
noteworthy, although clearly drunkenness and neglect of duty
were the most predominant forms of worker transgression. The
second table lists the number of Erie and C.B. & Q. men discharged by their respective grades of employ.[105]

The figures in tables 3.1 and 3.2 reveal that on the Erie and
C.B. & Q. Railroads, in the years designated, between 4 and 7
percent of the men employed were discharged annually for disciplinary reasons (or less than 1 percent of the total work force
each month).[106] The problem of industrial discipline on the nation's pioneer railroads thus appears to have been an inconsequential matter, hardly warranting the concern expressed by
early railway managers in corporate memoranda and letters and
editorialists in nineteenth-century railway trade journals. Yet, in

[104] *Record of Discharged Employees From the Service of the C.B. & Q. and
Leased Lines, February 1877–June 1892*, Chicago, Burlington & Quincy Railroad Papers, CBQ-33 1870 3.4. The ledger lists on a month-to-month basis the
names, positions, and reasons for dismissal of 8,279 men discharged from the
line during the fifteen-year period covered. For the purposes of this study, only
entries between February 1877—the first month listed—and December 1878
have been compiled. During that period, 811 employees, representing thirty-six
different occupations, were dismissed from the C.B. & Q. for seventy-six different
provocations.

[105] During the months of July and August 1877, a large number of C.B. & Q.
men were discharged for participating in the great railroad strikes of that summer.
Two sets of figures with strikers included and excluded are offered in tables 3.1
and 3.2 to give two perspectives on disciplinary actions within the firm.

[106] The Erie Railroad employed approximately 9,000 men in the early 1870s
and the C.B. & Q. employed 10,000 in the latter part of the decade. Percentages
of employees discharged annually are based on those total figures. Information
on aggregate employment for the Erie is available in Edward Mott, *Between the
Ocean and the Lakes*, p. 483; for the C.B. & Q., see Paul Black, "Development
of Management Personnel Policies," pp. 21–22. Paul Black has also calculated
discharge rates by reason and grade for the entire fifteen-year period covered by
the C.B. & Q. discharge ledger. His percentage figures are identical to those
generated by the two-year analysis reported in the text. See Paul Black, "Employee
Alcoholism on the Burlington Railroad, 1876–1902," *Journal of the West* 17:5–
11, and also his "Experiment in Bureaucratic Centralization," *Business History
Review* 51:444–459.

Table 3.1. Number and Percentage of Employees Discharged from the Chicago, Burlington & Quincy Railroad, February 1877–December 1878, and the Erie Railroad, January 1873– March 1873, by Reasons Given for Dismissal

Reason for discharge	C.B.&Q. Railroad			Erie Railroad	
	Number dis- charged	Percentage of total		Number dis- charged	Per- centage of total
		Strikers included	Strikers excluded		
Intemperance/intoxication/ drunkenness	150	18.5	22.0	23	14.6
Striker/ringleader of strike	128	15.8	—	2	1.3
Neglect of duty	99	12.2	14.5	22	14.0
Incompetence/incapable	61	7.5	8.9	49	31.2
No account	34	4.2	5.0	—	—
Garnished	32	3.9	4.7	—	—
Disobedience/disobeying orders	29	3.6	4.2	12	7.6
Quarreling/fighting	25	3.1	3.7	6	3.8
Worthless	23	2.8	3.4	—	—
Careless/carelessness	22	2.7	3.2	2	1.3
Lazy/loafing	22	2.7	3.2	4	2.5
Dishonest/lying	15	1.8	2.2	—	—
Collisions	15	1.8	2.2	—	—
Stealing/larceny	14	1.7	2.0	—	—
Dead beat	12	1.5	1.8	—	—
No good	12	1.5	1.8	—	—
Too much mouth/talked too much	12	1.5	1.8	—	—
Violating rules/neglect of time card rules	10	1.2	1.5	—	—
Negligence	10	1.2	1.5	5	3.2
Sleeping	7	.9	1.0	—	—
Hard, bad, vicious, rough character	7	.9	1.0	—	—
Failed to go when called	6	.7	.9	—	—
Impudent/impertinent/ incivility/insolent	6	.7	.9	—	—
Absent without leave/ nonattendence	5	.6	.7	4	2.5
Left switch open	4	.5	.6	—	—
Quit on his run/left engine	3	.4	.4	—	—
Immorality	3	.4	.4	—	—
Reckless running	3	.4	.4	—	—
Runaway	2	.2	.3	—	—
Insubordination	2	.2	.3	1	.6
Disorderly	2	.2	.3	2	1.3
Damaged cart	2	.2	.3	—	—

Table 3.1. Continued

Reason for discharge	C.B.&Q. Railroad			Erie Railroad	
	Number dis-charged	Percentage of total		Number dis-charged	Per-centage of total
		Strikers included	Strikers excluded		
Altered, changed pass	2	.2	.3	—	—
Irregularities in accounts	2	.2	.3	—	—
Conspiracy	2	.2	.3	—	—
Too slow	2	.2	.3	—	—
Tramp	1	.1	.1	—	—
Too independent	1	.1	.1	—	—
Minor	1	.1	.1	—	—
Insulted lady passenger	1	.1	.1	—	—
Misdemeanor	1	.1	.1	—	—
Bad reputation	1	.1	.1	—	—
Creating dissatisfaction among employees	1	.1	.1	—	—
Gave wrong name	1	.1	.1	—	—
Profane, vulgar language	1	.1	.1	1	.6
Spree	1	.1	.1	—	—
Forgetting train orders	1	.1	.1	—	—
Bad company	1	.1	.1	—	—
Refusing to help engineer	1	.1	.1	—	—
Not helping train	1	.1	.1	—	—
Family trouble	1	.1	.1	—	—
Misuse of property	1	.1	.1	—	—
Not answering dispatcher	1	.1	.1	—	—
Tampering	1	.1	.1	—	—
Fraud	1	.1	.1	—	—
Not a sound operator	1	.1	.1	—	—
Tampering with watch	1	.1	.1	—	—
Disloyal/unfaithful	1	.1	.1	1	.6
Smoking	1	.1	.1	—	—
Obtaining pass under false pretense	1	.1	.1	—	—
Refusing duty/not attending to duty	1	.1	.1	5	3.2
Inattention/inattention to duty	1	.1	.1	2	1.3
Unreliable	—	—	—	2	1.3
Unsteady	—	—	—	4	2.5
Did not give satisfaction/ did not suit	—	—	—	2	1.3
Inaccuracy and failure to keep up his work	—	—	—	1	.6
Reason not given	—	—	—	1	.6
Treacherous	—	—	—	1	.6
Tardiness	—	—	—	1	.6

Table 3.1. *Continued*

Reason for discharge	C.B.&Q. Railroad			Erie Railroad	
	Number dis- charged	Percentage of total		Number dis- charged	Per- centage of total
		Strikers included	Strikers excluded		
Permitting flagman to sign conductor's and engineer's name to orders	—	—	—	1	.6
Signing conductor's and engineer's name to orders	—	—	—	1	.6
By order of the president	—	—	—	1	.6
Request of E. O. Hill	—	—	—	1	.6
Total	811	98.9	98.9	157	99.5

absolute terms, disciplinary actions involved a good number of men—157 on the Erie in the first three months of 1873—and the lists fail to indicate how many additional workers were reprimanded, warned, fined, demoted, or suspended for problematic behavior. Discharge records also render little sense of how many derelictions were overlooked by local supervisors or were unseen.

Other qualifications come to mind. The question of dismissals and the career experiences of individual railwaymen is not illuminated by discharge records. A seemingly small percentage of workers may have been ousted each year for disciplinary reasons; this does not preclude the possibility that at some point in their working lifetimes, most nineteenth-century railway employees were dismissed for some kind of indiscretion. The reminiscences of men like Charles George, Harry French, and Herbert Hamblen are replete with stories of frequent run-ins with foremen and subsequent suspensions and discharges.

Second, aggregate monthly or annual figures hide important differentials among grades of workers. On the Chicago, Burlington & Quincy Railroad, trainmen accounted for 60 percent of all discharges. Since trainmen were roughly 20 percent of the entire work force, simple arithmetic indicates that close to 13 percent of all C.B. & Q. trainmen were being discharged each year. Discipline within the C.B. & Q.'s transportation department, therefore, was not an inconsequential concern. The Erie figures similarly reveal that clerical workers were a special problem on that line. While no more than 3 percent of all Erie employees, they comprised 17 percent of the discharged. At the rate they were being dismissed, 40 percent would have been discharged over a year's time.

The importance of grade is further illustrated in a document found in the archives of the Illinois Central Railroad. In 1897, as part of an effort to gather material for a company history, the line's officials asked J. B. Edams, a veteran machinist and master mechanic, to submit biographical information on all the engineers who had served under his charge in the North Division between April 1856 and April 1893. Edams provided material on 147 enginemen he had supervised over the course of thirty-seven years and listed their whereabouts. Fifty-three, or 36 percent, were still in the service of the I.C.; eleven, or 7 percent, had retired; and twenty-three, or 16 percent, were deceased. Edams could not recall the dispositions of another twenty-three men, while thirty drivers—a remarkable 25 percent of the group—had been discharged for disciplinary reasons.[107] Aggregate figures for the Illinois Central most likely would have obscured the extent to which discipline was a problem in this particular branch of operations and the degree to which discharge was a basic element in the work experience of I.C. locomotivemen.

Finally, inconsistencies between the Erie and C.B. & Q. discharge records are suggestive of the uneven and unpredictable nature of the disciplinary process. On the Chicago, Burlington & Quincy Railroad, drunkenness and neglect of duty accounted for more than a third of all infractions, with intemperance cited most frequently; on the Erie, however, incompetence prevailed far in excess of other reasons. Similarly, trainmen, and especially brakemen, on the C.B. & Q. were discharged at rates greatly disproportionate to their numbers in the work force, while station and track laborers accounted for a relatively small number of disciplinary cases. On the Erie, on the other hand, white collar employees were ousted in excessive figures, while the discharge

---

[107] Statement of J. B. Edams, April 1897, Illinois Central Railroad Papers, Historical Papers File, IC-2.91.

Table 3.2. Number and Percentage of Employees Discharged from the Chicago, Burlington & Quincy Railroad, February 1877–December 1878, and the Erie Railroad, January 1873–March 1873, by Grade of Employ

Grade of employee	C.B.&Q. Railroad				Erie Railroad	
	Number discharged		Percentage of total			
	Strikers included	Strikers excluded	Strikers included	Strikers excluded	Number discharged	Percentage of total
Trainmen	493	373	60.8	54.8	11	7.0
Conductors	64	40	7.9	5.9	0	0.0
Enginemen	39	37	4.8	5.4	1	.6
Firemen	48	48	5.9	7.0	1	.6
Brakemen	339	245	41.8	35.9	9	5.8
Baggagemen	3	3	.4	.4	0	—
Shop workers	161	155	19.9	22.7	38	24.2
Skilled mechanics	93	89	11.5	13.0	32	20.4
Unskilled mechanics	68	66	8.4	9.7	6	3.8
Station and track laborers	117	115	14.4	16.8	77	49.0
"Laborers"	39	39	4.8	5.7	18	11.4
Trackmen	—	—	—	—	29	18.5
Switchmen	57	55	7.0	8.0	19	12.1
Watchmen	6	6	.7	.9	2	1.3
Flagmen	2	2	.3	.3	2	1.3
Others	13	13	1.6	1.9	7	4.4
White-collar employees	19	19	2.3	2.8	27	17.2
Lower-level management	21	21	2.6	3.1	4	2.5
Total	811	683	100.0	100.0	157	99.9

rates for trainmen, especially brakemen, were extremely low. On two different railroads in roughly the same time period, remarkably different patterns emerged—an indication of the role that circumstance played in disciplinary matters.

IN THE EARLY years of rail transport development, inconsistency in fact marked the entire disciplinary process. Like recruitment, discipline was handled informally at the local level and with a good deal of individual discretion. The reasons men were chastised were often arbitrary; so, too, were specific punishments meted out. Family connections, subjective relationships with foremen, length of service, labor supply, and bureaucratic confusion were factors which intervened in the process. Despite the emergence of formal structures of management, discipline on the nation's pioneer railroads was administered without objective standards or fixed procedures.

When top level railroad managers decentralized the power of appointment, authority over disciplinary matters was also localized. Necessity was offered as the prime rationale. In large-scale, functionally divided, geographically dispersed organizations, high-echelon officials could not be bothered with the minute, day-to-day problems of employee control. Local authority, however, was also viewed as a positive good. After the violent strikes of July 1877, Charles Eliot Perkins, then vice president of the Chicago, Burlington & Quincy, was informed by President Robert Harris that a major grievance of the workers had been that top level management had left them under the unrestrained control of local officials. Perkins admitted that this was a justifiable complaint, but he added that it would be injurious to overall company discipline to interfere with the authority of foremen. "Men as a rule must be responsible to a power near at hand," he wrote.

You will never probably under any system, get absolute justice at all times. The best of us are not always just, and the lower down you go the greater the liability to error, and the stronger the influence of prejudices, sympathy and passion. But I do not esteem this to be a reason why you and I should undertake to interfere with the selection or dismissal of men in subordinate places. We might now and then prevent an injustice, but we should have a state of confusion and anarchy on the Railroad. The truth is that more men, who ought to be discharged, are kept in the service through the weakness and sympathy of those over them, then there are good men discharged through passion.[108]

Whatever the validity of Perkins's last comment, the truth was that decentralization without formal grievance procedures bred arbitrariness. Pioneer railwaymen were often disciplined for odd, subjective reasons. The discharge records of the Erie and Chicago, Burlington & Quincy Railroads include infractions like "bad reputation," "bad company," "family troubles," "dead beat," "too independent," "worthless," and "treacherous." Inconsistencies between the two lists further suggests that there was a wide latitude in interpreting supposed misdeeds. Why was "incompetency" so much more prevalent on the Erie? Were standards of judgment on this question more stringent? Similarly, was drunkenness more widespread on the C.B. & Q., or was it only less tolerated?

One interesting illustration of the subjective nature of disciplinary actions occurred on the Baltimore & Ohio Railroad. In August 1869, a B. & O. clerk was discharged with the official reason listed as "disrespectful remarks made to a colored woman." In a letter to the president of the line, W. Toole, master of transportation, explained why he had ordered the dismissal. Toole, it appears, had taken it upon himself to launch a crusade against the racist proclivities of B. & O. employees. "As you are aware," he wrote,

the 'negro question' has given the company and its officers much trouble for a long time past. During my attention to it, I became satisfied that a considerable portion of the trouble was caused by the foolish and often insolent deportment of some of the company's employees, and that their insolence consisted more in their manner than in their words. Knowing this to be the case, I determined to make an example of the first person who I might discover to be deporting himself so.[109]

---

[108] C. E. Perkins to Robert Harris, December 15, 1877, Chicago, Burlington, & Quincy Railroad Papers, Papers Concerning Employees, 1877–98, CBQ-33 1870 3.6.

[109] W. Toole to J. W. Garrett, August 24, 1869, Baltimore & Ohio Railroad Papers, file 1573.

If the reasons for disciplinary actions were often arbitrary, the penalties were even more so. It was left to local supervisors to determine whether a worker would either be informally warned, officially reprimanded, fined, demoted, temporarily suspended, dismissed with the possibility of future reinstatement, or permanently discharged. Even in cases involving accidents, which were generally reviewed by high level executives, discipline was meted out in a rather irregular fashion. Two conductors on the Boston & Worcester Railroad in 1841 were discharged for their role in a head-on collision, despite the fact that company officials admitted that the men were really not to blame.[110] Ten years later an engineer on the same line was only temporarily suspended for a similar kind of accident; this time the company noted that "mitigating circumstances" precluded a harsher penalty.[111] For his part in a collision in 1855, Henry Hutton, an engineer on the New Jersey Railroad, was demoted to work in the company's machine shop; while on the B. & O. in 1879 a driver was similarly suspended and then reinstated at reduced pay as a yard engineman.[112] The case of conductor Jake Nowland of the Eastern Railroad is probably the most incomprehensible. Declared responsible by the company, a court inquiry, and the Massachusetts railroad commissioners for one of the worst American train disasters of the nineteenth century—the Revere, Massachusetts collision of August 26, 1871 with thirty fatalities—Nowland was officially suspended from his position but remained in the company's employ and on the company's payroll for many years following the incident.[113]

In the absence of clear-cut standards and procedures, various factors entered into disciplinary decision making. Length of service was one. James Barnes, superintendent of the Western Railroad in the 1840s, took a strict position on dismissals for care-

[110] *Report of the Directors of the Boston & Worcester Rail Road Corporation to the Stockholders* (Boston, 1841), pp. 8–9.

[111] G. Twichell to D. N. Pickering, January 9, 1850, Boston & Worcester Railroad Papers, vol. 119.

[112] *Annual Reports of Railroad and Canal Companies of the State of New Jersey for the Year 1855* (Trenton, 1856), p. 20; M. M. Clements to J. W. Garrett, February 19, 1879, Baltimore & Ohio Railroad Papers, file 1573.

[113] Francis Bradlee, *The Eastern Railroad*, pp. 88–89.

lessness and disobedience of rules. In 1845, however, he rescinded a decision of a lower level official to suspend two conductors involved in an accident, citing their "long service and known qualities."[114] Another strong advocate of harsh sentences, James Clarke of the Illinois Central, in 1875 similarly overruled the dismissal of two conductors and an engineman in consideration of their past records and services.[115] Veteran status helped Jesse Dungan, a chronic alcoholic who worked in a machine shop on the Baltimore & Ohio Railroad. Despite his constant violation of company rules, he maintained his position. As his foreman explained, Dungan "has been dismissed for intoxication a number of times, but, on account of his being an old employee and in bad circumstances, and in every case promising reform, he has been reinstated again and again."[116] Dungan was luckier than a watchman on the Boston & Worcester road, who in 1850 was "seen under the influence of intoxicating drinks" and summarily discharged without any investigation.[117]

Labor supply was another consideration. In 1855 Abiel Rolfe, a station agent on the Boston & Lowell, complained to his superintendent about the shortage of "good help" during the busy freight season. Rolfe asked for permission to retain several men slated for disciplinary discharges.[118] The Pennsylvania Railroad during the 1850s faced difficulties recruiting and retaining skilled enginemen; as a result, management, as one historian has phrased it, "had to wink at peccadillos that would not be passed over so lightly now."[119] Robert Harris of the C.B. & Q. similarly noted in a letter to Charles Eliot Perkins that the company could not strictly enforce its regulations against drinking in the machine shops without losing most of its skilled blacksmiths and boil-

[114] James Barnes to George Bliss, December 28, 1845, Western Railroad Papers, case 3, Baker Library.

[115] Lightner, "Labor on the Illinois Central," p. 183.

[116] Master of Machinery to J. W. Garrett, June 26, 1867, Baltimore & Ohio Railroad Papers, file 1573.

[117] G. Twichell to D. N. Pickering, March 28, 1850, Boston & Worcester Railroad Papers, vol. 119.

[118] Abiel Rolfe to George Stark, November 2, 1855, Nashua & Lowell and Boston & Lowell Railroad Collection, vol. 199, Baker Library.

[119] Charles F. Carter, *When Railroads Were New*, p. 125.

ermakers.[120] When the Northern Pacific Railroad commenced operations, the line's general manager, Herman Haupt, was advised to proceed with caution in instituting a new program of strict discipline. The program, he was told by the company's vice president, could precipitate a strike at a "time when you need a large force to handle your transportation."[121]

Family and personal connections, so important in recruitment practices, also played a role in disciplinary proceedings. Edgar Custer, a veteran locomotiveman, recalls in his reminiscence, *No Royal Road*, being called into the office of his division superintendent to answer charges of running his engine at excessive speeds. "He was an old friend of my family. I felt rather hopeful." Custer's optimism was justified. He was only suspended for two weeks for an infraction which normally warranted automatic discharge.[122] In 1853, R. W. Hobart, a conductor on the Boston & Worcester Railroad, was informed by George Twichell, the line's superintendent, that many complaints had been received concerning his "unaccommodating spirits." Rather than order some form of discipline, Twichell suggested that they talk about the matter the next time Hobart visited his brother, who was a neighbor and close friend of Twichell's.[123] The extent to which family connections influenced discharge proceedings is revealed in a curious story told by Louis Loring about Calvin Stephens, the conductor of the first merchandise train on the Boston & Lowell Railroad:

In those days the freight conductor had almost unlimited control of merchandise and collected the money himself. One day Stephens had taken on over $500 freight charges, and on reaching Boston, got a "tip" in some way that the old Chelsea Bank was about to go under. He took his freight money over to the bank, and bought the money of the bank at a few cents on the dollar and turned in the $500 to the company in Chelsea Bank money. The bank failed the next day and the railroad held $500 worth of *worthless* money. Stephens was called up to explain,

---

[120] Paul Black, "Robert Harris," pp. 17–18.
[121] Quoted in Cochran, *Railroad Leaders*, p. 411.
[122] Quoted in Reinhardt, *Workin' on the Railroad*, pp. 122–126.
[123] G. Twichell to R. W. Hobart, June 18, 1853, Boston & Worcester Railroad Papers, vol. 158.

but merely said the bank was supposed to be sound the day before
when he took the money for freight, so he was let alone, the fact of his
being a nephew of the Appletons no doubt helping his case materially.[124]

Obviously, the personality of individual foremen was a most
important factor in disciplinary matters. There were the despots,
as one anonymous railwayman recalled in 1907 in an article in
the *Locomotive Engineer's Journal*: "Yes, the master mechanic
of 40 years ago or thereabouts was quite an important personage,
you may believe, who ruled his then submissive band like a
veritable Czar. If it suited his fancy to stop pay, that's all there
was to it. There was no redress."[125] Charles George, however,
remembered a different kind of supervisor: "All 'the boys' on
the road will swear by their superintendents, and no matter what
their grievances may be they feel that if they can only lay it before
the 'old man' it will be properly dealt with."[126] In truth there
were many kinds of foremen and, as Harry French related in
Railroadman, they ranged from the brutal and tyrannical to the
compassionate and fatherly.

Bureaucratic confusion and inertia also played their roles.
Workers often appealed successfully to higher officials to have
the discharge decisions of their local foremen reversed.[127] On the
Illinois Central, men dismissed from the northern division of the
line had little difficulty getting rehired on the southern branch.[128]
Three employees of the I.C. were even spared punishment when
management could not decide who was more responsible for an
accident. As general superintendent Edward Jeffrey explained
after investigating a collision of a train and a hand car, which
had resulted in the death of a bridge carpenter:

[124] Louis Loring, "Early Railroads in Boston," *The Bostonian* 1:306.

[125] Quoted in Richardson, *Locomotive Engineer*, pp. 246–247.

[126] Charles George, *Forty Years on the Rail*, p. 167. David Upton, a master
mechanic on the New York Central, was so beloved by the men under his charge
that they jointly raised over a thousand dollars to buy Upton a seven-piece silver
service for his new home. James Stevenson, "The Brotherhood of Locomotive
Engineers and Its Leaders, 1863–1920" (Ph.D. dissertation, Vanderbilt Univ.,
1954), p. 77.

[127] W. P. Smith to J. W. Garrett, May 1, 1865, Baltimore & Ohio Railroad
Papers, file 1573.

[128] Silas Bent to J. C. Jacobs, March 23, 1857, Illinois Central Railroad Papers,
J. C. Jacobs In-Letters, IC-1J2.1.

I consider the blame to be so evenly divided between the three men mentioned [a bridge supervisor, a yardmaster, and a locomotive engineer], that I don't see how we could consistently discharge one from the service without discharging the other two. I shall write a letter to each of the men severely reprimanding him for their parts in the transaction.[129]

Reinstatement finally complicated the whole disciplinary system. Discharged men were often taken back in as arbitrary a fashion as they had been dismissed. Conductor Thomas Wiley of the Baltimore & Ohio Railroad, discharged for drunkenness, was rehired after his fellow townspeople of Cumberland, Maryland, sent a petition to President Garrett attesting to Wiley's honorable and temperate character.[130] Strike pressure on the Erie Railroad in 1856 forced the reinstatement of fourteen of twenty-nine engineers dismissed for violating a new set of regulations.[131] George Barker of the Chicago, Burlington & Quincy was exonerated and rehired after signing a pledge to abstain from further drinking:

I hereby agree that if I am reinstated in the service of the Chicago, Burlington and Quincy Railroad Co., I will not so long as I shall be employed in this service as hereafter, drink any alcoholic liquor as a beverage or partake of it otherwise except as particularly and especially prescribed by a practicing physician—of which I will give notice to the superintendent of the necessity.[132]

If all else failed, a letter from a tearful wife could be employed to secure reinstatement. Each year, railroad managers received hundreds of such appeals, telling tales of woe and begging forgiveness. A letter from Rachael Grove to J. W. Garrett of the Baltimore & Ohio is most poignant. Mrs. Grove's husband, a machinist, was discharged from the B. & O. in 1867 for his participation in a strike. Mrs. Grove appealed for his reinstatement, citing his military record during the Civil War, his long

---

[129] Quoted in Lightner, "Labor on the Illinois Central," p. 85.
[130] Thomas Kaig to J. W. Garrett, August 23, 1865, Baltimore & Ohio Railroad Papers, file 1573.
[131] *Holley's Railroad Advocate*, October 11, 1856, p. 1.
[132] Quoted in Paul Black, "Robert Harris," p. 18.

service to the company and their desperately poor situation. She ended her letter:

Now dear Sir shall it be said at this time, when so many enemies of the country are being fully pardoned for the worst offenses, when every one feels that the faults of the truly penitent can well be forgiven; that the B. & O. RR, so famous for patriotism refused to be patient towards one who has given ten years of service.[133]

The corporate records of the Baltimore & Ohio Railroad do not reveal whether Mrs. Grove's request met with approval.

A FEW ADDITIONAL points concerning discipline deserve mention. The first is the subject of fines. In Victorian England, as the English historian Peter Kingsford has shown, fining was an integral part of the railway discipline system. British railway companies formally established financial penalties for specific infractions—one pound for drunkenness, seventeen shillings for neglect of duty, twelve shillings for insubordination—and strictly enforced the system through payroll deductions.[134] In the United States, the relative absence of fining practices is striking.

There are isolated manifestations of the use of fines. The rule book of the Rutland & Burlington Railroad in Vermont includes a clause that acts of negligence would result in the "withholding of pay."[135] The regulations of the Pennsylvania Railroad similarly contain a provision stating that fines "may be substituted" for dismissals, and that revenues obtained would be used to help defray expenses of disabled or sick employees.[136] Apparently, the Chicago, Burlington & Quincy Railroad experimented with the practice, for a list of grievances submitted to Robert Harris in 1876 includes the demand "that the system of fining engineers lately introduced be abolished."[137]

[133] Rachael Grove to J. W. Garrett, July 10, 1867, Baltimore & Ohio Railroad Papers, file 1573.
[134] Peter Kingsford, *Victorian Railwaymen*, pp. 22–27.
[135] Rutland & Burlington Railroad, *Rules and Regulations* (Rutland, Vermont, 1855), p. 5.
[136] Quoted in Sipes, *Pennsylvania Railroad*, pp. 255–256.
[137] Grievance Committee to Robert Harris, 1876, Chicago, Burlington & Quincy Railroad Papers, Miscellaneous, CBQ-33 1880 8.1.

The most extensive fining system was instituted in the late 1870s on the Iowa branch of the Illinois Central by division superintendent D. W. Parker. Parker insisted that employees under his command be liable for damages resulting from their carelessness. Between June and October 1878, sixteen employees were assessed accordingly: a switchman responsible for a derailment was charged $9.88 for the cost of repairs to the damaged switch; a conductor and brakeman were charged $30.87 and $18.53, respectively, for car repairs resulting from a collision; an engineer was assessed $15.00 for running into a cow; and a conductor was forced to pay for a ticket punch he had misplaced. The unkindest cut of all, though, was borne by a switchman named Knight, who was charged $6.20 for a broken urinal caused by rough switching.[138]

Besides these examples, there is little evidence in rule books or corporate records of the general use of fining practices on American railroads. There are indications that even when instituted, the system was strongly opposed. In 1876 the St. Louis & Southeastern Railroad demanded that its employees sign an agreement authorizing a fine of $20 for each violation of the company's rules. The threat of a strike by engineers and firemen succeeded in persuading the line's officials of the wisdom of withdrawing the proposal.[139] Harry French recalled that companies frequently deducted a portion of brakemen's wages to pay for flattened wheels, which were caused by the brakes being set too tightly. The system was broken by various work stoppages and an unusual lawsuit initiated by a brakeman who goes nameless in French's account. It appears that this trainman proved that he paid for a set of damaged wheels and that the railroad had retreaded the old ones and used them under a boxcar. The court awarded the brakeman a large sum of money as "rent" for the company's use of his wheels.[140]

One can only speculate about the reasons for the relative absence of fining systems on America's pioneer railroads. Perhaps in a nation of high labor mobility, the formal imposition of fines

[138] Lightner, "Labor on the Illinois Central," pp. 185–186.
[139] Stevenson, "Brotherhood of Locomotive Engineers," p. 131.
[140] Chauncey Del French, *Railroadman*, pp. 47–48.

was both impractical and self-defeating. Perhaps it went against the democratic grain of the society. American workers, also, possessed of the vote and political power and less constrained by strict class barriers, may have been more defiant and less willing to accept fining practices. The answer to the question lies in further cross-cultural and cross-industry studies of discipline systems.

A related issue concerns the law and employee control. In England, railroad managers were aided in their attempt to instill industrial discipline by Parlimentary decrees. The Railway Act of 1840, in particular, made the violation of private company rules a criminal offense subject to criminal prosecution.[141] In the United States, the role played by government in labor control was far more limited.

There were laws that did affect American railwaymen. By the mid-1870s, most state legislatures in the Northeast and Midwest had passed statutes making negligence, carelessness, and drunkenness punishable crimes in cases involving accidents and injuries.[142] Ordinances concerned with the stopping and sounding of bells at crossings, the making up of trains, abandoning engines, and the wearing of uniforms and badges were also enacted. Vermont even passed a law requiring conductors to read passages from Scripture to travelers riding on Sunday trains.[143] Only Michigan, however, established legislation approaching the comprehensiveness of Britain's Railroad Act. In 1855 the Michigan legislature passed a statute declaring that:

Any conductor, engineer, servant, or other employee of any railroad corporation, who shall willfully violate any of the written or printed rules thereof, in relation to the running of cars or trains for transportation of persons or property, shall be subject to a fine of not less than twenty-five, nor more than one hundred dollars, or to imprisonment in the county jail not more than six months.[144]

[141] Kingsford, *Victorian Railwaymen*, pp. 14–19.
[142] Charles Bonney, *Rules of Law for the Carriage and Delivery of Persons and Property by Railway* lists laws affecting railwaymen for each state. State statutes can also be found in state railroad commission reports throughout the period.
[143] John Stover, *American Railroads*, p. 125.
[144] Bonney, *Rules of Law*, p. 101.

Railroad executives did try to have more extensive legislation enacted. In 1854 John Griswold, director of the Illinois Central, wrote to Charles Eliot Perkins on the question. Griswold complained that there "was little or no discipline among employees" and expressed hope that the Illinois legislature would pass legislation "regulating Rail Road employes [and] making any disobedience of orders by which accidents are caused a penal offense." Griswold added that "We have taken measures to keep the members [of the Illinois legislature] in good humor by issuing invitations to them to ride over and examine the road during the session free of charge."[145] James Whiton, superintendent of the Boston, Concord & Montreal Railroad, similarly believed that governmental action was necessary to curb employee indiscipline. In a report prepared for the directors of his company, he recommended that they seek "legislation providing suitable penalties for disobedience of orders. At present the most flagitious disobedience can only be punished by dismissal from employment. . . . [We] need stronger action."[146]

The social and political structures of the country hampered management's efforts to secure assistance from government. In England, railroad executives could appeal to one body—Parliament—for dispensation. In America, various state legislatures had to be petitioned. More important, these assemblies were often hostile to railroad corporations. Executives expressed jealousy of their British counterparts on this score and lamented their fate.[147] James Clarke of the Illinois Central even insisted that legislation was futile since local public sentiment would make it difficult for railroads to procure indictments and convictions of their workers.[148]

Opposition to harsh discipline can even be seen at the federal level. In 1862, when the bill to charter the Pacific Railway Company was before Congress, Senator Samuel Pomeroy of Kansas proposed an amendment authorizing the company to enlist la-

[145] Quoted in Lightner, "Labor on the Illinois Central," pp. 108, 141.
[146] James Whiton, *Railroads and Their Management*, p. 65.
[147] Herbert Gutman, "Trouble on the Railroads in 1873–1874," *Labor History*, 2:229. See also letter of H. B. Ledyard to W. O. Hughart, February 6, 1883, quoted in Cochran, *Railroad Leaders*, p. 383.
[148] Cochran, *Railroad Leaders*, pp. 229, 537.

borers under military discipline. Pomeroy argued that the road would be beyond the pale of government and that some means of organizing laborers, who would be largely foreign-born, was necessary. Pomeroy's proposition was rejected by the Senate, 36 to 2.[149]

A third point concerns police surveillance and blacklists. The use of detectives to spy on employees dates back to at least 1855, when a group of Chicago-based railroads signed an agreement with Allan Pinkerton to have agents of his newly founded National Detective Agency supply information "concerning the habits or associations of the employees."[150] Pinkerton's services did not come cheap; the Illionois Central's share in the contract amounted to $8,000. Pinkerton also used the contract quickly to establish his reputation. Before the year was out, his investigation led to the well-publicized conviction of Oscar Caldwell, a conductor on the then Chicago & Burlington Railroad. For the indiscretion of stealing what the jury found to be a total of thirty-six dollars, Caldwell was sentenced to one year in the Illinois state penitentiary.[151]

The Caldwell case launched Pinkerton's career and his services thereafter were in great demand. In the 1860s he was hired by several companies to investigate employee thefts of revenue and property, and he was quick to publish pamphlets and books advertising the successful results of his espionage.[152] In later decades he would provide other services for strike-threatened railroad companies. Pinkerton's success spawned competitors, and each year railroad executives were besieged with circulars and offers from detective agencies boasting of their expertise in "testing employees" and of their agents' abilities to "mingle with strikers and ascertain their plans."[153]

Railroads also directly employed their own detectives to spy

[149] Lewis Haney, *A Congressional History of Railways in the United States From 1850 to 1887*, p. 63.

[150] Lightner, "Labor on the Illinois Central," p. 106.

[151] J. Victor Smith, *Trial of Oscar T. Caldwell, Late a Conductor on the Chicago and Burlington Line, For Embezzlement*, p. 35.

[152] Allan Pinkerton, *Tests on Passenger Conductors*, and also his *Report of the Trial of Frederick P. Hill*.

[153] File 1578, Baltimore & Ohio Railroad Papers.

on employees, though it is difficult to determine exactly when the "spotter" system began.[154] Through state legislation, railroad companies were further given authorization to deputize policemen. Ostensibly their function was to guard property and freight and protect passengers from thieves and con artists. Railroad policemen were known, however, to double as informers. John Boyle, a policeman on the Baltimore & Ohio Railroad was assigned, in addition to his normal duties, to observe the activities of watchmen, telegraph operators, and conductors and to see that section bosses did not draw pay for section hands not at work.[155] Railroad policemen, it should be pointed out, were not always loyal. In 1866, seven policemen on the B. & O. were discharged for assisting a group of striking repair shop workers.[156]

The first evidence of the use of blacklists occurs on the Erie Railroad in 1854. In that year, the Erie's management announced a plan to notify other railroads when they dismissed a man for cause. This action precipitated a successful work stoppage of engineers, and the line was forced to capitulate. The proposal was officially shelved.[157] In 1864 the Michigan Central drew up an actual blacklist of strikers and sent it to companies throughout the country.[158] Three years later Robert Harris of the Chicago, Burlington & Quincy, in correspondence with other railroad officials, formally raised the idea of keeping lists of discharged men and circulating them between companies.[159] The proposal was put into effect in 1871, though Harris had some misgivings. "Men of good character," he warned, "may have been dismissed for circumstantial reasons that should be acknowledged."[160] Finally, in 1873 leaders of eighteen southern railroads met to discuss their financial and labor problems and unanimously en-

[154] Clarence Ray, *The Railroad Spotter*.
[155] H. S. Dewhurst, *The Railroad Police*, pp. 14–19; John Boyle to J. W. Garrett, May 10, 1877, Baltimore & Ohio Railroad Papers, file 1578.
[156] J. C. Davis to J. W. Garrett, January 23, 1866, Baltimore & Ohio Railroad Papers, file 7559.
[157] Edward Hungerford, *Men of the Erie*, p. 141.
[158] Stevenson, "Brotherhood of Locomotive Engineers," p. 54.
[159] Robert Harris to J. Scheiter, September 21, 1867, Chicago, Burlington & Quincy Railroad Papers, Robert Harris Out-Letters, CBQ-3H4.1.
[160] Robert Harris to L. Carper, November 10, 1871, ibid.

dorsed the principle of circulating blacklists.[161] The concept was thus well accepted and practiced before the growth of trade unionism on the nation's rail lines and before some of the more dramatic strikes of the latter part of the century.

A last point concerns the unsystematic nature of disciplinary procedures on the nation's pioneer railroads. In April 1848, the New England Association of Railroad Superintendents met in its first convention. Among the many issues discussed was the question of discharging employees. A need for uniform rules and practices was recognized, for there were many complaints that workers were constantly claiming indulgences by citing the more lenient standards and procedures of other companies. The Association, however, failed to implement a definitive policy.[162] In the mid-1850s, James Clarke of the Illinois Central also tried to grapple with the problem, but his efforts at systemization met with little success. Discipline on the I.C. remained arbitrary and completely dependent on the personal judgment of local officers.[163] The matter remained ambiguous on all railroads until late in the century, when workers organized in unions demanded formal grievance procedures. Pressure for more bureaucratic standards and routines thus came from below, albeit in the name of fairness and justice. But that is a story for a later chapter.

[161] Stevenson, "Brotherhood of Locomotive Engineers," p. 106.

[162] *Reports and Other Papers of the New England Association of Railroad Superintendents, 1850* (Boston, 1850), p. 23. Various state railroad commissions also raised the issue of standardizing disciplinary proceedings. See *Annual Report of the Railroad Commissioner of the State of New York, 1855* (Albany, 1856), p. 372; *Report of the Railroad Commissioners of the State of Maine for the Year 1870* (Augusta, 1871), pp. 24–25; *Third Annual Report of the Massachusetts Board of Railroad Commissioners, January, 1872* (Boston, 1872), p. cxxxiii.

[163] Lightner, "Labor on the Illinois Central," pp. 112–114; also Silas Bent to J. C. Jacobs, March 28, 1857, Illinois Central Railroad Papers, J. C. Jacobs In-Letters.

4

THE REWARDS OF LABOR

FROM THE PROVERBIAL stick to the proverbial carrot: positive incentives as well as negative sanctions shaped railroad work in the nineteenth century. Diligence and loyalty had their rewards. Relatively high wages, bonus systems, a variety of fringe benefits, and definite opportunities for promotion to higher status and higher-paying positions—all this encouraged industriousness. But discipline was also self-engendered. Railroading offered a life of adventure, personal fulfillment, and camaraderie and the intrinsic rewards of such labor cannot be minimized.

MID-NINETEENTH-CENTURY railroad officials frequently exchanged ideas and information regarding wages, and the subject of employee compensation was discussed widely in the trade press. Although there hardly was unanimity, a good number of executives and editorialists spoke in favor of liberal wage policies. They marshaled various arguments. In an open labor market, the services of the "best qualified and most competent" men could only be secured by offering the "best" monetary incentives.[1] Niggardliness, moreover, ultimately endangered profits. "It is true economy to get the best men and pay them well," advised the *American Railway Times* in 1851. "Five or ten dollars saved per month on a switchman's wage makes a poor show for the thousands lost by the man's inefficiency."[2] High wages, finally, had symbolic value; a sign of management's good inten-

[1] *Report of the Investigating Committee of the Northern Railroad, May 1850* (Concord, N. H., 1850), p. 16.
[2] *American Railway Times*, July 24, 1851, p. 2.

Table 4.1. Average Daily Wages in Dollars of Twenty Railway and Nonrailway Occupations, 1840–79

Occupation	1840–1844	1845–1849	1850–1854	1855–1859	1860–1864	1865–1869	1870–1874	1875–1879
Railroad enginemen	1.99	2.04	2.17	2.31	2.46	3.08	3.38	3.35
Iron puddlers	2.81	3.00	2.60	2.54	3.30	4.59	4.41	3.13
Railroad conductors	2.08	2.23	2.32	2.45	2.62	3.26	3.31	3.06
Bricklayers	2.11	1.86	1.94	1.99	2.24	3.27	3.62	3.06
Blacksmiths	1.56	1.50	1.58	1.70	1.92	2.71	2.90	2.72
Skilled railroad shopmen	1.50	1.40	1.61	1.75	1.95	2.60	2.70	2.68
Machinists	1.41	1.40	1.48	1.54	1.74	2.54	2.60	2.26
Railroad agents	1.60	1.70	1.70	1.93	2.11	2.51	2.54	2.26
Railroad clerks	1.30	1.35	1.38	1.63	1.85	2.12	2.17	2.13
Woodworkers	1.50	1.50	1.53	1.54	1.77	2.42	2.39	*
Railroad firemen	1.12	1.12	1.18	1.32	1.36	1.80	1.85	1.82
Railroad brakemen	1.17	1.13	1.17	1.27	1.37	1.87	1.92	1.80
Teamsters	1.49	1.46	1.15	1.07	1.18	1.58	1.68	1.54
Unskilled railroad shopmen	.81	.95	1.01	1.08	1.30	1.81	1.73	1.50
Woolen weavers	*	*	.79	.88	.98	1.20	1.31	1.35
Miners	.79	.82	.94	1.02	1.31	1.80	1.91	1.34
Railroad track laborers	.95	.98	1.01	1.10	1.31	1.69	1.61	1.30
Railroad station laborers	1.02	.98	1.03	1.12	1.26	1.58	1.50	1.30
Common laborers	.84	.87	.95	.99	1.15	1.54	1.48	1.30
Cotton textile workers	.56	.61	.62	.62	.67	1.02	1.02	.84

* Insufficient data.

tions, they could serve to "create a strong sense of moral obligation" among railwaymen.[3] "Large pay," wrote John Garrett of the Baltimore & Ohio Railroad, "should secure great devotion to duty and great thoroughness and attention to the interests of the Company."[4]

The first two generations of American railwaymen received compensation that compared favorably with other pursuits. Table 4.1 compares the average daily wages of railroad workers with other occupations for the period 1840–79.[5] Changes over time and the vast spectrum of skill levels involved make generalizations hazardous, but on the whole the figures indicate that railwaymen were reimbursed as well or better than workers in comparable endeavors. Early American railroad companies may have had large pools of eager applicants at their disposal, but rapid expansion and excessive labor mobility apparently kept the wages of railroad workers relatively high in the nation's first five frenzied decades of rail transport development. A few methodological words of warning, though, are in order. Information on wages for the nineteenth century is scant and scattered. The figures listed in table 4.1 are to be viewed only as approximations. Wage rates are also poor indicators of actual income levels. On the negative side, they fail to reflect losses due to fines and purchases of tools and uniforms, and to the very irregular and seasonal nature of nineteenth-century work. On the plus side, wage rates also fail to include supplements to income generated by overtime work, bonuses, and the earnings of other members of the family. Finally, as averages, the figures listed in table 4.1 hide important variations, which will be discussed shortly.

Railwaymen's wages, relatively high in absolute terms, also kept pace with fluctuating prices. Table 4.2 compares percentage

[3] *Report of the Directors of the Boston & Providence Railroad* (Boston, 1849), p. 19.

[4] J. W. Garrett to W. P. Smith, December 5, 1864, Baltimore & Ohio Railroad Letterbooks, Maryland Historical Society. For a more conservative view on wages, see *Report of the Committee of Investigation of the Worcester and Nashua Railroad Company, March 20, 1856* (Worcester, Mass., 1856), p. 9; *Report of the Committee of Investigation of the Fitchburg Railroad Company, January 29, 1856* (Boston, 1857), p. 31.

[5] Sources and the procedures used in constructing table 4.1 are outlined in appendix C.

Table 4.2. *Percentage Changes in the Average Daily Wages of Railway and Nonrailway Labor Compared with Similar Changes in Cost-of-Living Indices, 1840–79*

| | Percentage changes in average daily wages | | Percentage changes in cost-of-living indices | | |
	Nonrailway workers	Railway workers	Warren & Pearson wholesale price index	Federal Reserve Bank index	Burgess index
1840–44	+ 1.3	+ 1.4	− 19	−15	− 2
1845–49	− .4	+ 8.0	− 1	− 6	+ 9
1850–54	+ 7.8	+ 6.5	+ 29	+19	+ 4
1855–59	− .5	+ 1.7	− 16	− 6	− 1
1860–64	+42.7	+20.0	+108	+56	+66
1865–69	+ 7.3	+13.4	− 18	− 7	−10
1870–74	− 2.8	− 8.0	− 7	− 3	−10
1875–79	− 9.5	+ 9.2	− 24	− 8	−15
1840–49	+ 4.4	+ 9.2	− 14	−15	+ 9
1850–59	+ 6.4	+15.7	+ 13	+17	+ 9
1860–69	+62.4	+35.4	+ 62	+56	+55
1870–79	−15.6	− 2.3	− 33	−13	−26

changes in the average wages of railway and nonrailway labor with similar changes in cost-of-living indices. The figures reveal that, except for the Civil War years of 1861–65, railwaymen throughout the time frame under study continually experienced gains in real income. Of equal interest is the fact that their wages either periodically rose at a greater rate or fell to a lesser extent than the wages of other workingmen. Again, caution is necessary. The percentage changes in wages reported in table 4.2 are combined averages for all railway and nonrailway occupations listed in table 4.1. Variations between positions are consequently obscured. Most important, information on prices for the nineteenth century is as scant and scattered as similar wage data. The price and cost-of-living indices constructed by economists rarely correspond as a result, so three different scales have been employed in table 4.2.[6]

Important wage differentials existed, and they deserve ex-

[6] Price and cost-of-living indices extracted from U. S. Department of Commerce, Bureau of the Census, *Historical Statistics of the United States, Colonial Times to 1957* (Washington, D. C., 1960), pp. 115, 127.

tended comment. One obvious point to be made concerns variations between grades of railwaymen: the higher the skill level,
the greater the level of compensation. As shown in chapter 2,
wage differentials between the top and bottom—between the
aristocrats of the industry, the locomotivemen, and the plebeian
track walkers and station hands—remained fairly constant
throughout the period at roughly a little more than 2:1 ratios.
During the Civil War years, this differential narrowed slightly
due to a comparatively greater increase in the demand for unskilled labor. It is interesting to note that wage information provided by Peter Kingsford in *Victorian Railwaymen* indicates that
in England wage distinctions between the top and the bottom
grew from approximately a 2:1 to 3:1 advantage between the
1840s and 1870s.[7] This suggests that English engine drivers ex-
acted a relatively higher premium than their American counterparts, and conversely, that there was a greater glut of unskilled
labor in England than in the United States. In direct comparison,
however, American railwaymen received significantly higher
compensation. Converting shillings into dollars reveals that nineteenth-century American railway workers—from track laborers
to locomotivemen—were paid on an average twice the rate of
their respective British counterparts.[8]

Regional differences were also important. For skilled positions,
especially, wages in the South were substantially higher than in
other parts of the country. In the mid-1850s, when northern
enginemen received between $55 to $60 a month, southern drivers were earning anywhere from $90 to $100.[9] This gap widened
during the Civil War years and then narrowed somewhat, but
still to the advantage of southern engineers. A reverse situation
existed for unskilled positions. Before the war, regional differentials are hard to measure since southern lines employed slave
labor. Afterwards, with the transformation to the wage system,
payroll records indicate that common station and track hands

---

[7] Peter Kingsford, *Victorian Railwaymen*, pp. 88–102.
[8] Zerah Colburn and Alexander Holley, *The Permanent Way*, p. 21; Edward
B. Dorsey, *English and American Railroads Compared*, pp. 48–49.
[9] *American Engineer*, July 11, 1857, p. 6.

received from 80 cents to $1.00 a day in the South and from $1.50 to $1.75 in the North.[10]

Wage differences between companies raise a third issue. Was there an advantage in working for certain lines—for example, for the longer, busier, more substantial, highly capitalized railroads whose earnings far outstripped their lesser established competitors? In 1878 the railroad commissioners of Illinois gathered complete wage data from the forty-eight railroad companies operating in the state.[11] For managerial positions, firm size and compensation proved to be highly related. The larger, busier, more endowed companies offered their managers significantly higher monetary rewards. For railwaymen below the level of station agent, however, it mattered little for which Illinois railway firm one worked. The relationship between company size and compensation for these employees was in most cases completely random.[12] With the exception of supervisory positions, the Illinois data suggest that skill level and region were more important in effecting wage distinctions than the nature of the firms in which mid-nineteenth-century American railwaymen toiled.

Finally, wages of specific occupational categories varied substantially even within given companies. In 1855 the management of the New York Central Railroad, in an annual stockholders' report, listed high and low income figures for several grades of workers. Agents, the report noted, earned anywhere from $10 a month to $166, conductors from $30 to $60, baggagemen from $30 to $40, enginemen from $50 to $78, firemen from $20 to $52, foremen from $60 to $100, carpenters from $20 to $52, and station porters from $10 to $52.[13] The wide ranges of income levels reported by the Central are not unusual. Similar variations

[10] These contentions are based on sources listed in appendix C.

[11] *Eighth Annual Report of the Railroad and Warehouse Commission of Illinois* (Springfield, Illinois, 1879), pp. 56–59.

[12] The Illinois survey included average yearly earnings for fifteen different occupational categories. This information was cross-tabulated with various indicators of firm size, and the resulting correlation coefficients are reported in table D.1 in appendix D with a methodological note.

[13] New York Central Railroad Company, *Report of a Committee, October 24, 1855* (Boston, 1855), p. 11.

can be cited from the payroll records and corporate reports of other companies.

Two factors appear to account for these discrepancies: the exact nature of the work performed, and the number of years in service to the company. Agents, clerks, and laborers assigned to busy central depots, for instance, generally received greater compensation than their counterparts employed at way stations along the line. Similarly, passenger train conductors, engineers, firemen, and brakemen frequently received higher wages than freight train operatives. In the shops, individual blacksmiths, machinists, and boilermakers earned income commensurate with their particular skills and duties.[14]

A loosely structured, informal seniority system also existed, though evidence from the written record is wanting on this subject. In 1843 the superintendent of transportation of the Western Railroad recommended yearly increments in conductors' salaries, but the line's directors shelved the proposal.[15] In 1865 the management of the Baltimore & Ohio Railroad formally approved a plan for annual increases for conductors, and the Illinois Central eleven years later introduced a system of increments for locomotivemen based on five-year intervals.[16] This is the extent of the documentation for such practices in corporate memoranda and reports. Available payroll accounts of mid-nineteenth-century railroad companies indicate, however, that men were paid according to length-of-service criteria. Workers who remained on company registers for long periods of time were consistently compensated at higher rates than less permanent employees. One extreme example is R. S. Dowd, a freight agent employed by the Hartford & New Haven Railroad. Dowd was the only employee located in both the line's surviving 1843 and 1870 payroll accounts (suggesting a minimum of twenty-seven years of service). In 1870 he earned a monthly salary of $166.67. No other agent

[14] Again, contentions here are based on sources listed in appendix C.

[15] *Proceedings of the Western Railroad Corporation with a Report of the Committee of Investigation, 1843* (Boston, 1843), p. 14.

[16] "Resolution Regarding Increase of Pay for Passenger Train Conductors, March 6, 1865," Baltimore & Ohio Railroad Papers, file 1461, Maryland Historical Society; David Lightner, "Labor on the Illinois Central Railroad, 1852–1900" (Ph.D. dissertation, Cornell Univ., 1969), pp. 168–170.

at the time received more than $100 a month, and $80 was the average.[17]

Intergrade, interregional, interfirm, and intragrade, firm-specific variations can thus be catalogued. The whole question of railwaymen's earnings is further complicated by three other considerations: first, that the methods employed to calculate earnings varied widely; second, that local supervisors often used great discretion in paying workers; and third, that railwaymen frequently were not paid at all for long periods of time or were else reimbursed in kind or in depreciated currency.

The daily wage figures presented in table 4.1 should not be read as evidence that all railwaymen between 1840 and 1879 were paid on the basis of per diem wage rates. Before the advent of union contracts, systems of payment varied considerably. Maintenance-of-the-way crews and shopmen generally were compensated according to daily wage figures and were paid only for days worked. Agents, foremen, clerks, station laborers, conductors, and brakemen, on the other hand, were either paid by the day or month or even annually. In the latter cases, there is confusion as to what actually constituted a normal or ample month's or year's work. Some companies prorated salary figures and reimbursed in effect only for days worked, while other firms paid straight salaries, not deducting for losses of time due to illness, absence, or seasonal factors. Agents, moreover, were often paid on a commission basis, or, if they handled the business of several companies, received compensation from several sources.[18]

The situation of engineers and firemen was even more complicated. Before the Civil War, drivers and their assistants were paid by the day or by the month. Companies set per diem wage rates or monthly salary figures without regard to the nature of the service performed—freight or passenger—the type of engine run, or the number of hours consumed. What constituted a normal day's or month's work remained a discretionary matter, although one hundred miles a day and twenty-five hundred miles a month emerged as the customary standards. Cabmen received

[17] For citation on payroll records see appendix C.

[18] These contentions are based on careful studies of the payroll records cited in appendix C.

no compensation for extra mileage or overtime caused by breakdowns and delays. Companies practiced different policies in paying salaried men during slack or unseasonal times.[19]

In the 1860s and '70s, carriers began to introduce piecework systems of payment into the industry. Under the straight mileage system, enginemen and firemen were compensated at fixed per-mile-run rates. Under the so-called "trip" system, companies established set schedules of payment for specific runs and reimbursed their cabmen accordingly. The move toward piecework methods of payment was economically motivated; rail firms now paid only for work performed. For the drivers and their assistants, the mileage and trip systems alleviated certain inequities and fostered others. Piecework allowed for compensation for all mileage covered and for the peculiar circumstances of specific trips. However, the cabmen under these systems were paid only when called and thus had no fixed, assured income; nor did established piecework rates take into account fluctuations in the number of hours required to complete runs, fluctuations most frequently caused by delays and mechanical failures. Once organized, enginemen and firemen would press for standardized union contracts establishing guaranteed incomes based on minimum hours and mileage requirements and including provisions for overtime and extra-mileage compensation.[20]

Before the advent of union contracts, the prerogative of fixing compensation also frequently remained in the hands of local supervisors.[21] Initially, boards of directors determined wages and salaries, but this function gradually devolved to lower level officials, along with hiring and disciplinary procedures.[22] Railroad managers and trade journal editors, like Henry Varnum Poor, openly advocated decentralization as the best means of rewarding individual performances within the context of large-scale work

[19] Reed Richardson, *The Locomotive Engineer*, pp. 112–113, 209.
[20] Ibid., pp. 45, 118, 144, 208.
[21] Ibid., pp. 155–156, 196.
[22] Examples of early boards of directors fixing salary levels of individual workers can be found in minutes of directors' meetings, vol. 4, p. 164 and vol. 8, p. 244, Boston & Worcester Railroad Papers, Baker Library, Harvard University; also, "Resolution, June 6, 1842," Auburn & Rochester Railroad Letterbook, 1840–51, New York Central Railroad Papers, Syracuse University Library.

organizations.[23] A committee investigating the management of the Northern Railroad in 1851 thus recommended entrusting the regulation of wages to local officials with the following argument: "Their familiarity with the duties and capacities of each individual will enable them to determine the value and importance of the service rendered by him to the Corporation."[24]

In those cases where companies did not post wage schedules unilaterally established by top echelon officers, individual workers entered into verbal agreements with local supervisors. Custom, prejudice, and similar subjective factors played as much a role here as strict economic considerations.[25] Needless to say, decentralization worked to the advantage of some workers and to the disadvantage of others. Clerks and station laborers employed under the supervision of Agent C. W. Perviel, for instance, were found by Baltimore & Ohio Railroad executives to be receiving frequent raises and to be paid in what was described as a completely liberal, "loose and unauthorized manner."[26] Letters in the same company's archives reveal that a Mrs. Turner was able to obtain for her son, a machinist's apprentice, a ten cent increase in his daily wage by pleading severe hardship with the boy's foreman.[27] A group of track workers on the Illinois Central in the 1850s, however, were not as fortunate. An investigation by I.C. officials discovered that, among other indiscretions, their supervisor employed and paid them at less than the suggested and recorded rate, while pocketing the difference.[28] Equally revealing is an incident chronicled by Harry French in his reminiscence, *Railroadman*. On one of his first jobs, which

[23] Alfred D. Chandler, Jr., *Henry Varnum Poor*, p. 156; *Report of the Executive Officers of the Baltimore & Ohio Railroad Company, on the Subject of Retrenchment* (Baltimore, 1842), p. 23; John C. Davis to Andrew Anderson, September 2, 1865, Baltimore & Ohio Railroad Papers, uncatalogued material.

[24] *Report of the Investigating Committee of the Northern Railroad, May 1850*, p. 17.

[25] Paul Black, "Robert Harris and the Problem of Railway Labor Management" (unpublished paper in author's possession), p. 13.

[26] W. P. Smith to C. W. Perviel, January 17, 1859, Baltimore & Ohio Railroad Papers, file 1461.

[27] D. W. Turner to J. W. Garrett, December 29, 1865, ibid.

[28] G. B. McClellan to L. H. Clarke, November 19, 1858, Illinois Central Railroad Papers, McClellan Out-Letters, IC-1M2.1, Newberry Library.

he had obtained through the intercession of his brother, Harry had reached an accord with his division superintendent to do both braking and telegraphing for $65 a month. When this supervisor transferred to another line, his replacement refused to recognize all existing arrangements, and Harry's monthly salary was summarily cut to $45. Harry had little recourse and was subsequently discharged for making an issue of the matter.[29]

Finally—and crucially—financial difficulties and currency shortages frequently forced railroad companies to withhold direct payments to employees. Workers on the state-owned and operated Philadelphia & Columbia Railroad, for instance, went without pay for four months in 1851, when the state legislature failed to pass a funding bill.[30] In the 1850s, employees on the Chicago, St. Paul & Fond du Lac Railroad frequently were not paid for five-month intervals, while in the 1870s men on the St. Joseph & Grand Isle waited upwards of six months for payday.[31] Harvey Reed in his reminiscence, *Forty Years A Locomotive Engineer*, even recalled working for the much-besieged Illinois-Midland Railroad for two years without receiving direct compensation.[32]

When unable to meet the usual monthly payrolls, companies resorted to stalling and payment in kind. The New Albany & Salem Railroad, located in Indiana, continually short on currency throughout the 1850s, issued meal and lodging tickets to its employees. The tickets represented a cash value of either fifteen or thirty cents. The line's paymaster was authorized to redeem the tickets in cash when presented by the public, but not when offered by employees.[33] After the Civil War, the almost completely bankrupt Norfolk & Western Railroad paid its workers in cornmeal, salt pork, shelter, and a promise of future pay.[34] Other hard-pressed companies advised employees to have land-

---

[29] Chauncey Del French, *Railroadman*, pp. 48–49.
[30] *Holley's Railroad Advocate*, May 2, 1857, p. 4.
[31] D. C. Prescott, *Early Day Railroading from Chicago*, pp. 28–29; B. A. Botkin and Alvin Harlow, eds., *A Treasury of Railroad Folklore*, p. 306.
[32] J. Harvey Reed, *Forty Years a Locomotive Engineer*, pp. 33–34.
[33] Frank Hargrave, *A Pioneer Indiana Railroad*.
[34] Hank Bowman, *Pioneer Railroads*, p. 121.

lords and merchants bill the lines directly.[35] The most frequently employed practice, though, in states which granted rail firms the privilege of printing money, was to reimburse workers partly in cash and partly in company notes which were redeemable at future dates.[36]

Currency shortages created obvious problems for employers and employees alike. In 1865 the Baltimore & Ohio Railroad was forced to extend the interval between payrolls from one month to two; the line subsequently found it difficult to compete for labor with local machine shops that were able to pay their men every two weeks.[37] Payless paydays were also a sure provocation for strikes and other job actions.[38] For workers, deferred payments meant a life in constant search of credit and constant debt. When paid in company-issued currency or other kinds of notes, they further faced the prospect of holding worthless paper if local merchants and landlords refused to accept it. The situation was not without its humorous aspects. George L. Anderson, a pioneer railwayman, recalled the following incident:

The St. Joseph and Grande Isle had a pretty hard sledding for the first four or five years. We worked six months in 1871 without pay. The company was short of equipment, and some of the fellows would get dissatisfied because of no pay, and they would sue the company, get judgement and levy on some locomotive or car, and tie up the little equipment the company had.[39]

The policy of paying workers by check on a regular weekly or biweekly basis did not come into practice until the 1890s.[40]

STUDIES OF WAGES and salaries often ignore the fact that workers either seek out or are presented with various means of supplementing incomes. For mid-nineteenth-century American rail-

[35] Reed, *Forty Years a Locomotive Engineer*, pp. 33–34.
[36] Bowman, *Pioneer Railroads*, p. 100, Thomas Cochran, *Railroad Leaders, 1845–1890*, pp. 179, 262–263.
[37] Thatcher Perkins to J. W. Garrett, July 28, 1865, Baltimore & Ohio Railroad Papers, file 468.
[38] Cochran, *Railroad Leaders*, p. 235.
[39] Botkin and Harlow, *Treasury of Railroad Folklore*, p. 306.
[40] Lightner, "Labor on the Illinois Central," p. 346.

waymen, a number of opportunities existed to increase their earnings above and beyond the recorded take-home pay. While some of these extra-income-producing activities had official sanction, others were either frowned upon and accepted, or else were clearly illegal. Railroad work did have the advantage, though, of offering these opportunities.

In an effort to encourage high productivity and efficiency, companies began experimenting in the 1850s with a variety of bonus or premium systems. After a strike of engineers in 1854, the Erie Railroad held out to each driver the offer of a monthly prize of five dollars for running without an accident.[41] The Pennsylvania, the Reading, the Boston, Concord & Montreal, the Little Miami, and the Ohio & Mississippi Railroads similarly adopted early plans for awarding monthly and yearly premiums to engineers and firemen who had the best record on fuel consumption. Bonuses ranged anywhere from five to fifty dollars a month.[42] The Baltimore & Ohio Railroad also instituted a premium system for its enginemen and extended the idea to include shopmen and track repair crews. A fifty-cents-a-week increment was offered to shop apprentices for "good conduct," while section men were tempted with year-end bonuses for having the least broken tracks.[43]

Rail lines also experimented with nonmonetary incentives to boost productivity. In 1855 Superintendent McCallum of the Erie Railroad instituted a system of posting monthly reports listing the line's enginemen and their respective records on fuel consumption. In an annual stockholders' report, McCallum duly noted that the practice "has tended to excite, amongst the engineers employed, an honorable emulation to excel . . . [and] a

[41] *Colburn's Railroad Advocate*, January 19, 1856, p. 1.

[42] Chandler, *Henry Varnum Poor*, p. 165; *Colburn's Railroad Advocate*, June 28, 1856, p. 1, and November 24, 1885, p. 1; *The Railroad Gazette*, October 9, 1875, p. 414; H. D. Bacon to Engineers of the Ohio & Mississippi Railroad, March 16, 1860, Baltimore & Ohio Transportation Museum, display case; James Stevenson, "The Brotherhood of Locomotive Engineers and Its Leaders, 1863–1920" (Ph.D. dissertation, Vanderbilt Univ., 1954), p. 124.

[43] Resolution of the Board of Directors of the Baltimore & Ohio Railroad, May 14, 1873, Baltimore & Ohio Railroad Papers, file 9679; Memorandum of W. N. Bolling to J. Garrett, August 26, 1867, ibid., file 8056.

satisfactory improvement has taken place [in fuel savings]."[44]
Trade journal editors quickly hailed McCallum's innovation and
recommended its adoption throughout the industry.[45] Other nonmonetary incentive programs were also suggested and tried. The
Delaware, Lackawanna & Western Railroad awarded diplomas
for faithful service, and the railroad commissioners of Maine in
1873 recommended that the rail lines in the state, "as an in-
ducement for disciplined and careful behavior," award merit
badges to deserving employees.[46]

Beyond structured bonuses and premiums, railwaymen also
received occasional monetary rewards for unusual or meritorious
actions. John Sweeney, an engine house foreman, was awarded
one hundred dollars by the Illinois Central in 1861 for his efforts
in saving a valuable property during a fire.[47] Another I.C. employee, John Whitney, a locomotive fireman, received a gold
watch for his part in preventing an approaching train from hur-
tling into two trains which had already collided.[48] The board of
directors of the Baltimore & Ohio Railroad in February 1864
similarly presented engineman William Lemmon with a five
hundred dollar reward for avoiding an accident, which would
have resulted from another employee's negligence.[49] Other actions also warranted special citation. It was customary to award
the first engineer who crossed a new bridge ten or twenty dollars
for testing the structure and risking his life.[50] Trainmen on special
runs carrying political candidates, foreign dignitaries, or prom-

[44] *Reports of the President and Superintendent of the New York and Erie
Railroad, September 30, 1855* (New York, 1856), p. 56.

[45] *Colburn's Railroad Advocate*, November 24, 1855, p. 1; *Railway Times*,
February 18, 1860, p. 66.

[46] George D. Phelps to D. H. Potterer, November 17, 1855, Letterbooks of
George D. Phelps, 1845–1856, Delaware, Lackawanna & Western Railroad
Papers, Syracuse University Library; *Report of the Railroad Commissioners of
the State of Maine for the Year 1873* (Augusta, Maine, 1874), p. 10.

[47] William Osborn to John Sweeney, February 21, 1861, W. H. Osborn Out-
Letters, Illinois Central Railroad Papers, IC-106.1.

[48] Silas Bent to John Whitney, May 15, 1857, J. C. Clarke Out-Letters, Illinois
Central Railroad Papers, IC-1C5.1.

[49] Resolution of the Board of Directors of the Baltimore & Ohio Railroad,
February 11, 1864, Baltimore & Ohio Railroad Papers, file 9679.

[50] *The Railroad Gazette*, July 30, 1870, p. 410.

inent stockholders were given small gratuities.[51] Workers not participating in strikes also often received monetary gifts.[52] Loyal enginemen on the Pennsylvania Railroad in 1877 were given two hundred dollar supplements to their normal take-home pay.[53] Finally, in prosperous years, top executives occasionally authorized surplus monies to be dispersed at the discretion of local supervisors to diligent, faithful workers.[54]

Railway employees also discovered their own means for increasing their incomes. Some methods, as discussed in chapter 2, were obviously illegal—the embezzlement of fares and the theft of coal, lumber, tools, and other company property for sale or private use. Railway workers also stole from freight cars and accepted goods from riders in lieu of fares. A group of early conductors on the Boston & Lowell Railroad, for instance, were discovered eating shipments of oysters and were severely censured.[55] Harvey Reed in his reminiscence similarly recalled taking boots from a freight car when he was a young fireman.[56] Locomotivemen also customarily permitted farmers, sheepherders, and ranch hands to ride in the cab for a nominal fee; conductors and brakemen on freight runs collected fares from hobos; and passenger conductors and brakemen on the Concord and the Rock Island Railroads were frequently caught accepting eggs, butter, vegetables, grain, clothes, and household wares from salesmen and other travelers in return for free passage.[57]

Railroad workers had at their disposal other means of supplementing income which were legal but not officially sanctioned. Baggagemen and porters received tips that constituted a signif-

---

[51] G. Clinton Gardner to Frank Thomas, June 6, 1876, G. Clinton Gardner Letterbooks, Eleutherian Mills Historical Library.

[52] *Holley's Railroad Advocate*, October 11, 1856, p. 1.

[53] *Railroad Gazette*, January 4, 1878, p. 3.

[54] Cochran, *Railroad Leaders*, p. 242.

[55] Louis Loring, "Early Railroads in Boston," *The Bostonian* 1:306.

[56] Reed, *Forty Years a Locomotive Engineer*, pp. 28–29.

[57] Stewart Holbrook, *The Story of American Railroads*, p. 340; Gilbert Lathrop, *Little Engines and Big Men*, p. 69; *Rock Island Magazine*, October 1922, p. 12; State of New Hampshire, *Hearing in the Matter of the Concord Railroad Corporation vs. George Clough and Trustees* (Concord, N. H., 1869), pp. 10–11.

icant portion of their total earnings.[58] Passengers often gave gifts
to favorite conductors on holidays and special occasions. Charles
George received a watch as a token of appreciation from loyal
riders on the Vermont Central.[59] A group of patrons similarly
presented a two hundred dollar silver tea set to John B. Adams,
a veteran conductor on the Western Railroad. A local newspaper
noted the presentation: "There is hardly a man living upon the
line of the railroad between Springfield and Albany who is not
indebted to Mr. Adams for kind attention to his wife, mother
or sister."[60] Pioneer conductors also sold water at a penny a cup
and were known to accept "bribes" from male passengers who
were seeking entrance to the ladies' cars.[61]

Train crews at times exhibited impressive ingenuity and enterprise. On the Eastern Railroad, trainmen would buy fruits,
vegetables, and poultry at stations in New Hampshire and sell
them at sizable profit to Boston provision dealers.[62] In Indiana
during the 1850s, engineers on the New Albany & Salem Railroad frequently stopped their trains en route so that crewmen
could buy berries, eggs, and chestnuts from local farmers. They
then sold this produce at major stations along the line.[63] The
practice was tolerated by company officials until it drew newspaper comment. In 1857 an editorial in the Crawfordsville *Review* remarked that it was time the Postmaster General added
an extra car to the New Albany & Salem Railroad runs to make
room for the mails that were being crowded out by shipments
of produce being carried on by trainmen. The practice was then
officially prohibited.[64]

By far the most common way to earn additional money was
to perform transport-related odd jobs. While employed as a conductor, Harry French carried messages and packages for a fee

[58] Holbrook, *Story of American Railroads*, p. 269.
[59] Charles George, *Forty Years on the Rail*, p. 186.
[60] Botkin and Harlow, *Treasury of Railroad Folklore*, p. 160.
[61] Bowman, *Pioneer Railroads*, p. 99; Isaac Hinckley to J. W. Garrett, December 21, 1866, Baltimore & Ohio Railroad Papers, file 3089.
[62] Francis Bradlee, *The Eastern Railroad*, p. 54.
[63] Frank Hargrave, *A Pioneer Indiana Railroad*, p. 151.
[64] Holbrook, *Story of American Railroads*, p. 116.

and even shopped for people living along the line. Harry also came into some additional cash when he was rewarded for assisting in a birth on his train.[65] Charles George also kept busy with extra-income-earning chores. As he related:

Conductors often turn an honest penny by carrying on a little commission business and thus accommodating the patrons of their roads. Those who run through rural districts get farmers' products and sell them to city buyers at a good profit. In the early days of my running the Waukegan train, I made quite a good deal of money by purchasing goods in Chicago for my passengers in Waukegan. I took all this trade to Potter Palmer who is now known the world over for his magnificent hotel and great wealth, but who in the days of which I speak had just started in the dry goods business house of Marshall Field & Company. Mr. Palmer never forgot me at Christmas time, and he always gave me my owns goods at cost.[66]

Railroad companies tried to put a halt to such activities. In 1840 the directors of the Northern Railroad formally prohibited the line's conductors from carrying letters and packages except for the firm. To appease the men, who faced losses in earnings, the directors voted to increase their conductors' salaries.[67] W. R. Arthur, general superintendent of the Illinois Central Railroad, in 1863 similarly warned company agents, conductors, and trainmen against carrying letters. The line had received complaints from the Post Office Department, he noted, adding that it was a violation of federal laws punishable by fifty dollar penalties to convey mail not prepaid with official stamps.[68] Finally, Robert Harris of the Chicago, Burlington & Quincy took a strong stand against the private business activities of freight and station agents. Faced with a variety of problems—creditors of agents placing liens on the company, agents shortweighing and tying up company freight cars with their own shipments—Harris in 1870

[65] French, *Railroadman*, p. 138.
[66] George, *Forty Years on the Rail*, pp. 182–183.
[67] Charles Kennedy, "The Early Business History of Four Massachusetts Railroads," *Bulletin of the Business Historical Society* 25:197.
[68] Circular from W. R. Arthur to Agents, Conductors, and All Train-Men, November 10, 1863, Illinois Central Railroad Case, American Antiquarian Society Library.

ordered C.B. & Q. agents to terminate all their private business activities related to transport. The problem, however, persisted.[69] Harris also collaborated with express companies and other railroads to fix agents' salaries. Whenever an agent was offered supplemental income in the form of commissions for doing business with express firms or other lines, Harris ordered a reduction in the employee's C.B. & Q. compensation.[70]

A final means of increasing income was volunteering for extra work. Most companies did not pay for overtime. The following regulation from the rule book of the Long Island Railroad was commonplace: "All persons, at any hour, are expected to perform whatever service may be required of them without any stipulation as to extra pay."[71] At the discretion of local supervisors, railwaymen did often receive additional money for extra trips or for working extreme hours.[72] A few companies, like the Chicago, Burlington & Quincy, even adopted formal overtime payment procedures. An investigation in 1876, in fact, revealed that overtime was a major source of income for C.B. & Q. employees. More than two-thirds of the conductors studied earned additional pay from extra work, the average recipient augmenting his income by upwards of 30 percent. Half the brakemen investigated also supplemented their incomes in this manner, increasing their earnings by 25 percent.[73] With the advent of formal union contracts, overtime payments became standard.

AMERICA'S pioneer railroad companies also offered their employees a number of fringe benefits. To reduce transiency and attract what superintendent Herman Haupt of the Pennsylvania Railroad termed "reliable men with families," many lines built

[69] Paul Black, "The Development of Management Personnel Policies on the Burlington Railroad, 1860–1900" (Ph.D. dissertation, Univ. of Wisconsin, 1972), pp. 284–285.

[70] Ibid., p. 288; Paul Black, "Robert Harris," pp. 15–16.

[71] *Report of Committee of the Long Island Railroad Co. in Relation to the Accident on the 28th Day of August, 1865* (Long Island City, N. Y., 1865), p. 4. See also Richardson, *Locomotive Engineer*, p. 147.

[72] Payroll records cited in appendix C contain notations for overtime payments and special reasons given.

[73] Paul Black, "Development of Management Personnel Policies," p 297.

accommodations to house their workers.[74] This included single-family dwellings, tenements near stations and in shop towns, and barracks for section gangs living along the line.[75] Sleeping quarters in depots and roundhouses were also provided for men on layovers.[76] In most cases, workers paid rent above and beyond their take-home pay to live in company-built lodgings.[77] A property list in the archives of the Baltimore & Ohio Railroad, however, indicates that division officers, agents, and most foremen were supplied housing rent-free.[78] An interesting aside here is provided by the Atlantic & Great Western Railroad. In the early 1860s, the company announced a plan to rent houses and lots to the line's employees. The plan included a provision that after ten years of faithful service, ownership of the property would be signed over to the worker for a nominal fee.[79] There unfortunately is no evidence to indicate how this early example of welfare capitalism fared in practice.

The number of workers provided with company-built homes and the costs are difficult to ascertain. Two surviving documents—a payroll record and a rent list from the Northern Railroad—provide a partial answer. In 1850 the company leased property to thirty-eight individuals, twenty-five of whom were employees. The line at the time employed 140 men, which means that about 18 percent of the firm's work force were residing in company-owned housing. These workers paid rent ranging from

[74] Herman Haupt to J. E. Thomson, August 5, 1852, Herman Haupt Letterbook, Historical Society of Pennsylvania. In 1889 the U. S. Commissioner of Labor surveyed 427 railway firms and discovered that 174, or 41 percent, furnished some kind of housing for their employees. See *Fifth Annual Report of the Commissioner of Labor, 1889* (Washington, D. C., 1890), p. 21.

[75] Thatcher Perkins to J. W. Garrett, July 28, 1865, Baltimore & Ohio Railroad Papers, file 468; *Report of the Directors of the Boston and Maine Railroad* (Boston, 1870), p. 7; *Report of the Board of Managers of the Mine Hill and Schuylkill Haven Railroad Company, 1857* (Philadelphia, 1857), p. 12; G. B. McClellan to W. H. Osborn, October 29, 1857, McClellan Out-Letters, Illinois Central Railroad Papers, IC-1M2.1.

[76] Warren Jacobs, "The Fall River Line Boat Train," *Railway and Locomotive Historical Society Bulletin*, no. 2, p. 8; Joseph Kirkland to J. N. Perkins, November 17, 1856, Joseph Kirkland Out-Letters, Illinois Central Railroad Papers, IC-1K3.1.

[77] Lightner, "Labor on the Illinois Central," p. 125.

[78] Property of the B. & O. RR, Baltimore & Ohio Railroad Papers, file 1942.

[79] *American Railroad Journal*, March 19, 1864, p. 292.

1 to 19 percent of their take-home pay, with 11 percent the average. All grades of workers were involved, and there was little correlation between position occupied and percentage of income paid to the firm in rent.[80]

Free passes and shipping privileges represented two other benefits. Company policies on the former practice varied considerably. Some firms only allowed employees free transportation to work or on company business, while others extended the privilege to all times and even to family members. Robert Harris of the Chicago, Burlington & Quincy especially favored the broadest use of passes, as he wrote, to "cultivate among all the employees of the Co. a feeling of sympathy with the Road." C.B. & Q. men and their families could ride free at all times on any of the divisions of the line.[81] It was also customary for companies to give veteran employees moving to other parts of the country letters stating claims to free passage on other roads. Carriers similarly paid the moving expenses of recruits, especially new managers, agents, clerks, and skilled enginemen and machinists.[82]

The Chicago, Burlington & Quincy Railroad, in particular, permitted employees to benefit in various ways from the company's business. In the 1860s, workers were allowed to ship packages at 50 percent of the normal rates (the figure was raised to 80 percent in the 1870s).[83] The line also delivered coal to employees from the company's mines at per cost freight charges and sold lots of company-owned land to groups of workers at reduced prices.[84]

[80] Documents can be found in *Report of the Investigating Committee of the Northern Railroad*, pp. 33–35.

[81] Robert Harris to N. D. Munson, February 27, 1872, Harris Out-Letters, Chicago, Burlington & Quincy Railroad Papers, CBQ-3H4.1., Newberry Library; Paul Black, "Development of Management Personnel Policies," p. 335.

[82] *Report of the Committee for Investigating the Affairs of the Boston and Providence Railroad Corporation* (Boston, 1857), p. 16; H. E. Woods to George Stark, September 11, 1856, Nashua & Lowell and Boston & Lowell Railroad Papers, vol. 201, Baker Library; Baldwin & Whitney to William McKee, November 15, 1842, Baldwin Locomotive Papers, Outgoing Letters, 1842–1843, Historical Society of Pennsylvania.

[83] Paul Black, "Development of Management Personnel Policies," p. 343.

[84] Ibid., p. 344; *Railroad Gazette*, September 21, 1877, pp. 426–427.

Nineteenth-century rail firms extended a number of other, miscellaneous benefits. During the Civil War, carriers helped their employees obtain exemptions from the draft, lent them money to pay bounty fees, and sometimes paid the fees in full.[85] John Garrett, president of the Baltimore & Ohio, even used his influence and contacts in the War Department to assure that B. & O. employees captured by Confederate soldiers would be the first released in prisoner exchanges.[86] Companies like the Boston & Albany, the Vermont Central, and the Passumpsic & Connecticut Rivers Railroad established libraries for their workers during the 1850s and '60s.[87] Other railroads such as the Cleveland & Pittsburgh and the C.B. & Q. built reading and waiting rooms.[88] The Atlantic & Great Western in 1864 even donated $150,000 to help furnish a lodge hall for the newly formed Brotherhood of Locomotive Engineers.[89]

Finally, companies granted certain fringe benefits which were not quite officially sanctioned. As will be shown in the next chapter, at the discretion of local supervisors gratuities were often awarded to injured men and to the families of employees killed in service. Local foremen also placed older, veteran workers in less demanding positions rather than discharge them, and were known to lend money from the companies' coffers to em-

[85] File 568 of the Baltimore & Ohio Railroad Papers contains hundreds of letters indicating the intense efforts the company pursued to help employees obtain deferments.

[86] J. W. Garrett to John L. Wilson, August 14, 1862, Baltimore & Ohio Railroad Letterbooks, Maryland Historical Society; J. W. Garrett to Mrs. Mary Ann Coleman, August 31, 1863, ibid.

[87] Colburn's Railroad Advocate, June 2, 1855, p. 3, April 19, 1856, p. 4; A Catalog of the Circulating and Consulting Departments of the Boston & Albany R. R. Library (Boston, 1868). A printed circular issued by the librarian of the Boston & Albany Railroad Library offers an amusing aside. The librarian asked all supervisors to inform workers about the opening of the library and further beseeched them to recover books loaned to employees who were discharged. See H. C. Bixby to Agents and Heads of Departments of the Boston & Albany Railroad, January 12, 1869, Boston & Albany Railroad Case, American Antiquarian Society Library.

[88] The Railroad Gazette, January 7, 1871, p. 341; Memorandum of C. E. Perkins on Waiting Rooms for Employees, December 8, 1883, Chicago, Burlington & Quincy Railroad Papers, Memorandum President's Office, 1878–1900, CBQ-3P4.92.

[89] Stevenson, "Brotherhood of Locomotive Engineers," p. 77.

ployees in hardship.[90] Vacations were even granted. W. Spaulding, a station agent on the Illinois Central, gave James Sharky, a laborer, time off for illness in 1865 while keeping him on the line's payroll.[91] A clerk on the Chicago, Burlington & Quincy was similarly extended a leave to attend to sick relatives.[92] Granting vacations, in fact, had semiofficial approval on the C.B. & Q. Top management personnel accepted leave-giving as a proper means of engendering loyalty and rewarding diligence, but wanted the practice to remain a secret prerogative of local supervisors. The following passage from a memorandum issued from the office of President Charles Eliot Perkins in the 1880s illuminates this point:

Men may take leaves only with permission. Those who work by the day, month or week, and are paid for overtime should not receive pay when on leave. Those who are called for extra work occasionally without compensation, should not be under strict rules. Advisory for local officers to decide to give short vacations without having their pay stopped. . . .

The service will be positively benefitted by letting him [the employee] understand that if he is zealous in the Company's behalf he will be allowed to leave without losing pay for the two or three weeks he is absent. . . . In short, it is important that the officers of the company, great and small, should take and show an active interest in the welfare of those under them in the service. . . .

It is not expedient to post this memoranda. Expedient to have officers of the company instructed privately, that they may, at their discretion, give vacations, subject to approval as above, to men of good standing, without loss of pay, in accordance with the foregoing. . . .

Thus the vacation without loss of pay be understood to be, what in fact is, a reward for good conduct, and does not come to be regarded as a vested right.[93]

[90] Cochran, *Railroad Leaders*, p. 87; Robert Harris to C. H. Chappell, November 11, 1872, Chicago, Burlington & Quincy Railroad Papers, Harris Out-Letters, CBQ-3H4.1.
[91] W. Spaulding to J. C. Jacobs, December 22, 1856, Illinois Central Railroad Papers, J. C. Jacobs In-Letters, IC-1J2.1, Newberry Library.
[92] E. E. Fayerweather to C. E. Perkins, February 28, 1880, Chicago, Burlington & Quincy Railroad Papers, Miscellaneous Papers, CBQ-G5.3.
[93] Memorandum of C. E. Perkins, January 30, 1886. Memoranda President's Office, 1878–1900, Chicago, Burlington & Quincy Railroad Papers, CBQ-3P4.92.

In spite of everything that has just been said, it should be emphasized that America's pioneer railroad companies were hardly paternalistic or philanthropic in their dealings with employees. Benefits were largely nominal and loosely and narrowly distributed. Unlike European concerns, America's early railroad companies did not build churches, schools, or social halls, or establish savings institutions or burial societies. Most significantly, by 1880, American rail companies lagged far behind their European counterparts in providing medical insurance and pension benefits—a subject to be further examined in the next chapter.[94]

FOR MANY railwaymen, "working on the railroad" represented more than a job. It was a life's commitment, a career. Promotions were an integral part of the work, as men could look forward to advancing from low-skilled, low-paying posts to more responsible, secure, highly compensated positions. Promotions, though, not only meant increased income and a chance to have a greater voice in assignments—some men could even hope to assume managerial roles—it also presaged greater status and prestige. Harry French recalled that, when he was first promoted from baggageman to passenger conductor, the social standing of his family changed overnight. He and his wife now received invitations to parties and other social gatherings and became respected members of their community.[95]

Before the 1860s, there is little evidence that railroad companies followed a fixed policy of filling vacancies from within the ranks. There is an indication in Benjamin Latrobe and Jonathan Knight's 1838 study of the management of the nation's lines that the Boston & Lowell Railroad did not even practice what was to become the standard procedure of elevating firemen to engineers. Latrobe and Knight reported:

[94] For the welfare programs of European railroad companies, see Kingsford, *Victorian Railwaymen*, chaps. 7, 9 and 10; F. Jacqmin, *Railroad Employes in France*, pp. 16–35. One fringe benefit of the work that has not been discussed here, but was mentioned in an earlier chapter, concerns access to information on employment opportunities. Compared with other workers, railwaymen were at a decided advantage in learning of job possibilities.

[95] French, *Railroadman*, p. 61.

A common hand is here preferred for a fireman, because as is alleged, he aspires less to become an engineer, and is, consequently, more contented with his pay and situation than if he were a mechanic, possessing knowledge of his engine, such as to fit him to take charge of it.[96]

This policy, though, may have been motivated by ethnic considerations. In relating the same practice, Louis Loring, a nineteenth-century railroad buff, recalled:

In the early days on the Boston and Lowell only Irishmen were employed as firemen, for the characteristic reason that when they once learned to fire, they were satisfied to work in that capacity as long as they lived, while a Yankee would no sooner learn to fire then he would know all about running an engine and want to be promoted to the position of engineer.[97]

By the late 1860s, promotion from the ranks became an announced, settled practice within the industry.[98] Railroad managers and trade journal editorialists expressed themselves in favor of various promotion schemes, citing the following general justifications for their introduction. Filling vacancies from among those already in service first solved immediate labor supply and recruitment problems. The practice also operated as an effective apprenticeship system. Workers were educated and received education on the job as they served under men they eventually would replace. The railroads did not have to invest in training facilities or rely on outside institutions. Finally, and most important, promotions became a basic part of the reward structure of railway work and were an incentive for diligent and loyal behavior.[99] "This Company," announced John Henry Devereux, general manager of the Lake Shore & Michigan Southern in 1871, "as a rule rewards faithful service by promoting its employees in each distinct Department and selects its best men to

---

[96] Jonathan Knight and Benjamin Latrobe, *Report Upon the Locomotive Engines and the Police and Management*, p. 18.

[97] Loring, "Early Railroads in Boston," p. 306.

[98] Cochran, *Railroad Leaders*, pp. 89–90.

[99] *American Railroad Review*, March 14, 1861, p. 152; *Railroad Gazette*, October 9, 1875, p. 413; Richardson, *Locomotive Engineer*, p. 154; Paul Black, "Robert Harris," p. 8.

fill places of responsibility and trust."[100] Perkins of the Chicago, Burlington & Quincy similarly implored officials of the line to grant frequent promotions. "In that way, and in that way only can you get the zeal and esprit so essential to economy and efficiency."[101]

The career patterns of mid-nineteenth-century American railwaymen can be illustrated by drawing on information contained in the Illinois Central Railroad's biographical compendium of "representative" employees published in 1900.[102] The career lines of the 155 workers who were born before 1850 have been mapped.[103] Although these men cannot truly be considered representative—as will be shown, not all railwaymen experienced upward occupational mobility—their careers followed patterns that are typical for those workers who were promoted.

Illinois Central locomotivemen had their own career ladders. Close to one-third began railroading in their late teens as shop or enginehouse hands and became firemen in their early twenties; approximately half entered the trade directly as firemen in their early twenties, while the rest commenced railroad work as skilled mechanics, brakemen, or construction and station laborers.

A four or five-year apprenticeship as fireman preceded advancement to ranks of driver. Young engineers then normally remained in freight work for ten years before elevation to passenger service, the most prestigious and highest paying of nonmanagerial, blue-collar railway positions. Promotion to scheduled passenger runs also represented a well-earned relief from the irregular, long-haul, frequent night duties of freight work.

Not every Illinois Central driver climbed in step. T. J. Pimm, for instance, began his career as a roundhouse laborer at twelve, advanced to fireman a year later, and first assumed control of a freight engine at eighteen. William Smith became a passenger locomotiveman at twenty-one, after only a year of freight service and three years of firing. Edward Stearns, on the other hand,

---

[100] Quoted in Cochran, *Railroad Leaders*, p. 313.

[101] Ibid., p. 431.

[102] Illinois Central Railroad, *History of the Illinois Central Railroad*.

[103] Graphic representations of the careers of the 155 "representative" Illinois Central employees born before 1850 can be found in appendix E with a methodological note.

entered the trade as a fireman at the age of thirty-nine and became a passenger engineer at fifty-one. Charles Chevalier similarly was not promoted to passenger service until the age of sixty. The "normal" career, however, followed this pattern: laborer at eighteen, fireman at twenty-one, freight driver by twenty-six and passenger locomotiveman by thirty-five.

The career lines of Illinois Central pioneer conductors form a separate but almost identical configuration. Instead of entering as firemen, close to 50 percent of the conductors began railroad work in their early twenties as brakemen. The other half commenced as station hands, firemen, and shop and enginehouse laborers—also in their early adult years. An apprenticeship in braking of four to five years was then a normal prerequisite for advancement to freight conductorships. After ten years of work in freight service, the last step involved elevation to the status of passenger conductor.

Again, there were exceptions to the general pattern. James Colquhous became a brakeman at twenty, a freight conductor at twenty-one, and a passenger conductor at twenty-two. Silas Mabey entered the trade as a station laborer at eighteen, two years later moved up to brakeman, and was appointed freight conductor at twenty-four. Mabey, however, never advanced to passenger service. In contrast, John Smith first began his railway career at thirty-seven as a fireman, became a freight conductor at forty-two, and waited until the age of fifty-eight to be promoted to passenger runs. The normal pattern, however, was laborer at twenty, brakeman at twenty-two, freight conductor at twenty-six, and passenger conductor at thirty-six.

The career histories of Illinois Central local level officials are as varied as their titles. While the patterns for shop and engine or roundhouse foremen are fairly straightforward, those for station agents, yardmasters and trainmasters defy easy assessment. For shop foremen, the most frequent course followed was entrance to the trade at eighteen as a shop hand, from four to six years' service as an apprentice, advancement then to the level of skilled mechanic, and, after fourteen or fifteen years of devoted duty, appointment at the age of forty to managerial jobs. Enginehouse supervisors similarly assumed their positions in their early forties and were generally recruited from the ranks of passenger train engineers.

A few case histories will illustrate the difficulties in delineating career patterns among local Illinois Central station agents. Charles St. John, for instance, entered the trade at the tender age of nine as a station hand. At twelve he became a telegraph operator, and just three years later received an appointment as depot master. In contrast, both John C. and John H. Wilson became station agents at the age of fifty-three, after more than thirty years of service in various lesser posts. A final unusual case was James Rasbach, who began railroading as a brakeman at the age of thirty-six and just one year later accepted a depot agency.

While the patterns varied, the most frequent route to a station agency was through apprenticeship as a station clerk. If a typical agency career had to be defined, it would be the following: entrance to the trade as a laborer in the late teens, advancement to a clerical post in the early twenties or direct assumption of a clerkship at that same age; subsequent promotion to assistant depot head after ten years of service and/or direct appointment to a station agency in the mid-to-late thirties. The average age at which Illinois Central depot masters assumed their posts was 35.7 years, though the range in ages was from fifteen to sixty-one—just one indication of the amount of variation in these career lines.

Equally inconsistent were the occupational patterns of local I.C. yard foremen and trainmasters. One yard supervisor, James Williams, for example, assumed his post at the age of thirty-seven without any prior railroading experience (he formerly had been superintendent of a southern plantation), while Patrick Boyle rose to yardmaster at the early age of twenty-two after only two years of service as a construction worker and brakeman. Illinois Central local trainmasters similarly came from the varied ranks of freight and passenger conductors and yard, shop and enginehouse foremen, and assumed their positions at disparate ages.

The careers of I.C. division officials—the line's middle level management—were also uniform in some cases and dissimilar in others. A majority of the company's early division roadmasters began their careers as construction or track laborers. In their early thirties they rose to local supervisory posts, most frequently as track foremen, and then to division roadmasterships in their mid-forties. The division master mechanics similarly had consistent careers: most began as shop hands or firemen, later became freight and passenger engineers, were promoted to local shop or enginehouse foremanships, and then elevated to division heads in charge of the regional operation and maintenance of the rolling stock. While one master mechanic obtained his appointment at the young age of twenty-eight, the others characteristically reached their career destinations in their middle to late forties. For the general division agents, however, no overall pattern existed. Most normally served early apprenticeships as station clerks, but their careers from that point followed widely divergent paths.

The careers of the I.C.'s earliest division superintendents are probably the most interesting of all. Under the Illinois Central's departmentalized, divisional structure, division superintendents wielded great power and authority. Lords of their personal realms, they in effect were general managers of small-to-medium-size railroads. The careers of these men are impressive. All but one began railroading in their mid-to-late teens as construction and station laborers, clerks, and brakemen. The exception entered the trade in a supervisory capacity as a station agent (and at the unusually young age of eighteen). Their careers then proceeded apace. By their mid-twenties, they occupied positions as passenger conductors or local foremen. Promotion to divisional posts came in their early thirties; and between the ages of thirty-seven and forty-three, they received appointments to division superintendencies. These men climbed up the organizational ladder, or more accurately, the organizational escalator, with all due dispatch.

Finally, information is available on the careers of four early I.C. central office department heads. Like the road's division superintendents, these men started railroading in their early adult years at low level posts, rose quickly through the ranks to achieve divisional offices in their early forties, and then moved up to central headquarters at an average age of fifty.

From the reconstruction of the careers of early Illinois Central Railroad employees, two points stand out. First, the occupational

Table 4.3. *Average Ages of Illinois Central Employees upon Reaching Their Career Destinations*

Final position	N	Average age reaching final position	Standard deviation	Age range
Passenger locomotivemen	51	34.9	7.7	19–61
Passenger conductors	25	36.1	7.8	22–58
Local officials	40	38.1	11.1	15–64
Division officials	26	43.2	7.6	27–59
Central headquarters officials	4	49.3	6.2	41–58

hierarchy of railroad work was also an age hierarchy. The higher the level of authority, the older the average age at which men attained their final positions (see table 4.3). Workers who rose to the very top echelons, though, generally had foreshortened, encapsulated careers. Passenger conductors and locomotivemen, for instance, reached their professional destinations at the age of thirty-five or thirty-six. For many officials, such train service represented a stepping stone to the managerial ranks. These employees characteristically climbed quickly up the ladder, often occupying passenger conductorships or drivers' positions by their mid-twenties.

Secondly, the careers of mid-nineteenth-century American railwaymen varied extensively. Patterns are discernable but exceptions abound. This point raises the issue of procedures and the very handling of promotions. Variations are prominent, because an absence of system characterized the entire process.

In the early period, boards of directors handled promotions in a formal manner. Superintendents nominated men for advancement; the directors then checked the candidates' credentials and finally voted their approval. The corporate minutes of the Boston & Worcester Railroad accordingly reveal that on July 10, 1843, board members, after considerable discussion, unanimously agreed to promote Joseph Moore, a conductor, to a station agency.[104] An interesting exception to this procedure in-

[104] Minutes of directors' meetings, vol. 5, p. 38, Boston & Worcester Railroad Papers.

volved pioneer engine drivers. Before the 1850s, railroad companies apparently granted locomotivemen the privilege of personally appointing their own successors.[105] The origins of this custom and its eventual demise remain obscure.

With growth in size and complexity of operations, and the bureaucratic decentralization of authority, the power to award promotions passed to local supervisors. Occasionally, dynamic chief officers, like James Clarke of the Illinois Central, took a direct hand in conferring advancements, yet such usurpations of power became less frequent.[106] More important, by default local foremen assumed complete control in this area of decision making. Pioneer railroad executives generally set no specific standards or requirements for promotions, nor did they establish formal testing procedures or fixed length-of-service schedules. When guidelines were issued, they usually consisted of vague directives stipulating the personal qualities expected in men slated for advancement.[107]

The Chicago, Burlington & Quincy Railroad provides a lone instance of top officials establishing a few definitive criteria. In 1870, for example, Robert Harris, citing reasons of safety, formally prohibited the elevation of illiterate firemen to locomotiveman status. Local supervisors apparently followed Harris's order scrupulously, for a survey taken in 1885 revealed that the line then employed a good number of men who had been firing for over twenty years without receiving promotions because of their inability to read.[108] During his tenure as president of the C.B. & Q., Perkins similarly instructed local officials to favor married men for promotion over the allegedly less responsible, more transient single workers.[109]

The question of who received promotions, the criteria that

---

[105] Richardson, *Locomotive Engineer*, p. 114.

[106] Lightner, "Labor on the Illinois Central," p. 116.

[107] See, for instance, the guidelines issued by Herman Haupt, Superintendent of the Pennsylvania Railroad. Herman Haupt to General A. I. Rumfort, June 23, 1852, Herman Haupt Letterbook.

[108] Paul Black, "Development of Management Personnel Policies," pp. 232–233.

[109] Richard Overton, *Burlington Route: A History of the Burlington Lines*, p. 181.

applied, and the timing of advancements thus rested in the hands of local officials. Harvey Reed recalled the following circumstances surrounding his advance from fireman to locomotive driver. His supervisor called him into his office without warning and asked him a few questions about the running of an engine. This served as his test for promotion.[110] Another pioneer driver remembered that in the 1850s and '60s, "when a Master Mechanic was to promote a fireman, he would call him into his office and question him regarding breakdowns on the road. Then he would send him alone to a pair of main driving wheels and they [sic] had to set all the eccentrics right, before he would promote them [sic]."[111]

It was only in the 1880s that companies first began to introduce formal testing procedures. The Illinois Central adopted a written test of thirty technical questions for firemen in 1881.[112] Henry Brockholst Ledyard, president of the Michigan Central, following the lead of civil service reformers, similarly instituted in 1887 a system of competitive exams for passenger conductorships that were offered every sixty days.[113] With the advent of union contracts and seniority clauses, the process was further routinized on a widescale basis and made less arbitrary.[114]

In the absence of formal standards and procedures, it is not

---

[110] Reed, *Forty Years a Locomotive Engineer*, p. 31.

[111] B. C. Vaughan, "Early Recollections," *Railway and Locomotive Historical Society Bulletin*, no. 7, p. 71.

[112] Lightner, "Labor on the Illinois Central," p. 241.

[113] Cochran, *Railroad Leaders*, pp. 91, 405.

[114] Certain complications in the promotion process have not been mentioned. Railwaymen did not always seek to rise to new positions. Transfers to better working situations or runs were often desired substitutes to changes in job category. Moreover, railway workers collectively fought one kind of promotion system. In the 1870s many railroad companies, in order to encourage loyalty, adopted classification systems within grades of work. Locomotivemen would thus be labeled first, second, and third grade engineer and be paid accordingly while basically performing the same work. The creation of artificial status distinctions between workers was strongly opposed, especially since the awarding of grades remained in the hands of local foremen. Seniority principles would be championed as the only equitable system for granting promotions and wage increases. See Cochran, *Railroad Leaders*, p. 379; Richardson, *Locomotive Engineer*, pp. 146, 213; Letter of Grievance Committee to Robert Harris, 1876, Chicago, Burlington & Quincy Railroad Papers, Miscellaneous, CBQ 33 1889 8.1.

surprising that nonmeritorious factors frequently played an important role in promotion decisions during the pioneer days of railway travel. Family, personal, and political connections helped. A federal commission investigating the railroad industry during the First World War noted in its report that nepotism was rampant in the early years of development. A "master mechanic might have a favorite nephew who, after firing an engine for six months, might be given the best passenger run on the road."[115] Letters in corporate archives similarly reveal that prominent stockholders and politicians intervened to secure promotions for relatives and friends.[116]

Railroad companies also granted advancement for certain acts of loyalty. During the initial period of the 1877 strike, the management of the Baltimore & Ohio Railroad announced that all faithful employees would be rewarded by having their names placed first on the list for promotion.[117] Herbert Hamblen similarly recalled an incident where a telegraph operator and a conductor had received promotions for offering what turned out to be false testimony favoring their company in a liability suit.[118] Finally, if need be, new positions could be bought and sold. Railwaymen frequently offered their supervisors gifts at holidays and special occasions in hopes of special dispensation.[119] Eugene Mahoney, a pioneer engineer on the Jersey Central, recalled that promotion on that line depended on two to fifteen years of service and "the price was gold watch chains, rocking chairs, bottles of wine, poultry, quails and cigars." "The Master at Jersey City had so many cigars on hand at one time," Mahoney added, "that he placed them on sale in a cigar store on Communipaw Avenue."[120] As Robert Harris sadly concluded in a letter discussing the process of promotion, "Personal preference, from one cause or another, more generally determines the selection."[121]

[115] U. S. Eight Hour Commission, *Report of the Eight Hour Commission* (Washington, D. C., 1918), p. 307.
[116] Cochran, *Railroad Leaders*, p. 407.
[117] Holbrook, *Story of American Railroads*, p. 247.
[118] Herbert Hamblen, *The General Manager's Story*, p. 61.
[119] Richardson, *Locomotive Engineer*, p. 153.
[120] Stevenson, "Brotherhood of Locomotive Engineers," p. 7.
[121] Clive Stott, "Robert Harris and the Strike of 1877" (M.A. thesis, Univ. of Western Ontario, 1967), p. 185.

IT IS IMPOSSIBLE to devise tests that would precisely identify those factors which permitted some men to rise through the ranks and those which acted to limit the chances of others. Assembling a representative and meaningful sample of both "climbers" and "dawdlers" itself would present enormous difficulties; finding relevant biographical information about both groups would further render the whole task unfeasible. Material contained in the career sketches of Illinois Central railwaymen does afford a limited means of approaching the problem. While the information does not permit a strict comparison of the promoted and unpromoted, it can be used to compare those who rose quickly through the ranks with those whose careers progressed at a less accelerated pace.

When the Illinois Central employees are divided between "fast" and "slow" climbers, father's occupation and marital status emerge as important factors in the speed of promotion.[122] Fast risers tended to be sons of businessmen, professionals, and skilled workers. Conversely, sons of farmers, unskilled laborers, and, most surprisingly, sons of railwaymen, advanced less quickly. Married men also tended to advance faster than single workers. Other influences—a railwayman's place of origin, his religious or ethnic background, his educational achievements, having had relatives in the trade, the number of companies he worked for, his political affiliation, and the size of his family—proved less predictive of how quickly he rose in the occupational hierarchy of the company. Two exceptions deserve mention. Years of schooling did not prove to be an important factor in the advancement process for Illinois Central employees as a whole; yet I.C. conductors who completed high school were much more likely to rise quickly than those who had not progressed beyond grade school. Foreign-born local supervisors, surprisingly, also tended to advance sooner to their career destinations than their native-born counterparts.

An answer to the question of who succeeded in railway work— who advanced quickly to top positions—then, is not straightforward. Social background had a definite influence, although

---

[122] Table F.1 in appendix F lists correlation coefficients between the speed of promotion of Illinois Central employees and various socioeconomic and career factors. A methodological note is also included.

having a father or other relative in the trade was not necessarily an asset for Illinois Central railwaymen (at least in rising quickly). What exactly placed men from better backgrounds at an advantage is unclear (especially since formal education was not a requisite for fast advancement). Married men also did well, but whether they climbed quickly because they were favored or were just pushing harder to maintain their families is a question without a readily available answer. Literary evidence suggests that married railwaymen did receive special dispensation from management; the fact that number of offspring was not associated with pace of promotion also points to the role of managerial decisions in the fortunes of married workers. In general, a fairly open occupational structure existed on the Illinois Central Railroad in the mid-nineteenth century. A man's class background and marital status affected his chances for promotion, but with no other sociodemographic factors playing a role, luck, circumstance, and of course, merit, must have figured formidably in career experiences as well.

A last question to be asked concerns numbers. How many men, or what percentage of the work force, received promotions? How common was the experience? Railroad folklore is replete with rags-to-riches success tales. James Clarke, for example, general manager of the Illinois Central Railroad, started his career as a track walker on the Baltimore & Ohio.[123] Tom Scott, influential president of the Pennsylvania Railroad, similarly entered railroading as a station clerk.[124] Do such stories, and even the careers of the so-called "representative" Illinois Central employees, obscure the reality of most railwaymen being frozen into low-level positions, and that few experienced upward mobility?

The issue is not simple. On one hand, the occupational structure formed a pyramid with limited room at the top; not everyone could possibly rise. On the other hand, supervisors filled vacancies from within the ranks, which meant that many railwaymen did advance. A significant portion of the work force was also

[123] Cochran, *Railroad Leaders*, p. 46.
[124] Bowman, *Pioneer Railroads*, p. 110.

Table 4.4. Career Dispositions of 1,987 Railwaymen over a Two-Year Period

Company	Years	Stayed in same position		Moved up		Moved down		Moved out	
		N	%	N	%	N	%	N	%
Hartford & New Haven RR	1851–52	138	44	19	6	0	0	154	50
Hartford & New Haven RR	1868–70	381	44	42	5	0	0	441	51
Cleveland & Toledo RR	1864–66	291	36	69	8	3	1	449	55

comprised of temporary hands; for these employees, railroad work had the advantage of either providing extra income or provisional employment in bad times. Are these men to be included in the equation? Finally, even if the above or similar kinds of conceptual problems could be ironed out, the data for the nineteenth century are so scarce that a definitive answer is impossible.

The problem can be attacked partially, however, by following men through surviving payroll records and noting changes in their occupational titles. Three nineteenth-century account books from the Hartford & New Haven and the Cleveland & Toledo Railroads have been employed for this purpose.[125] Each payroll covers a period of twenty-four months. The fortunes of close to two thousand workers have been traced accordingly and the findings are reported in an encapsulated form in table 4.4.

This table reveals that after two years, between 5 and 8 percent of the original cohort of workers still employed by their respective companies had moved up in the occupational hierarchy. Roughly another 40 percent still listed on the payrolls had not changed their positions. The largest group, however, more than half, had disappeared from the companies' books. Brakemen, baggagemen, and firemen made the greatest advances. Approximately 20 percent of them moved up during the two-year period,

[125] Hartford & New Haven Railroad, Payroll Records, 1850–1853, 1868–1870, New York, New Haven & Hartford Railroad Papers, vols. 90 and 91, Baker Library; Cleveland & Toledo Railroad, Payroll Records, 1864–1867, New York Central Railroad Papers, Syracuse University Library.

a figure far greater than their percentage of the total. White-collar workers, especially clerks, also fared well, with between 9 and 12 percent of them moving up to higher status positions. Not surprisingly, conductors, enginemen, and skilled shop mechanics, in particular, achieved the smallest gains. With a limited number of supervisory posts to be occupied, they enjoyed the fewest opportunities for promotion.

At first glance, the fact that 7 percent of the work force moved upward occupationally is not impressive. What has to be carefully considered, though, is the dispositions of those employees who disappeared from the companies' rolls. Many of these men undoubtedly occupied temporary posts; the great majority of them were unskilled laborers. On the basis of published reminiscences and the career sketches of Illinois Central employees, it is also safe to assume that a good number of those who left went to accept higher status positions on other lines. If only one in five of the men who disappeared in this way moved both "out" and "up," the total figure for employees granted promotions during a given twenty-four-month period rises to between 15 and 18 percent. These figures suggest that approximately one in every six railwaymen advanced through the ranks every two years. These men served as highly visible and important examples. They were symbols of the basic beneficence of the system—objective proof that diligence and loyalty had their rewards.

A DECENT day's pay, various opportunities to increase earnings, a number of fringe benefits, and genuine prospects for a more rewarding future—railroading had much to offer. But the lure of the road extended far beyond these extrinsic advantages. Every farm boy dreamed of becoming a railwayman because the work itself provided its own justification.

Railroadmen took pride in their work. Charles Dickens, traveling in America, found the country's pioneer train conductors to be proud men of class and bearing.[126] They engaged in polite and literate conversation. They wore top hats and lilac kid gloves

---

[126] Botkin and Harlow, *Treasury of Railroad Folklore*, p. 159.

and carried silverplated lanterns and gold timepieces. The "swankiest" were even known to sport solid gold ticket punches.[127] In the early days, conductors also printed their own tickets. John Bradley, employed by the Hartford & New Haven Railroad around the time of the Civil War, added a personal touch. For the entertainment of his passengers, he devised riddles and had them stamped on his checks.[128] In the early days, too, conductors were so much the captains of their charges that many companies, instead of designating trains by numbers, named specific trips after their conductors. One of the first printed schedules thus reads, "Jones to meet Brown at Jericho."[129]

For the nation's pioneer locomotive engineers, too, workmanship and the dignity of labor were not idle concepts. They were deeply felt, practiced ideals. An early railroad traveler vividly recounted this impression: "We could not but note the Engineer's bearing as he mounted his steed. He patted the glittering brazen knobs, here and there, as a man might a favorite animal."[130] Pioneer drivers guarded their machines as prized and personal possessions. With the assistance of their firemen, they devoted great care and effort to keeping the engines finely tuned, well-oiled, and brightly polished. On layovers or days off, it was not uncommon for drivers to spend their leisure time at the roundhouse scrubbing headlights, shining whistles and bells, and buffing the brasswork.[131] Enginemen also often presided over the selection of color schemes and designs for their machines.[132] An early locomotive on the Pennsylvania Railroad was so proudly fashioned and bedecked:

Although the stack, firebox, and part of the steam dome are painted black, the rest of the engine exhausts the rainbow. Wheels and pilots are not only red but vermilion red. The boiler is eggshell blue. The tender is a delicate rose, with the railroad's title done in a flowing ribbon and surrounded by curlicues in gold. The outside of the cab is gorgeous

[127] Ibid., p. 160.
[128] Ibid., p. 161.
[129] Richardson, *Locomotive Engineer*, p. 97.
[130] Quoted in ibid., p. 104.
[131] Ibid., p. 105; John Stover, *The Life and Decline of the American Railroad*, p. 20.
[132] Richard Reinhardt, ed., *Workin' on the Railroad*, p. 122.

with scroll work in gold and underneath the window a painting showing a Bengal tiger obviously stalking some unseen prey in a jungle as green as emerald. The name plate, set well forward on the boiler, is in great Barnum-type letters, TIGER; another jungle painting appears on the side of the headlight, and to top everything off an American flag flows from a special bronze socket atop the pilot.[133]

Pioneer locomotivemen fought stubbornly to maintain the dignity of their service. They opposed measures which usurped their power, even to the extent of resisting innovations like telegraphic orders.[134] They found it a particular injustice when many roads, following Cornelius Vanderbilt's lead, ordered all decorative work to be removed from engines and all machines to be painted black. The commodore, chief stockholder and manager of the New York Central, thought American locomotives too gaudy. He objected especially to the bright paint, brass ornamentation, scrollwork, and idyllic portraits. An industrious nation, he held, could ill afford to be frivolous or nihilistic. In line with his sober, corporatist ideology, he prescribed standard funereal black for all Central engines.[135] Locomotivemen duly countered such initiatives by organizing to raise subscriptions to buy their own adornments, especially banners and buntings for holidays and other special occasions.[136]

Finally, pioneer locomotivemen also resisted, though with little success, attempts by the major carriers in the mid-1870s to introduce continuous engine running. From the earliest days, machines were traditionally assigned to specific drivers and were in operation only when the enginemen were on duty. The drivers assumed responsibility for their operation and upkeep. Under the new plan, engines were to be in constant use, being handled by different train crews at each juncture. This change in procedures emerged as a major grievance of locomotivemen, for it effectively destroyed the close tie established between man and machine. On some lines, like the Illinois Central, enginemen

---

[133] Holbrook, *Story of American Railroads*, p. 33.
[134] Stover, *Life and Decline*, p. 26.
[135] Richardson, *Locomotive Engineer*, pp. 174, 255; Holbrook, *Story of American Railroads*, p. 90.
[136] *Railroad Gazette*, July 30, 1870, p. 410.

succeeded in convincing management that continous running was less efficient and more costly. Extra men had to be hired to make repairs normally handled by the drivers; disinterested locomotivemen also tended to overwork the machines. If the enginemen had no vested or inherent interest in the maintenance of the engines, the drivers warned, rapid deterioration of the rolling stock was inevitable.[137]

Conductors and locomotivemen thus derived great personal satisfaction from their work. The historical record is wanting for other grades of railwaymen, but one can assume that intrinsic rewards figured prominently in the experiences of most rail workers. Railroad work, after all, was new, intriguing, and uncommon labor. As Charles George recalled the 1840s: "In those days passengers made a great deal of railwaymen."[138] Railroading also held out the lure of adventure, travel, and escape. The work experience, finally, was one shared by men of similar strength and daring. The case for a life on the line was perhaps best put by an anonymous pioneer trainman. His words, slightly overdramatic to be sure, echo sentiments that all mid-nineteenth-century railwaymen could easily have affirmed: "I've heard of the call of the wild, the call of the law, the call of the Church. There is also the call of the railroads."[139]

[137] Lightner, "Labor on the Illinois Central," pp. 171–176.
[138] George, *Forty Years on the Rail*, p. 149.
[139] Quoted in Richardson, *Locomotive Engineer*, p. 102.

5

THE PERILS OF LABOR

≡

EXPERIENCE generally squared with expectations. Railroading beckoned and provided. Men answered the call of the road and found that the work offered genuine material and personal rewards. Yet, there is another side to the story, one much less sanguine. Mid-nineteenth-century American railwaymen labored under constant adversity. Certain negative aspects of the work—payless paydays, capricious supervision—have already been mentioned. Here attention will focus on even harsher realities. Railroad employment was erratic and without guarantees, the hours of service long, and most crucially, railway workers toiled under the ever-present and pressing threat of accidents and the high probability of injury and death. Along with the satisfactions of labor came great uncertainties and risk.

IN 1870 AND 1872, Marcellus Bliss, a locomotive engineer on the Wisconsin Central, kept a complete record of his daily activities in two personal diaries.[1] Among other items, he listed his exact work assignments—whether he was on the road, in the shop, on layovers or off. The patterns of employment that emerge from Bliss's records are interesting. Bliss occupied a permanent position on the line; during the two years in question he worked roughly the same aggregate number of days. Yet, the number of days he worked each month fluctuated dramatically over the course of each year. The pattern of his employment for 1870

---

[1] Diaries of M. N. Bliss, 1870, 1872, Bliss Family Diary Collection, Historical Society of Wisconsin.

also varied considerably from that of 1872. These findings are illustrated in the accompanying figure.

Marcellus Bliss's record of attendance on the job points to a basic reality of railroad work in the nineteenth century: that even for those steadily employed, employment was irregular and uncertain. From one month to the next, workers rarely knew how many days they would be called. For the average railwayman—especially the per diem wage earner—the ramifications were enormous. Aggregate yearly earnings, for instance, might have remained the same, but the income available each month often fluctuated substantially. A watchful eye on personal and family expenses had to be maintained as a result, and careful budgeting was required. If need be, provisional employment in other trades might be sought during slack times. Since there is no indication in Marcellus Bliss's diaries that he ever considered or held any secondary jobs, one can assume that, in addition to being highly paid, he was a salaried employee as well.

Seasonal demands and weather conditions played a key role in fluctuations of employment. Men generally worked a full complement of days each month when the roads were busiest and freight and passenger traffic at their peaks. Employment in all branches of the trade thus tended to rise sharply in the autumn, when the hauling of agricultural products reached its crest, and to decline in the winter. A slight rise would occur in the spring, when intensive efforts were needed to repair winter-torn roadbeds, while a leveling-off would follow in the summer months.[2] Inclement weather also contributed to irregular employment. A series of snowstorms in January 1872 kept Marcellus Bliss off the job for twenty-eight days. Bliss also worked but ten days in March 1870 because of an unspecified illness—a finding that highlights the obvious but easily ignored reality that sickness, injury, attendance to personal affairs, and even strikes and wars, figured in fluctuating work patterns. Unanticipated events and happenings likewise could upset normal employment routines. In August 1867, a contingent of machine shop employees on the Baltimore

---

[2] David Lightner, "Labor on the Illinois Central Railroad, 1852-1900" (Ph.D. dissertation, Cornell Univ., 1969), p. 225. See also table 5.2 in this chapter.

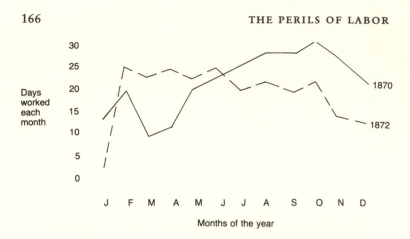

Days worked each month

Months of the year

Marcellus Bliss's record of attendance on the job, 1870 and 1872.

& Ohio Railroad were temporarily dismissed when a fire completely destroyed their plant.[3]

Additional factors were involved in the problem of job uncertainty. Railwaymen, as has been shown, labored under the constant threat of disciplinary discharges. Local foremen dispensed justice in a subjective manner that warranted genuine concern and fear. Security of employment was also subject to the vicissitudes of the economy. During periods of recession or currency shortages—or when particular firms were beset by financial difficulties—it was standard procedure for railway executives to order immediate staff and wage reductions.[4] Even in normal times, efforts at cost cutting jeopardized jobs. The practice of doubleheading, for instance, which involved the hitching of two locomotives together to pull twice as many cars as a single engine, was introduced to halve the number of employed con-

[3] J. L. Davis to J. W. Garrett, August 30, 1867, Baltimore & Ohio Railroad Papers, file 1573, Maryland Historical Society.

[4] Lightner, "Labor on the Illinois Central," pp. 81, 151, 158; *Twenty-Third Annual Report of the President and Directors to the Stockholders of the Baltimore and Ohio Rail Road Company* (Baltimore, 1848), p. 7; Minutes of Board of Managers, November 23, 1853, Delaware, Lackawanna & Western Railroad Papers, Syracuse University Library; George Phelps to D. H. Dotterer, December 2, 1854, Letterbooks of George D. Phelps, 1854–56, ibid.; *Ninth Annual Report of the Directors of the Western Rail-Road Corporation* (Boston, 1844), p. 14; Thomas Cochran, *Railroad Leaders*, p. 163.

ductors and brakemen.[5] It should be noted, though, that there were limits to the number of men that could be cut before services were severely curtailed. High fixed costs and debts prevented railway managers from either instituting substantial short-term reductions during normal periods or from closing down operations during business slumps. A railroad, in this respect, was not a textile mill. A modicum of service had to be maintained, which meant that a core work force had to be steadily employed. Company archives are thus replete with letters from harried local foremen explaining their reasons for not carrying out ordered staff reductions.[6] For some favored men, railway work then did have the advantage of offering fairly constant employment even in bad times. Other railroad workers, though, were not as fortunate in escaping the iron hand of the market economy.

Organizational changes also affected employment prospects and security. To avoid unnecessary duplications, railway managers often eliminated certain positions following mergers and consolidations. Men were either dropped outright or forced to accept inferior positions.[7] Internal reorganizations similarly threatened jobs. In 1867 Cornelius Vanderbilt of the New York Central announced a restructuring of divisional boundaries, which obliged most Central employees to choose between moving their homes, living apart from their families, or being dismissed.[8] Finally, the very fact that nineteenth-century railway companies had changing, ill-defined manpower needs made job insecurity to a certain extent an inevitability. Men frequently reported to work only to find that their services were not needed. Vivid evidence of this is provided in the letters of John Newell, chief engineer on the Illinois Central in the 1860s. Newell's correspondence with local foremen reveals that track crews, for in-

[5] Reed Richardson, *The Locomotive Engineer*, p. 163.

[6] Lightner, "Labor on the Illinois Central," p. 84; *Report of the Executive Officers of the Baltimore & Ohio Rail Road Company, on the Subject of Retrenchment* (Baltimore, 1842), p. 8; *Eighth Annual Report of the President and Directors to the Stockholders of the Baltimore and Ohio Rail Road Company* (Baltimore, 1834), p. 36.

[7] Cochran, *Railroad Leaders*, pp. 311, 315.

[8] James Stevenson, "The Brotherhood of Locomotive Engineers and Its Leaders" (Ph.D. dissertation, Vanderbilt Univ., 1954), p. 132.

Table 5.1. Number and Percentage of Railway Employees Working Stated Number of Days in 1889

Days worked	Number of employees	% of employees
0– 25	56,404	25.1
26– 50	25,684	11.5
51–100	31,014	13.8
101–150	18,861	8.4
151–200	14,122	6.3
201–250	12,393	5.5
251–300	17,816	7.9
301–365	48,272	21.5

stance, were assembled, enlarged, reduced, and abolished with astonishing frequency.[9]

If the reasons for employment fluctuations and uncertainty are manifold and varied, they are at least fathomable. What is extremely difficult to assess, though, is the precise magnitude of the problem. How irregular was the work? What percentage of the work force was affected and to what degree? High levels of transiency, the fact that many men were hired purely as temporary hands, and a paucity of hard data complicate a thorough evaluation of the issue.

The United States Bureau of Labor did investigate the question of the steadiness of employment in the railroad industry in 1889, and its findings, though not applicable to the time frame under study here, are revealing. The Bureau examined the payroll accounts of sixty of the largest companies then operating in the country. The number of days worked between April 1, 1888 and March 30, 1889 were calculated for close to 225,000 employees. The results of this inquiry are summarized in table 5.1.[10]

The Bureau discovered that 58.8 percent of the total number of employees working on the roads under study were employed less than six months. More than a quarter of the group, in fact, were actually on various company books for less than twenty-five days. If five and a half or six days a week of work is considered the norm for the nineteenth century, then the Bureau's

[9] Lightner, "Labor on the Illinois Central," p. 89.
[10] *Fifth Annual Report of the Commissioner of Labor, 1889: Railroad Labor* (Washington, D. C., 1890), p. 82.

figures indicate that only an approximate one quarter of the railwaymen surveyed were working a full complement of days in 1888 and 1889.

There are, of course, obvious problems with the Bureau's data. Men were not linked across payroll records. A railroad employee could have worked three one-hundred-day stints for three different firms. In that case he would have been counted three times in the 51–100 days worked category, when in actuality he had been employed for 300 days. Since job hopping between companies was a fairly common practice, the figures in table 5.1 are clearly weighted toward the lower end of the scale. The Bureau also made no attempt to filter out purely provisional positions; a vast number of individuals included in the 0–25 days worked category surely must have been temporary hands. Again, the figures are slanted in one direction. Yet, even with these qualifications, the Bureau's statistics are so unevenly distributed that it is safe to draw even the cautious conclusion that less than a majority of nineteenth-century railwaymen found constant employment in the trade. If one also assumes that employment conditions stabilized over the course of the century, as was suggested in chapter 2, then in the pre-1880 period with which this study is concerned the problems of job fluctuations and uncertainty were probably greater in magnitude than is suggested by the Bureau of Labor's study for 1889.

The Bureau's investigation also discovered that not all railwaymen were equally affected by the problem. Highly skilled workers tended to be employed a greater number of days per year than men on the lower rungs. While only 15 percent of the brakemen surveyed, for instance, worked three hundred days or more in 1888-89, over 40 percent of the enginemen were employed full time.[11] Data from the pre-1880 period confirm that a clear relationship existed between grade of employment and days worked. Table 5.2 contains information culled from the 1852 payroll account of the Hartford & New Haven Railroad. Average number of days worked each month has been calculated

[11] Ibid., p. 136.

Table 5.2. Average Number of Days Worked Each Month for Nine Grades of Railwaymen, Hartford & New Haven Railroad, 1852

Position	Jan.	Feb.	Mar.	Apr.	May	June	July	Aug.	Sept.	Oct.	Nov.	Dec.	Average number of days worked during year
Lower-level management	26.0	25.8	25.3	25.2	25.4	26.0	26.0	25.3	26.0	26.0	25.7	26.0	308.7
White-collar	26.0	26.0	21.8	23.3	21.9	23.7	22.3	25.3	26.0	24.9	26.0	26.0	293.2
Conductors	26.0	26.0	23.0	26.0	26.0	26.0	26.0	26.0	26.0	26.0	26.0	26.0	309.0
Baggagemen	26.0	25.8	23.8	26.0	23.4	26.0	24.0	24.0	24.4	26.0	23.1	24.2	296.7
Brakemen	20.0	18.6	23.5	20.9	21.4	23.6	18.5	18.8	25.4	20.8	23.3	17.8	252.5
Engineers	25.9	23.6	24.1	24.8	25.9	24.8	25.9	26.0	26.0	26.0	25.8	26.0	303.8
Firemen	24.0	19.4	22.1	24.3	26.0	23.1	26.0	24.3	23.2	25.8	22.6	20.4	281.2
Skilled shopmen	24.3	21.4	20.3	21.6	23.1	22.6	22.8	23.1	23.0	22.6	23.5	23.2	271.5
Unskilled labor	16.0	18.1	16.8	14.4	18.6	16.3	15.3	17.9	20.9	15.4	17.8	15.2	202.7
Average days worked per month for whole force	23.8	22.7	22.3	22.9	23.5	23.6	23.0	23.4	24.5	23.7	23.7	22.6	
			Low							High			

for nine grades of workers. Fluctuations in employment between grades and seasonal variations are clearly illustrated.[12]

Type of work was as important a factor as grade level in employment fluctuations. Men who worked indoors, for example, were less likely to be affected by changing weather conditions. A report issued by the Baltimore & Ohio Railroad in 1855 thus indicated that employees engaged in the machinery department worked on the average five more days per month than those workers employed in transportation.[13] The report was based on calculations for the month of February, a time of year when inclement weather normally curtailed train service. Since work in the shops was less affected, the men there remained more fully occupied. Finally, length of service also appears to have played a role in steadiness of employment. Analysis performed on data extracted from the 1852–54 and 1868–70 payroll records of the Hartford & New Haven Railroad revealed very strong, statistically significant correlations between the number of months men were on the company's books and the number of days they were engaged each month.[14] Long-term employees, in other words, tended to work fuller complements of days. Literary evidence suggests that veteran workers were either offered or guaranteed greater work time and the opportunity to have constant employment. Moreover, irregular and uncertain job conditions acted indirectly to encourage diligent and loyal behavior among railwaymen. The chance for continuous employment served as an informal work incentive. Since assignments were in the hands of local foremen, it proved both advantageous and wise to remain in the good favor of one's superior.[15] The arbitrary control of workloads by local supervisors became

[12] Hartford & New Haven Railroad, Payroll Record, 1851–53, New York, New Haven & Hartford Railroad Papers, vol. 90, Baker Library, Harvard University.

[13] *List of Officers & Employees in the Service of the Baltimore & Ohio Rail Road Company with their Occupation and Salary, February, 1855* (Baltimore, 1855), p. 97.

[14] When number of months employed was cross-tabulated with days worked per month, the Pearson correlation coefficients were 0.63 for the 1851–53 payroll account of the New Haven & Hartford Railroad and 0.54 for the 1868–70 record. Level of statistical significance was 0.001 in each case.

[15] Richardson, *Locomotive Engineer*, pp. 171–172.

a festering grievance which railwaymen would take up once they were organized to advance and protect their mutual interests.

While it is extremely difficult to measure the precise magnitude of the problem, irregular and uncertain employment conditions in the industry were serious enough to generate great concern among railway executives. In 1849, stockholders of the Baltimore & Ohio Railroad, for instance, were informed in an annual report that the company was facing obstacles in securing the services of reliable mechanics. Work in the shops was erratic and unsteady, and permanent employment could not be offered. Good men were reluctant to take jobs. B. & O. officials planned to solve the problem by converting the shops, which were purely repair facilities, into car and engine building plants. When men were not fully engaged in the upkeep of old equipment, their time would now be occupied in the construction of new rolling stock.[16] The directors of the Western Railroad in Massachusetts similarly announced plans in 1853 to start building locomotives in company-owned and operated facilities. This move, too, was justified as an effort to secure a corps of dependable, skilled mechanics by regularizing shop employment.[17]

Attempts to deal with the problem in other branches of the trade were less concerted. The general issue of employment fluctuations and uncertainty was recognized and discussed, and concern was voiced, but few concrete recommendations were offered. Railway executives for the most part decried the arbitrary control of work assignments by local supervisors. They issued instructions to foremen to divide employment as fairly and evenly as possible. They even made certain suggestions: that married, older workers be favored for retention over younger, single men during periods of retrenchment; and that men laid off during

---

[16] *Twenty-Third Annual Report of the President and Directors to the Stockholders of the Baltimore & Ohio Railroad Company* (Baltimore, 1849), p. 8.

[17] Stephen Salsbury, *The State, the Investor and the Railroad*, pp. 272–273. In the late 1880s the managers of the Chicago, Burlington & Quincy tried to regularize employment for shop workers in another way. They decided to move the shops to a town where there were other employment opportunities, so that during slack times men could find provisional jobs. See Cochran, *Railroad Leaders*, p. 472.

slack times be the first considered for reemployment when conditions improved.[18]

Only in a few cases, however, were substantive measures taken to insure job security for nonshop workers. These exceptions deserve mention. During the Civil War, many companies offered guarantees, sometimes written, of continued employment to men leaving to serve in the army.[19] The Baltimore & Ohio similarly made deliberate efforts during the war to keep all B. & O. employees fully occupied by moving them from destroyed portions of the road to operating areas.[20] By far the most innovative action, though, was attempted by Robert Harris of the Chicago, Burlington & Quincy. In the early 1870s, Harris initiated an experiment establishing a system of guaranteed work time for C.B. & Q. enginemen and firemen. Over the years, Harris had received petitions from cabmen complaining that they frequently reported to duty only to be informed by their supervisors that there was no work. Their employment was unsteady and uncertain and so was their income. To assuage the men and deal with a very real problem, Harris proposed to guarantee to those men who were ready to work a payment for nine-tenths of the normal monthly load no matter how many days they were actually employed. If the drivers and their assistants worked a complete complement of days, they would of course be paid in full. Harris's plan was in effect only a short period, for the Panic of 1873 and the economic downturn that followed forced the C.B. & Q. to abandon the experiment.[21] Harris remained convinced, though, of the importance of offering workers guaranteed work time. After the strikes of July 1877, he ordered a study that disclosed that one-fourth of the C.B. & Q. engineers surveyed worked less than the normal load. On this and other evidence, he concluded that much of the unrest of the summer could be attributed to the fact that "there is not an opportunity

[18] Cochran, *Railroad Leaders*, pp. 271, 274, 295, 388.

[19] *Report of the Board of Managers to the Stockholders of the Mine Hill and Schuylkill Haven Railroad Company, 1864* (Philadelphia, 1864), p. 42.

[20] *Thirty-Fourth Annual Report of the President and Directors to the Stockholders of the Baltimore & Ohio Railroad* (Baltimore, 1860), p. 42.

[21] Robert Harris to George Chalender, October 29, 1873, Chicago, Burlington & Quincy Railroad Papers, Harris Out-Letters, CBQ-3H4.1, Newberry Library.

for full employment."[22] Harris's initiatives represented a pioneer effort to deal concretely with job fluctuations and uncertainty. Guaranteed work time, as has been mentioned before, became an early goal and demand of organized railwaymen.

Finally, there is some evidence to indicate that pioneer railway workers tried to create equal employment opportunities among themselves. A veteran engineer on the Kanawha & Michigan Railroad reported in 1894 that drivers on that line practiced an old custom of regulating train mileage to spread the work. "Our little family," he noted, "have agreed among ourselves for the regular men to make $100 and get off, then let the extra men have the rest during the slack season."[23] The driver referred to this informal arrangement as following custom; unfortunately, other evidence confirming the practice and indicating its prevalence is lacking.

WHEN THEY HAD the opportunity to work, mid-nineteenth-century railwaymen generally put in long hours. A precise accounting of the length of the work day, though, presents difficulties. Before 1880 no studies were undertaken on the subject; figures are available, but they are scant and scattered. More important, the idea and practice of a standardized day had not fully emerged yet. Control over the number of hours worked remained in the hands of local foremen.[24] Most often immediate needs and circumstances dictated how much time men spent on the job each day. The management of the Baltimore & Ohio in 1854 could thus describe in an annual report to stockholders the following kind of situation: "For two months [April and May] the entire equipment of the Road was in constant use; extra trips without number were made by the engines, and the men in charge as enginemen and conductors, were for weeks deprived of needful rest."[25]

[22] Robert Harris to J. M. Forbes, August 2, 1877, Chicago, Burlington & Quincy Railroad Papers, Harris In-Letters, CBQ-3H4.1.

[23] Quoted in Richardson, *Locomotive Engineer*, p. 337.

[24] Ibid., Dan Mater, "The Development and Operation of the Railroad Seniority System," *Journal of Business of the Univ. of Chicago* 13:398.

[25] *Twenty-Eighth Annual Report of the President and Directors to the Stockholders of the Baltimore and Ohio Railroad Company* (Baltimore, 1854), p. 57.

In "normal" times, most mid-nineteenth-century railwaymen worked between ten and twelve hours a day, six days a week. In the 1850s, for instance, track repair crews on the Illinois Central put in a twelve-hour day. They reported to work at six in the morning and broke off at the same hour in the evening. One hour was allowed for dinner. By the mid-1870s, the number of hours worked each day by I.C. trackmen had been reduced to ten.[26]

Shop workers generally worked a ten or eleven hour day. They reported at 7:00 A.M., had time off for dinner between twelve and one, and quit at six. On Saturdays, it was customary to leave work an hour early, although the men were expected to clean and put away their tools after five.[27] When and how this tradition emerged is difficult to ascertain. In 1873 Charles Eliot Perkins, then vice president of the Chicago, Burlington & Quincy, wrote Robert Harris, general superintendent of the line, asking him why men were allowed to leave early on Saturdays without having their pay reduced accordingly. Harris replied that as long as he could remember, workers in the shops walked off at 5:00 P.M. to end the work week, and it was assumed that they would not be penalized. Harris counseled Perkins against fomenting an issue. It was custom, he noted, "One of those things that goes a long way, at least someway, towards preventing those combinations by which 'unions' are constantly hurting themselves and bothering everyone else." On Harris's advice, no action was taken.[28]

Office workers, too, were expected to put in a twelve-hour day. On the Baltimore & Ohio Railroad in the late 1850s, clerks were obliged to report to work at 7:00 A.M. and to leave no earlier than seven at night.[29] It is unclear from surviving mem-

[26] Lightner, "Labor on the Illinois Central," pp. 76–77, 156.

[27] Ibid.; Time Roll, September 1867–February 1869, Illinois Central Railroad Papers, Time Books, IC-3.9; *Rules for the Government of Persons Employed in the Machinery Department, Illinois Central Railroad to Take Effect June 1, 1878*, Illinois Central Railroad Papers, IC-11M2.2.

[28] Robert Harris to C. E. Perkins, June 19, 1872, Chicago, Burlington & Quincy Railroad Papers, Robert Harris Out-Letters, CBQ-3H4.1.

[29] W. P. Smith to J. W. Garrett, June 25, 1859, Baltimore & Ohio Railroad Papers, file 15213.

oranda whether B. & O. office personnel worked a five or six-day week.

The hours of trainmen were the least fixed and the most subject to variations and fluctuations. Seasonal factors, breakdowns, and scheduling delays rarely allowed for a "normal" day's work. In general, however, enginemen, firemen, brakemen, and conductors before the 1880s worked a seventy-hour week—twelve hours on weekdays and ten on Saturdays.

Exceptions to the norm, however, abound. Conductors on the Brooklyn Railroad in the early 1860s, for instance, were expected to remain on duty fourteen hours a day.[30] John Garrett of the Baltimore & Ohio wrote that twelve hours constituted a standard day's work on that line, although he admitted that B. & O. freight trainmen usually worked anywhere from sixteen to twenty hours.[31] Railroad trade journals in the 1870s similarly reported that train crews were normally on duty between fifteen and seventeen hours.[32]

At times, trainmen even worked far in excess of the figures mentioned. Herbert Hamblen relates in his reminiscence, *The General Manager's Story*, an instance when an engineer was on continuous service for fifty-two hours. Hamblen noted that this driver refused to obey an order to make an additional trip and was summarily fired.[33] Articles appearing in the *Locomotive Engineer's Journal* similarly cited cases of train crews operating upwards of a week with only brief periods of rest.[34] This apparently was not unusual. In 1883 the Bureau of Labor concluded, after an investigation into the high rates of accidents on American railroads, that excessive hours of work were a prime cause. The Bureau offered the following example as a typical occurrence:

A freight train gang left the starting point at 11:10 A.M. and returned at 7:10 the next morning, at the end of twenty hours. At 8:00, within

---

[30] *American Railway Review*, May 16, 1861, p. 295.

[31] J. W. Garrett to W. P. Smith, August 29, 1863, Baltimore & Ohio Railroad Letterbooks.

[32] *Railway Times*, September 30, 1871, p. 310; *Locomotive Engineer's Journal*, November 1871, p. 491.

[33] Herbert Hamblen,*The General Manager's Story*, p. 189.

[34] Quoted in Richardson, *Locomotive Engineer*, pp. 151–152.

an hour of the time of their arrival, they took out another train, returning at 4:40 P.M., at the end of eight hours and a half. Three hours after their arrival at 7:30, they began work again, returning at 10:30 A.M. the next day, at the end of fifteen hours, having been on duty 43½ hours, with the exception of fifty minutes intermission at one time, and three hours at another. "Of course," says one of the brakemen, "I went out with my train the same night." It was on this road that one of the brakemen, overworked on a freight train, fell asleep at his post and was run over and killed by the train he was sent to flag.[35]

Before 1880 railway executives strongly resisted attempts to reduce hours of work in the industry. Railwaymen, for their part, generally supported the eight-hour reform movement of the late 1860s and celebrated the passage of legislation on the state level limiting the length of the work day. Such measures, however, proved ineffective against management intransigence.[36] The following letter from John Douglas, president of Illinois Central to William Osborn, director of the I.C., is revealing. Written in May of 1867, after the Illinois legislature had enacted an eight-hour measure, the letter indicates how easily companies circumvented the law:

At the last session of our Legislature a bill was passed hurriedly and without our knowledge limiting the hours of labor to eight per day, to take effect May 1. Yesterday was a general holiday and the men had a large demonstration which passed off peacefully. . . . The companys leading into this city have all decided to employ the men by the hour working ten hours a day, and we are acting with the balance.[37]

Reducing hours through union contracts became a major goal and accomplishment of organized railway workers after the 1880s. States continued to pass legislation, but it was not until the passage in 1916 by Congress of the Adamson Act, which awarded the eight-hour day to the nation's railwaymen, that government initiatives afforded meaningful protection.[38]

[35] Charles Clark, "The Railroad Safety Movement in the United States" (Ph.D. dissertation, Univ. of Illinois at Urbana, 1966), p. 53.

[36] Paul Black, "Robert Harris and the Problem of Railway Labor Management" (unpublished paper in author's possession), pp. 24–25.

[37] Cochran, *Railroad Leaders*, p. 316.

[38] Albert Fishlow, "Productivity and Technological Change in the Railroad Sector, 1840–1910," in *Output, Employment, and Productivity in the United States after 1800*, p. 612. A bill to limit employment of railway employees for

Before the 1880s, the question of overtime payments also remained as unsettled an issue as the length of the work day.
Printed rule books indicate that most companies adopted the
straightforward policy that employees were to perform all tasks
assigned to them without expecting extra compensation. Available payroll records, however, indicate that men were often paid
for overtime work, though in a rather unsystematic fashion. On
the same line, some workers would receive additional pay for
services rendered beyond normal working hours, while others,
putting in the same extra time, would not. Similarly, while some
employees received lump sums for their extra labor, others were
reimbursed according to strict overtime payment formulas.[39]

Unfortunately, one finds little discussion of the issue of overtime prior to 1880 in either printed or manuscript corporate
records. From the absence of formal consideration, the fact that
men did receive extra compensation, and the haphazard manner
in which such awards were dispensed, it can be assumed that
the matter of overtime payments, like the actual fixing of the
length of the work day, remained a prerogative of local supervisors. Here memoranda in the archives of the Baltimore & Ohio
Railroad shed some light. Before 1854, the B. & O. allowed men
overtime compensation in all cases according to a complex system of awards. In that year, the company adopted a new policy
of "no allowance for extra time." The company, however, did
provide for exceptions. In cases of "unusual work" or "exceptional delay," men could be offered compensation, but only at
the discretion of local officers.[40] It is unclear how widespread
the practice of local prerogative was in overtime matters in the
industry. Important railroads, like the Illinois Central and Chicago, Burlington & Quincy, did institute formal systems of over-

over twelve consecutive hours in each twenty-four-hour period was introduced
in Congress in 1884 and defeated; in 1907, Congress passed the Hours of Service
Act limiting employment to sixteen consecutive hours in any given twenty-four-
hour period. See Lewis Haney, *A Congressional History of Railways in the United
States from 1850 to 1887*, p. 317; Richardson, *Locomotive Engineer*, p. 251.

[39] These contentions are based on careful studies of the payroll records cited
in appendix C.

[40] W. P. Smith to J. W. Garrett, September 2, 1863, Baltimore & Ohio Railroad
Papers, file 1461.

time payments. Employees on these lines, who occupied positions where the length of the work day could be fixed with some degree of certainty—like shopmen, track repair crews, station hands, and clerical personnel—were paid at time and a half for extra labor. The arrangements for trainmen were more complex, involving accounting for extra time spent during delays and breakdowns.[41] Overtime compensation became a standardized and fixed feature of the work after the 1880s with the advent of union contracts.[42]

A final area of contention involving hours was the question of Sunday work. Nineteenth-century railroad companies faced stiff public pressure to curtail or terminate operations on the Sabbath. Much concern for the moral well-being of railwaymen was voiced.[43] Citizens of Hampden County in Massachusetts thus sent the following petition to the managers of the Western Railroad in March 1848, calling for an end to Sunday train running:

We believe that conscientious men, whose services are most valuable, will not labor for the company, if required to work on the Sabbath, and that many, who would otherwise be good and worthy citizens will be overcome by the temptation, by their habitual neglect of the institutions of religion, become at length immoral, and bring up their children in impiety.[44]

Over the course of the century, moral considerations generally gave way to economic ones. In 1869 Robert Harris of the Chicago, Burlington & Quincy could write that "for more than ten years this Road has been run on the principle of giving to its employees Sunday as a day of rest."[45] Ten years later, Harris sadly admitted that the road could only handle its increased traffic by running trains on the Sabbath. To enable as many

[41] Lightner, "Labor on the Illinois Central," p. 165; Paul Black, "The Development of Management Personnel Policies on the Burlington Railroad, 1860–1900" (Ph.D. dissertation, Univ. of Wisconsin, 1972), p. 296.

[42] Richardson, *Locomotive Engineer*, pp. 218–220.

[43] L. F. Dimmick, *Discourse on the Moral Influence of Rail-Roads*, p. 94.

[44] Petition on labor on the Sabbath, March 1848, Western Railroad Papers, case 2, Baker Library.

[45] Robert Harris to C. H. Chappell, March 22, 1869, Chicago, Burlington & Quincy Railroad Papers, Harris Letterbooks, CBQ-3H4.1.

employees as possible to enjoy their well-earned day of rest, Harris did try to limit Sunday running. He was quick to point out, though, that his motivations were not particularly religious. A proper day's rest, he argued, would insure that C.B. & Q. men would be more industrious on the job.[46]

A similar pattern emerged on the Illinois Central. In 1868 John Douglas, president of the I.C., could inform the New York Sabbath Commission that "Sunday labor on this Railroad is reduced to strict necessity for its good effect on employees."[47] During the 1870s, the line, however, gradually increased its Sunday train service. Religious organizations lodged repeated complaints. I.C. officials countered by justifying their actions in a rather amusing and disingenuous way. Answering a petition from the Reverend Rufus W. Clark, William Ackerman, president of the I.C. in 1882, thus wrote:

I would beg to say, so far as my own observation goes, I think there has been a gradual improvement in the morals of Railway employes throughout the country during the past 10 years, less of intoxication, greater regard for the observance of the Lord's day and a higher standard of morality generally prevails; owing largely to the efforts made by the officers of the leading lines of the Country to afford their men the advantage of reading rooms and other conveniences. I do not believe it is possible to abolish Sunday trains, so the best we can do is to reduce the number to a minimum.[48]

By the 1880s, most companies abandoned all pretense of curtailing Sunday operations. As Henry Brockholst Ledyard of the Michigan Central noted, it was just an "impossibility . . . to [do] way with Sunday work." Ledyard did attempt to placate his critics by ordering the company's shops closed for one hour on Sundays to allow men an opportunity to attend religious services. He similarly arranged to have a coach set aside on each train where passengers and trainmen could worship. The wheels of the Central, however, kept turning.[49]

[46] Cochran, *Railroad Leaders*, p. 46.
[47] Ibid., pp. 210–211.
[48] Ibid., p. 245.
[49] Ibid., pp. 387, 402.

EMPLOYMENT was erratic and uncertain, and the hours were long. But an even greater specter haunted nineteenth-century American railwaymen. Railroad work was dangerous. Accidents were not just common; they were an integral component of the work. If many men ultimately escaped accidental injuries and death, the fear and threat of such happenings were inescapable and hung over everyone working on the line.

In the early years, especially, the level of technological development was primitive at best, and working conditions were dramatically unsafe. Most companies, for instance, operated their trains on single tracks. Sidings were provided for the passage of oncoming trains, so precise coordination of train movements was imperative. Crude scheduling and signaling systems, and the very unpredictable manner in which early locomotives ran, resulted in frequent collisions.[50] Faulty roadbed and track conditions, and poorly built bridges and overpasses constructed more often than not with thrift rather than safety in mind, contributed their share to early train wrecks and derailments.[51]

Boiler explosions also frequently occurred. The first recorded train accident in America involved just such an explosion on the South Carolina Railroad in 1830. The fireman on the train, a slave hireling, was blamed for not releasing a steam valve in time. Early boilers even when carefully tended, though, were rarely reliable. To protect passengers, many lines placed "barrier" cars piled high with bales of cotton or sand bags between the engines and the coaches. Little protection, though, was afforded the men in the cab.[52]

Pioneer locomotive drivers and firemen went unprotected as well from inclement weather and flying sparks and smoke. In the early years, there was much resistance by the traveling public to the introduction of covered cabs; passengers wanted to keep a close scrutiny on the drivers and their assistants, demanding their constant alertness and attention to duty. Only gradually

[50] Richardson, *Locomotive Engineer*, pp. 97, 117.

[51] Ibid., pp. 177–178. Traction was very poor on the early roads. A plague of grasshoppers in Pennsylvania in 1836 almost brought all train service there to a halt until a sandbox was added to the locomotive to provide greater traction. See John Stover, *The Life and Decline of the American Railroad*, p. 20.

[52] Stewart Holbrook, *The Story of American Railroads*, p. 27.

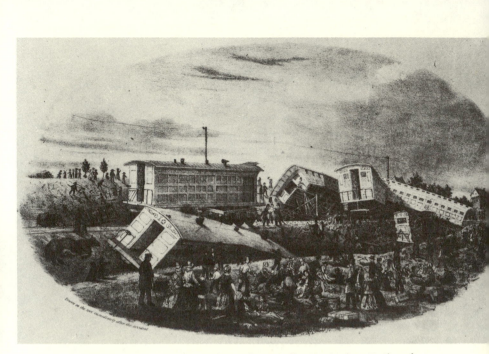

A depiction of a train wreck on the Camden & Amboy Railroad, August 29, 1855. (Courtesy of Smithsonian Institution.)

were canvas coverings adopted; wooden and then metal cabs first became common in the 1850s. Before that time, cabmen were totally exposed to the elements. Early engineers and firemen in New England suffered from frostbite in the wintertime. Cabmen everywhere were endangered by flying sparks from the fire stacks of the engines. One pioneer driver thus remembered that one could always tell a member of an engine crew in those days by the holes burned in the back of his vest.[53]

The absence of automatic braking and coupling devices made the work of the brakemen the most hazardous of all. When the engineer blew the whistle for "down brakes," brake crews scurried to their posts on top of the cars to turn the brake wheels. Normally assigned to two or three cars, the brakers often found themselves manning five or six as companies sought to reduce

[53] Ibid., pp. 38, 115; Richardson, *Locomotive Engineer*, p. 95; Stover, *Life and Decline*, p. 20.

their operating staffs. While running from car to car, it was easy to slip and fall, or to be hit by overhead obstructions. The work was particularly dangerous at night or during storms. Augustus Shaw, a veteran brakeman of twenty-five years, thus described the hazards of his job to a congressional investigating committee in 1890:

Say, for instance, it is a bad night—what we call a blind night on the road—sleeting, raining, snowing, etc. We hear the call for "down brakes." Of course we cannot always be on top of the train. During cold weather we go into the caboose occasionally to warm ourselves. We are called out by a signal of "down brakes." We get out on top of the train. We find that the top of the cars are completely covered with sleet. In attempting to get at those brakes a great many brakemen lose their lives, slip off the cars and again, even if they do reach the brakes, it is more often the case than it is not that they find that the brakes are frozen up, and they cannot twist them. That again occasions danger. They cannot set the brakes at all, cannot set the dog, cannot twist the brake. What we call the dog is the little piece of iron which catches onto the ratchet wheel. As no brakes are set, all will depend on the engine to stop the train, and if the train was going with any speed it would take some time to stop it.[54]

Coupling, too, claimed the limbs and lives of many a brakeman. In the early years, when the link-and-pin coupling system was used, the brakeman had to stand between cars in order to guide the link attached to the drawbar of one car into the side opening of the drawhead of the other. At the same time he would be poised to drop a heavy pin through a hole in the top of the drawhead, which would pass through the opening of the link and establish a couple. The pieces, however, rarely fitted neatly—especially with cars manufactured by different companies—and as the brakeman wrestled with the various parts, the chances of having his fingers and hands crushed were enormous.[55] The job was so hazardous that "old time" brakemen were often recognized by missing fingers or crippled hands. When applying for new jobs, they carried vivid proof of their experience, and fore-

[54] Quoted in Clark, "Railroad Safety Movement," p. 20.
[55] Ibid., pp. 29, 111.

The hand brake system made the job of brakeman particularly peril-
ous. (Reprinted from T. C. Clarke et al., *The American Railway*,
New York, 1889.)

men looking for veteran workers were known to consider missing
fingers an apt qualification for employment.[56]

Brakemen also risked their very lives while coupling cars. As

[56] John Stover, *American Railroads*, pp. 151–152.

one part of the train was moved slowly back to be hitched to stationary cars, brakemen often ran alongside guiding the links and pins. If they tripped or had their feet caught in a switch, they easily could be run over by the train. If they were standing between cars and the whole system of drawheads and drawbars collapsed, they could be crushed to death. Brakemen were also crushed by deadwoods, which were wooden blocks placed on the ends of cars both to absorb the impact of coupling and to protect them if the drawbar collapsed.[57]

Finally, to add to the perils of the job, pioneer brakemen and their fellow trainmen faced repeated danger from marauding hold-up gangs and attacking Indians.[58] Train crews on the Michigan Central in the late 1840s were even frequently set upon along the route by angry farmers who had been refused compensation from the company for livestock killed or disfigured by Central trains.[59]

Workers in the transportation department, however, were certainly not the only railwaymen exposed to unsafe or risky conditions. Accidents routinely occurred in the machine and repair shops and the roundhouses. Exploding boilers, crude tools, unreliable machines, primitive forges, scattered pieces of metal, and the very bustle of activity in the shops took their toll. Shop men received serious burns and bruises and were in constant danger of losing limbs.

The work of yard crews and station hands was arduous and hazardous, too. Whether in switching or coupling cars, or in hauling and loading heavy freight, there was ample chance for injury. The yards, especially, were busy places, and despite precautions, men frequently were hit by shunting engines and cars accidently set in motion. Finally, track repair workers encountered their share of adversity. Fixing railbeds and replacing tracks involved backbreaking labor. Handcars, used by track crews to travel from point to point, were also particularly dangerous. It

---

[57] Clark, "Railroad Safety Movement," p. 57.
[58] B. A. Botkin and Alvin Harlow, eds., *A Treasury of Railroad Folklore*, p. 187; Keith Bryant, Jr., *History of the Atchison, Topeka and Santa Fe Railway*, p. 56.
[59] Hank Bowman, *Pioneer Railroads*, p. 77.

was not uncommon for men to be thrown from the cars while manning the cranks.

Grisly evidence of the extent of the hazards of railway work is provided by accident reports compiled by nineteenth-century railroad companies. In the early years many carriers listed detailed information on employee injuries and fatalities in annual stockholder reports. Later, state railroad commissions demanded full accounting of all mishaps, which were also printed in annual statements. What follows is a small sample drawn from the tens of thousands of such reports. The accounts impart the very horror often experienced in the work. In some cases, too, the reports provide a brief but meaningful insight into the lives of mid-nineteenth-century railwaymen. It is rather discomforting to learn even this much about these anonymous Americans because of the gruesome manner in which they were either killed or maimed.

From the *Sixth Annual Report of the Norfolk County Railroad:*

June 26, 1852. Orpheus Holmes, a very worthy man, who has been employed on the road as a brakeman since it was opened, and who had recently been appointed conductor of the freight train, was instantly killed by his head coming in contact with a bridge, while standing on top of a box car.[60]

From the *First Annual Report of the Old Colony and Fall River Railroad Company:*

April 29, 1854. Jeremiah Harrington, road repairer, while relieving another man in turning the hand-car, was caught by the crank and thrown in front of the car upon the track. He was seriously injured in the spine, so as to produce paralysis of arms and legs, of which injury he died.[61]

From a *Report of the Central Railroad Company of New Jersey, January 1, 1855:*

September 1, 1854. Michael Darren, in attempting to pass from one loaded dirt car to another, while the train was in motion, fell between

[60] *Sixth Annual Report of the Norfolk County Railroad Company to the State of Massachusetts* (Boston, 1853), p. 140.

[61] *First Annual Report of the Old Colony and Fall River Railroad Company to the State of Massachusetts* (Boston, 1855), p. 189.

The coupling of cars accounted for the greatest number of accidental injuries and deaths suffered by pioneer railwaymen. (Drawing by Peter Copeland. Courtesy of Smithsonian Institution.)

the cars and was killed. He had arrived in this country but a few days previous, and was in the employment of the company.[62]

From a *Report of the Hudson River Railroad to the State Engineer & Surveyor of the State of New York:*
    June 7, 1865. F. F. Graves, conductor, was killed while coupling cars

[62] *Annual Reports of Railroad and Canal Companies of the State of New Jersey, 1855* (Trenton, 1855), p. 21.

at Hastings. Until a short time previous to the accident resulting in his death, Mr. Graves had been serving in the capacity of locomotive engineer, which position he had filled for many years, with credit to himself and the company. On account of ill health, occasioned by the severe duties of his position, he was appointed conductor, and in his zealousness for the company's welfare, met with the accident causing his death.[63]

Prior to 1880 and even 1890, railroad companies resisted all attempts to introduce safety devices like the automatic air brake and the automatic coupler. The Westinghouse brake, for instance, was first tried in 1869. By 1873 it had been improved to the point where the legislature of Michigan passed the first state statute mandating its use.[64] Few companies operating in Michigan, however, felt obliged to abide by the dictates of the law. In Illinois and other states, moreover, railroads joined forces effectively to block passage of safety-device measures.[65]

The carriers opposed the adoption of safety improvements on several grounds. They argued first that the state could and should not interfere with the day-to-day operations of the roads. They further insisted that inventions like the air brake had not been fully tried and tested, and that it was foolish to force acceptance of less than perfect mechanisms. More to the point, the carriers argued that the costs were much too high. Few railroads could afford to invest in such capital improvements. Ever responsive to public opinion, railway executives even maintained that the state would be fostering monopoly by dictating which devices were to be adopted. The carriers clearly had the Westinghouse Air Brake and Jenney Car Coupler Companies in mind, the pioneers in the field and the two leading producers at the time.[66]

The railroads were joined in their opposition to new safety legislation by state railroad commissions. Throughout the 1870s, the influential railway commission of Massachusetts, headed by Charles Francis Adams, Jr., advised against precipitate actions by the legislature. Railroad managers, not legislators, the commissioners warned, were in the best position to assess their needs.

[63] *Annual Report of the State Engineer & Surveyor of the State of New York of the Year Ending September 30, 1866* (Albany, 1867), p. 285.

[64] Clark, "Railroad Safety Movement," p. 74.

[65] Ibid., p. 348; Lightner, "Labor on the Illinois Central," p. 364.

[66] Clark, "Railroad Safety Movement," pp. 184–189, 210.

The link-and-pin couple.
(Courtesy of Association of
American Railroads.)

The railroad corporations of Massachusetts, moreover, "were sufficiently liable for the operation of their roads." Further "legal encumbrances to make them operate more safely or efficiently" were not required.[67]

American railway workers did not immediately champion the adoption of safety devices, either. Locomotive engineers at first opposed the introduction of air brakes. The operation of the brake represented an extra function to them for which they were not guaranteed additional compensation. By 1874, sentiments had changed, and the drivers, under the auspices of the Brotherhood of Locomotive Engineers, came out solidly in favor of passage of safety air brake legislation.[68] There was also some disagreement among brakemen and conductors concerning the merits of various automatic coupling systems. The principle itself was not opposed. Support for new coupling devices, however, was less than wholehearted among switchmen whose very job security was threatened by their adoption.[69]

Strong opposition by railway managers combined with equivocation by state railroad commissioners and an absence of unanimity among railwaymen acted to delay passage of legislation forcing the introduction of safety devices. It was not until 1893, a full twenty-five years after the invention of both the automatic brake and couple, that Congress narrowly passed the Safety Appliance Act. This bill made it unlawful for common carriers

[67] Ibid., p. 259.
[68] Ibid., p. 167.
[69] Ibid., chap. 5.

engaged in interstate commerce to operate after January 1, 1898, without power driven wheel brakes and mechanisms for operating the trains' brake systems on all locomotives. The act also required automatic couplers on all cars and a sufficient number of cars to have power brakes so that hand brakes would not be necessary.[70] In the twenty-five years of delay between invention and widespread application, the lives and physical well-being of tens of thousands of American railwaymen had been imperiled needlessly.

A PRECISE accounting of the numbers injured and killed while in rail service before 1889 is impossible. In that year the newly established Interstate Commerce Commission began collecting data on accidents from all railroad companies operating in the country. Before that time, the process of gathering information on casualties was carried out at the state level, but only in states having railroad commissions. The quality and extent of reporting for the pre-1880 period varies considerably from state to state and from year and year.

The 1889 ICC statistics are informative, and since they provide the only complete and reliable base to measure the extent of the hazards of nineteenth-century railway work, they merit examination and comment.[71] For the year ending June 30, 1889, the ICC reported that 1,972 railwaymen had been killed on the job and 20,028 men were injured. Railroad employees accounted in that year for 34 percent of all railway accident fatalities and 76 percent of all such injuries (passengers accounted for 5 percent of the fatalities and 8 percent of the injuries, while "other persons" comprised 61 percent of the deaths and 16 percent of the injuries). In 1889, 704,443 men held positions on the nation's rail lines, which means that in that year one out of every 357 employees was killed in service and one out of every thirty-five injured.[72] The commission found these figures particularly dis-

[70] Ibid., p. 237; Richardson, *Locomotive Engineer*, p. 250.

[71] *Second Annual Report on the Statistics of Railways in the United States to the Interstate Commerce Commission for the Year Ending June 30, 1889* (Washington, D. C., 1890), p. 36–38.

[72] The figure of 704,443 men includes all workers who found employment in the railroad industry in 1889 during the course of the year. It does not represent discrete positions in the trade, which were probably two-thirds of that number.

tressing, pointing out that in England the equivalent statistics for 1889 were one worker in 875 killed and one in 158 injured.

Statistics were also offered on causes of accidents and grades of employees involved. Coupling and uncoupling of cars accounted for 16 percent of all fatalities and 34 percent of all injuries experienced by American railwaymen in 1889. Falling from trains and engines resulted in one-fourth of all deaths and 10 percent of all injuries. Collisions and derailments were responsible for 15 percent of the fatalities and 7 percent of the injuries. A broad range of other kinds of accidents accounted for the rest.

When broken down by grade, the figures are particularly startling. Trainmen—engineers, firemen, conductors, and brakemen—led the most precarious existences by far. While they constituted approximately 20 percent of the entire work force, they accounted for 60 percent of all fatalities and 56 percent of all injuries. The next largest group of employees listed together by the commission were switchmen, flagmen, and watchmen, who represented 12 percent of those killed in service and 11 percent of those injured. The hazards faced by train crews are made even more vivid when put in per capita terms. In 1889, for every 117 trainmen employed, one was killed; for every twelve, one was injured. The ICC found these figures distressing, too, for in England the corresponding statistics were one trainmen in 329 killed and one in thirty injured.

Information provided by state and company reports for the pre-1880 period, though scattered and incomplete, generally conform to the picture presented by the ICC data for 1889. In Wisconsin, for instance, between 1874 and 1880, railway employees accounted for 42 percent of all railway accident fatalities and 74 percent of all injuries; in Michigan between 1872 and 1879, for 39 percent of all accidental deaths and 61 percent of all injuries; in New York, between 1856 and 1880, for 33 percent of all fatalities and 45 percent of all injuries.[73] In Massachusetts and Connecticut the figures are slightly lower. In these two states,

[73] Robert Hunt, *Law and Locomotives*, p. 155; statistics for Michigan and New York compiled from accident reports listed in the *Annual Reports of the Commissioner of Railroads of the State of Michigan, 1872–79*, and the *Annual Reports of the State Engineers & Surveyor of the State of New York, 1856–80*.

The yards of the Baltimore & Ohio Railroad, Baltimore, Maryland, in the early 1880s. The work of yard crews was arduous and dangerous. (Courtesy of Association of American Railroads.)

passenger service was proportionately greater than in states to the west, where the bulk of traffic was in freight haulage. Passengers, as a result, suffered a greater proportion of the casualties there. Accordingly, in Connecticut, between 1857 and 1880, railwaymen accounted for 24 percent of all accidental deaths and 36 percent of all injuries; in Massachusetts between 1847

and 1871, for 31 percent of all fatalities and 25 percent of all injuries.[74]

Employment statistics on the state level are either unreliable

[74] *Third Annual Report of the Board of Railroad Commissioners, January 1872* (Boston, 1872), p. cxxii; statistics for Connecticut compiled from data in *Annual Reports of the General Railroad Commissioners of the State of Connecticut, 1857–80.*

or nonexistent for the pre-1880 period, making per capita estimates difficult. In 1855, the railroad commission of New York reported that 18,012 men were employed on the state's operating railway lines. That is the first and last time before 1880 that the commission published aggregate figures on employment. In 1855, thirty-three railwaymen were reported killed in accidents in the state and forty-one were injured, which means that one railway worker in 546 died in service, while one in 439 was injured.[75] Fairly reliable aggregate figures are also available for Illinois, Iowa, Michigan, and Massachusetts in the mid- and late 1870s.[76] The annual per capita calculations there range from one in 272 to one in 695 killed and one in 97 to one in 571 injured.

Two points are interesting about the pre-1880 state figures: they are all more favorable in terms of fatalities and injuries than the data presented by the ICC in 1889; over time, too, the per capita rates for men killed and injured become larger, implying a worsening situation. This suggests that either the pre-1880 data are incomplete and suspect and that no conclusions are warranted, or that over the course of the nineteenth century, accidents became more numerous and frequent both relatively and absolutely as the work became more hazardous. Intuitively, the latter contention seems most plausible. As the railroads increased their operations, as passenger and freight traffic multiplied, the demands on workers increased proportionately. So, too, did the chances for mishaps and casualties.

For the pre-1880 period, available evidence also indicates that coupling and falling from trains were the most common causes of accidental injuries and deaths. In Massachusetts, between 1847 and 1871, falling off trains accounted for 29 percent of all fa-

[75] *Annual Report of the Railroad Commissioners of New York, 1855* (Albany, 1856), p. 342.

[76] Statistics compiled from accident reports listed in the *Annual Reports of the Boards of Railroad Commissioners of the State of Illinois*, 1878–1880, *Iowa*, 1878–80, *Michigan*, 1872–80, and *Massachusetts*, 1867–80. A recently completed study of accident rates on the Atchison, Topeka & Santa Fe Railroad for the late nineteenth century reveals identical figures to the ones reported here. See James Ducker, "Men of the Steel Rails" (Ph.D. dissertation, Univ. of Illinois at Champaign-Urbana, 1980), p. 7.

talities and 19 percent of all injuries; coupling for 18 percent of all deaths and 20 percent of all injuries; derailments and collisions for 12 percent of all deaths and 19 percent of all injuries; "striking overhead obstructions" for 19 percent of all fatalities and 18 percent of all injuries; and a host of "other" reasons for 21 percent of all deaths and 24 percent of all injuries.[77] Figures for Connecticut for the period 1857–80 and New Jersey for 1853–80 are roughly equivalent.

Pioneer trainmen were also exposed to the greatest risks of accidental injuries and deaths. In Connecticut, between the late 1850s and 1880, enginemen, firemen, conductors, and brakemen accounted for 60 percent of all employee injuries and 57 percent of all such fatalities; in Massachusetts, for 55 percent of all injuries and 64 percent of all accidental deaths.[78] A study prepared by the managers of the Illinois Central Railroad in 1884 further highlights the correlation between type of employment and liability to injury and death. For the ten-year period, 1874–84, the company found that the proportion of employees suffering a disabling injury was:

1 in 167 office and station workers
1 in 36 machinery department employees
1 in 30 road department employees
1 in 20 men in train service
1 in   7 men in switching service.

The report did not specify which workers were represented in the category of "switching service"; whether switchmen and brakemen assigned to switching and coupling chores are included is unclear. The report also listed figures on fatalities. Here, too, the relationship between type of work and exposure to risk is

[77] *Third Annual Report of the Board of Railroad Commissioners, January, 1872* (Boston, 1872), pp. cxx–cxxii. Figures for Connecticut and New Jersey compiled from accident statements listed in both states' railroad commission reports for years indicated in the text.

[78] Statistics for Connecticut and Massachusetts compiled from accident statements listed in both states' railroad commission reports for the years indicated in the text.

dramatic. Between 1874 and 1884 the proportions of I.C. employees involved in accidents resulting in death were:

1 in   2,120 office and station workers
1 in   1,090 machinery department employees
1 in   360 road department employees
1 in   120 men in train service
1 in   90 men in switching service.[79]

Three general points can be made from the above figures. First, accidents resulting in employee injuries and deaths contributed to a certain extent, albeit slight, to the general labor turnover problem discussed in chapter 2. Men disappeared from company payroll records because of accidental disabilities and fatalities. Second, and on a related issue, accidents also resulted in losses in overall efficiency and productivity. From available data, it is clear that during the nineteenth century approximately 3.5 percent of the nation's railway work force at any given moment were disabled.[80] This represents not only a loss in labor power, but in labor experience and expertise as well. Finally, the sad plight of the nation's pioneer brakemen must be emphasized. Brakemen led the most precarious of lives. Though no more than 10 percent of the total work force, state data from the pre-1880 period for Massachusetts, Connecticut, and New Jersey indicate that brakemen accounted for 35 to 50 percent of all injuries and fatalities suffered during railroad mishaps.[81] Whether in coupling cars or braking, the perils of their labor were staggering. At times the pressure of the work could become unbearable. Suicide even loomed as a desirable alternative. A reporter for a Baltimore

[79] Lightner, "Labor on the Illinois Central," p. 263.

[80] The figure of 3.5 percent emerges from statistics provided by the ICC in 1889 and from available pre-1880 state-level data. It is confirmed by a report issued in 1894 showing that on the Pennsylvania, Baltimore & Ohio, and Burlington Railroads—lines employing about 17 percent of the nation's railroad task force—between 3.1 and 3.8 percent of their respective work forces were disabled at any one given moment in time. See Emory Johnson, "Railway Departments for the Relief and Insurance of Employes," *Annals of the American Academy of Political and Social Science* 6:92.

[81] These figures again have been compiled from accident statements listed in the railroad commission reports of the states mentioned.

newspaper filed the following report after interviewing a group
of B. & O. brakemen in the summer of 1877:

In two instances, it is said, brakemen after the loss of rest and under
the depression of reduced wages, etc., have purposely thrown themselves
under the wheels. Nearly all the men talked with said at one time and
another when melancholy, they had meditated about stepping over the
bumpers and meeting instant death.[82]

WORKERS disabled in accidents and the widows and families of
deceased railwaymen faced a grim and uncertain future. In making claims for compensation for their losses, the legal system
offered little or no relief. Railroad companies often granted gratuities to injured men and sometimes paid hospital and funeral
expenses, but only in an informal and unsystematic fashion.
Structured, comprehensive insurance programs for railwaymen
did not emerge until the 1880s.

In the early years, the courts ruled in favor of the railroads in
practically all employee liability suits. Judges generally applied
the common law principle of implied contract in assessing the
merits of claims. Under implied contract, the courts held that an
employee in engaging to serve a master accepted all conditions
of such service, including all the ordinary risks incident to his
employment. In entering into hire, the employee even accepted
the risk of negligence on the part of a fellow servant. In their
printed rule books, railroad companies accordingly warned
workers that they had no legal right to receive compensation for
any injury.[83]

The first railroad employee liability case to be brought before
an American court involved a fireman by the name of Murray
who was employed by the South Carolina Railroad. Injured in
an accident in 1838, he sued the line, but the court ruled in the
defense's behalf. Finding that the mishap had been caused by the
negligence of the locomotiveman for whom Murray fired, the
court declared that the South Carolina Railroad Company could

[82] Robert Bruce, *1877: Year of Violence*, p. 45.
[83] Clark, "Railroad Safety Movement," pp. 219, 223.

not be held liable for employee injuries resulting from the carelessness of fellow servants.[84]

In 1842 a similar case came before the courts of Massachusetts.
A decision here, handed down by Chief Justice Shaw, became
the precedent for future suits. The case involved a complaint
brought by Nicholas Farwell, an engineer on the Boston &
Worcester Railroad. Farwell had been disabled when a careless
switchman left a switch open, resulting in a derailment. Farwell
sought an award on the grounds that the company had failed to
exercise sufficient care by employing an incompetent switchman.
The award was denied, the court ruling that:

He who engages in the employment of another for performance of
specified duties and services, for compensation, takes upon himself the
natural and ordinary risks and perils incident to the performance of
such services, and in legal presumption the compensation is adjusted
accordingly. And we are not aware of any principle which should except
the perils arising from the carelessness and negligence of those who are
in the same employment. These are the perils which the servant is as
likely to know, and against which he can as effectively guard, as the
master. They are perils incident to the service, and which can be as
distinctly forseen and provided for in the rate of compensation as any
other. To say that the master shall be responsible because the damage
is caused by his agents, is assuming the very point which remains to be
proved.[85]

Subsequent court decisions and the passage of legislation on
the state level slowly eroded to a certain extent the precedent set
in the Farwell case. In several rulings in the 1850s and '60s, the
courts declared that the Farwell decision did not completely ab-
solve management from the responsibility of providing and insuring safe equipment and working conditions.[86] A brakeman in
New Hampshire thus was awarded damages when he proved
that his injuries were the result of his company's negligence in
not properly keeping the track free of snow and ice.[87] A fireman

[84] Samuel M. Lindsay, "Report on Railway Labor in the United States," in
Reports of the Industrial Commission on Labor Organizations, p. 895.
[85] Clark, "Railroad Safety Movement," pp. 219, 223.
[86] Ibid., p. 220.
[87] American Railroad Journal, September 20, 1862, p. 727.

in New York employed by the Western Railroad similarly received an award of $3,500 after being disabled in a boiler explosion. He apparently had notified officials of the Western on several occasions of defects in the boiler, but no repairs were made. The court ruled that his injuries resulted from the actual negligence and malfeasance of the company, and that the Western was liable for damages.[88]

More important were statutory modifications of the fellow servant rule. Under the Farwell decision, judges generally extended the concept of fellow servant to include agents and managers of the corporation. Railroad companies in this way were not held liable for injuries or fatalities caused by the orders of foremen or supervisors. Before 1880 several states enacted legislation reversing this interpretation and rendering railroads subject to damages in consequence of the neglect and deeds of their agents. These states included Georgia (1855), Iowa (1862), the territory of Montana (1873), Kansas (1875), and Wisconsin (1875). These laws also generally expanded the grounds upon which railroad corporations could be held responsible for injuries and represented first steps in the slow evolution of the concept of *employer* liability.[89]

Despite gradual liberalization in laws and interpretations, the courts in the early period did not represent a source of relief for mid-nineteenth-century railwaymen. In many ways it is not surprising that, even with the great number of accidents, so few personal-injury and wrongful-death actions were initiated against the railroads.[90] Railway workers either had little access to legal assistance, did not want to jeopardize their chances of receiving voluntary gratuities from their employers, feared for their future employment, or else calculated quite rationally that the possibilities of ultimately winning in court were quite slim. Cases also took time. Records in the archives of the Baltimore & Ohio Railroad reveal that suits remained unsettled at various levels of

[88] Ibid., April 21, 1855, p. 252.
[89] Clark, "Railroad Safety Movement," pp. 226–232; Paul Black, "Development of Management Personnel Policies," p. 369; Lindsay, "Report on Railway Labor," pp. 898–899; Charles C. Bonney, *Rules of Law for the Carriage and Delivery of Persons and Property by Railway*, pp. 95–100, 143–150.
[90] Hunt, *Law and Locomotives*, p. 89.

the legal system for upwards of ten to twelve years.[91] Even with bona fide claims, unpredictability marked the whole judicial process. As Robert Hunt, a leading student of nineteenth-century legal actions involving railroads, has commented: "As often as not ultimate recovery [of employee claims], put through the wringer of a suit at law, rested on fortuitous circumstances quite unrelated to the merits of the controversy. . . . The court[s] wended [their] way, granting recovery here and denying recovery there."[92]

Two documents are available that can give some inkling of the exact degree to which legal actions proved fruitless. In 1875 the St. Louis & Southeastern Railroad reported to the railroad commissioners of Illinois on damages claimed and paid to employees by the company in the course of the year.[93] They included the following: one injured yardman sued for $10,000 and was awarded $47.66; an injured switchman claimed $5,000 and received $500; another switchman asked for $1,000 and received $100; an injured brakeman similarly asked for $200 and was awarded $15. Two families of killed brakemen claimed $15,000 and $10,000 in damages, respectively, and received no award. The St. Louis & Southeastern further reported that twenty-seven injured employees and the family of one deceased worker chose not to bring suits against the company. Of these twenty-eight cases the company decided to award fourteen with gratuities amounting to $934.50. Clearly only a small percentage of the railwaymen involved in accidents on the road saw fit to bring the St. Louis & Southeastern to court; of these only half were successful. Those who made no claims appear to have fared better than those who did.

Further evidence on the subject is provided in the annual report of the railroad commissioners of Illinois for 1876. In that year, the fifty-three railroad companies operating in the state reported paying $3,654.70 in damages to employees killed or injured

[91] J. W. Garrett to T. Perkins, August 15, 1864, Baltimore & Ohio Letterbooks. An enormous backlog of liability cases also existed on the Atchison, Topeka & Santa Fe Railroad in the late nineteenth century. See Ducker, "Men of the Steel Rails," p. 84.

[92] Hunt, *Law and Locomotives*, p. 153.

[93] *Fifth Annual Report of the Railroad and Warehouse Commission of the State of Illinois* (Springfield, Ill., 1876), p. 239.

while on duty. During that year, 102 railwaymen had been injured in accidents in the state and 262 killed. Only twenty-four
of these workers received damages amounting to the above figure. The report did not state how many claims were actually
filed. What is of interest, too, is that in the same year the fifty-
three railway companies operating in Illinois reported paying
$119,288.24 in damages for livestock killed and $26,100.29 for
property burned by locomotives.[94] Property clearly took prece-
dence over life and limb in Illinois in the 1870s. In this respect,
a slave master had a greater chance of collecting on damages if
his leased slave was injured or killed in an accident than a wage-
earning railwayman.[95]

Finally, while the law only rarely functioned to promote the
welfare of railwaymen, it could at times be used directly against
them. Nineteenth-century railway workers were subject to criminal prosecution in cases where their overt negligence, carelessness, or malfeasance resulted in injury or death to others, especially passengers. Evidence does suggest, though, that public
sentiment against railroad companies often worked to the advantage of railroad employees, as local juries were reluctant to
prosecute workingmen of the community.[96] The ultimate threat
of indictment and conviction, nevertheless, remained ever present.

ON AN INFORMAL, discretionary, and completely voluntary basis,
American railway companies in the nineteenth century did offer
limited relief to employees involved in accidents. Companies frequently paid medical expenses of injured men or awarded them
flat charitable grants. While recuperating, disabled men were also
often kept on the payroll. The Boston & Worcester Railroad in
the 1830s and '40s paid injured men deemed deserving of support

---

[94] *Sixth Annual Report of the Railroad and Warehouse Commission of the
State of Illinois* (Springfield, Ill., 1876), pp. 444–445.

[95] Robert C. Black III, *The Railroads of the Confederacy*, p. 30.

[96] *American Railroad Journal*, September 10, 1853, p. 583; documents accompanying letter of William Osborn to J. W. Brooks, March 31, 1862, Illinois
Central Railroad Papers, W. Osborn Out-Letters, IC-106.1.

full wages.[97] Other lines offered only partial pay during periods of incapacitation. Robert Harris, general superintendent of the Chicago, Burlington & Quincy, advised officials on that line to offer half wages plus medical costs. "If we pay in full," he warned, "there are many men who will take advantage of it, and we will be obliged to watch them with great closeness. Half pay keeps them from want and gives them an incentive to go to work as soon as they can. In some instances the circumstances will justify payment in full."[98]

Railroad companies further attempted to aid disabled employees by making special efforts to employ them in less demanding tasks.[99] Stockholders of the Fitchburg Railroad thus learned in the company's annual report of 1849 the following about a brakeman who had fallen from the top of a freight car and been run over: "His leg was amputated, and he recovered and is now in the employ of the company as an assistant clerk in the freight department."[100] Injured trainmen on the New York & Erie Railroad in the 1850s were similarly placed in clerical or depot positions; officials on the Illinois Central made a practice of allowing disabled brakemen and others to occupy spots as flagmen and watchmen; and on the Chicago, Burlington & Quincy, the Chariton branch of the road, where there was only limited freight service, was reserved for old and crippled engineers and firemen.[101] The C.B. & Q. also offers an example of an unusual form of relief afforded an injured railwayman. In 1871 a machinist, George Emerick, lost a limb when his clothing caught in a revolving shaft. Hearing that Emerick's house was

[97] Minutes of directors' meetings, vol. 2, p. 264, Boston & Worcester Railroad Papers, Baker Library.

[98] Robert Harris to H. Hitchcock, February 10, 1870, Chicago, Burlington & Quincy Railroad Papers, Harris Out-Letters, CBQ-3H4.1.

[99] Paul Black, "Robert Harris," p. 26; report on Jeremiah Hayes, February 10, 1846, Western Railroad Papers, case 3, Baker Library.

[100] *Seventh Annual Report of the Fitchburg Railroad Company to the State of Massachusetts* (Boston, 1849), p. 47.

[101] Edward Mott, *Between the Ocean and the Lakes*, p. 401; Lightner, "Labor on the Illinois Central," pp. 125–126; Paul Black, "Development of Management Personnel Policies," pp. 379–380.

badly in need of repair, superintendent Harris authorized the head of the company's building department to rebuild his home.[102]

Railroad companies also extended relief to widows and the families of railwaymen killed while in service. Carriers sometimes paid medical fees and donated burial expenses. They also offered direct monetary awards.[103] In the first accident involving a company employee, the Boston & Albany Railroad made a $500 payment, which was roughly equal to one year's wages to the widow of Hiram Bridges, a freight train engineer.[104] The Illinois Central gave Mrs. Mary Cross an award of $250 when her son, a brakeman, who was her sole surviving support, was killed in a mishap.[105] In 1853 the board of managers of the Delaware, Lackawanna & Western Railroad likewise voted to continue paying the salary of a deceased engineer to his widow for four months.[106] The widow of a station agent on the Boston & Worcester Railroad was not only presented with a $200 gratuity; she also received an additional full month of her husband's salary and was allowed to remain in a company-owned house rent-free for an extended period.[107]

Railroad companies helped the families of employees killed in accidents in other ways. Herbert Hamblen recalled an instance where the widow and children of a fatally injured car repairer were given employment in a car-cleaning gang.[108] Letters in the company archives of the Baltimore & Ohio Railroad reveal that widows frequently wrote company managers beseeching them to employ their elder sons.[109] Finally, the Galena & Chicago Union Railroad offered one widow an unusual gratuity. At her

[102] Ibid., p. 378.
[103] Lightner, "Labor on the Illinois Central," p. 127.
[104] Salsbury, *State, Investor and Railroad*, p. 105.
[105] Cochran, *Railroad Leaders*, p. 296.
[106] Minutes of the Board of Managers of the Delaware, Lackawanna & Western Railroad, November 9, 1853, Delaware, Lackawanna & Western Railroad Papers.
[107] Minutes of directors' meetings, vol. 7, pp. 126–127, Boston & Worcester Railroad Papers.
[108] Hamblen, *General Manager's Story*, p. 25.
[109] File 1466, Baltimore & Ohio Railroad Papers.

request, the company presented her with a sewing machine so that she could earn her own living.[110]

In extending relief to injured railwaymen and the families of employees killed while on duty, the motives of nineteenth-century railroad managers were not entirely benevolent. Companies went out of their way to announce publicly and to warn employees that they were absolutely under no obligation to award gratuities.[111] Some firms, like the New Haven & Hartford Railroad, declared forthrightly that in practically no circumstances would grants of relief even be considered.[112] Some railway executives regarded gratuities as merely a means of maintaining good public relations.[113] Others, like Robert Harris, envisioned corporate benevolence as a way of encouraging loyalty. "In so far as this [paying allowances] would indicate to our men," Harris wrote, "that we were disposed to consider the misfortune of those who faithfully served us, I think we would find a full return."[114] Charles Eliot Perkins, ever the cold rationalist, frowned on the practice, but nonetheless countenanced relief giving as a matter of "business expediency."[115] The true justification lay elsewhere. In offering relief to needy families of the disabled and deceased, all nineteenth-century companies made the recipients sign comprehensive waivers agreeing not to bring suits against the firms.[116] Furnishing awards thus provided the roads with a clear and facile avenue for avoiding legal liability. A few copies of such releases survive. The following is taken from the archives of the Illinois Central, and was signed by one Emma Leffingwell, the wife of an I.C. employee, on November 13, 1858:

[110] D. W. Yungmeyer, "Selected Items From the Minute Book of the Galena and Chicago Union Railroad Company," *The Railway and Locomotive Historical Society Bulletin*, no. 65, pp. 28–29.

[111] *Rules and Regulations for Running the Trains on the North Pennsylvania Railroad* (Philadelphia, 1875), p. 3; *Forty-First Annual Report of the Philadelphia, Wilmington & Baltimore Railroad Company* (Philadelphia, 1879), p. 15; Lightner, "Labor on the Illinois Central," pp. 123–124.

[112] Cochran, *Railroad Leaders*, p. 261.

[113] Ibid., p. 261.

[114] Robert Harris to J. Joy, November 10, 1869, Chicago, Burlington & Quincy Railroad Papers, Harris Out-Letters, CBQ-3H4.1.

[115] Memorandum of C. E. Perkins, January 17, 1885, Chicago, Burlington & Quincy Railroad Papers, Memoranda President's Office, 1878–1900, CBQ-3P4.92.

[116] Paul Black, "Robert Harris," p. 27.

Whereas, the Illinois Central Rail Road Company has agreed to pay the undersigned Mrs. Emma Leffingwell, widow of Frederick O. Leffingwell, her late husband, the sum of Three Hundred Dollars for the loss of Frederick O. Leffingwell her late husband from injuries sustained by him while in the employment of the said Company, upon their Rail Road, and resulting in his death.

And the undersigned Mrs. Leffingwell having agreed to accept the said sum of Three Hundred Dollars in full payment and satisfaction of all claims and demands for the said loss and injuries.

Now in consideration of the receipt of the said sum of money this day paid me by the said Illinois Rail Road Company the receipt whereof is hereby acknowledged, I the undersigned Emma Leffingwell have and hereby accept and receive the said sum of money in full satisfaction and discharge of the said Company from all claim and demand which I may or can have by reason of such loss and injuries. And I hereby release and discharge the said Company from all and every claim arising therefrom.[117]

The entire process of dispensing relief—who received grants and how much—was also fairly arbitrary. Robert Harris, in fact, argued that an absence of fixed rules and procedures should mark the process. "Avoid any particular practice lest it might become a common law," he warned the line's officials. If the men ascertained patterns and precedents, their claims would become more numerous and demanding.[118] On most roads the power to award gratuities was generally delegated to divisional superintendents. Settlements for less than $500 were made routinely without consulting central office executives. Small grants could even be made at the local level at the discretion of local foremen and supervisors.[119] Attitudes toward offering restitution, it should be pointed out, frequently changed. On the Illinois Central, for instance, in the 1870s a new administration, which looked with a jaundiced eye on corporate charity, ushered in a period of retrenchment. Financial awards, which once were fairly liberal,

[117] Waiver of Emma Leffingwell, November 13, 1858, Illinois Central Railroad Papers, IC-3.92.
[118] Robert Harris to H. Hitchcock, March 16, 1875, Chicago, Burlington & Quincy Railroad Papers, Harris Out-Letters, CBQ-3H4.1.
[119] Paul Black, "Development of Management Personnel Policies," p. 375.

were now considered only in cases where legal actions against the company seemed likely and potentially successful.[120]

An employee's previous standing in the firm, rather than his actual needs, appears to have played an important role in the decision process. A circular issued by the Louisville, New Orleans & Texas Railroad informed workers on that road that, while the company followed the practice of not awarding compensation, exceptions would be made based "on the circumstances of the case and previous good conduct."[121] A memorandum in the archives of the Baltimore & Ohio Railroad similarly indicates that officials were advised to judge the merits of a claim "on what the conduct of the party has been in reference to providence, ability displayed, courage and assertions for the interest of the Company."[122] Cases on the Illinois Central were often decided on whether the claimant was "deserving" or not.[123] The grade of an employee also figured in the size of the award. If a brakeman and a locomotive driver were both injured in an accident, it was not unusual for the engineer to receive a substantially greater gift.[124]

An injured railwayman or his widow could do little to insure corporate benevolence. Victims tried to help their cases by accompanying their claims with letters from clergymen and fellow townspeople attesting to their grievous circumstances.[125] Nothing was guaranteed. The unpredictable and discretionary nature of relief giving is revealed in the following letter of January 1873 from A. M. Mitchell, general superintendent of the Illinois Central, to I.C. President John Newell, describing how he settled two claims:

Some ten days since, O'Connor a brother of the Fireman that was killed by Engine No. 128 running (broken rail near Peotone February 5) asked

[120] Lightner, "Labor on the Illinois Central," pp. 187–188.

[121] Quoted in Clark, "Railroad Safety Movement," p. 11.

[122] H. Evan to James Howison, January 14, 1863, Baltimore & Ohio Railroad Letterbooks.

[123] Lightner, "Labor on the Illinois Central," p. 124.

[124] Minutes of directors' meetings, vol. 3, pp. 217–218, Boston & Worcester Railroad Papers.

[125] Theodore Snow to Western Railroad Company, July 20, 1850, Western Railroad Papers, case 3; petition to the directors of the Western Railroad on behalf of Mrs. Marcy, 1841, ibid., case 1.

what the company proposed to do in the way of settlement. I replied that it had been the custom of the company to meet surgical and burial expenses and in case a family or parents were in need made small donations. Some other conversation followed and he left saying he would call again. He called yesterday asked if the company were ready to settle. I asked him what terms a settlement was proposed. He stated the sum of $4000, the only proposition he had to make. I answered that it would not be accepted.

Shortly after he left Ed Davis the Engineer that run the Engine and whose ankle was badly broken called and asked to have a settlement of his case (previously he had been promised his pay as Engineer while off duty). I asked him what settlement he desired. He said if the company paid him $1000 for settlement for lost time and injury he would sign a release. I accepted the proposition and the money was paid him.[126]

American railway firms continued to dispense relief in an ad hoc discretionary fashion through the 1870s. While European railroads began establishing structured, inclusive insurance programs as early as mid-century, interest in and acceptance of such proposals came only very slowly in the American industry.[127] In 1889, the newly formed Interstate Commerce Commission found that of the top eighty-five companies operating in the country, only twelve had instituted some kind of formal insurance plan.[128]

Before the 1880s a few attempts were directed at establishing insurance programs, but they were either half-hearted, short-lived, or short-sighted. A constitution of the Boston & Worcester Railroad Mutual Benefit Association dated 1855 exists, but there is no evidence that the company-sponsored and managed society actually ever functioned.[129] Memoranda in the firm's archives, in fact, indicate that ten years later, in January 1865, the directors of the B. & W. considered the subject of insuring employees and tabled the matter indefinitely.[130] Herman Haupt, superintendent of the Pennsylvania Railroad, similarly spoke eloquently in the

[126] A. M. Mitchell to J. Newell, January 4, 1873, Illinois Central Railroad Papers, IC-1N6.3.

[127] Johnson, "Railway Departments," p. 70.

[128] *Third Annual Report of the Interstate Commerce Commission, December 1, 1889* (Washington, D. C., 1889), p. 342.

[129] *Constitution of the Boston & Worcester Railroad Mutual Benefit Association* (Worcester, Mass., 1855).

[130] Minutes of directors' meetings, vol. 8, p. 308, Boston & Worcester Railroad Papers.

1850s of the need for establishing relief programs, but it was only twenty-five years after his retirement from the line that the Pennsylvania took action on the issue.[131]

Robert Harris of the C.B. & Q. characteristically supported a variety of schemes. In 1868 he joined other Chicago railway executives in establishing the Provident Life Insurance and Investment Company. Harris's motives here were not wholly philanthropic. The association represented for him an attempt to counter the more corrupt private insurance companies in the field; he also hoped to entice C.B. & Q. engine drivers away from the newly formed Brotherhood of Locomotive Engineers, which had its own relief program. Harris's organization became insolvent within a year's time. In 1872 he then authorized agents of the Travelers Life and Accident Insurance Company to solicit business from Burlington employees and even arranged for automatic payroll deductions to be paid to the firm. This move effectively placed the Travelers Company in a privileged position, and hampered agents of other insurance groups. Finally, in 1873 Harris helped set up another company-sponsored relief plan, the Protective Association of the Employees of the C.B. & Q. and Leased Lines, but this effort, too, failed to achieve its intended goals.[132]

Illinois Central officials also experimented with various proposals. In the 1860s, the road established the Illinois Central Relief Club, a compulsory insurance program supported by deductions from wages amounting to one-half of one percent of monthly earnings. The funds were to be used to aid sick and injured men, help with funeral expenses, and make small contributions to the families of deceased employees. The plan sparked opposition from Illinois Central workers, who found the compulsory payments a hardship. The club was then transformed into a voluntary society and disappeared after four years of operation following losses in membership and declining financial reserves.[133]

---

[131] *Valedictory Address of the General Superintendent of the Pennsylvania Railroad to the Officers and Employees of the Company* (Philadelphia, 1859).

[132] Paul Black, "Development of Management Personnel Policies," pp. 388–389, 399.

[133] Lightner, "Labor on the Illinois Central," p. 128.

One successful experiment in the early period deserves mention. In 1869 the newly completed Central Pacific Railroad built the nation's first hospital devoted exclusively to the care of railwaymen. An absence of medical services in the region of the country served by the line provided the rationale behind the plan. The hospital was financed by employee contributions of fifty cents a month, automatically deducted from wages. Central men were entitled to free admission and medical attention at the hospital in cases of sickness or injury while in the service of the company. Retired employees were also eligible for treatment. The Central Pacific's Railroad Hospital served as a model for other companies in later years.[134]

In the late 1870s, interest in insurance programs intensified. In 1876 the Philadelphia & Reading Railroad Company established an accident and life insurance system for its workers and contributed an initial endowment of $25,000. Employees paid premiums based on grade of employment and wages. The benefits they received varied accordingly.[135] The railroad strikes of 1877 were, however, the precipitating force behind renewed concern for employee relief services. Railway executives began actively to look to insurance programs as a means of assuaging their growing disgruntled and rebellious employees.

Immediately following the violence of July and August 1877, officials of the Chicago, Burlington & Quincy, for instance, heatedly debated the issue in a flurry of interoffice memoranda. True to color, Vice President Perkins strongly opposed all insurance proposals. "Nothing would in my judgement do more to destroy in the end all zeal and esprit-de-corps than to adopt any plan of giving to our employees something for nothing." "Merit," he added, "and merit alone should be rewarded."[136] John Griswold, chairman of the board, truly frightened by the events of the summer, disagreed. We "had better be thinking it over," he wrote referring to a proposed insurance plan that the company would

[134] *Annual Report of the Board of Directors of the Central Pacific Railroad Company to the Stockholders* (Sacramento, Calif., 1873), p. 8; A. N. Towne to C. E. Perkins, January 30, 1880, Chicago, Burlington & Quincy Railroad Papers, Papers concerning Employees, 1877–1889, CBQ-33 1870 3.6.

[135] Circular of the Philadelphia & Reading Railroad Company, April 3, 1877, ibid.

[136] C. E. Perkins to R. Harris, December 7, 1877, ibid.

endow with a $100,000 contribution. "And I think without any undue haste that the sooner these plans are elaborated and adopted the better, in order to show the men that while we would not submit to their dictation we still have their interest at heart and are desirous of making them understand that the interests of the corporation and their own are mutual."[137] President Harris naturally concurred with Griswold's judgment, declaring again that a company-sponsored and managed program would be an effective means of luring trainmen from allegiance to their brotherhoods.[138] Divisions within the managerial ranks, however, led to inaction. No plan was adopted, and it took another disastrous and bitter strike eleven years later before C.B. & Q. officials moved to establish a comprehensive, permanent relief program.[139]

The violence of 1877 also caused concern among officials of the Illinois Central. In direct response, they formed the Illinois Central Railroad Mutual Benefit Association. The society, however, enrolled few employees and passed out of existence rather obscurely.[140] It remained, then, for the Baltimore & Ohio to initiate the most enduring and influential insurance program of all. Under John Garrett's leadership, the Baltimore and Ohio Employe's Relief Association was established in 1880. This plan was unique in that the B. & O. assumed all costs of administration. The company also donated a large initial endowment and made membership compulsory. B. & O. employees paid set monthly premiums equivalent to a day's wages and received fixed benefits commensurate with their contributions to the fund. They were covered for fifty-two weeks of sickness (indefinitely for recovery from accidents) and were eligible also for death benefits. Upon joining the plan, B. & O. employees agreed to the stipulation that acceptance of awards represented a waiver of the legal right to initiate damage suits, a feature of all early railroad company insurance programs. In its first year of operation, the B. &

---

[137] Cochran, *Railroad Leaders*, p. 344.

[138] Memorandum. Plan of a Life Insurance Fund and an Accident Insurance Fund, Chicago, Burlington & Quincy Railroad Papers, Papers Concerning Employees, 1877–1898, CBQ-33 1870 3.6.

[139] Stevenson, "Brotherhood of Locomotive Engineers," pp. 99–100.

[140] Lightner, "Labor on the Illinois Central," p. 141.

O. relief association processed 4,167 claims. It became the model for insurance systems established by other major trunk lines in succeeding years.[141]

On the whole, pioneer railwaymen were forced to fend for themselves. Many applied to private insurance companies for policies, but they were frequently turned down. One veteran engine driver from Chicago remembered being rejected by two commercial firms. "I did not receive a policy, simply because I was a Locomotive Engineer," he noted, "which they classed as 'extra hazardous.' "[142] Private insurance companies were also notoriously unreliable and often times fraudulent. They charged high premiums and increased them almost at will.[143] As Herbert Hamblen recalled, "On account of their hazardous calling," pioneer railwaymen were compelled to "carry all the life and accident insurance they are able to, at enormously heavy rates."[144]

Railway workers also turned toward cooperative self-help. In 1867, the newly formed Brotherhood of Locomotive Engineers set up the Locomotive Engineers' Mutual Life Insurance Association, which rendered needed assistance to disabled members and their widows and orphans.[145] Other brotherhoods that came into existence later followed suit and it can be assumed that pioneer railwaymen relied on community and ethnically based mutual aid societies as well. Railway workers also acted in less formal ways to extend charity. Despite opposition from management, they made a point of honoring their fellow workers by draping cars on the occasion of a death. More important, railwaymen at an early date established the custom of collecting contributions for sick, disabled, or killed comrades.[146] In Poughkeepsie, New York, for example, employees on the Hudson River Railroad traditionally raised more money among themselves for

[141] *First Annual Report of the Baltimore and Ohio Employes' Relief Association* (Baltimore, 1881), pp. 3, 10, 14–15, 77; Johnson, "Railway Departments," pp. 67–73.

[142] Quoted in Richardson, *Locomotive Engineer*, p. 132.

[143] Stevenson, "Brotherhood of Locomotive Engineers," p. 91. Lightner, "Labor on the Illinois Central," p. 128.

[144] Hamblen, *General Manager's Story*, pp. 220–221.

[145] Richardson, *Locomotive Engineer*, pp. 132–135.

[146] Robert Harris to H. Hitchcock, April 22, 1872, Chicago, Burlington & Quincy Railroad Papers, Harris Out-Letters, CBQ-3H4.1.

the city's St. Barnabas Hospital than was donated by their employer, Cornelius Vanderbilt.[147] The custom of informal mutual
assistance had its genesis in the very realities of the trade. As
Harry French in his reminiscence *Railroadman* recalled, "Reckless indeed was the worker who 'passed up the hat' when it was
offered; one never knew when it would be going around for him
or his widow."[148]

FOR THOSE who survived the ardors and perils of the work, old
age brought little comfort and little relief from the insecurities
and uncertainties of railway employment. The work could be as
erratic and unsure, the hours as long, and the tasks as risky for
old men as for young.

An informal seniority system, though, did emerge in the early
period. Managers rewarded veteran workers with choice assignments, placed older men in less demanding positions usually
without reductions in pay, and generally promoted them first in
good times and dismissed them last in periods of retrenchment.
Custom, however, marked the whole process, and seniority rights
depended totally on management's good will and grace. Pioneer
railwaymen obviously lost all such privileges when transferring
to new lines, and there were no guarantees that officials would
act consistently or indiscriminately.[149] Clearly defined and enforced seniority rights became an important early aim of organized railwaymen. With few exceptions, the first written agreements reached between managers and railway unions contain
seniority clauses. One can infer that the brotherhoods sought to
formalize and guarantee what had already been customary.[150]

American railroads not surprisingly also lagged far behind
their European counterparts in instituting formal pension plans.
In France, Germany, and England, carriers at an early date introduced superannuation funds to which both employees and

[147] Clyde and Sally Griffen, *Natives and Newcomers*, p. 221.
[148] Chauncey Del French, *Railroadman*, p. 195.
[149] Mater, "Development and Operation" pp. 393–403; Richardson, *Locomotive Engineer*, pp. 114–115.
[150] Mater, "Development and Operation," pp. 392–394; Richardson, *Locomotive Engineer*, pp. 104, 154, 228–229.

employers made contributions.[151] In America the idea was little discussed. Robert Harris as usual spoke in the 1870s of the moral responsibility of railroad companies to provide pensions, but he was a lone voice.[152] The Baltimore & Ohio Railroad did establish the nation's first railroad pension plan in 1884 as part of its overall relief program; it was not until the turn of the century, however, that other firms followed suit.[153]

The Baltimore & Ohio pension program fixed sixty-five as the age at which men, who had worked for the company for at least ten years, could retire and be eligible for benefits. B. & O. pensioners received relief in accordance with the grade of the last position they occupied and the number of years in service to the company. Awards varied from 20 to 35 percent of daily earnings when employed.[154] The real significance of the B. & O. plan lies in its establishing a definite date at which men could retire. For B. & O. employees a new stage of life was thus created, for there now existed a formal distinction between a man's working and postworking life. Before the 1880s, it is unclear exactly when and if railwaymen retired. In fact, the entire issue of when laboring people left the work force in the nineteenth century is itself very uncertain. Musing on this subject in December of 1877, Robert Harris concluded that there were actually very few old men in the trade. The number of railway workers who survived, succeeded and were promoted, and stuck to railroading was small. As he noted, "The charm of the life soon wears away [for young and middle-aged men] and they drift into other avocations before they get old."[155] Yet every pioneer railroad had its celebrated and honored old-timer, its Pop. And one can only assume that in the early years, these hearty souls toiled on the line quite literally to their dying days.

[151] Johnson, "Railway Departments," pp. 83–84; F. Jacqmin, *Railroad Employes in France*, p. 6.

[152] Paul Black, "Development of Management Personnel Policies," p. 361.

[153] Edward Hungerford, *The Story of the Baltimore and Ohio Railroad*, vol. 2, pp. 320–321; Holbrook, *Story of American Railroads*, p. 214.

[154] Johnson, "Railway Departments," pp. 85–86.

[155] Robert Harris to J. N. Griswold, December 10, 1877, Chicago, Burlington & Quincy Railroad Papers, Harris In-Letters, CBQ-31B1.5.

6

THE RAILWAYMEN: A SOCIAL PROFILE[1]

≡

FROM RECRUITMENT through promotion, old age, retirement, and death, the stages in the occupational life cycle of the first two generations of American railwaymen have been outlined. A focus on the work experience provides an extensive but incomplete portrait of the lives of these workers. Their social backgrounds and characteristics, their personal histories and private affairs have been touched upon and traced in passing. Here a direct attempt will be made to sketch in the details.

NINETEENTH-CENTURY railroad work was a world inhabited by men. Males comprised almost the entire work force of the nation's pioneer railroads, even in clerical positions that women came to occupy and dominate within the industry in the twentieth century. An occasional female employee can be found in early payroll records. Two women, out of a task force of 850, are listed in the accounts of the Hartford & New Haven Railroad in 1870: Mrs. Julia Sullivan, who assisted her husband, Michael, in cleaning cars (earning $3.50 a day between them), and Mrs. T. L. Hatch, who took care of the depot at Newington, Connecticut. For her efforts, she received seventy-five cents a day.[2]

---

[1] Much of the information contained in this chapter has been retrieved from the computer data bank of the Philadelphia Social History Project. I would like to thank the Project's director, Professor Theodore Hershberg of the University of Pennsylvania, for allowing me access to this information, and members of his staff for their kind assistance.

[2] Payroll Record, March 1870, Hartford & New Haven Railroad, New York,

One finds occasional mention of female employees in other sources as well. Herbert Hamblen in his reminiscence recalled an instance where the widow and children of a car repairer killed while in service were given employment in a car-cleaning gang.[3] Letters in the archives of the Delaware, Lackawanna & Western Railroad similarly reveal that George Button, a telegraph operator, was granted permission to license and employ his two sisters as operators. Button pleaded their case by noting that "little opportunity offers a lady for lucrative employment."[4] An article in the *American Engineer* in July of 1857 further indicates that black women in the South were commonly employed on southern railroads. "There is a colored woman on every passenger train," the report noted, "to carry water and wait on ladies, and who sells fruit to such as choose to buy."[5] Without further information it can only be assumed that these women were either hired or purchased slaves.

The issue of hiring women on a more formal basis was rarely discussed. To deal with the pressing problem of embezzlement, the railroad commissioners of Massachusetts in 1870 recommended an end to the collection of fares by conductors on trains, the building of more stations, and the hiring of women as clerks. As the commissioners noted, "The expense of employing ticketmasters in such stations could be obviated by selecting females for such duties."[6] There is no indication that railroad lines in the state followed this advice. It would not be until the turn of the century that rail companies began to staff their burgeoning, labor-saving-machine equipped offices with low-paid workers drawn from the nation's growing pool of women educated in high schools.[7]

New Haven & Hartford Railroad Papers, vol. 91, Baker Library, Harvard University.

[3] Herbert Hamblen, *The General Manager's Story*, p. 25.

[4] George Button to John Brisbin, February 13, 1865, Delaware, Lackawanna & Western Railroad Papers, Counsel's Letters, box 1, Syracuse University Library.

[5] *The American Engineer*, July 11, 1857, p. 6.

[6] *First Annual Report of the Massachusetts Board of Railroad Commissioners* (Boston, 1870), p. 64.

[7] Maurine Greenwald, "Women Workers and World War I," *Journal of Social History* 9:154–177.

Robert Harris of the Chicago, Burlington & Quincy not surprisingly was a lone innovator on the question of female labor. Harris, a champion of various reform causes, was somewhat of a feminist. He initiated, for instance, a secret policy of issuing half-fare tickets to women music teachers. It was "not on account of the particular vocation in which they were engaged," an aide to Harris explained, "but because so few avenues of support are open to women—and, for the most part, giving so little remuneration." "We favor the 'Women's Movement,' " he added, "to the extent of giving this slight advantage over the sterner sex."[8]

Harris backed his principles with even more definitive action. On December 3, 1869, Harris, with a good deal of fanfare, authorized the hiring of Miss Minnie Rockwell as a telegraph operator and clerk at the Burlington station in Earl, Illinois.[9] Miss Rockwell became the first female operating employee on the line. Her salary was fixed at $40.00 per month—double the ordinary amount for beginning station assistants—but her tenure was short-lived. Her supervisor, antagonistic to the experiment from the outset, complained immediately of her incompetence. He also noted that she was forever clamoring about the uncleanliness of the depot. Worst of all, Miss Rockwell had apparently become a curiosity, attracting the attention of a "rowdy element" who disrupted the running and routine of the station. Whether she quit or was fired is unclear, but by January 1870 Harris was looking for another female candidate to take her place.[10] Harris's experiments with hiring women were dropped when he left the C.B. & Q. and were not fully reinstituted by company executives until the late 1890s.

If railway work was a man's world, it was also a young man's world. Nearly half of the workers employed on the nation's early railroads were men in their twenties and early thirties.[11] The

[8] Paul Black, "The Development of Management Personnel Policies on the Burlington Railroad, 1860–1900" (Ph.D. dissertation, Univ. of Wisconsin, 1972), p. 248.

[9] Robert Harris to E. Gannon, December 9, 1869, Chicago, Burlington & Quincy Railroad Papers, Harris Out-Letters, CBQ-3H4.1, Newberry Library.

[10] Paul Black, "Development of Management Personnel Policies," pp. 248, 250.

[11] Age statistics are based on information drawn from the Philadelphia Social History Project data bank. The age profile of Philadelphia railwaymen should not be significantly different from workers in other parts of the country.

youthful age profile of the industry is not difficult to understand. A majority of railway workers occupied unskilled and semiskilled positions as trackmen, station hands, yard laborers, and brakemen. Carriers deliberately hired young men at low wages to staff these jobs. The trade necessarily had a youthful air.

Among the young men hired by the country's pioneer railroad companies were a sizable contingent of minors below the age of twenty-one. Child and teenage labor, however, never became as great an issue on the railroads as it did in the textile industry and mining. Early railroad managers actually held ambivalent attitudes on the question of employing youngsters. Some executives insisted that the grueling nature of the work required recruiting workers who were young and energetic and able to endure hard labor. In rejecting an application for employment on the grounds of age, John Garrett of the Baltimore & Ohio wrote to one job seeker that "our service requires, almost without exception, young men who can bear fatigue and exposure, and those who are older, who are especially experienced in railway affairs."[12] The managers of the Chicago, Burlington & Quincy Railroad, for similar reasons, adopted a strict policy of not hiring firemen over the age of twenty-five.[13]

Yet the employment of minors concealed potentially vexing problems. Newspaper reports of accidents detailing the gruesome injuries or fatalities of teenage employees did little to improve the already tarnished reputations of unpopular railroad companies. More important, under common law, firms could be held liable to claims by parents in cases of accidents to minors, especially if the young men were employed without parental consent. Losses of such suits forced companies to adopt strict policies restricting employment in train, station and yard service to no one under the age of twenty-one, and to no applicants below eighteen in the shops.[14] Shop hands between the ages of eighteen

[12] John Garrett to C. Billingsley, May 17, 1866, Baltimore & Ohio Letterbooks, Maryland Historical Society.

[13] Paul Black, "Development of Management Personnel Policies," p. 307.

[14] Ibid.; Erasmus Hudson to President and Directors of the Western Railroad Company, November 15, 1847, Western Railroad Papers, case 2, Baker Library; John Garrett to John Wilson, August 21, 1866, Baltimore & Ohio Railroad Letterbooks; Master of Transportation to J. W. Garrett, September 27, 1879, Baltimore & Ohio Railroad Papers, file 1559.

and twenty-one were usually enrolled in formal apprenticeship programs where parental approval was required.

While railroad executives guarded against the employment of minors, teenagers and even children could be found occupying positions in the trade throughout the early years. Census figures reveal that between 4 and 6 percent of the men engaged in the industry during the nineteenth century were below the age of twenty-one.[15] In fact, two-thirds of the 155 Illinois Central railwaymen, whose careers were examined earlier, began railroading in their minor years, one actually at the age of nine, two at twelve and thirteen, respectively, two at fourteen, and eight at fifteen.[16] Evidence from railroad reminiscences also confirms that it was not uncommon for males to enter the trade at rather young ages. Harry French, for example, began telegraphing at fourteen.[17]

French's career was unusual; most boys hired by pioneer railroads held menial positions at best. The Erie Railroad, for instance, employed youngsters as waterboys who went through the cars with long-spouted cans of water and glasses to serve thirsty passengers.[18] The New Albany & Salem line in Indiana also engaged trainboys. One of the first was W. W. Garrott, who made his initial run at the age of thirteen in 1856. He was responsible for lighting and tending stoves and lamps in the cars and for distributing fruit, candy, and newspapers, as well as fresh drinking water, to travelers. Garrott received no regular wage, but in his reminiscences he recalled making as much as $40 a month in tips and commissions.[19]

Newsbutchers were another integral part of the early railroading scene. These were young boys hired by franchised news agencies, not the lines themselves, to distribute papers, books, and refreshments on the trains. From railway folklore, it appears that the boys delighted in maintaining a notorious image. They were an unruly and rude lot, and many lines, like the Chicago, Burlington & Quincy, seriously considered terminating the prac-

[15] Philadelphia Social History Project data bank.
[16] Illinois Central Railroad, *History of the Illinois Central Railroad and Representative Employees.*
[17] Chauncey Del French, *Railroadman*, p. 32.
[18] Stewart Holbrook, *The Story of American Railroads*, p. 66.
[19] Ibid., pp. 115–116.

Drinking water was supplied to passengers in the early days of railroading from spouted kettles carried by waterboys and conductors. (Courtesy of United States Envelope Company, Paper Cup Division.)

tice of contracting out newspaper distribution. These companies decided to sell reading material and food directly to the traveling public and hire their own young vendors, who were to be placed under the watchful eye of train conductors.[20]

Most nineteenth-century rail lines also instituted formal apprenticeship programs in the shops and even in the depots. Robert Harris, for instance, arranged for teenage boys to learn telegraphy at local stations. A student paid for his education and, after a fixed period of training, he could be hired as a depot assistant.[21] An even more formal situation prevailed in the shops. A young man, typically fifteen years of age, would sign with his parents' consent a legal "Indenture of Apprenticeship," binding him to service for a fixed number of years, usually four to six, at a set minimum daily wage. In return, companies generally provided apprentices with room and board and the promise of instruction in "the Trade and Business."[22] Papers in the archives of the Baltimore & Ohio Railroad reveal that B. & O. officials were quite stringent in holding young men to their obligations.

[20] Ibid., chap. 35; Thomas Cochran, *Railroad Leaders, 1845–1890*, p. 440.
[21] Paul Black, "Development of Management Personnel Policies," p. 205.
[22] Examples of apprenticeship agreements can be found in the Illinois Central Railroad Papers, Historical Items, IC-3.6, box 1A, Newberry Library.

They resorted to legal action to return runaways and generally insisted that full terms of apprenticeship be served.[23] It is also interesting to note that several southern rail lines in the antebellum period established formal shop apprenticeship programs as part of long-range plans to form a corps of white workers, particularly among machinists and firemen.[24]

Finally, no account of child labor on the railroads would be complete without mention of the ubiquitous callboys—youngsters usually below the age of ten—hired to notify trainmen that they were on call.[25] The trick of their trade was to learn which workers frequented which saloons and how to wake a man up at his home as gently as possible. Callboys became the source of many legends; from callboy to company president was the railroads' version of the rags-to-riches myth of nineteenth-century America.

Young men dominated the trade, but they, of course, did not comprise the entire work corps of the nation's early railroads. The occupational hierarchy of the industry represented an age hierarchy as well, as has been shown earlier. Upper-grade, skilled and high-paying positions generally were occupied by experienced men in their forties and fifties. Some young people rose extremely quickly, older employees could be found in lesser posts—especially among discriminated groups, like blacks and the Irish—and in frontier areas all posts tended to be held by younger men; yet, the positive relationship between age and grade of employ remained fairly constant.

Every line was also graced by a cadre of old-timers, the Pops, who labored to their dying days and cultivated their own reputations. Their numbers, too, were not inconsequential. Railway workers over the age of sixty-five represented close to 3 percent of the total during the early years.[26] These veterans served an important function in providing a link to past traditions and

[23] J. C. Davis to J. W. Garrett, September 6, 1860, Baltimore & Ohio Railroad Papers, file 4304.

[24] *Colburn's Railroad Advocate*, January 5, 1856, p. 3; *Semi-Annual Report of the Directors of the South Carolina Canal and Rail-Road Company* (Charleston, S. C., 1834), p. 5.

[25] Holbrook, *Story of American Railroads*, p. 266.

[26] Philadelphia Social History Project data bank.

transferring to the younger majority of men a sense of the dignity of their trade.

THE YOUNG MEN hired by the nation's first railroads came from a variety of social backgrounds, although an agrarian heritage was most common. Close to 40 percent of the Illinois Central railwaymen listing their fathers' occupations were sons of farmers. Of the rest, 28 percent were sons of unskilled or skilled workmen, 18 percent of businessmen, 16 percent of railwaymen, and 4 percent of professionals.[27] The group is probably atypical and overrepresentative in their upper-status origins. What can be inferred, though, is that a majority of early railwaymen came from farm families. Certainly in rural areas, it was not unusual for the sons of farmers to work part-time, or even full-time, for the railroads in hopes of accumulating sufficient savings to purchase their own homesteads.[28] The portrait presented in many nineteenth-century reminiscences of the orphaned teenager leaving the family farm in search of fortune and adventure on the railroads holds more than a grain of truth.[29] Once hired, as mentioned earlier, a worker's socioeconomic background appears to have been an important factor in rising quickly through the ranks, with men from loftier origins faring better. However, having a father in the trade did not necessarily guarantee one's future success.

The ethnic composition of America's first generations of railroad employees was as varied as their social backgrounds. Region played an important role here. The names listed in payroll records for early New England rail lines, for instance, especially among lower-grade workers, are predominately Irish in character. Germanic surnames similarly outweigh others in midwestern railroad account books. In the South, during the antebellum period, blacks, mainly hired and purchased slaves, comprised the vast bulk of the work force. Time period is also a consideration when

[27] Illinois Central Railroad, *History of the Illinois Central Railroad and Representative Employees.*

[28] James Ducker, "Men of the Steel Rails" (Ph.D. dissertation, Univ. of Illinois at Urbana–Champaign, 1980), pp. 124–126.

[29] Charles George, *Forty Years on the Rail*, p. 17.

analyzing ethnicity. Most of the nation's original corps of enginemen were of English descent, having immigrated to the United States with English-built locomotives.

Native-born white Americans, however, generally dominated the trade in both absolute terms and status during the early years. In Philadelphia between 1860 and 1880, roughly 80 percent of the railwaymen living in the city were white males of native ancestry, a figure entirely disproportionate to their numbers in the population at large. Irish immigrants accounted for approximately 15 percent of all rail workers, German arrivals for 3 percent, and black Americans for less than 1 percent. In the same time period, whites born in the United States were but 50 percent of the population in the city; Irish-born, 25 percent; German-born, 13 percent; and blacks, 5 percent. So overwhelming was the presence of native whites in the railway industry in Philadelphia that in only two other trades in the city—printing and bricklaying—did they represent as large a proportion of the work force (while in an immigrant-dominated industry like shoemaking, old-stock Americans composed only 46 percent of the total).[30] Philadelphia may represent an anomalous case, but little evidence exists to indicate that the native white presence was less pervasive elsewhere.

White males born on these shores also dominated the social hierarchy of railroad work. In 1880, for example, while 20 percent of the native whites held jobs as general laborers in Philadelphia, 48 percent of the Irish, 60 percent of the Germans, and 93 percent of the blacks were similarly engaged. Conversely, close to 40 percent of the old-stock Americans occupied white-collar supervisory and clerical posts, while less than one-quarter of the Irish, 18 percent of the German, and none of the blacks were so advantaged. A strong association between ethnicity and occupational position clearly existed in the early years of the industry.

A few qualifications are in order. An exact correspondence between ethnic affiliation and grade level did not prevail. Native white Americans occupied positions on the lower rungs of the

---

[30] Figures on ethnicity for Philadelphia railwaymen are provided in table G.1 included in appendix G. A methodological note accompanies the table.

railway occupational scale and men of Irish descent presided over top echelon positions as well. More important, by 1880 the social structure of the industry had become less rigid. Railwaymen of Irish and German heritage were now holding upper and lower management spots in nearly the same proportions as their native white counterparts, and second generation immigrants were experiencing greater success in the trade than their ethnic kinsmen born in the Old World.[31] The lessening influence of ethnicity is also manifest in the careers of Illinois Central employees, for ethnic identity proved a poor predictor of their ability to rise with dispatch through the hierarchy. The railroad industry, in fact, proved a boon to many immigrant groups, particularly the Irish. Between 1830 and 1880, the trade expanded rapidly and genuine and growing employment and promotion opportunities materialized for both native and foreign-born Americans, with one great proviso: that one's skin color was white.

The almost total exclusion of blacks in the northern part of the railway industry during the mid-nineteenth century, even in the most menial of positions, is striking. In the 1860 census for the city of Philadelphia, not a single black male is listed as holding a position in the railroad trade. In 1870 only twelve men are so designated; in 1880, thirteen. While black Americans represented more than 4 percent of the city's total work force, they accounted for less than 1 percent of the railwaymen working and residing in Philadelphia.[32]

There is also an almost complete absence of mention of blacks in the northern industry in corporate records, railway trade papers, or reminiscences. An occasional reference can be found. In the 1840s, the Philadelphia & Columbia Railroad employed Sam Jones as a baggageman. He was thought to be the first black to be hired by a Pennsylvania company.[33] From travelers' accounts, it appears that the New York Central employed black baggage-

[31] See table G.2 in appendix G.

[32] A similar situation prevailed in towns where workers from the Atchison, Topeka & Santa Fe Railroad resided. See Ducker, "Men of the Steel Rails," p. 162.

[33] Charles F. Carter, *When Railroads Were New*, pp. 124–125.

men at stations and black porters on sleeping cars.[34] George Pullman, of course, began hiring ex-slaves as Pullman porters and conductors in the late 1860s, though they remained totally under the hire, management, and pay of Pullman officials.[35] Aside from these examples, indications are that blacks were not employed on northern lines; they were not hired on the Chicago, Burlington & Quincy, nor on the northern division of the Illinois Central.[36] Railroad companies servicing Philadelphia apparently did not make a practice of giving employment to blacks either.[37] Although no one discussed the issue or articulated reasons for the absence of blacks, it is probably safe to assume that racial discrimination in the North, pure and simple, was the root of the problem.

An opposite situation for blacks prevailed in the South, especially before the Civil War. In the antebellum period, blacks manned the southern railroads. They comprised almost the entire core work force of station, yard, and track laborers, as well as brakemen, firemen and shop mechanics. There is evidence that black slaves even drove trains, though that was strictly prohibited by state laws.[38] Whites, of course, occupied all managerial and clerical positions, as well as conductorships. After emancipation, blacks in the South were relegated to low level positions as porters and laborers, a process hastened by the discriminatory policies of the all-white railway brotherhoods.[39] The railway industry provides a case in point where blacks under slavery attained

[34] Alvin Harlow, *The Road of the Century*, p. 153.

[35] Holbrook, *Story of American Railroads*, pp. 321–330.

[36] Paul Black, "Development of Management Personnel Policies," p. 253; David Lightner, "Labor on the Illinois Central Railroad, 1852-1900" (Ph.D. dissertation, Cornell Univ., 1969), pp. 227–228.

[37] More blacks may have worked for railroads in Philadelphia than the census figures imply. Blacks hired by railroads in the city may have listed their occupation simply as "laborer" and not "railroad laborer"—making a precise accounting impossible. Still, this problem should effect the results compiled for other ethnic groups in a fairly similar fashion. The almost complete absence of blacks with any titles in the railroad industry is still striking.

[38] Robert C. Black III, *The Railroads of the Confederacy*, p. 30; *Articles and Charters of the Chesapeake, Ohio and Southwestern R. R. Co.* (Louisville, Kentucky, n.d.), p. 75; *American Engineer*, July 25, 1857, p. 20.

[39] Reed Richardson, *The Locomotive Engineer*, p. 189; see also Hugh Hammett, "Labor and Race," *Labor History* 16:470–484.

and occupied skilled positions denied to them as freedmen. In the twentieth century, black participation in the trade would increase both in the North and South, but only recently under fair employment standards.[40]

Finally, from whatever social or ethnic background, few railwaymen in the early years entered the trade with the benefits of formal education. Attendance at school is one aspect of childhood and adolescence that is rarely mentioned in nineteenth-century reminiscences. Of the men included in the Illinois Central Railroad's biographical compendium, moreover, only one-fourth reported any schooling. Of these, 47 percent had completed grade school; 42 percent, high school; and 11 percent, college. With the exception of I.C. conductors, level of educational attainment did not prove an advantage in career advancement.

The general lack of schooling is reflected in the low recorded literacy rates for the first two generations of American railwaymen. Half of the men signing payroll vouchers on the Hartford & New Haven Railroad in April 1868 did so with an "X."[41] A study conducted on the Chicago, Burlington & Quincy Railroad in 1871 similarly indicated that more than a third of the line's engineers could not read their train orders at all.[42] The railroad industry developed during the nineteenth century without great reliance on the concurrent expansion of public school education.

ANY COMMENTARY on the personal lives of mid-nineteenth century railwaymen runs the risk of unwarranted generalization. Surviving evidence is much too scarce, scattered, and without pattern. For every pioneer railwayman who carefully fashioned the image of "boomer" or roustabout, there were others who righteously maintained the honor of the profession. These workers garnered reputations as respectable family men, home owners, and worthy members of their communities.

In an attempt to mold a stable, diligent, and loyal work force,

[40] Howard W. Risher, Jr., *The Negro in the Railroad Industry*, chaps. 5–6.
[41] Payroll Record, April 1868, Hartford & New Haven Railroad, New York, New Haven and Hartford Railroad Papers, vol. 91.
[42] Paul Black, "Robert Harris and the Problem of Railway Labor Management" (unpublished paper in author's possession), p. 12.

railway lines generally favored married men in hiring and promotions.[43] Only in a few instances, where conditions were particularly rustic or primitive, did companies adopt policies which
placed single men at an advantage.[44] Available statistical materials indicate that railway workers married and formed families
in proportions similar to the population at large.[45]

Railroad work, however, did prove disruptive of normal family
life. Men frequently were on the road for long periods of time
and away from home. When employment was uncertain or irregular they also often left their families in search of new opportunities. In the West, it was not uncommon for married men
to live in boardinghouses temporarily before sending for their
wives and children in hopes of settling permanently.[46] Forced
tranfers could then necessitate further moves.

The lure of railroading, too, created conflicts with family ties.
Many a pioneer railway worker preferred to spend his leisure
hours not at home, but rather at the roundhouse polishing his
engine, or at the depot, or the local railwaymen's saloon ex-
changing tales and enjoying the company of his comrades. Family
crisis is a constant theme in nineteenth-century railway reminiscences. Herbert Hamblen left his home several times to take new
positions, his family joining him months later.[47] Hamblen's career in railroading was so varied, extensive, and preoccupying
that he had little time to enjoy the comforts of home and family
life. Harvey Reed also frequently traveled in search of employment, leaving his family behind. At one point he was blacklisted
for his trade union activity and had no alternative but to move.[48]

[43] Herman Haupt to J. E. Thomson, August 5, 1852, Herman Haupt Letterbook, Historical Society of Pennsylvania; Thatcher Perkins to J. W. Garrett, July
20, 1865, Baltimore & Ohio Railroad Papers, file 468.

[44] Paul Black, "Development of Management Personnel Policies," p. 206; Paul
Black, "Robert Harris," p. 9.

[45] Eighty percent of the sample of Illinois Central employees were married,
while close to 60 percent of the railwaymen residing in Philadelphia in 1880
were listed in the manuscript census as married. The latter figure corresponds
to the percentage married for Philadelphia's adult population at large. Figures
compiled from the Philadelphia Social History Project data bank.

[46] Ducker, "Men of the Steel Rails," p. 161.

[47] Hamblen, *General Manager's Story*, pp. 285, 292, 300.

[48] J. Harvey Reed, *Forty Years a Locomotive Engineer*, pp. 39, 43.

A roundhouse in Norwalk, Ohio, in the late nineteenth century. The roundhouse was a place of work and social interaction. (Courtesy of Association of American Railroads.)

The most poignant tale is told by Harry French. After he became a passenger conductor, Harry married his sweetheart, Molly. They then bought a home and established themselves as respectable members of their community. This life, however, soon proved too sedentary for "boomer" Harry, and, after much quarreling and bickering, he persuaded Molly to move West. There railroading was as wild and woolly as it once had been in the East. Molly, who had aspirations of becoming an actress, never happily adjusted to her new circumstances. She particularly objected to Harry's incessant drinking and smoking and to his rude friends. During one of his frequent long-term jaunts, job-hopping from line to line much like a hobo, Molly fell in love with a lodger in their home. Harry returned and, after a period of turbulence, they agreed to a divorce. Harry later remarried, but his habits did not change. His second wife, however, proved more tolerant of his railroading mania.[49]

There is no means to gauge accurately the extent to which the

[49] French, *Railroadman*, pp. 60–61, 82, 87, 101, 104, 124, 128.

occupation had a disruptive influence on family life. Reliable divorce or separation statistics listed by occupation are non-existent for the period under study. Mid-nineteenth-century railway reminiscences, and simple intuition, suggest that the work was not conducive to "normal" family relations. This is borne out in contemporary studies. The sociologist William Cottrell has written extensively on the subject. The "place relationships of railroaders are always in flux," Cottrell found from his interviews and observations. "The influence of institutions which mold and form character, that serve to give stability to personality, that provide the nexus between person and locality are continually broken by their movement. The creation of the family is delayed, and its formation altered by reason of long periods of shifts in location." "The pattern of social relationships set by the occupation," Cottrell specifically concluded, "prevents normal relationships between wife and husband, father and child."[50]

The personal dilemmas that Cottrell depicted for modern-day railwaymen are echoed in the reminiscences of their pioneer forebears, in the repeated references to moving, time demands, family crises, and the hold that the work had on the men's fancies. Certainly, not all railwaymen faced unfortunate family situations. Stable family relationships, given the nature of the work, were just particularly difficult to establish and maintain.

The work also tended to foster social isolation. Forced by company decree or sheer necessity to live near stations, shops and engine houses, railwaymen often resided in segregated communities near their work. Physical separation and the transient and time-consuming nature of the work limited contact and involvement with the larger community. Cottrell notes the problem for twentieth-century railway workers and its consequences. "Contacts with the church and the school are transitory," for families of railwaymen. "Membership in other place groups, such as fraternal or recreational organizations, is made difficult. Participation in government and the community is made purely secular and pecuniary." As a result, Cottrell concluded, "Status is more and more dependent upon a financial rating."[51]

[50] William Cottrell, *The Railroader*, pp. 59, 76.
[51] Ibid.

Writing in the nineteenth century, pioneer railwayman Herbert Hamblen described the same process but in less academic terms. The dimensions of the problem and its consequences are remarkably similar.

From the very nature of their employment, railwaymen and their families are usually compelled to live isolated from the general community, near the roundhouses, shops and yards where they are employed. Being steady, hard-working men, with tolerably regular incomes, and the hope of permanent employment and promotion, they are induced to mortgage their salaries for years in advance to build homes for themselves and families. . . .[52]

Hamblen's comments are telling, especially on the personal and social quandaries of the railroad life. His portrait, however, fits most but not all nineteenth-century railwaymen. Railroad workers living in small-to-medium size railway-shop and crossroads towns generally resided in isolated and segregated parts of their communities.[53] In large, sprawling, economically diverse cities, railwaymen neither formed, or were forced to form, easily identifiable enclaves. In nineteenth-century Philadelphia, for example, railroad workers never clustered residentially as a group or by specific occupation or even by ethnicity. They blended unobtrusively into the urban landscape.[54]

The problem of meeting mortgage payments is also overemphasized by Hamblen. Only a minority of railwaymen in the nineteenth century achieved the benefits of home ownership. Supervisors and upper-grade employees, as well as older workers in general, owned homes to a greater extent than the mass of younger, lesser skilled and lower paid workers.[55] There was one notable exception. Permanence of position and residence greatly influenced the chances for proprietorship. Stably situated shop-

[52] Hamblen, *General Manager's Story*, pp. 220–221.

[53] Ducker, "Men of the Steel Rails," p. 155.

[54] Computer mappings of railwaymen in Philadelphia by place of residence revealed no significant clusters, with one exception of Irish-born laborers. Otherwise railway workers distributed themselves throughout the city. This finding is displayed in statistical form in table G.3 in appendix G.

[55] Statistics on home ownership for Philadelphia railwaymen in the late nineteenth century can be found in table G.4 in appendix G. A methodological note is included.

men were more likely to be home owners than the more aris-
tocratic conductors and locomotivemen, whose frequent transfers and moves forced them into the renter class. What they lost
in real property, however, they made up in personal holdings.
Census enumerators invariably found the personal wealth of
trainmen to be greater than their real worth and greater than
the personal property holdings of other railway workers.[56] Type
of work in the trade effected in this way the individual investment
and spending patterns of early railwaymen.

Railroad work, finally, did not absolutely preclude involvement in the associational and civic life of the communities in
which railwaymen resided. Workers joined local clubs and societies when possible. They also fraternized with nonrailway people, but usually with fellow town members of similar estate and
status.[57] A conductor might join a local lodge of the Masons, an
association not readily joined by trackmen or station porters.

Railroad workers also participated in local politics—rarely,
however, as a group. Of the Illinois Central men reporting their
political affiliation, there was an even division between Democrats and Republicans, with a smattering of independents. Nineteenth-century railroad executives actually took an interest in
the political sentiments of their employees. In 1880 Henry Broadholst Ledyard, general manager of the Michigan Central, wrote
a memorandum asking supervisors of workers living in the town
of Niles to stress to their men the importance of the defeat of a
local bond issue which did not favor the line.[58] Officials on the
Northern Pacific in the early 1880s similarly discussed supporting
the campaign of an employee who was running for a local office,
although they feared that his loss might be interpreted as a rebuff
of company policies.[59]

Other lines, however, took strong stands against interfering
in the political affairs of their workers. After receiving complaints

[56] Statistics on personal wealth for railwaymen in the city of Philadelphia in
the late nineteenth century can be found in table G.5 in appendix G. On the
differences in real and personal property holdings of conductors and locomotivemen, also see Ducker, "Men of the Steel Rails," pp. 170–171.

[57] Ducker, "Men of the Steel Rails," pp. 180–183.

[58] Quoted in Cochran, Railroad Leaders, p. 381.

[59] Ibid., p. 421.

from both political parties that supervisors were coercing men to vote in certain ways, managers of the Erie in 1876 released a firmly worded order prohibiting such practices.[60] During the late 1850s, the Illinois Central tried to impress upon its workers that on the job they owed their loyalties solely to the company, and that party or sectional feelings could not be allowed to interrupt the smooth running on the road.[61] During the 1860s and 1870s, the I.C. also took a strong stand against officials influencing employees on political matters; however, in 1896 the company actively encouraged workers to oppose William Jennings Bryan.[62]

Railroad workers did not begin to act on political matters in a concerted way until late in the century. They mobilized collectively to seek legislation specifically aiding them on hours of work and conditions of safety. As a group, railwaymen also apparently opposed various populist party candidates; they viewed populist calls for the regulation of railroad shipping rates as a potential threat to their incomes.[63] For the most part, however, railwaymen in the nineteenth century never formed what can be deemed a cohesive or definitive political voting bloc.

The pattern of social life thus varied. Some railroaders lived as boomers, others not; some resided in isolated communities, others in variegated towns and cities; some were able to fashion stable family ties, others encountered numerous obstacles; some became involved in activities within their communities, many found it impossible given the nature of the work. Through the welter of experience, though, one characteristic remains common. Whatever the individual differences, the social lives of mid-nineteenth-century American railway workers revolved around each other. A closely knit social world existed among railwaymen, even when their forged bonds were not reinforced by physical proximity.

[60] Receiver's Order, no. 12, Erie Railroad Company Papers, Letterbook of Incoming Correspondence and Miscellany, Syracuse University Library.

[61] J. C. Clarke to Phineas Pease, March 20, 1857, Illinois Central Railroad Papers, J. C. Clarke Out-Letters, IC-1C5.1.

[62] Lightner, "Labor on the Illinois Central," p. 328.

[63] On the political activity of railwaymen in the late nineteenth century, see Ducker, "Men of the Steel Rails," chapter 6.

The camaraderie of work extended to off the job. Railwaymen socialized primarily with other railwaymen. Social relations, however, were structured by the work itself, for railwaymen generally fraternized with workers in the same branches of the trade. Some men actually had few alternatives. Maintenance-of-the-way crews lived together out on the road, often in homes of their section bosses. They comprised a strange mixture of young immigrants, farm boys, and college men seeking respite from the boredom of study in the romance of hard labor. Trackmen were invariably bachelors who lived, worked, drank, and caroused together in the absence of other company. They also developed their own language and attitudes toward their duties. "Section men are not supposed to work," was a favorite refrain of pioneer track walkers.[64]

For similar reasons, shopmen also formed distinct social groupings. They usually lived in small, isolated rural shop towns and fraternized among themselves accordingly. Many nineteenth-century companies deliberately fostered their isolation. These lines located shop facilities in the pristine countryside to keep shop workers from the corrupting influence of the more rambunctious and, not incidentally, better-organized trainmen. Companies endeavored especially to limit contact between shop crews and the independent-minded aristocrats of the trade, the locomotive drivers.[65]

Among trainmen a different situation prevailed. Alternatives existed, but through a conscious process of selection and rejection, engineers, conductors, brakemen, and firemen formed social ties within their own grades which were based on shared work and career experiences. This process reinforced the craft distinctions created, maintained, and encouraged by railroad managers.

Engine drivers established their own social world, complete with singular customs and traditions and a developed argot. Firemen were allowed entry into this private universe, but only as junior members. Cabmen accordingly spent a good portion of their leisure hours in each other's company. They exchanged

[64] Richard Reinhardt, ed., *Workin' on the Railroad*, pp. 209–210.
[65] Ibid., p. 140; Carter, *When Railroads Were New*, p. 125.

visits at their homes with their wives and children and attended special dinners and outings together; there were also the countless hours either consumed at the roundhouse passing information and telling tales or in reveling at their favorite saloons and poolhalls.[66] Every railway town and city, in fact, had its well-known haunts that were the exclusive domain of engine drivers and their assistants. Herbert Hamblen recalled even being denied a room at a boardinghouse which catered solely to engineers and firemen. He was a lowly brakeman at the time. As he noted: "Thus I took my first lesson in railroad caste, and it was thoroughly impressed on both my mental and physical person."[67]

Enginemen and firemen formed close but potentially factious ties. They worked together as a team and the master-apprenticeship relationship strengthened the link. Veteran drivers thus often recalled with great affection the first enginemen they fired for. James Chadbourne, for instance, fondly remembered getting up at the break of day as a young fireman to make up his train and prepare the engine for his fatherly mentor who came late to work because he helped his handicapped wife in the mornings.[68] In some instances, despite their age and skill gaps, drivers and firemen even established closer bonds than they did with their own peers. Cabmen on unscheduled, long-haul, night freight runs shared more in common with each other than they did with their usually older, more stable and conservative counterparts in passenger service.[69] Relations, however, were certainly not always saccharine and frictionless. Some notoriously tyrannical drivers treated their firemen more like slaves than apprentices, and they were remembered accordingly. In bad times, especially, relations easily soured. When companies announced cutbacks during periods of retrenchment, it became a serious matter whether enginemen were to be laid off or demoted, thereby replacing the now endangered firemen. This festering issue, among others, was

[66] Lawrence Doherty, "The Wheeler Station," *The Railway and Locomotive Historical Society Bulletin*, no. 49, p. 93.

[67] Hamblen, *General Manager's Story*, p. 30.

[68] James Chadbourne, "Recollections," *Railway and Locomotive Historical Society Bulletin*, no. 4, pp. 15–16.

[69] Hamblen, *General Manager's Story*, pp. 214–215.

responsible for the creation of separate craft unions among locomotive engineers and firemen.

Pioneer train conductors established their own social nexus. Rail transport, in fact, had hardly been in its infancy when the nation's conductors fashioned a distinctive manner and dress. Adorned in top coats and fine silk hats, ever tending to the comfort of their passengers, and wary of insubordination in the ranks, they appeared the epitome of taste and responsibility.[70] There was a certain amusing hypocrisy to their pose: though it was public knowledge that embezzlement of fares was common, early conductors oozed with respectability. Through their shared values and work and career experiences, they also identified with each other and formed close friendships. In his reminiscence, Charles George recalled organizing a dance in 1850 for conductors from the New York Central, Vermont Central, Rutland & Burlington, and Hudson River Railroads.[71] Occupational grade allegiances, here, clearly outweighed company ties. George more readily fraternized with conductors from other lines than he did with workers in other grades in his own company. When George later moved to Chicago, he had little trouble discovering the favorite meeting places of conductors and established his first acquaintances with men of his own grade.[72]

The conductors' apprentices—railway brakemen—were not welcomed into the fraternity of their masters, even as junior partners. Their youth, bachelor status, income, general rowdiness, and most important, the perils of their labor, set them apart from all other railwaymen. The brakemen, to be accurate, also set themselves apart and formed their own social communities based largely on a shared sense of their own daring and do. Brakemen stayed in the same cheap boardinghouses and caroused together at the same bars and brothels.

Divisions within the work place thus became divisions outside of work. Railwaymen fraternized primarily with other railwaymen, and especially with workers in the same grade of employment. There was, of course, nothing inevitable about this. Lasting

[70] George, *Forty Years on the Rail*, pp. 37–38.
[71] Ibid., p. 64.
[72] Ibid., pp. 183–184.

friendships were formed with men not in the trade; similarly, and with one important exception, workers did socialize with men in other branches of the industry.

The exception is an interesting one. From the earliest days of train travel, relations between conductors and engineers remained bitter and hostile. Pioneer conductors and drivers vied for the right to be deemed proper captains of their charge. For various reasons, they also developed fairly discordant manners, bearings, and conceptions of the dignity of their respective functions. The hardy, dauntless enginemen considered the farcically adorned, posturing conductors to be dandies at best. The custom thus immediately emerged that the cab was off bounds to them. The proud and dignified conductors, for their part, judged the drivers to be but a coarse and uncultured lot. Matters were not enhanced by company officials, who insisted that these rivals for respect and fame spy and report on each other.[73]

The animosity became the stuff of legends. The most frequently recounted tale deserves telling. Whether the incident actually occurred, of course, is beside the point. Apparently in 1842, one Ebenezer Ayres, a conductor on the New York & Erie Railroad, contrived a primitive signal system connecting the coaches with the engine by stretching a rope over the top of the cars to the cab and tying a block of wood to the engine. Ayres then explained to his driver, Abraham Hammil, that, when he wanted the train stopped, he would tug the rope, and the jiggling wood block would be a signal for Hammil to blow the whistle for "down brakes" and to cut the steam. Hammil, however, refused even to entertain the thought of having his authority usurped and proceeded to dismantle Ayres's primitive signal system. Ayres then repaired the rope, which Hammil once again cut. The dispute was finally resolved in an epic fast and furious fisticuff, which Ayres won. Legend holds that his victory established for all time the conductor's supremacy on the train.[74]

Whatever the actual relations, railwaymen shared a rich informal and formal associational life together in their off hours.

[73] *Colburn's Railroad Advocate*, December 22, 1855, p. 3; Edward Hungerford, *The Story of the Baltimore and Ohio Railroad, 1827-1927*, vol. 1, p. 48.
[74] Hank Bowman, *Pioneer Railroads*, pp. 70-71.

Two conductors on the New York Central Railroad. The photograph was taken in 1864. (Reprinted from Hank Bowman, *Pioneer Railroads*, New York, 1954.)

While much leisure time was actually spent conversing at depots, roundhouses, and shops, the center of social activity was the saloon. Drink and drinking were basic ingredients in the diets and lives of pioneer railwaymen. Just as the nature of their work cannot be fully appreciated without considering the perils of their labor and the inescapable reality of accidental injuries and death, the work of nineteenth-century railway workers is equally incomprehensible without understanding the ever present importance and role of alcohol.

Pioneer railwaymen are the best spokesmen on the subject. Harry French remembered that be began drinking hard liquor at the age of fifteen when he was a telegraph operator. He started on this lifelong habit, as he recalled, because "all railroad men drank."[75] In 1910 William Lynch, a veteran driver on the Nashville, Chattanooga & St. Louis Railroad, similarly reminisced:

[75] French, *Railroadman*, p. 12.

HARPER'S WEEKLY.

JOURNAL OF CIVILIZATION

Vol. XVII—No. 854.]   NEW YORK, SATURDAY, MAY 10, 1873.   [WITH A SUPPLEMENT. PRICE TEN CENTS.

Entered according to Act of Congress, in the Year 1873, by Harper & Brothers, in the Office of the Librarian of Congress, at Washington.

A gallant engine driver and his fireman depicted on the front
cover of *Harper's Weekly*, May 10, 1873.

Many changes have taken place on the road in the last 54 years. In former times the first place to go after putting away the train was to the saloon and tank up on booze and play cards, get drunk and fight. But now we hardly ever hear of a railroadman getting drunk. They all seem to be sober and perfect gentlemen.

Lynch even recalled an instance where the use of alcohol was required:

In earlier days there was much said in regard to the use of whiskey and sometimes it was forced on us in place of water. In 1854 a bad Cholera epidemic was raging in Nashville and when we roustabouts had nothing else to do we had to work in the freight house and were not allowed to drink water but instead a bucket of French brandy and a tin dipper were at each door and we had to drink that or nothing.[76]

Drinking provided the railwaymen with both an escape and a community. The case for understanding the intemperate ways of the nation's pioneer task force of railway workers was most aptly presented by an anonymous railwayman writing in the *Locomotive Engineer's Journal* in 1869. "Inured to danger," he wrote, early railwaymen "instinctively cultivate a disposition for reckless and excitable habits. During their trips, the fever of excitement was kept up by the influence of strong drink; and many a man had gained the reputation of being a swift runner and making almost impossible time when he was half drunk." Afterwards, "they would congregate in grogshops and beer saloons to recount over their wonderful adventures on the road." The anonymous correspondent then offered an ultimate explanation for their insobriety. Railwaymen "would drink to soothe their grievances and demonstrate mutual sympathy; drink evil and bad luck to some obnoxious and tyrannical official and drink long life and continued prosperity to themselves."[77]

Railroad workers also engaged in more formal and orthodox associational activities. Railwaymen on the Chicago, Burlington & Quincy, for instance, in 1859 inaugurated the first annual

[76] Quoted from Jesse C. Burt, Jr., "The Savor of Old-Time Southern Railroading," *Railway and Locomotive Historical Society Bulletin*, no. 84, pp. 38–39.

[77] *Locomotive Engineer's Journal*, September 1869, p. 403.

employees' ball.[78] On other lines, workers helped establish rail-waymen's libraries, social halls, buying cooperatives, and burial societies.[79] Many of these ventures were only short-lived. In April 1872, the Railroad Young Men's Christian Association was founded in Cleveland by George Myers, a station agent, who had been holding prayer meetings for workers in a room at his depot. Chapters of the Railroad "Y" spread throughout the country. The organization provided members with clean, com-fortable lodging and recreation, reading and prayer rooms, Bible lectures, and study groups and hymn fests. In the 1880s, the Railroad YMCA received financial assistance from several rail lines.[80]

Pioneer railwaymen engaged in one other kind of formal as-sociational activity that proved both critical to the history of American railway workers and the American railway industry as a whole—trade unionism. By 1877 engineers, conductors, and firemen had established their own fairly stable, nationally based union organizations. While these associations emerged and op-erated primarily as protective agencies, they also fulfilled im-portant fraternal functions. Local union lodge halls built by pi-oneer trainmen served for informal gatherings as well as organized meetings, lectures, and socials. Initiation rites, secret oaths, and other rituals marked brotherhood occasions. Active women's auxiliaries were also an integral part of some locals. Railroad workers joined national unions both to protect their material interests and for the comradeship provided by lodge members.[81]

As informal social relations among railwaymen were struc-tured by the work itself, so too was the process of union for-mation. Despite one attempt in the early period and repeated efforts after 1877 to organize railwaymen on an industrial basis, a strict craft union approach came to dominate within the Amer-ican railway trade almost immediately. The common experience

[78] R. C. Overton, *The First Ninety Years*, p. 59.

[79] *Colburn's Railway Advocate*, June 2, 1855, p. 3; Ducker, "Men of the Steel Rails," p. 124.

[80] John Moore, *The Story of the Railroad "Y,"* pp. 275–277.

[81] On the fraternal function of the brotherhoods, see Ducker, "Men of the Steel Rails," chap. 8.

of being employees failed to dissolve the divisions of skill and status that materialized among railwaymen.

The National Protective Association of Locomotive Engineers, founded in November 1855, represents the first recorded attempt to form a bona fide trade union organization by American railway workers. The association owed its existence to the firing of thirteen engine drivers by the Baltimore & Ohio in 1854. Deciding that their only protection lay in organization, they called for a convention of drivers. It met on November 5, 1855, with seventy-one delegates from fourteen states and fifty-five railroads in attendance. The Association was formally established at the convention, and a constitution was written which included provisions for officers, chartering, finances, and membership requirements. The constitution emphasized the key complaint of the engineers—that, as the railroad industry had expanded, inexperienced and incompetent men who depressed wages and displaced veteran drivers had been brought into the trade. The association called on the nation's rail lines to hire only association members who were sober, literate, responsible, and competent.

Plans were also laid at the convention for the publication of a journal, *The Railroad Operator*, which among other items was to discuss the "various relations of Capital and Labor." Not a single issue appears ever to have been printed. The Protective Association met again in 1856 and 1857 and then held no further meetings. The organization, fragile at the outset, failed to survive the depression of 1857. Local groups did persist and they laid the foundation for the formation of the Brotherhood of Locomotive Engineers in 1863.[82]

The Brotherhood of Locomotive Engineers, the first permanent trade union organization of American railway workers, and still the most influential of the railway brotherhoods, grew out of a series of disputes in the early 1860s between the management of the Michigan Central Railroad and its drivers. The wages of Central engineers had been increased in the spring of 1862. These

---

[82] Richardson, *Locomotive Engineer*, p. 180; James Stevenson, "The Brotherhood of Locomotive Engineers and Its Leaders" (Ph.D. dissertation, Vanderbilt Univ., 1954), p. 26; *Colburn's Railroad Advocate*, December 22, 1855, p. 3.

gains, however, were offset by a company decision to increase the number of hours of work and the required number of runs. Central's management then quixotically reversed itself by announcing wage cuts in the fall. After this move, thirteen disgruntled Central engineers met in the home of William Robinson, who had been secretary of the National Protective Association. They decided to call a general meeting for May 5, 1863, where the Brotherhood of the Footboard was formally established. The organization soon spread, and in August of that year a national organization was formed—the Brotherhood of Locomotive Engineers—with William Robinson as Grand Chief.[83]

The BLE's constitution of 1863 granted local units almost complete autonomy. The following year brotherhood members engaged in a series of strikes and were soundly defeated. These reverses produced a crisis in the new organization, and Grand Chief Robinson, a defender of local initiative and activism, was ousted in favor of Charles Wilson at the union's convention in 1864. Wilson quickly forced through a complete reorganization of the brotherhood. Local units now were directed to report all grievances to the Grand Chief, who was to act as a sole mediator. If he failed to reach an accord with a company, approval for strike action then had to be obtained from a majority of locals within the union. Wilson's virtual no-strike plan remained in effect throughout his tenure, which terminated with his own ouster in 1874.[84]

Wilson succeeded in stamping the organization with a definite conservative character. He argued that locomotive drivers could best attain improvements in wages and working conditions not through belligerent actions, but by proving through their conduct and efficiency that they were worthy of better treatment. Under Wilson's leadership, amendments were added to the union's constitution restricting membership to men of good moral character, whites, literates, persons at least twenty-one years of age, and engineers in good standing with a minimum of one year's experience. Other regulations established strict codes of discipline.

[83] Richardson, *Locomotive Engineer*, pp. 120–123.
[84] Ibid., pp. 136–139; Stevenson, "Brotherhood of Locomotive Engineers," pp. 56–68.

Brotherhood men could be censured or expelled for conduct
deemed unbecoming a member of the organization. Each month
the union's journal published lists of disciplined drivers. Offenses
included improper language, dishonesty, drunkenness, insolence,
fraud, desertion of family, and immorality. Wilson envisioned
this disciplinary system as a means to permit the union to sub-
stantiate its claim to being a wholesome force, one that railroad
managers could easily recognize and with which they could con-
fidently negotiate.[85]

Wilson also insisted that the brotherhood's major function
was to serve as a mutual aid society. To this end, various accident,
death benefit, and burial insurance programs were established
during his reign.[86] Despite these measures, opposition to his con-
ciliatory policies gradually grew within the organization. Wilson's orders for brotherhood men to break unauthorized strikes
and his dictatorial expulsion of rebel locals especially sparked
internal dissension. In 1874 he was ousted as Grand Chief and
replaced by Peter M. Arthur who led the brotherhood for the
next quarter century. Wilson, however, bequeathed a conservative legacy to the union which persists to this very day.[87]

The two other brotherhoods that emerged in the early period
functioned only as benevolent societies. The Order of Railway
Conductors of America owed its inception to the organizing
activities of conductors on the Illinois Central Railroad. In 1868,
they formed a fraternal association dubbed the "Conductor's
Union." Chicago, Burlington & Quincy men then established a
second lodge. A national convention was held in 1869 where the
Brotherhood of Conductors was formally established. (The name
was changed in 1878 to the Order of Railway Conductors of
America.)

The ORC remained a fraternal society until 1890. A mutual
life insurance program was established for members, and lodges
were built where conductors fraternized and heard temperance
lectures. In 1877 the ORC adopted a strict no-strike policy which

---

[85] Richardson, *Locomotive Engineer*, pp. 122–132; Stevenson, "Brotherhood
of Locomotive Engineers," pp. 56–68.

[86] Richardson, *Locomotive Engineer*, p. 123.

[87] Stevenson, "Brotherhood of Locomotive Engineers," pp. 80, 117–118.

provided for expulsion of members who engaged in such activities. In 1885 the order decided to permit officers to assist in settling disputes, and the anti-strike clause was officially dropped from the society's constitution five years later.[88]

Circumstances surrounding the formation of the Brotherhood of Locomotive Firemen were fairly similar. The union was founded at Port Jervis, New Jersey, in December 1873 by Joshua Leach as a mutual benefit society. Upon joining, a member received a certificate that constituted a life insurance policy of one thousand dollars. Members paid monthly premiums of fifty cents.[89] The Brotherhood of Locomotive Firemen did not affect a more active trade union stance until the 1880s, when a young fireman by the name of Eugene Victor Debs assumed a leadership role in the organization.

These were the only permanent organizations of railwaymen to be established before 1880. Other railway workers made attempts to organize in the early period, but their efforts were short-lived and ineffective. Letters, for instance, in the archives of the Baltimore & Ohio reveal that a "Machinists' Union" was formed on that line in 1873.[90] The organization disappeared as mysteriously as it emerged. There is even evidence that a valiant attempt was made in the early years to form an industrial union of railwaymen. The Railroad Man's Protective Union was founded as such in St. Louis in 1865, but it passed from the scene before constituting a threat.[91] There is also the strong possibility that other organizations that have left no historical traces came into existence. Railwaymen not enrolled in the three original brotherhoods began to form stable, visible, and active unions in the 1880s and '90s. This occurred at the same time that American railway workers became engaged in a series of violent confrontations with their employers that brought this country as close to massive civil disorder as it has ever been.

[88] Clyde E. Robbins, "Railway Conductors," *Studies in History, Economics and Public Law* 61:15–22, 123.

[89] Charles Clark, "The Railroad Safety Movement in the United States" (Ph.D. dissertation, Univ. of Illinois at Urbana, 1966), p. 168.

[90] Machinists' Union to J. W. Garrett, April 28, 1873, Baltimore & Ohio Railroad Papers, file 3089.

[91] Stevenson, "Brotherhood of Locomotive Engineers," p. 87.

7

THE LEGACY
OF THE EARLY YEARS:
CONCLUSIONS

≡

IN THE MAJORITY of cases a man's employment depends not alone upon his good behavior, ability and trustworthiness, but upon the whim of his superior; he is hired for no specific time, holds no contract with his company that secures him employment, and is liable to be discharged at any moment without warning.—*Locomotive Engineer's Journal*[1]

FOR THE THIRD and fourth generations of American railwaymen, conflict and turmoil marked their working days. In the last quarter of the nineteenth and first quarter of the twentieth centuries, American railroad workers and their supporters within the communities in which they resided fought a succession of pitched battles with agents of management and the law that resulted in alarming losses in life, limb, and property. The tracks, shops, stations, and yards of the nation's railroads became staging grounds for open class warfare. The same period also witnessed the emerging and growing application of state power to order and stabilize industrial relations within the trade, heightened efforts by railway executives to develop new methods of personnel control, and further expansion of trade union formation and organizing among American railwaymen who sought to undo the more

[1] *Locomotive Engineer's Journal*, December, 1875, p. 640.

arbitrary and uncertain conditions of their labor through the securing of collective contracts.

The above events and developments have certainly not escaped the notice of historians. The violence attending American labor disputes at the turn of the century and the general militancy of American workers—railwaymen notably included—went unmatched in the western industrializing world and continues to draw scholarly interest. The failure of American working people during the same period to translate vigilance into sustained, independent, class-based oppositional political activity has been a related and equal source of debate, puzzlement, and inquiry. The more riveting and celebrated happenings of the modern era, however, should not obscure the reality of relations between railway workers and managers in the early years. A golden age of peaceful coexistence never prevailed; overt collective confrontations that are less well known and documented occurred. Problems and issues that emerged in the early years—particularly, the discretionary power and authority of local supervisors—and remained unattended and unresolved became the festering sores and legacies with which later workers and executives in the trade would have to contend.

THE FIRST STRIKE of American railwaymen is customarily dated to a work stoppage of engineers on the Erie Railroad in 1854. Abundant evidence in newspapers and corporate archives indicates that there had been a significant number of disputes of consequence before that time. As was noted in an earlier chapter, firemen on the Boston & Worcester Railroad in the 1840s staged a successful protest that succeeded in changing a company decision to adopt an engine that would have required extensive stoking. Apparently 1854 was not the first year that executives on the Erie Railroad encountered employee resentment. An article in the *Paterson Intelligencer* of May 18, 1853 reported that yard workers on the Erie had walked off their jobs in anger over deteriorating working conditions. The report further noted that the men had been replaced by a gang of "poor darkies" who later became the object of an attack by the aggrieved striking white workers.[2] An annual statement to stockholders of the Baltimore & Ohio Railroad in 1853 similarly contains an oblique reference to trouble on that line. The directors of the road sadly informed investors that unanticipated expenses had risen during the year, including the "sum of $26,290, as incurred in the increase of wages made at time of the 'Strike'. . . ."[3]

The Erie Strike of 1854 and one that followed two years later, however, certainly deserve credit as the first major job actions on an American railroad. Both strikes attracted national attention and concern and are of interest because they came in protest against administrative and operational regulations and only tangentially involved the question of wages and hours. They are of significance, too, because they occurred on the railroad that was the first to introduce a systematic plan of bureaucratic management.

The strike of 1854 occurred after Daniel McCallum replaced Charles Minot as general manager of the line.[4] Minot, a former locomotive driver, had enjoyed a close rapport with engineers on the road. McCallum, a firm believer in tight management, had come into office determined to enforce a new set of regulations that he had written while serving as a division superintendent on the line. Minot, in fact, had resigned his post after refusing to institute McCallum's rules, which the directors of the Erie had voted to adopt.

Two regulations in particular raised the ire of drivers on the road. The first—the infamous Rule 6—declared that every engineer was to be held accountable for running off a switch at a station, even if the switch had been set improperly by a switchman. Enginemen were expected to slow down at each station, whether or not they were stopping, and to check the switches for themselves. They received further orders to take no person's word on the matter and were warned that they could run past

---

[2] Walter Arndt Lucas, *From the Hills to the Hudson*, p. 254.

[3] *Twenty-Seventh Annual Report of the President & Directors of the Baltimore and Ohio R. R. Company* (Baltimore, 1853), p. 31.

[4] Thorough accounts of the Erie strikes of 1854 and 1856 can be found in Edward Hungerford, *Men of the Erie*, pp. 140–143; Edward Mott, *Between the Ocean and the Lakes*, pp. 430–434; *Holley's Railroad Advocate*, October 11, 1856, p. 1.

nonstop stations without checking the switches only at their own risk, with the company reserving the right to decide whether the running was reckless or not. The second regulation that fomented bitterness and tension took the form of an announcement that the Erie would post notices of engineers dismissed from service and send them to other lines (in effect, an early form of black-listing).

After peacefully submitting protests against the new rules, engineers on the Erie decided to walk off their jobs on June 17, 1854, demanding the abrogation of the regulations. The move quickly paralyzed the line, and McCallum was forced to capitulate. He changed Rule 6 to satisfy the disgruntled men and announced that the company would both institute fair hearings before dismissals and drop all plans to post and distribute lists of discharged drivers. The engineers returned to work on June 27, the matter apparently settled. This attempt to tighten discipline on the Erie, as well as similar efforts on other lines at the time, served as a prime motive for the calling of the convention of enginemen in 1855 that led to the establishment of the National Protective Association of Locomotive Engineers.

Peace, however, was short-lived on the Erie. Despite McCallum's concessions, twenty-nine engineers were discharged for running off switches during the two-year period following the strike. In September 1856, Erie drivers once again formed a protest committee and presented a new list of grievances to the directors of the road. This time they not only called for the elimination of Rule 6, but also for payment of wages when their engines were in the repair shops and when they were ready for duty; they also asked for free passes for engineers from other railroads when they traveled on the Erie, a privilege already extended to conductors. The engineers also took up the cause of their firemen by demanding wage increases for them.

The board of directors rejected the demands almost completely. They also proceeded to order the discharge of all members of the grievance committee. Erie drivers quickly reacted by refusing to run their engines, and traffic on the line soon came to a standstill. The company advertised for new enginemen, but few accepted the offer. Striking drivers retaliated with various acts of sabotage, and many left to take positions on lines to the West. The strike dragged on for six months and gradually ended without a settlement and McCallum eventually resigned. The loss of revenue during the strike and the cost of damage to the rolling stock proved to be disastrous. More than half a million dollars were lost, and the strike proved instrumental in sending the Erie into bankruptcy and receivership in 1859.

Labor problems did not abate on the Erie. Serious strikes occurred there again in 1860 and 1874.[5] Other lines also experienced labor disorders during the early years, although few were as publicized as those on the Erie. Conductors walked off their posts on the Baltimore & Ohio Railroad in 1857, protesting against a new regulation that held them responsible for broken seals on freight cars and for loss of merchandise. The conductors succeeded in halting traffic on the line by breaking switches and encouraging mob attacks on the trains.[6] Additional local walkouts beleaguered B. & O. officials, with particularly damaging strikes occurring in 1859, 1864, 1869, 1874, and 1876. B. & O. railwaymen in different grades of employ cooperated during these early protests. Plans for a general strike were actually formulated in 1859; in 1866 seven hired policemen were even discharged for assisting a group of striking shop workers.[7]

Publicized strikes also occurred on the Illinois Central in 1858, 1862, and 1867, the Michigan Central in 1865, the Chicago, Burlington & Quincy in 1876, and the Reading Railroad in 1870.[8] During the latter confrontation, striking Reading men

---

[5] Mott, *Between the Ocean and the Lakes*, pp. 434–438.

[6] *Holley's Railroad Advocate*, May 23, 1857, p. 3.

[7] File 5747, Baltimore & Ohio Railroad Papers, Maryland Historical Society, contains memoranda and letters concerning strikes on the line in the 1850s, 1860s, and 1870s. See also J. C. Davis to J. W. Garrett, January 23, 1866, file 7559, ibid.

[8] David Lightner, "Labor on the Illinois Central Railroad, 1852–1900" (Ph.D. dissertation, Cornell Univ., 1969), pp. 117, 142; James Stevenson, "The Brotherhood of Locomotive Engineers and Its Leaders" (Ph.D. dissertation, Vanderbilt Univ., 1954), p. 64; Grievance Committee to Robert Harris, 1876, Chicago, Burlington & Quincy Railroad Papers, Miscellaneous, CBQ-33 1880 8.1, Newberry Library; J. B. Gowen to G. A. Nicholls, March 1, 1870, Reading Railroad Papers, Eleutherian Mills Historical Library.

wreaked havoc on the line's switches and tracks. Pioneer railway workers showed little aversion to engaging in physical violence.

The first generations of American railwaymen learned to cooperate with each other in their protests as did their adversaries in management. During a strike of enginemen on the Galena & Chicago Union Railroad in 1864, companies in the Chicago area successfully collaborated to supply strikebreakers.[9] The strike is significant because it was the first important job action called and led by the newly formed Brotherhood of Locomotive Engineers. It also occurred during the Civil War and seriously affected troop and supply movements to the northern armies. The defeat of the engineers during the strike was largely responsible for the adoption by the Brotherhood of Locomotive Engineers of a more conservative stance.

Archival and newspaper searches thus reveal that the early years of American railroading were etched by organized group conflict—conflict to match the daily individual confrontations that occurred between railwaymen and their supervisors over matters such as recruitment practices, training, discipline, compensation, workloads, promotions, and accidental injury and death benefit awards. The exact number of formal labor disputes will never be known. The incidents of record not only give clear indications of the very existence and extent of unrest in the early period, but also render some notable patterns. Pioneer railwaymen protested in concert; they received support from other members of their communities; destruction of private property was a tactic frequently employed, as a matter of course; and the conditions and regulations under which they labored were as critical to them as the matters of hours of work and compensation. Early American railroad workers thus established traditions of protest to be followed by their descendants.

HARDLY A YEAR went by in the late nineteenth and early twentieth centuries without at least one significant and easily documented strike of railwaymen. A number of these confrontations have entered the pantheon of America's most dramatic and conse-

[9] Stevenson, "Brotherhood of Locomotive Engineers," pp. 47–48.

quential labor struggles: the spontaneous nationwide railway strikes of July 1877; the so-called Gould strikes of 1885 and 1886 involving the Knights of Labor; the Great Burlington Strike of 1888; the momentous Pullman strike and boycott of 1894 featuring the leadership of Eugene V. Debs; the bloody Illinois Central Railroad, or as it was dubbed at the time, Harriman Strike of 1911-1914; the threatened strike of the four major brotherhoods of trainmen in 1916 that led to the intervention of President Woodrow Wilson and the passage of the Adamson Act imposing the eight-hour day on the industry; and finally, probably the largest action of all, the strike of railway shopmen in 1922 that engaged more than 400,000 workers.[10]

Sandwiched between the "great" battles of the period was an unending succession of other less dramatic, though no less intense, railway labor disputes and protests. Serious walkouts erupted on rail lines serving Buffalo, New York in 1891, on the Great Northern Railroad in 1893, and the Atchison, Topeka & Santa Fe in 1904.[11] Countless smaller, fleeting, both spontaneous and organized job actions unfolded; a precise enumeration is impossible. By the turn of the century, American railroads stretched across the continent and were visible signs of the nation's progress—but progress achieved and accompanied by severe social stress and turmoil.

The railway labor confrontations of the modern era are not

[10] Standard accounts of the railroad strikes mentioned can be found in the following. For the railroad strikes of 1877: Robert Bruce, *1877: Year of Violence*, and Philip Foner, *The Great Labor Uprising of 1877*. For the Gould strikes of 1885–1886: Henry Pelling, *American Labor*, pp. 70–72; Philip Foner, *History of the Labor Movement in the United States*, vol. II, pp. 50–53, 83–86. For the Burlington strike of 1888: Donald McMurray, *The Great Burlington Strike of 1888*. For the Pullman strike and boycott of 1894: Almont Lindsay, *The Pullman Strike*. For the Harriman strike of 1911–1914: James Green, *The World of the Worker*, p. 189; David Montgomery, *Workers' Control in America*, p. 107; Carl Graves, "Scientific Management and the Santa Fe Railway Shopmen of Topeka, Kansas, 1900–1925" (Ph.D. dissertation, Harvard Univ., 1980), pp. 310–311. For the threatened strike of trainmen in 1916 and the passage of the Adamson Act: Arthur Link, *Woodrow Wilson and the Progressive Era, 1910–1917*, pp. 235–239. For the railway shopmen's strike of 1922: Green, *World of the Worker*, pp. 120–121, and Graves, "Scientific Management," pp. 263–290.

[11] Foner, *History of the Labor Movement*, pp. 253–254, 257–259; Graves, "Scientific Management," pp. 75–123.

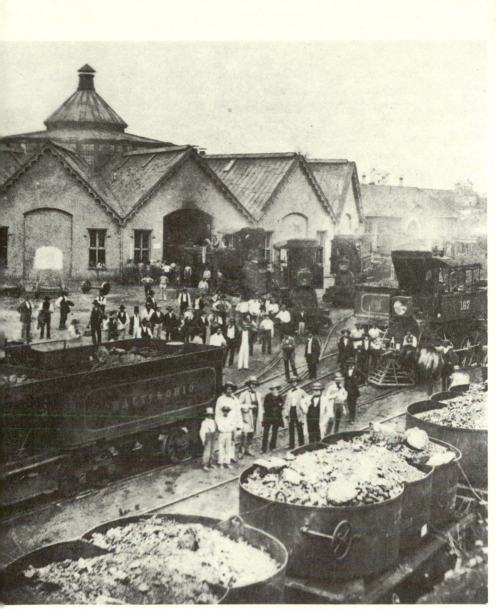

The shops of the Baltimore & Ohio Railroad at Martinsburg, West Virginia. The photograph was taken during the Civil War. The great railroad strikes of 1877 began at Martinsburg on July 16 of that year. (Courtesy of Baltimore & Ohio Railroad.)

easily or simply characterized. Some strikes involved already organized railroad workers and their efforts to gain more inclusive contracts and improved benefits; others represented attempts by railwaymen largely neglected by the existing brotherhoods to organize and secure their own collective bargaining rights and agreements. The announcements of cutbacks in compensation and rewards sparked some incidents; the implementation of new programs—like scientific management and piece rate schemes—provoked others. During some struggles, exceptional class solidarity across skill levels and trades was manifest, while scabbing, jurisdictional disputes and labor fratricide marked others. Most railway job actions similarly occurred during business contractions and had bad times as their backdrop, while a few erupted during moments of general prosperity. Finally, a number of confrontations can be understood by simple reference to local conditions and immediate shop-floor grievances and concerns, while others can only be fathomed by appreciation of larger events, developments, and contexts—most notably, the effects of depressions, social and political mobilizations, and war.

Throughout the welter of particulars, a few patterns and points do draw attention. The violence accompanying railway labor disputes three and four generations ago is striking. July 20, 1877: twenty demonstrators killed, seventy wounded in Pittsburgh during a confrontation between railwaymen and their supporters and the troops brought to the city to force the movement of strike-bound trains; the next night Pittsburgh was lit up by a red glow as rioters destroyed and burned almost the entire property and rolling stock of the Pennsylvania Railroad. April 9, 1886: seven workers killed in a battle with police in East St. Louis during the second Gould strike. July 1894: the toll reached twenty-five killed and sixty injured as railwaymen throughout the country in support of striking Pullman Company workers walked off their jobs and paralyzed the nation's commerce and transport. Guerrilla skirmishes and gunplay marked the three-year Harriman strike, provoking a special congressional inquiry. The summer of 1922: violent encounters occurred in various western towns as state militia were called in to establish order during the railway shopmen's strike. While the levels of outward physical conflict subsided, the persistence of violence is noteworthy.

Railwaymen throughout both the early and later years were also joined in protest by other members of their communities. The greater and lesser known labor struggles of the nineteenth and early twentieth centuries have to be understood as community uprisings as well. Striking railwaymen tapped a reservoir of submerged rancor in many towns and cities and gathered support from both working-class and middle-class peoples—from common day laborers, skilled workers, small businessmen, and local professionals.[12] As social historian Herbert Gutman and others have found and noted, community supporters rallied to the cause of railroad workers to protest against economic conditions and hard times, and more important, to challenge the growing, encroaching political and economic power of concentrated capital, a power destructive of cherished republican ideals and a power best symbolized by the nation's first and largest corporations, the railroads.[13] Railwaymen fought for better working standards and they and their community allies struggled together for the maintenance of a democratic capitalism and polity.[14]

[12] Surviving arrest records, in fact, reveal that railwaymen rarely were in the ranks of the most rebellious and law-breaking of demonstrators. See: Leonard Wallock, "The B & O 'Monopoly' and the Baltimore Crowd" (Master's thesis, Columbia Univ., 1974), pp. 29–37; Richard Schneirov, "The 1877 Great Upheaval in Chicago" (unpublished paper in author's possession), pp. 30–37.

[13] On community support for railwaymen see: Herbert Gutman, "Workers' Search for Power" in H. Wayne Morgan, ed., The Gilded Age; Herbert Gutman, "Trouble on the Railroads in 1873-1874," Labor History 2:215–235; Shelton Stromquist, "Community Structure and Industrial Conflict in Nineteenth-Century Railroad Towns" (Paper read at the convention of the Organization of American Historians, New York, April 1978, in author's possession); also Wallock, "The B & O 'Monopoly,' " and Schneirov, "1877 Great Upheaval."

[14] Some qualifications are in order on the issue of the community nature of railway labor uprisings. During the early and later years a definite ecological pattern of protest emerged. Not every community possessed of rail facilities and a cohort of railway workers were bitten by the fever of insurrection. During periods of strife, towns connected by the same rail lines experienced remarkably different levels of disorder. Cities in the East tended to be less effected than those in the West. In general, fervid protest and activity throughout the years 1877–1922 occurred in communities where one or more of the following conditions prevailed: in rail centers where the railroads dominated the local economy and where railway workers represented a significant segment of the work force; in

Finally, during the disputes of the early and later years, rail-waymen voiced a constant, though not always newsworthy, grievance. The complaint against the discretionary power of im-mediate supervisors surfaced and reappeared in every strike men-tioned, as did demands to limit their sway. The capricious rule of foremen proved an often hidden but fundamental issue of contention fueling anger. An anonymous correspondent to the *Locomotive Engineer's Journal* stated the case well. In account-ing for the violence of July 1877, he wrote: "The uprising was the natural result of premeditated, preconcerted causes—the re-sult of arbitrary rules and unjust discrimination allowed officers and operations, a culmination of stupid mismanagement and the fruits of unwise policies, and explosion was as unexpected as would be a thunderbolt from a cloudless sky."[15]

Again during the Pullman Strike of 1894, the arbitrary power of supervisors was the common denominator of complaint. An official demand of the strikers was an end to the "constant har-assment of foremen."[16] A federal commission established to in-vestigate the disorders later collected testimony and was inun-dated by tales of favoritism and nepotism, the violent tempers

---

places where local businessmen and professionals were dependent on the trade and purchases of residing railwaymen; in towns served by single rail companies where monopoly power of rate setting and service provision fostered resentment; in newly settled areas not possessed of established or entrenched elites or folk-ways; in rail centers with relatively large yard facilities and sizable contingents of younger and potentially more rebellious yard workers, switchmen and brake-men; and in towns and cities where railwaymen, even though a highly transient population, formed cohesive, identifiable residential communities. Chicago, Pitts-burgh, and Martinsburg, West Virginia—not New York City, Philadelphia, or Burlington, Iowa—represented predictable sites for enraged confrontation. Also, while community support and agitation on behalf of railwaymen extended into the 1920s (in the shopmen's strike of 1922, for example), it did not maintain the high pitch of the early years. Railwaymen's strikes generally became less spontaneous and more organized, less characterized by grass roots insurgency, and less general in scope. The persistence of violence even into the twenties emphasizes the relative nature of change. The points made here are substantiated by Wallock and Schneirov and argued most succinctly by Stromquist. I have dealt with the issue of the geography of protest at length in "The Railwaymen of Philadelphia, 1860–1880: A Socio-Demographic Portrait" (Paper read at the convention of the Social Science History Association, Cambridge, Massachusetts, November 1979).

[15] Quoted in Reed Richardson, *The Locomotive Engineer*, p. 165.
[16] Quoted in Richard Edwards, *Contested Terrain*, p. 60.

and often brutal acts of foremen and their despotic character.[17] The revelations came as something of a surprise, since the investigators had expected wages and hours of work to be the only grievances of note. The following interview with Franklin Mills, a discharged Baltimore & Ohio employee, is instructive:

COMMISSIONER KERNAN: What was the feeling among the employees on the Baltimore and Ohio with regard to striking prior to the time they struck?

MILLS: It was not very favorable.

COMMISSIONER KERNAN: Had there been any cuts in wages about which they were dissatisfied?

MILLS: Not lately. The most of the difficulty on the Baltimore & Ohio was favoritism, pets and maladministration of some of the petty officers.[18]

The United States Strike Commission of 1895 also heard from Charles Naylor, a local officer of the American Railway Union and a fireman on the Pittsburgh, Fort Wayne & Chicago Railroad. Naylor placed the disruptions of a year earlier in the clearest perspective. "In a large number of roads," he testified, "there was a feeling among the employees that they were almost in a helpless condition to stand against the oppression of the petty officials, and the petty officials took advantage of that feeling and deviled the men, just as their particular temperament at the moment led them to do so."[19] Such testimony and the violence of the age gave a clear message. A new system of relations—a new social contract—between railway management and labor had to be forged and developed.

GOVERNMENT officials became one party to developments.[20] Civil disorder, significant losses of lives and property, successive threats to the nation's commerce, and pressure from influential corporate interests provided ample justification for state intervention. Fed-

[17] Edwards, *Contested Terrain*, pp. 58–61.
[18] Quoted in ibid., p. 61.
[19] Quoted in ibid., p. 61.
[20] Standard accounts of evolving government policy on railway labor disputes can be found in Gerald Eggert, *Railroad Labor Disputes*, and Leonard Lecht, *Experience Under Railway Labor Legislation*.

eral judges took the first initiatives. Starting in July 1877, United States circuit court judges began issuing stern injunctions to strikers and their leaders—against interference with the operations of lines in receivership, secondary boycotts, unlawful assembly, blocked passage of the U.S. mails, and restraints of trade—that effectively limited protest activity. In this way the federal judiciary assumed the lead in setting governmental policy on railroad labor disputes during the late nineteenth century.

Federal executives moved slowly to exert their authority. During the riots of 1877 and the Pullman strike and boycott of 1894, Presidents Hayes and Cleveland heeded the pleas of state officials and backed various judicial orders by sending federal troops to quell disturbances and secure the safe movement of trains. Not until 1916 and Woodrow Wilson's almost single-handed settlement of a threatened nationwide walkout of trainmen was the full force of the President's office used to deal with the problem. Meanwhile, support was gradually growing in Congress for legislative solutions.

In 1886, after a congressional investigation of the Gould strikes, Congress began considering a number of measures aimed at establishing arbitration procedures for the railroad industry. Two years of debate and wrangling produced a bill which created a three-member mediating panel that was granted limited powers to affect and enforce settlements. More forceful and permanent procedures were then enacted with the passage of the Erdman Law in 1898 and the Newlands Act in 1913, although the voluntary participation of contending parties remained a feature of both pieces of legislation. Government participation in railway labor matters dramatically increased during World War I and was further codified in the Transportation Act of 1920; a final stage of Congressional activity, forty years in the making, was reached with the Railway Labor Act of 1926, which, in amended form, stands as the basic law that applies to this day. The act detailed procedures for the initiation of contract talks privately between unions and carriers and for later mediation and then arbitration by government-sponsored boards of conciliation. A thirty-to-sixty-day cooling-off period was also provided for and the President was given last resort emergency power personally to settle disputes. Government involvement in railway labor affairs served as a precedent for other industries.

The turbulence of the period also forced a response from top railroad executives who were both frightened and perplexed by unfolding events. Their sense of surprise, bewilderment, and fear was best voiced by Charles Eliot Perkins. In a letter to John Forbes, a director of the Chicago, Burlington & Quincy, Perkins, then vice president of the line, described his reaction to the events of the summer of 1877: "The strike was inaugurated [on the C.B. & Q.] on Wednesday, July 25. I confess that I felt like a Doctor dealing with a new and unknown malady."[21] Perkins, true to form, then went on to diagnose the disease. Workers, he noted, were living in an age of extravagance and had unrealistic expectations. To prove his point he harkened back to a time twenty-five years before when he proudly and comfortably lived on $30 a month as a station clerk. Perkins failed to add, however, that he owed his first job and much of his later success to his marriage to Forbes's niece.

A cure for their troubles was imperative, and railway managers embarked on an almost frantic search for explanations and answers. Prior to the great strikes of 1877, top executives generally left decisions on labor affairs to circumstance and subordinates. The seriousness of the new situation now demanded closer attention to such matters on their part. The anxious exploration for means of engendering greater loyalty among employees is trenchantly illustrated in a chain of well-preserved and remarkable letters and memoranda that passed between officers of the Chicago, Burlington & Quincy Railroad during and after the railroad strikes of 1877.

The strikes had hardly reached Chicago when C.B. & Q. officials began voicing grave misgivings about the announced wage reductions that had sparked disorder. John Griswold, a director of the line, thus wrote to the road's president, Robert Harris, on July 24: "This concerted outbreak of employees puts a somewhat different aspect upon matters, and had we anticipated it so soon I should not have been in favor of cutting the lower

---

[21] C. E. Perkins to J. Forbes, August 2, 1877, Chicago, Burlington & Quincy Railroad Papers, Perkins Letterbooks.

A depiction of the burning of a roundhouse in Pittsburgh during the great railroad strikes of July 1877. (Reprinted from *Harper's Weekly*, August 11, 1877.)

grades." Griswold then backed off somewhat, counseling that the company remain firm with the cutback decision, so as not to appear acting out of fear. He heartily recommended, though, that a plan to increase wages when dividends exceeded 8 percent be seriously considered as a way to win back the allegiance of C.B. & Q. men.[22]

Once tensions had subsided, President Harris seized the initiative, and, in an almost daily outpouring, barraged Burlington executives with reforms aimed at preventing further disorders. He first advised that the company be more sensitive to the financial plight of its employees, and that the personal consequences of wage reductions be weighed before implementation. He further seconded Griswold's suggestion that a plan be devised to have wages raised as the company's net earnings increased. In discussing compensation, Harris also tried to revive interest in an idea that he had championed in the early 1870s: the guaranteed income. Citing statistics on monthly income fluctuations, he argued that a sure means to reinstill loyalty would be to guarantee eight- or nine-tenths wages to every employee whether or not there was work to be assigned.[23]

Another reform strongly espoused by Harris was the written contract. In several letters to Griswold, he argued that the company could not expect to "stimulate enthusiasm" among employees if they remained under the often arbitrary rule and supervision of local foremen. To deal with the problem, he favored instituting written contracts which would clearly stipulate fixed ground rules for compensation, dismissals, promotions, and seniority rights. The rules would be in effect for the stated life of the agreements. Harris also foresaw establishing grievance procedures to handle contract ambiguities and disputes.[24] Finally, he argued forcefully for the implementation of company-spon-

---

[22] J.N.A. Griswold to Robert Harris, July 24, 1877, Chicago, Burlington & Quincy Railroad Papers, Perkins Letterbooks.

[23] Robert Harris to J. M. Forbes, July 31, 1877, Chicago, Burlington & Quincy Railroad Papers, Harris In-Letters, CBQ-31B1.5; see excerpts of Harris's letters in Thomas Cochran, *Railroad Leaders, 1845–1890*, pp. 252–253.

[24] Cochran, *Railroad Leaders*, pp. 353, 355; Robert Harris to J. N. Griswold, August 2, 1877, Chicago, Burlington & Quincy Railroad Papers, Harris In-Letters, CBQ-31B1.5.

sored and administered accident and death benefit insurance programs.[25]

Between early August and mid-December, Harris staunchly defended his proposed reforms. In addition to his major concerns, he also spoke in favor of welcoming back strikers without penalties and of abolishing Sunday freight service so all C.B. & Q. men could enjoy the Sabbath.[26] Harris's plans were considered and debated by Burlington officials, but at every point he met stiff resistance from Charles Eliot Perkins. Involved in an organizational power struggle with Harris at the time, Perkins pecked away at each proposal. Taking a strict laissez-faire position, and opposed to any and all corporate philanthropy and paternalism, he argued over and over again that "Merit and merit alone should be rewarded."[27] Ultimately Perkins's views prevailed and action on all of Harris's reforms was tabled. Harris gave up his effort to improve relations with employees and soon retired from the line that he had served diligently and faithfully for nearly twenty years.[28]

Executives on the other roads engaged in a similar search for explanations and remedies. In the years following the riots of 1877, many ultimately came to side with Perkins's stern, tight-fisted approach. Henry Broadholst Ledyard of the Michigan Central, for instance, proposed that railroad managers adopt more definite plans to coordinate their response to worker demands.[29] Others further argued for a determined attack on the existing brotherhoods. G. Clinton Gardner, general manager of the Pennsylvania Railroad in the late 1870s, ordered the immediate dis-

[25] Cochran, *Railroad Leaders*, pp. 349, 354–355; Memorandum, Plan for a Life Insurance Fund and an Accident Insurance Fund, Chicago, Burlington & Quincy Railroad Papers, Papers Concerning Employees, 1877–98, CBQ-33 1880 3.6.

[26] Clive Scott, "Robert Harris and the Strike of 1877" (Master's thesis, Univ. of Western Ontario, 1967), pp. 85–86, 113.

[27] C. E. Perkins to R. Harris, December 7, 1877, Chicago, Burlington & Quincy Railroad Papers, Papers Concerning Employees, 1877–98, CBQ-33 1880 3.6; Memorandum of C. E. Perkins on Supply and Demand, August 6, 1877, Chicago, Burlington & Quincy Railroad Papers, Perkins Letterbooks.

[28] Richard Overton, *Burlington Route*, pp. 159–160; Bruce, *1877: Year of Violence*, p. 304.

[29] Cochran, *Railroad Leaders*, p. 397.

missal of all employees who were members of unions and held his division superintendents accountable for identifying union men.[30] The swift discharge and blacklisting of insurgent strikers and strike leaders similarly was upheld as a necessary defensive maneuver. Finally, legislative action to outlaw strikes garnered support as a possible remedy. James C. Clarke, president of the Illinois Central in the 1880s, believed that in legislation establishing the Interstate Commerce Commission, the inclusion of a clause prohibiting work stoppages would be a much-needed first step toward curbing unrest. To that end, he applied pressure on Illinois congressmen.[31]

However, a growing number of leaders in the industry favored more positive approaches. Their answers varied, but in general this group agreed that the loyalty of railroad employees could be regained only through benevolent means. The most naive among them simply believed in the power of exhortation. The problem, they held, was one of poor public relations. Railway employees should be told that company interests were ultimately their own, and that patience would have its just rewards. To assist in this campaign, executives advised that the popular press be used to inform workers and the public at large of management's good intentions. Officials of the Illinois Central even paid the expenses of a YMCA evangelist to help spread the word.[32]

Other managers had more specific, tangible proposals. One positive answer was to reward the loyal. On the New York Central, following the strikes of 1877, William Vanderbilt distributed $100,000 to men who maintained allegiance to the line.[33] Loyal workers on the Pennsylvania similarly received bonuses in their pay vouchers.[34] On the Reading Railroad, all employees who refused to join the strike were immediately promoted or placed at the top of promotion lists.[35]

---

[30] G. Clinton Gardner to Frank Thomson, June 30, 1877, G. Clinton Gardner to Robert Pitcairn, July 20, 1878, G. Clinton Gardner Letterbook, Eleutherian Mills Historical Library.

[31] Cochran, *Railroad Leaders*, p. 301.

[32] Ibid., pp. 397, 472; *Annual Report of the Louisville & Nashville Railroad Company, 1877–78* (Louisville, Kentucky, 1878), p. 9.

[33] Bruce, *1877: Year of Violence*, p. 302.

[34] *Railroad Gazette*, January 4, 1879, p. 3.

[35] Resolution of Board of Managers, April 17, 1877, Reading Railroad Papers.

The violent response of railwaymen to announced wage cuts also served to convince many executives of the folly and danger of such unilateral actions. The riots in this way acted to set a floor on acceptable wages. When reductions were proposed on the Illinois Central following the Panic of 1893, the line's general superintendent reminded his board of directors about the events of 1877. The point needed no further elaboration and the plan to cut wages was summarily tabled.[36] High wage policies and even profit sharing similarly became much-discussed reforms during this period.

Extending accident and death benefit insurance, however, proved to be the most popular solution. Following the lead of the Baltimore & Ohio Railroad, practically all of the major trunk lines established insurance programs during the 1880s. Even Perkins came to see the merits of extending insurance relief to C.B. & Q. employees, although it took the disastrous Burlington Strike of 1888 to change his mind.[37] Railroad executives devised their insurance plans clearly to engender loyalty: employees generally were not eligible to receive benefits if they maintained membership in brotherhood programs. Railroad managers also considered other welfare reforms. The B. & O. established a savings plan and a pension program which became models for other railroads. During this period several lines built free medical care facilities and even old-age homes for their employees.[38]

The turbulence of the post-1877 years also brought to the attention of high officials the problem of the pervasive and often onerous power of local foremen. Standardizing procedures thus became recognized as a key answer to lessening tensions. Henry Ledyard in 1886 accordingly proposed the idea of competitive examinations for recruitment and promotion.[39] A. N. Towne, general superintendent of the Central Pacific Railroad, similarly argued in favor of fixed grievance procedures and a system of

---

[36] Lightner, "Labor on the Illinois Central," p. 204.

[37] Stevenson, "Brotherhood of Locomotive Engineers," pp. 99–100.

[38] Emory Johnson, "Railway Departments for the Relief and Insurance of Employes," *Annals of American Academy of Political and Social Science* 6:88–90; Illinois Central Railroad, *History of the Illinois Central Railroad Company and Representative Employees*, p. 713; Stewart Holbrook, *The Story of American Railroads*, p. 214.

[39] Cochran, *Railroad Leaders*, p. 91.

fines and suspensions to replace the practice of dishonorably discharging men.[40] In 1887 a Standard Code was drawn up by the American Time Convention (the forerunner of the Association of American Railroads), which created a uniform set of rules and regulations to apply to all lines.[41] This meant that men who moved from company to company would not be dismissed for behavior acceptable on one road but not on another. The notion of guaranteed work assignments and income was also discussed.[42]

Finally, the events of the late nineteenth and early twentieth centuries convinced a small group of railway executives of the value of recognizing trade unions as legitimate bargaining agents. In the 1870s Dean Richmond, president of the New York Central, became one of the first railway officials to encourage the growth of the Brotherhood of Locomotive Engineers. Richmond believed that the organization had a beneficial influence on Central drivers, and he commended BLE leaders for maintaining order on the line.[43] On the Illinois Central, the Brotherhood, while not encouraged, was patiently tolerated by I.C. officials, who found it convenient to meet with union leaders to discuss grievances.[44] Frederick Kimball, president of the Norfolk & Western Railroad, likewise welcomed Knights of Labor organizers to the road as a stabilizing force. These cases were certainly isolated and the officials involved were exceptional.[45] Most executives eventually came to recognize the value of dealing with the brotherhoods as a means of preventing violent confrontations, but only after organized railwaymen, through strike pressure, convinced them of the wisdom of such policies.

FOR RAILWAY WORKERS, the post-1877 period represented a time of both outward protest and intense behind-the-scenes union organizing activity. Before 1877 only three stable brotherhoods

[40] A. N. Towne to Robert Harris, December 4, 1877, Chicago, Burlington & Quincy Railroad Papers, Harris In-Letters, CBQ-3H4.6.

[41] Richardson, *Locomotive Engineer*, pp. 169, 248.

[42] Cochran, *Railroad Leaders*, p. 236; Bruce, *1877: Year of Violence*, p. 302.

[43] Stevenson, "Brotherhood of Locomotive Engineers," p. 67.

[44] Lightner, "Labor on the Illinois Central," p. 178.

[45] Cochran, *Railroad Leaders*, pp. 33, 374.

Table 7.1. *Organizational Information on the Seventeen Principal Railway Brotherhoods Established before 1901*

Craft group	Union initials	Date established	Date of first agreement	% of workers organized in each craft by 1890
Locomotive engineers	BLE	1863	1875	81
Conductors	ORC	1868	*	61
Locomotive firemen	BLF&E	1873	1876	54
Boilermakers	IBBISB	1880	1892	*
Brakemen	BRT	1883	1887	23
Trackmen	M of W	1886	1892	*
Telegraphers	ORT	1886	1892	*
Machinists	IAOM	1888	1892	*
Sheet-metal workers	SMWIA	1888	*	*
Blacksmiths	IBBDF	1889	1892	*
Carmen	BRCA	1891	1901	*
Electricians	IBEW	1891	1917	*
Clerks	BRC	1898	1906	*
Stationary firemen and oilers	IBFO	1898	*	*
Signalmen	BRSA	1901	1907	*

* Information unavailable or not applicable.

had emerged. By 1901 thirteen additional well-established railway craft unions had joined the field. Railway workers discovered organization to be a first step toward solving their problems. The written contract served as the next most important goal. Table 7.1 notes dates of formation of all brotherhoods established by 1901; dates of first agreements signed and percentages of men enrolled in each craft by 1890 are also listed.[46]

The Brotherhood of Locomotive Engineers led the way in negotiating for written contracts. It signed the first known written railroad labor agreement with William Vanderbilt of the New York Central in 1875. The contract is noteworthy for, among

[46] Figures for the table compiled from Dan Mater, "The Development and Operation of the Railroad Seniority System," *Journal of Business of the Univ. of Chicago* 13:395; Charles Clark, "The Railroad Safety Movement in the United States" (Ph.D. dissertation, Univ. of Illinois at Urbana, 1966), pp. 188–189.

other items, it established the principle of a guaranteed minimum daily wage. Clause 1 accordingly stipulated that passenger and freight engineers were to receive three and one-half cents per mile run, "excepting when the run is under 100 miles for which $3.50 per day will be paid." The notion of guaranteed income was extended a year later, when the brotherhood negotiated its second agreement with the New Jersey Central Railroad. This contract fixed compensation at a basic ninety dollars a month for twenty-six hundred miles of driving or less.[47]

In the next twenty-five years, the BLE entered into formal agreements with various railroads. These early contracts included detailed provisions for guaranteed wages, mileage and hour limitations, fixed rest periods, compensation for overtime, extra service, and excessive delays, as well as seniority rights and grievance and disciplinary procedures. As more items became negotiable, contracts increased in size, scope, and complexity.[48]

Wage agreements in particular became tediously long and complex, taking into account all possible circumstances and eventualities. There was a slow evolution from the simple daily or monthly wage to the trip and straight-mileage payment plans, to the combination daily guarantee and mileage system, and finally to what was termed the "dual pay basis" form of compensation. Under the latter arrangement, men were paid at fixed per mile rates with both a set number of hours and miles considered a guaranteed minimum day's labor. An example is provided in the following clause from a BLE contract signed in 1886 with the St. Paul, Minneapolis & Manitoba Railroad: "All first class engineers shall be paid at the rate of 3 and 9/10ths cents per mile. . . . Twelve hours or less, or one hundred miles or less to constitute a day's work."[49] As this example illustrates, matters became further complicated with the introduction of classification schemes. Many contracts reached during this period by the BLE, in fact, established different, well-defined wage calculations for drivers by years of service, type of service—passenger, freight, or yard—and even by the type of engine handled.[50]

[47] Richardson, *Locomotive Engineer*, pp. 196, 209.
[48] Ibid., chapter 12.
[49] Ibid., p. 210.
[50] Ibid., pp. 172, 210–212, 220.

Complex wage agreements protected brotherhood engineers against arbitrary methods of compensation. Men were to be paid exactly for the work they performed, which was now to be limited to driving. Any services provided above and beyond what was defined as a standard day's labor were covered by separate, equally well-defined overtime pay arrangements.[51] Contracts also provided for greater security and certainty in other aspects of the work experience. Engineers on the Missouri Pacific in 1885, for instance, received a written guarantee that the company would cease its practice of fining workers.[52] Locomotivemen on the Wabash, St. Louis & Pacific Railroad similarly secured written assurance that they would not be called for duty until an hour before scheduled departures.[53] A far-reaching contract signed on the Illinois Central in 1886 contained a number of unusual security measures: I.C. drivers received guarantees that they would be placed in positions as firemen during slack periods and not be discharged; they were also promised full wages if they reported to work and their runs were delayed or canceled.[54]

Other railway brotherhoods were able to secure protective measures for their members. The Brotherhood of Railway Trainmen dates its history from 1883, when eight brakemen met in a caboose in Oneonta, New York, in the yards of the Delaware & Hudson Railroad, to form a benevolent association. Encouraged by Eugene Debs, the Oneonta group soon launched a national campaign to organize railroad brakemen and to enlarge the benefit association's function to include trade union activities.[55] In one of the first contracts negotiated, the BRT secured a regulated system of promotion for its members. Under the terms of the agreement, brakemen were eligible after three years or 72,000 miles of service to take an examination in operating rules and train orders to qualify for conductorships. If a brakeman passed the test and all positions were filled, he was to be placed on a standby list.[56]

A group of thirty-two white-collar employees on the Missouri

[51] Ibid., pp. 226–227.
[52] *Locomotive Engineer's Journal*, May 1885, p. 276.
[53] Ibid., April 1883, p. 193.
[54] Richardson, *Locomotive Engineer*, pp. 224, 228–229.
[55] Joel Seidman, *The Brotherhood of Railway Trainmen*, pp. 1–2.
[56] Ibid., pp. 7–8.

Pacific and Missouri, Kansas & Texas Railroads formed the Order of Railway Clerks in December 1899 (the name was later changed to the Brotherhood of Railway and Steamship Clerks, Freight Handlers, Express and Station Employees when the organization expanded its scope and jurisdiction).[57] The new association signed its first significant agreement with executives of the New York, New Haven & Hartford Railroad. It included an important clause granting the brotherhood the right of representation in appeals of disciplinary actions taken against union members.[58]

A final example was the Brotherhood of Maintenance of the Way Employees, founded in 1887. In April 1902, representatives of the brotherhood signed with the East St. Louis & Suburban Railway Company what was probably the most comprehensive early railway labor agreement for lower-grade workers reached to date. It gave trackmen the right to a speedy, fair, and impartial trial in the event of disciplinary charges; the right to be represented at hearings by fellow workers of their own choosing; the right of appeal to the general manager; pay for time lost because of improper discharges; a nine-hour day, pro rata pay for the tenth hour on Sundays; promotion based on seniority; the recognition of seniority during force reductions; and free passage on the line after six months of service. The contract also established set wage schedules and fixed pay periods along with grievance procedures.[59] Through organization and such written contracts, railwaymen in all branches of the trade methodically sought to gain control over various aspects of the work experience and to write their own collective work rules to match the rules written by management. Their success was due in no small part to the more disorderly strike activity in which they engaged at the same time.

The third and fourth generations of American railwaymen thus fought, organized, and bargained to bring order to their working

---

[57] Nixson Denton, *History of the Brotherhood of Railway and Steamship Clerks, Freight Handlers, Express and Station Employees*, p. 19.

[58] Ibid., p. 24.

[59] Willard Hertel, *History of the Brotherhood of Maintenance of Way Employees*, p. 53.

lives, an order their forebears never had the good fortune to know. Railway workers during the early years of rail transport development entered large-scale enterprises, which, as historians like Alfred Chandler and Thomas Cochran have aptly emphasized, were bureaucratically shaped and structured by rather sophisticated businessmen. Yet, as has been shown repeatedly in this study, the work experience for the average nineteenth-century American railwayman remained a function of his personal relations with supervisors and foremen. Despite rules, regulations, and strict hierarchies of authority and accountability established from on high, local officials handled recruitment, discipline, job assignments, compensation, promotions, and accidental injury and death benefit awards, as well as other aspects of the work, in arbitrary and discretionary ways.[60]

With this perspective, the efforts of railwaymen in the post-1877 period to organize and secure written contracts takes on new meaning. In the name of fairness, justice, and security, railway workers allied to demand further bureaucratic standards and procedures to control as much of the work experience as possible. They both lost and gained in the process. Workers who had achieved special privileges through personal connections had to sacrifice their advantages to the common good. A certain amount of the romance, adventure, and spontaneity of the work was also forfeited. For instance, the renaissance men of the trade, the locomotive drivers, no longer fiddled, jiggled, pampered, and tuned their engines. That now belonged strictly in the domain of shop work, and the drivers were to be paid only for the work stipulated in the contract. Railwaymen, by the turn of the century, as veteran driver William Lynch noted, had become both sober and sobered. In a sense, by fighting the arbitrary rule of supervisors and demanding more formal standards, they con-

---

[60] In the past few years a number of studies about other industries have been published that also place great emphasis on the critical role played by foremen in industrial conflict and labor process development. (These works appeared after my own observation of this phenomenon in the railroad industry and were encouraging corroborations of the major argument of this book.) These studies include: Daniel Nelson, *Managers and Workers*; Edwards, *Contested Terrain*; and Michael Burawoy, *Manufacturing Consent*.

tributed to the bureaucratization and routinization of their own work.

Yet, at the same time, they also gained substantial control over the work situation and how they were to be treated as men and employees. This was not, to be sure, workers' control in the pure sense of worker seizure of the ownership and management of the means and processes of production. Rather, they secured control of the work experience, control over even seemingly trivial aspects of work which made their lives more secure, if not more autonomous.[61] As railroad corporations in the same period privately organized through pooling agreements and mergers to undo ruinous competition within the industry, and as government officials tried to rationalize industrial relations in the trade, so railway workers organized to undo competition among themselves to create conditions of stability. No one wanted an unfettered or uncontrollable marketplace, despite the rhetoric and public worship of individualism and free enterprise.

The role played by workers in demanding stricter standards and procedures also adds a new perspective to the whole question of bureaucratization. Pioneer railway managers imposed bureaucratic structures on the work situation, which proved to be dysfunctional in day-to-day labor relations. Conflicts stemming from worker frustration with arbitrary local supervision produced pressure from below for greater standardization. Bureaucratization thus represented both a structure and a process—a process which was dialectical in nature. Bureaucratic work organizations in this light developed not solely as the handiwork of farsighted businessmen, as entrepreneurial or Great Man theorists would have us believe; nor were they the results of some naturally emanate, inevitable, uniform movement toward greater degrees of rationality and organization, as glib modernization theories imply; but rather they emerged as part of a complex

---

[61] The form of worker power achieved by railwaymen—control over the work experience if not the productive process—has not been amply highlighted in recent studies and debates on workers' control movements. For various sides to the debate see: Montgomery, *Workers' Control in America*; Burawoy, *Manufacturing Consent*; and Jean Monds, "Workers' Control and the Historians," *New Left Review* 97:81–104.

unfolding process involving people, conscious decision making, personal interests, and human conflict.

Finally, throughout this study, various cross-cultural comparisons have been made and they offer some suggestions, if not conclusions, about work and laboring people in America. American railwaymen were part of a worldwide economic revolution, yet the nature of their work experience was shaped in many important respects by peculiar American circumstances and institutions. They labored, for instance, in a country with a federal system of government. American railway managers, as a result, could not easily or certainly secure legislation or judicial rulings that would have facilitated the disciplining of their labor forces. American railway workers and their supporters also possessed full citizenship and the vote; they wielded significant political power that was often manifest in hostility to railroad corporations at the level of local and state government. The political structure, though, in one way functioned to their disadvantage. In countries with strong, active central governments, railway workers were able to secure insurance protection guaranteed by the state decades before American workers received such benefits by bringing economic pressure on individual companies.

American railwaymen also worked in a country that did not have a highly fixed system of class distinctions, where a democratic republican ideology prevailed. In Britain, railway managers were able to superimpose the British class system on authority relations within the firm; class sanctions thus encouraged labor regimen (though paternalism had some advantages in greater corporate benevolence). In America, foremen, supervisors, and even high-level executives who rose from the bottom found the authority they possessed to be less sanctified. It is both symbolic and characteristic that when grade-specific uniforms were first proposed by railway managers, the idea met with bitter derision and opposition. The wearing of uniforms and insignia by civilian workers was deemed degrading in a democratic society.[62] Dem-

[62] Alfred D. Chandler, Jr., *Henry Varnum Poor*, p. 321; Charles F. Carter, *When Railroads Were New*, p. 145; Morris, *Railroad Administration*, pp. 264–265; *Colburn's Railroad Advocate*, August 11, 1855, p. 3; *American Railroad Journal*, September 1, 1855, p. 555.

ocratic ideals, in this way, offer one possible explanation for why American railwaymen and their supporters in the post-1877 period were at the same time highly militant, but not politically radical. As freeborn citizens of the republic, they refused to countenance unjust and unfair treatment and resorted to violent means to protest their circumstances.[63] Yet, the same egalitarian ideology promised opportunity and freedom for every hard-toiling American; in their eyes the system—especially if they could exert some control over the work experience—needed no revolution.

[63] For a recent study on railwaymen and republican ideology, see Nick Salvatore, "Railroad Workers and the Great Strike of 1877," *Labor History* 21:522–545.

APPENDIXES

≡

A. Table 2.4

TABLE 2.4 was constructed by gathering daily wage information on railroad workers and common laborers starting in 1838, when the first figures for operating railwaymen are available. Wages were then averaged over the time periods noted in the table. Differentials were created by dividing the indicated figures. Daily wage data for railway workers were compiled from the sources listed below. The locations of these materials can be found in the bibliography of this manuscript. In a few cases, where the title of the source is not indicative of where it was located, the archive where it was discovered is noted in parenthesis.

Baltimore & Ohio Railroad, printed payroll lists, 1842, 1852, 1855.
Boston & Maine Railroad, annual stockholders reports, 1849–1868.
Boston & Providence Railroad, investigatory reports, 1840, 1849.
Boston & Worcester Railroad, manuscript payroll records, 1849–1851, 1855.
Boston, Concord & Montreal Railroad, investigatory report, 1857.
Cape Cod Railroad, annual stockholders report, 1858.
Charlotte & South Carolina Railroad, annual stockholders report, 1856.
Chesapeake & Ohio Railroad, annual stockholders report, 1868.
Chesire Railroad, annual stockholders reports, 1850–1852.
Cleveland & Toledo Rail Road, manuscript payroll records, 1864–1867 (New York Central System Archives, Syracuse University Library, Syracuse, New York).
Concord Railroad, annual stockholders report, 1850.
Connecticut & Passumpsic Rivers Rail Road, manuscript payroll list,

1856 (Elijah Cleveland Business Records, University of Vermont Library, Burlington, Vermont).

Fall River Railroad, annual stockholders reports, 1850–1851.

Fitchburg Railroad, annual stockholders report, 1856.

Hartford & New Haven Railroad, manuscript payroll records, 1845–1847, 1851–1853, 1868–1870.

Illinois Railroad and Warehouse Commission, annual reports, 1878–1879.

Minnesota Railroad Commission, annual report, 1872.

New York & New Haven Railroad, annual stockholders report, 1860.

Northern Railroad, investigatory report, 1850.

North Carolina Railroad, annual stockholders reports, 1865, 1871.

Old Colony Railroad, annual stockholders reports, 1849–1850.

Philadelphia & Reading Railroad, investigatory report, 1846.

Philadelphia, Wilmington & Baltimore Railroad, annual stockholders reports, 1842, 1849–1850.

Sandusky, Dayton & Cincinnati Railroad, annual stockholders report, 1858.

South Shore Rail Road, annual stockholders report, 1854.

Virginia & Tennessee Railroad, annual stockholders report, 1860.

Western Railroad, manuscript payroll record, 1842, investigatory report, 1843.

Worcester & Nashua Railroad, annual stockholders report, 1856.

"Report, Engineer's Office, Baltimore & Ohio Railroad (May 14, 1838)," *Railway and Locomotive Historical Society Bulletin*, no. 13 (1927).

"Salaries on the Central Railroad," *American Railroad Journal*, December 15, 1855, p. 802.

United States Department of Labor, Bureau of Labor Statistics, *Bulletin No. 64: History of Wages in the United States from Colonial Times to 1929* (Washington, D.C., 1934).

Wage information on common labor was gathered from the following sources:

Edith Abbott, "The Wages of Unskilled Labor in the United States, 1850–1900," *The Journal of Political Economy* 13 (June 1905).

United States Department of Labor, Bureau of Labor Statistics, *Bulletin No. 64: History of Wages in the United States from Colonial Times to 1929* (Washington, D.C., 1934).

Yearly wages figures used to construct the averages listed in table 2.4 for station and track hands, locomotive engineers, and common laborers are presented in the accompanying table.

	Average daily wages (in dollars)		
Year	Railroad track and station laborers	Railroad locomotive engineers	Common laborers
1838	.80	2.00	*
1839	*	*	*
1840	1.00	2.00	1.02
1841	*	*	*
1842	.93	2.00	.95
1843	.90	1.96	.94
1844	*	*	.98
1845	.90	2.00	.93
1846	.90	2.15	.91
1847	.90	2.00	.91
1848	*	*	.93
1849	.99	2.12	.93
1850	.96	2.12	.92
1851	.99	2.20	.93
1852	.96	2.15	.95
1853	1.02	2.27	.98
1854	1.14	2.28	.95
1855	1.10	2.57	.99
1856	1.23	2.25	1.00
1857	1.16	2.35	1.01
1858	1.03	2.55	1.04
1859	1.15	2.38	1.03
1860	1.45	2.54	1.03
1861	1.27	2.42	1.03
1862	1.14	2.11	1.04
1863	1.29	2.42	1.25
1864	1.38	2.66	1.44
1865	1.63	2.89	1.63
1866	1.63	3.00	1.64
1867	*	*	1.60
1868	1.55	3.18	1.63
1869	1.75	3.50	1.68
1870	1.75	3.50	1.65
1871	1.50	3.45	1.66
1872	1.58	3.16	1.66
1873	*	2.50	1.66

* Reliable figures not available.

B. Tables 2.5 and B.1 through B.7

Table 2.5 was constructed from three separate manuscript payroll records of the Hartford & New Haven Railroad located in the New York, New Haven & Hartford Railroad Company Papers in Baker Library of Harvard University. Volume 89 of the collection is a payroll account covering the period September 1844–April 1847; volume 90 is a record of employees on payroll from August 1850–June 1853; and volume 91 is a similar account for the period April 1868–March 1870. Account books between these three periods were missing.

Since volume 91 covered the shortest time frame and enclosed an exact two-year period, a decision was made to make three separate tracings of men over two-year spans. Since over 35,000 combined entries were potentially involved, a second, more important decision was made to employ sampling procedures. The time and money in eventual computer costs of tracing every employee was not deemed worthy of the effort.

The following sampling technique was used. For volume 89, every entry in the April 1845, September 1845, March 1846, September 1846, and March 1847 payroll listings was recorded and keypunched on IBM cards; for volume 90, every entry for April 1851, September 1851, March 1852, September 1852, and March 1853; for volume 91, every entry for April 1868, September 1868, March 1869, September 1869, and March 1897. For volume 89, every entry included an employee's name, location in the payroll book, number of days worked in the month, and daily wages; for volumes 90 and 91, an employee's specific job title was available and it was also recorded. This procedure allowed for the tracing of men across six-month time periods over a total of twenty-four months.

Once every entry was keypunched, employees were linked across six-month periods first using an IBM sort program and then by hand. All the usual linking problems, especially with common names, were encountered. It was unclear whether Thomas Murphy, laborer, listed in April 1868 was the same Thomas Murphy, laborer, enumerated in September 1869; an even more difficult problem arose if the Thomas Murphy found in the September 1868 payroll was listed as a brakeman; was he promoted or was he a different individual? Matters were simplified when employees' middle names or initials were included; also knowing a man's location in the payroll account proved of value, since the formats of the accounts were fairly consistent. Men were considered "linked" across six-month payroll periods only if certainty had been established.

Once the tracing was completed, the estimated number of months employed in the company was calculated according to the schema in the accompanying table.

The sampling technique employed to produce the figures in table 2.5

Particular sampling month(s) found in payroll account*	Possible range of months employed	Possible average	Category assigned by number of months employed
1	1– 5	2.5	1– 6
1–2	6–11	8.5	7–12
1–3	12–17	14.5	13–18
1–4	18–23	20.5	19–24
1–5	24	24.0	19–24
2	1–10	5.5	1– 6
2–3	7–16	11.5	7–12
2–4	13–22	17.5	13–18
2–5	19–23	21.0	19–24
3	1–11	6.0	1– 6
3–4	7–17	12.0	7–12
3–5	13–18	15.5	13–18
4	1–11	6.0	1– 6
4–5	7–12	9.5	7–12
5	1– 6	3.0	1– 6

* Key to column one: 1 = First April; 2 = First September; 3 = First March; 4 = Second September; 5 = Second March.

is certainly not ideal. What is important is that the technique was employed consistently for all three payrolls, so that comparisons between the three are valid. Also a test of the technique was attempted by linking every entry in volume 89 across the two-year span for all twenty-four months. The numbers involved were small enough to warrant the experiment. The results from this extended total-population approach were practically identical to those derived from sampling on a six-month basis.

For the 1851–53 Hartford & New Haven Railroad study, the correlation between length of service and position in the railway occupational hierarchy was Contingency $C = 0.31$ at the 0.001 level of significance. For the 1868–70 study, the comparable figures are Contingency $C = 0.29$ at the 0.001 significance level.

Tables B.1 through B.7 that appear at the end of this appendix provide turnover figures for six other railroads in the time period under study. Details on the procedures employed to construct these tables follow.

Table B.1 was constructed from volume 107 of the Boston & Worcester Railroad Papers at Baker Library of Harvard University. The volume is a manuscript payroll account listing men employed by the line on December 1, 1849, 1850 and 1851, and on November 30, 1855. All entries for the first three rolls were recorded and keypunched on IBM cards; the entries were first linked by an IBM sort program and then by hand. No sampling was involved. Listings of specific occupational titles allowed for the occupational breakdown illustrated in the table.

Table B.2 was constructed from a payroll account of the Cleveland & Toledo Railroad Company found in the archives of the New York Central Railroad at Syracuse University Library. The account covered the period February 1864–April 1867. The numbers involved warranted a similar sampling procedure as employed with the Hartford & New Haven accounts. Employees were sampled from the February 1864, November 1864, February 1865, August 1865, and April 1866 listings. Entries were keypunched, linked, and counted using the same techniques described for table 2.5.

For the 1864–66 Cleveland & Toledo Railroad Company study, the correlation between length of service and position in the railway occupational hierarchy was Contingency $C = 0.32$ at the 0.001 level of significance.

Table B.3 was constructed from a handwritten list of blacksmiths, carpenters, machinists, engineers, and firemen employed by the Western Railroad during the year 1842. Men were listed on a monthly basis. The record was found in the corporate papers of the Western Railroad at Baker Library of Harvard University. Entries were keypunched and linked across the twelve months covered by the roll. No sampling was involved.

Table B.4 was constructed from a printed list of officers, conductors and enginemen employed by the Eastern Railroad, which indicated the number of years each man had served the company. The list can be found in the *Annual Report of the Directors of the Eastern Railroad Company* (Boston, 1848), pp. 10–11.

Table B.5 was constructed from information included in the annual stockholders' reports of the Boston and Maine Railroad. Between 1849 and 1868, the names, positions, and wages and salaries of most of the line's employees were listed in the reports. These entries were keypunched and linked by hand to derive the count of average years of service by grade level presented in the table. No sampling was involved.

Table B.6 was constructed from a handwritten list of men employed in the car and locomotive departments of the Chicago, Burlington & Quincy Railroad in May 1860, 1861, and 1862. The roll was drawn by John Van Nortwich, then president of the C.B. & Q., and can be found in the Burlington Company archives in the Newberry Library (under the listing CBQ-2.8). If an employee was enumerated once, he was counted as serving one full year; if listed two or three times, he was counted as remaining with the line for two full years.

Table B.1. Turnover Analysis for the Boston & Worcester Railroad, 1849–51

Grade level	Total number employed	Number employed, by years			% employed, by years		
		1	2	3	1	2	3
Upper-level management	8	3	1	4	38	12	50
Lower-level management	64	18	13	33	28	20	52
White-collar	37	11	10	16	30	27	43
Conductors	15	5	0	10	33	0	67
Baggagemen	9	0	0	9	0	0	100
Brakemen	84	56	12	16	67	14	19
Enginemen	32	4	3	25	13	9	78
Firemen	25	9	8	8	36	32	32
Skilled shop mechanics	132	56	29	47	42	22	36
General unskilled labor	417	253	69	95	61	16	23
Total force	823	415	145	263	50	18	32

Table B.2. *Turnover Analysis for the Cleveland & Toledo Railroad, 1864–66*

Grade level	Total number employed	Number employed, by months				% employed, by months			
		1–6	7–12	13–18	19–24	1–6	7–12	13–18	19–24
Upper-level management	21	4	3	3	11	19	14	14	53
Lower-level management	123	35	6	9	73	29	5	7	59
White-collar	171	87	17	18	49	51	10	10	29
Conductors	32	8	2	1	21	25	7	3	66
Baggagemen	48	28	6	1	13	58	13	2	27
Brakemen	141	95	19	11	16	67	14	8	11
Enginemen	60	17	3	3	37	28	5	5	62
Firemen	95	54	16	2	23	57	17	2	24
Skilled shop mechanics	374	184	59	24	107	49	16	6	29
Unskilled shop mechanics	138	78	24	10	26	57	17	7	19
Station and track labor	989	640	107	82	160	65	11	8	16
Total force	2192	1230	262	164	536	56	12	7	25

Table B.3. *Turnover Analysis for the Western Railroad, 1842*

Grade level	Total number employed	Average number of months employed	Number employed, by months				% employed, by months			
			1–3	4–6	7–9	10–12	1–3	4–6	7–9	10–12
Blacksmiths	19	6.30	8	3	1	7	42	16	5	37
Carpenters	20	5.05	10	4	1	5	50	20	5	25
Machinists	63	3.90	41	7	8	7	65	11	13	11
Enginemen	30	6.50	9	6	8	7	30	20	27	23
Firemen	46	4.70	26	9	2	9	57	20	4	19
Total force	178	4.90	94	29	20	35	53	16	11	20

Table B.4. Turnover Analysis for the Eastern Railroad, 1836–47

Grade level	Total number employed	Average number of years employed	Number employed, by years		% employed, by years	
			1–5	6–10	1–5	6–10
Upper-level management	8	6.0	5	3	63	37
Conductors	13	3.7	10	3	77	23
Enginemen	23	2.5	21	2	91	9
Total force	44	3.5	36	8	82	18

Table B.5. Turnover Analysis for the Boston & Maine Railroad, 1849–68

Grade level	Total number employed	Average number of years employed	Number employed, by years				% employed, by years			
			1–5	6–10	11–15	16–20	1–5	6–10	11–15	16–20
Upper-level management	22	7.4	13	2	2	5	59	9	9	23
White-collar	25	4.0	19	3	3	0	76	12	12	0
Agents	123	6.2	75	20	14	14	61	16	11	12
Conductors	47	6.3	31	8	3	5	66	8	3	5
Enginemen	77	6.7	47	12	6	12	61	16	8	15
Total force	294	6.2	185	45	28	36	63	15	10	12

Table B.6. Turnover Analysis for the Chicago, Burlington & Quincy Railroad, 1861–62

Grade level	Total number employed	Number employed, by years		% employed, by years	
		1	2	1	2
Enginemen	29	7	22	24	76
Firemen	29	19	10	66	34
Machinists	39	13	26	33	66
Machinists' apprentices	17	9	8	53	47
Boilermakers	15	3	12	20	80
Blacksmiths	21	9	12	43	57
Blacksmiths' helpers	25	15	10	60	40
Engine wipers	22	20	2	91	9
Painters	13	4	9	31	69
Carpenters	79	30	49	38	62
Total force	289	129	160	45	55

Table B.7. Length of Service of Engineers Employed by the Chicago, Burlington & Quincy Railroad, 1877

Number of years in company's service	Number	%
Less than 5 years	147	47
5 years and less than 10 years	106	34
10 years and less than 15 years	43	14
15 years and less than 20 years	14	4
20 years and less than 25 years	4	1
Total	314	100

The figures in table B.7 were taken from Clive Scott, "Robert Harris and the Strike of 1877" (Master's thesis, Univ. of Western Ontario, 1967), p. 156.

C. Table 4.1

Data on railwaymen's wages were compiled from the following sources and averaged over the time periods indicated in table 4.1. The location of most of these sources can be found in the bibliography of this manuscript. Where the title of a source is not indicative of where it was located, the reference or archive where it was discovered is noted in parentheses.

Baltimore & Ohio Railroad, printed payroll lists, 1842, 1852, 1855.

Boston & Maine Railroad, annual stockholders reports, 1849–1868.

Boston & Providence Railroad, investigatory report, 1840.

Boston & Worcester Railroad, manuscript payroll records, 1849–1851, 1855.

Boston, Concord & Montreal Railroad, investigatory report, 1857.

Cape Cod Railroad, annual stockholders report, 1858.

Charlotte & South Carolina Railroad, annual stockholders report, 1856.

Chesapeake & Ohio Railroad, annual stockholders report, 1868.

Chesire Railroad, annual stockholders reports, 1850–1852.

Chicago, Burlington & Quincy Railroad, list of wages, 1873 (Chicago, Burlington & Quincy Railroad Papers, Robert Harris Out-Letters, pp. 492–493, CBQ-3H4.1, Newberry Library).

Connecticut & Passumpsic Rivers Railroad, manuscript payroll list, 1856 (Elijah Cleveland Business Records, University of Vermont Library, Burlington, Vermont).

Fall River Railroad, annual stockholders reports, 1850–1851.

Hartford & New Haven Railroad, manuscript payroll records, 1845–1847, 1851–1853, 1868–1870.

Illinois Central Railroad, list of wages, 1855 (David Lightner, "Labor on the Illinois Central Railroad, 1852-1900," Ph.D. diss., Cornell University, 1969, pp. 72–73).

Illinois Railroad and Warehouse Commission, annual reports, 1878–1879.

Maine Railroad Commissioners, annual reports, 1874, 1876.

Minnesota Railroad Commission, annual report, 1872.

New York & New Haven Railroad, annual stockholders report, 1860.

New York Central Railroad, annual stockholders report, 1855.

Northern Railroad, investigatory report, 1850.

North Carolina Railroad, annual stockholders reports, 1865, 1871.

Philadelphia & Reading Railroad, investigatory report, 1846.

Philadelphia, Wilmington & Baltimore Railroad, annual stockholders reports, 1842, 1849–50.

Sandusky, Dayton & Cincinnati Railroad, annual stockholders report, 1858.

South Shore Rail Road, annual stockholders report, 1854.

Virginia & Tennessee Railroad, annual stockholders report, 1860.

Western Railroad, manuscript payroll record, 1842, investigatory report, 1843.

Worcester & Nashua Railroad, annual stockholders report, 1856.

United States Department of Labor, Bureau of Labor Statistics, *Bulletin*

No. 64: History of Wages in the United States from Colonial Times to 1929 (Washington, D.C., 1934).

Information on wages of nonrailroad workers were compiled from the following sources:

Edith Abbott, "The Wages of Unskilled Labor in the United States, 1850–1900," *Journal of Political Economy* 13 (June 1905).

Robert Layer, *Earnings of Cotton Mill Operatives, 1825–1914* (Cambridge, Mass., 1952).

United States Department of Labor, Bureau of Labor Statistics, *Bulletin No. 64: History of Wages in the United States from Colonial Times to 1929* (Washington, D.C., 1934).

D. Table D.1

Table D.1 lists Pearson correlation coefficients for firm size and average yearly earnings for fifteen different railroad occupational categories. The cases studied are forty-eight rail carriers operating in the state of Illinois in 1878. Eleven indicators of company size are used and the results reported in the text are consistent across each. The data for this analysis can be found in the *Eighth Annual Report of the Railroad and Warehouse Commission of Illinois* (Springfield, Illinois, 1879), pp. 56–59.

Table D.1. Pearson Correlation Coefficients for Firm Size and Average Yearly Earnings of Fifteen Occupational Categories, Forty-Eight Illinois Railroad Companies, 1878 (Levels of significance noted in parentheses)

	No. of employees	Length of line	Aggregate common-preferred stock
Division superintendents	.75 (.00)	.75 (.00)	.75 (.00)
Master mechanics	.57 (.00)	.50 (.00)	.60 (.00)
Road masters	.36 (.02)	.29 (.05)	.42 (.02)
Station agents	.27 (.04)	.25 (.05)	.29 (.04)
Clerks	−.16 (.18)	.09 (.31)	−.05 (.39)
Conductors	.01 (.47)	.16 (.15)	.08 (.31)
Engineers	.07 (.34)	.24 (.06)	.12 (.25)
Firemen	.10 (.27)	.13 (.21)	.09 (.30)
Brakemen	−.17 (.14)	−.07 (.39)	−.16 (.19)
Flagmen-Switchmen	.27 (.07)	.03 (.45)	.27 (.08)
Shopmen	−.19 (.14)	.11 (.27)	−.12 (.26)
Telegraph operators	.03 (.44)	.07 (.36)	−.10 (.33)
Section foremen	.07 (.33)	.11 (.23)	.17 (.15)
Laborers	−.11 (.25)	−.07 (.34)	−.05 (.39)
Other employees	−.09 (.30)	.11 (.27)	.11 (.29)

Table D.1. Continued

	Aggregate bonded-floating debt	Total cost of construction and equipment	Total train mileage
Division superintendents	.66 (.00)	.79 (.00)	.84 (.00)
Master mechanics	.50 (.00)	.56 (.00)	.58 (.00)
Road masters	.14 (.25)	.35 (.10)	.45 (.01)
Station agents	.19 (.13)	.19 (.19)	.31 (.03)
Clerks	.07 (.35)	−.03 (.45)	.04 (.42)
Conductors	.12 (.24)	−.01 (.48)	.01 (.48)
Engineers	.12 (.24)	.02 (.46)	.11 (.23)
Firemen	.11 (.25)	.11 (.30)	.21 (.12)
Brakemen	−.10 (.29)	−.16 (.23)	−.12 (.25)
Flagmen-Switchmen	.01 (.48)	.15 (.26)	.21 (.15)
Shopmen	−.23 (.11)	−.22 (.17)	−.18 (.17)
Telegraph operators	−.07 (.37)	.02 (.49)	−.15 (.41)
Section foremen	.22 (.09)	.08 (.35)	.13 (.22)
Laborers	−.05 (.38)	−.22 (.16)	−.04 (.41)
Other employees	.07 (.35)	−.02 (.46)	.26 (.08)

	No. of freight tons	No. of passengers
Division superintendents	.73 (.00)	.82 (.00)
Master mechanics	.47 (.01)	.50 (.00)
Road masters	.46 (.01)	.44 (.01)
Station agents	.28 (.06)	.45 (.00)
Clerks	.03 (.46)	.03 (.45)
Conductors	.08 (.33)	.19 (.15)
Engineers	.12 (.26)	.20 (.15)
Firemen	.11 (.27)	.30 (.05)
Brakemen	−.12 (.26)	.03 (.44)
Flagmen-Switchmen	.20 (.26)	.34 (.05)
Shopmen	−.18 (.18)	.04 (.41)
Telegraph operators	.11 (.30)	.03 (.46)
Section foremen	.02 (.47)	.17 (.19)
Laborers	.08 (.34)	.09 (.33)
Other employees	.26 (.09)	.16 (.20)

	Gross earnings	Gross expenses	Net earnings
Division superintendents	.85 (.00)	.85 (.00)	.82 (.00)
Master mechanics	.52 (.00)	.53 (.00)	.51 (.00)
Road masters	.40 (.01)	.40 (.01)	.49 (.01)
Station agents	.31 (.10)	.31 (.02)	.30 (.02)
Clerks	.03 (.43)	.03 (.43)	.03 (.32)
Conductors	.11 (.25)	.08 (.30)	.13 (.20)
Engineers	.16 (.15)	.14 (.18)	.18 (.12)
Firemen	.17 (.14)	.13 (.20)	.21 (.09)
Brakemen	−.07 (.33)	−.11 (.24)	−.02 (.46)
Flagmen-Switchmen	.26 (.08)	.22 (.12)	.29 (.06)
Shopmen	−.13 (.24)	−.18 (.16)	.07 (.35)

Table D.1. Continued

	Gross earnings	Gross expenses	Net earnings
Telegraph operators	.06 (.38)	.04 (.41)	.07 (.36)
Section foremen	.13 (.20)	.11 (.24)	.15 (.17)
Laborers	−.05 (.39)	−.07 (.34)	−.02 (.46)
Other employees	.13 (.23)	.13 (.23)	.12 (.24)

NOTE: Levels of significance are listed because of the problem of missing information. Not all forty-eight companies were included in every cross-tabulation. In some instances, the operation was performed on a sample of the whole population of Illinois railroad firms. Pearson's *r* measures the strength and direction of a linear relationship between two variables. It ranges from −1 to +1. As *r* approaches its limits, we can assume there is a strong linear relationship. An *r* of 0 implies no correlation.

E. Figures E.1 through E.5

In Figures E.1 through E.5 the career lines of 155 Illinois Central railwaymen born before 1850 are mapped. Fifty-nine I.C. locomotive engineers are included in figure E.1; twenty-six conductors in figure E.2; forty local officials in figure E.3; twenty-six division officials in figure E.4; and four central office department heads in figure E.5.

Information to construct the career lines was derived from a biographical compendium of "representative" Illinois Central Railroad employees compiled and published by the carrier in 1900 (the exact citation: Illinois Central Railroad, *History of the Illinois Central Railroad and Representative Employees* [Chicago, 1900]). Short biographic and career sketches of several thousand I.C. workers are included in the volume. For the purposes of this study, only the 155 men in the compendium born before 1850 were selected for analysis.

Information contained in the sketches allowed for a reconstruction of the careers of each member in the sample. The men were then grouped into five categories by last position achieved in the firm. Some individuals in each category had unique occupational histories. They received their own line in the maps. Most followed fairly consistent patterns; these careers have been collapsed into single lines and the reported entry dates and intervals between career steps are average figures. For example, in figure E.1 the first locomotiveman mapped had a unique career. He entered railroading at the age of thirty as a skilled mechanic; at the age of thirty-four he became a freight engineer and at thirty-nine a passenger driver. Twenty-three I.C. engineers, on the other hand, had similar and more traditional occupational histories, and their careers are mapped as one in the right-hand column. These men entered the trade as firemen at an average age of twenty-one, were then promoted to freight engineer at an average age of twenty-four, and were finally elevated to passenger driver status at an average age of thirty-five years.

Two points need mention. Information for men who did not start their careers in railroading with the Illinois Central are included in the road's biographical compendium. Entry dates in the tables thus represent ages at which I.C. employees actually entered the trade and not just the firm. Second, the I.C. volume offered no clues as to the criteria employed in the selection of these so-called typical workers. As noted in the text, while the 155 men included in this study probably cannot be considered representative of the entire work force of early I.C. employees, their careers are indicative of those who were promoted.

Figure E.1. Career Lines of Fifty-Nine Locomotive Engineers Born before 1850 and Employed by the Illinois Central Railroad

Number of locomotivemen in each career line																	
1	1	2	1	1	1	1	1	1	3	1	5	2	7	3	3	2	23
SM	FE	CL	DL	DL	DL	BR	BR	BR	BR	RL	RL	SL	SL	SL	FR	FR	FR

Starting position:

Age	SM	FE	CL	DL	DL	DL	BR	BR	BR	BR	RL	RL	SL	SL	SL	FR	FR	FR
10																		
11																		
12											RL							
13											FR							
14																		
15				DL														
16																		
17			CL		DL													
18						DL	BR	BR			FE		SL	SL	SL	FR		
19									BR			RL		FR			FR	
20		FR				FR	BR		FR			RL	FR					
21					YL		FC	FE	FR				FR	FE				FR
22		FE	FE	RL			FR		FE									
23						FE			FE									
24							PE				FR	FE						FE
25																		
26									FE					PE				
27			FR	FR	PE													
28			FE				FE					FE				FE		
29		PE																
30	SM	PE			FE													
31																		
32							PE											
33																		
34	FE													PE			PE	
35																		PE
36																		
37																		
38																		
39	PE											PE						
40																		
41											PE							
42				PE														
43																		
44																		
45																		

KEY: SM = Skilled Mechanic; FE = Freight Engineer; CL = Construction Laborer; DL = Depot or Station Laborer; YL = Yard Laborer; BR = Brakeman; RL = Round or Engine House Laborer; SL = Shop Laborer; FR = Fireman; PE = Passenger Engineer.

Figure E.2. *Career Lines of Twenty-Six Conductors Born before 1850 and Employed by the Illinois Central Railroad*

	Number of conductors in each career line										
Starting position:	1 TG	1 RL	1 SL	1 SL	1 SL	2 FR	2 FR	4 DL	1 DL	2 BR	10 BR
Age: 15											
16											
17			SL						DL		
18				SL				DL			
19			YD		SL			BR			
20						FR			BR		
21		RL			BR	FR					
22	TG		BR			BR					BR
23		BR	FC								
24		FC		SM				FC			FC
25	BR			BR		FC			FC		
26											
27	FC			FC			FR			BR	
28											
29											
30											
31			PC								
32							FC				PC
33											
34											
35					FC						
36									PC		
37								PC			
38										PC	
39	PC										
40		PC									
41											
42											
43						PC	PC				
44					PC						
45											
46											
47				PC							
48											

KEY: TB = Telegraph Operator; BR = Brakeman; FC = Freight Conductor; PC = Passenger Conductor; RL = Round or Engine House Laborer; SL = Shop Laborer; YL = Yard Laborer; SM = Skilled Mechanic; FR = Fireman; DL = Depot or Station Laborer.

Figure E.3. Career Lines of Forty Local Officials Born before 1850 and Employed by the Illinois Central Railroad

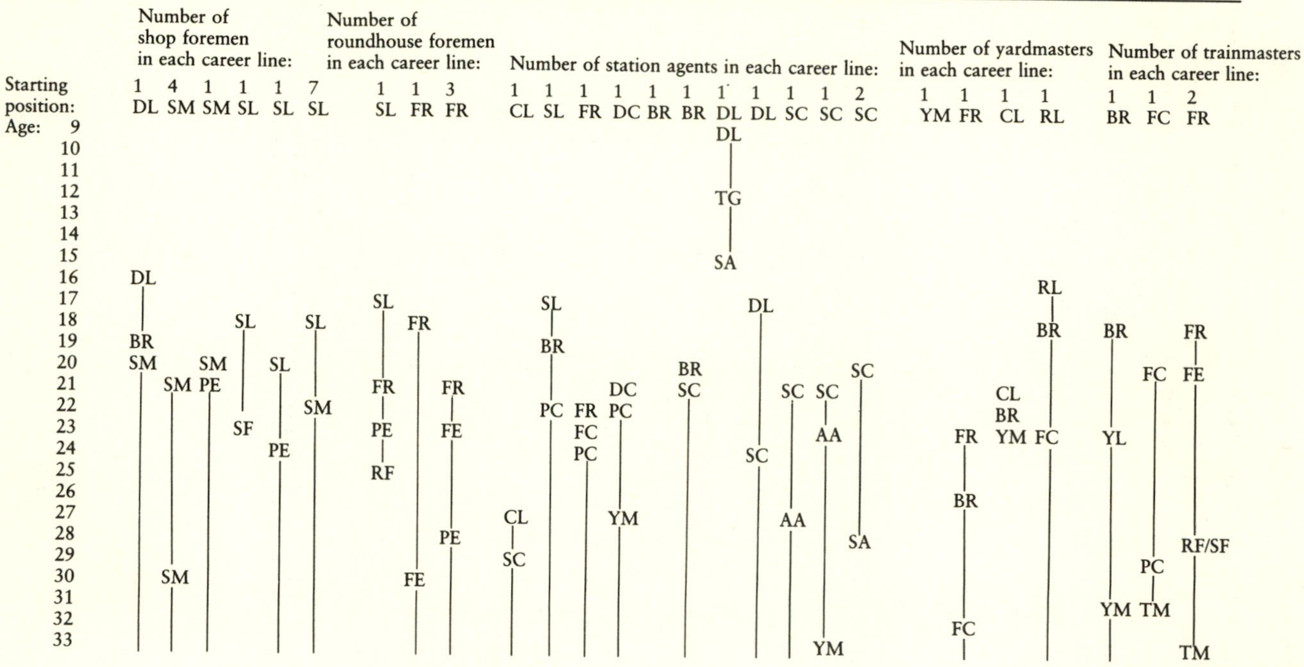

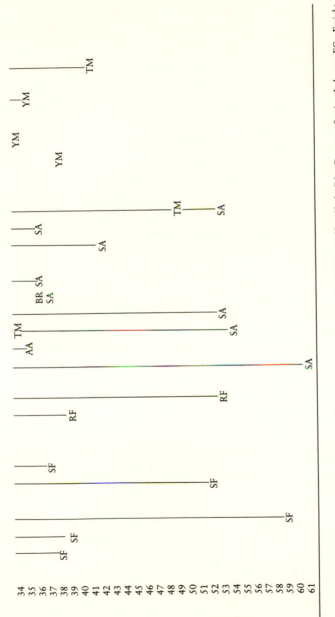

KEY: AA = Ass't. Station Agent; BR = Brakeman; CL = Construction Laborer; DC = Division Office Clerk; DL = Depot or Station Laborer; FC = Freight Conductor; FE = Freight Engineer; FR = Fireman; PC = Passenger Conductor; PE = Passenger Engineer; RF = Round or Engine House Foreman; RL = Round or Engine House Laborer; SA = Station Agent; SC = Station Clerk; SF = Shop Foreman; SL = Shop Laborer; SM = Skilled Mechanic; TG = Telegraph Operator; TM = Trainmaster; YM = Yard Master.

Figure E.4. Career Lines of Twenty-Six Division Officials Born before 1850 and Employed by the Illinois Central Railroad

Number of roadmasters in each career line:					Number of master mechanics in each career line:					Number of general agents in each career line:				Number of division superintendents in each career line:								
1	1	1	1	2	1	1	1	2	2	1	1	1	1	1	1	1	1	1	1	1	1	1
TG	SM	TL	CL	CL	SL	SM	FR	FR	FR	BR	CL	SC	SC	SC	CL	SA	SC	SC	DL	DL	BR	BR

Starting position / Age: 15–31

(Career-line chart with position codes: TG, SM, TL, SC, SA, CL, SL, FR, PE, SM, FE, PE, SF, MM, BR, SC, SA, SC, AA, MM, FE, BR, FR, TD, TG, SC, DC, SC, DL, SC, FC, TM, TD, SA, PC, PC, BR, FC, PC, DL, BR.)

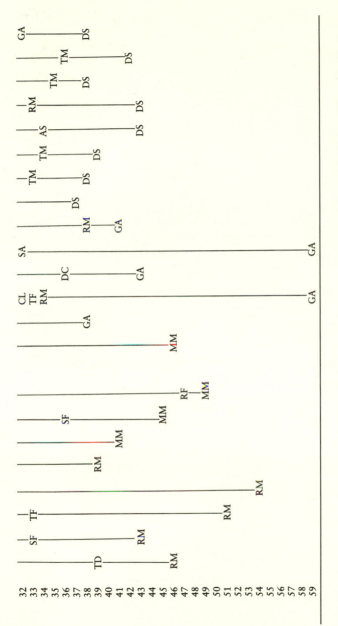

KEY: AA = Ass't. Station Agent; AS = Ass't. Division Superintendent; BR = Brakeman; CL = Construction Laborer; DC = Division Office Clerk; DL = Depot or Station Laborer; DS = Division Superintendent; FC = Freight Conductor; FE = Freight Engineer; FR = Fireman; GA = General Agent; MM = Master Mechanic; PC = Passenger Conductor; PE = Passenger Engineer; RF = Round or Engine House Foreman; RM = Road Master; TD = Train Dispatcher; TF = Track Foreman; TG = Telegraph Operator; TL = Track Laborer; TM = Trainmaster.

*Figure E.5. Career Lines of Four Central Office Department Heads Born before
1850 and Employed by the Illinois Central Railroad*

Starting position:	General superintendent of telegraphs TG	Chief engineer CL	Superintendent of transportation SC	General manager DL
Age: 19			SC	
20			SA	
21				DL
22	TG			SL
23				TD
24		CL		
25				
26				
27		TF		
28				FC
29			GA	
30	SA	RM		
31				YM
34				RM
35			DS	
41		AE	ST	
42	DT			DS
47				GM
51		CE		
58	GT			

KEY: TG = Telegraph Operator; CL = Construction Laborer; SC = Station Clerk; DL = Depot Laborer; SL = Shop Laborer; SA = Station Agent; TD = Train Dispatcher; TF = Track Foreman; FC = Freight Conductor; YM = Yard Master; RM = Roadmaster; DT = Division Sup't. of Telegraphs; DS = Division Superintendent; GA = General Agent; AE = Ass't. to Chief Engineer; GT = General Sup't. of Telegraphs; CE = Chief Engineer; ST = Sup't. of Transportation; GM = General Manager.

F. Table F.1

Table F.1 lists correlation coefficients for speed of promotion with various socio-demographic and career factors. The cases analyzed are 155 Illinois Central Railroad employees born before 1850 whose biographic sketches are included in the road's compendium of "representative" I.C. workers compiled and published in 1900. The information in these sketches was coded, keypunched and transformed into a computerized data base.

Creation of table F.1 involved the following steps. The sample was first divided between "fast" and "slow" risers. Men who advanced from their first to last positions within fifteen years were defined as "fast" climbers; the others as "slow." A dichotomous dependent variable, speed of promotion, was then cross-tabulated with the twelve independent variables listed in table F.1. All these factors were reclassified into nominal or ordinal form (the categories for ethnicity, the most ambiguous variable, were old stock and immigrant). Contingency tables were first generated for the sample population as a whole and then for I.C. engineers, conductors, local officials, and division level officers. Since there were only four central office department heads, a separate analysis was not performed for them. Contingency Coefficient C is used as a measurement of association in this table since the dependent variable was ordered categorically and the independent variables were either ordered or unordered categorically. Contingency Coefficient C ranges from 0 to 1 (from 0 to 0.77 in the case of 2 x 2 tables); high values indicate a strong relationship between the independent variables and speed of promotion.

One qualification needs comment. The cell sizes in this analysis in many instances were quite small. The problem was compounded by missing data. Therefore, it is not unexpected that so few of the correlations are significant at the 0.05 level. Noteworthy, however, are the few highly correlated, statistically significant results—particularly, father's occupation and marital status—that emerged despite the low number of cases.

Table F.1. Correlates of Speed of Promotion (Levels of significance reported in parentheses)

	All railwaymen	Engineers	Conductors	Local officials	Division officials
Year of birth	.04 (.71)*	.04 (.98)*	.13 (.95)*	.05 (.99)*	.00 (.61)*
Place of birth	.11 (.64)	.11 (.88)	.20 (.76)*	.51 (.00)	.24 (.69)
Father's occupation	.32 (.04)**	.34 (.37)**	.49 (.19)	.50 (.09)**	.38 (.57)**
Religion	.01 (.83)**	.36 (.23)**	.26 (.60)**	.08 (.57)**	.17 (.50)
Ethnicity	.08 (.57)	.05 (.96)	.19 (.43)	.07 (.98)**	.29 (.29)
Education	.06 (.93)**	.37 (.49)**	.62 (.08)**	.49 (.23)**	.44 (.24)
Previous occupation	.32 (.12)**	.37 (.49)**	.60 (.19)**	.44 (.24)**	.25 (.50)**
Marital status	.25 (.00)**	.08 (.81)*	.01 (.50)*	.31 (.09)*	.27 (.41)*
Number of children	.08 (.45)	.05 (.91)	.11 (.90)	.32 (.10)	.20 (.37)
Relatives in railroad work	.04 (.69)*	.01 (.87)*	.18 (.58)*	.20 (.34)*	.16 (.75)*
Number of different companies worked for	.09 (.51)*	.14 (.56)*	.23 (.48)*	.22 (.36)*	.24 (.45)*
Political affiliation	.37 (.22)**	.50 (.50)**	.50 (.51)**	.70 (.14)**	.33 (.64)**

* Entire population included in tabulation; no missing information.

** Missing information eliminated more than half of the cases in these tabulations.

NOTE: Contingency Coefficient C was used as a measurement of association in this table since the dependent variable was ordered categorically and the independent variables were either ordered or unordered categorically. Contingency Coefficient C ranges in value from 0 to 1 (from 0 to 0.77 in the case of 2 × 2 tables); high values indicate strong relationships between independent variables and speed of promotion.

G. Tables G.1 through G.5

Data included in the tables in this appendix were drawn from the Philadelphia Social History Project data bank. Information on the project can be found in Theodore Hershberg, "The Philadelphia Social History Project: A Methodological History" (Ph.D. dissertation, Stanford University, 1973).

Table G.1 lists railwaymen in Philadelphia for three census years by grade of employ and ethnicity. Comparisons to the population at large are also given; figures on total population include only males over the age of eighteen, or the total male work force, and come from Hershberg, p. 294. Figures in the text for employment in the printing, bricklaying and shoemaking industries also are drawn from Hershberg, pp. 278–281.

The correlation between ethnicity and position in the trade, using Contingency Coefficient C, was 0.47 in 1860, 0.34 in 1870 and 0.28 in 1880, an indication of the decreasing rigidity of the industry's social structure. In all three census years, measurements of association were statistically significant at the 0.01 level. Contingency C was used because both independent and dependent variables were unordered and categorical.

Table G.2 lists railwaymen in Philadelphia in the census year 1880 by position and ethnicity, with ethnic affiliation broken down by generation. The correlation between ethnicity by generation and place in the trade using Contingency Coefficient C was 0.37 at the 0.01 level of statistical significance. The table clearly indicates that second generation immigrants occupied better positions in the industry to a greater extent than their first generation counterparts.

Table G.3 gives figures on residential segregation for Philadelphia railwaymen during three census years and is broken down by grade of employ and ethnicity. Figures in the third column of the table indicate the number of railwaymen in any category who lived in one grid space in the city (a grid space represents a block and a half square unit established for analytic purposes by the Philadelphia Social History Project). The absence of clustering among railwaymen is best depicted graphically through computer mappings. These maps would have occupied an inordinate space in this manuscript; they are available from the author upon request.

The figures on native white American railwaymen are not weighted in this analysis as they are in tables G.1 and G.2. The Philadelphia Social History Project sampled but one-sixth of the so-called NWAs in 1860 and one-ninth in 1870 and 1880 (the figures on the Irish, Germans, and

Table G.1. Philadelphia Railwaymen by Grade Level and Ethnicity, 1860, 1870, 1880

Position in the industry	NWA N	NWA %	Irish N	Irish %	German N	German %	Black N	Black %
1860								
Upper management	18	6	1	1	0	0	0	0
Lower management	60	21	8	12	0	0	0	0
White-collar	18	6	1	1	0	0	0	0
Conductor	96	33	8	12	0	0	0	0
Locomotive engineer	18	6	10	14	0	0	0	0
Fireman	6	2	1	1	0	0	0	0
Brakeman	42	15	16	23	4	100	0	0
Shopman	18	6	1	1	0		0	0
Laborer	12	4	25	35	0	0	0	0
Total	288	99	71	100	4	100	0	0
Percentage of total		79		20		1		0
Total in population	70,014	53	37,718	28	20,411	15	5,554	4
Percentage of total population								
1870								
Upper management	99	6	6	1	0	0	0	0
Lower management	90	5	5	1	2	3	0	0
White-collar	459	28	40	13	6	10	0	0
Conductor	414	25	49	16	11	18	0	0

Engineer	180	11	44	14	9	14	1	6
Fireman	45	3	19	6	3	5	0	0
Brakeman	153	9	21	7	6	10	4	24
Shopman	27	2	12	4	0	0	0	0
Laborer	189	11	118	38	26	41	12	70
Total	1656	100	314	100	63	101	17	100
Percentage of total		81		15		3		1
Total in population		94,473		38,024		23,956		5,773
Percentage of total population		58		23		15		4
1880								
Upper management	9	1	1	1	0	0	0	0
Lower management	126	5	20	5	5	5	0	0
White-collar	819	33	67	18	13	13	0	0
Conductor	306	12	17	5	6	6	0	0
Engineer	234	10	27	7	2	2	1	7
Fireman	117	5	13	4	1	1	0	0
Brakeman	324	13	41	11	11	11	0	0
Shopman	36	2	5	1	1	1	0	0
Laborer	495	20	178	48	59	60	14	93
Total	2466	101	369	100	98	99	15	100
Percentage of total		84		12		3		1
Total in population		147,915		38,605		26,500		9,525
Percentage of total population		66		18		12		4

key: NW/A = Native white American.

Table G.2. Philadelphia Railwaymen by Grade Level, Ethnicity,
and Generation, 1880

	Old stock		2nd Irish		1st Irish	
Position in the industry	N	%	N	%	N	%
Upper management	9	1	0	0	1	1
Lower management	90	5	18	4	20	5
White-collar	594	35	117	28	67	18
Conductor	198	12	63	15	17	4
Engineer	171	10	27	7	27	7
Fireman	63	4	18	4	13	4
Brakeman	216	13	81	20	41	11
Shopman	36	2	0	0	5	1
Laborer	306	18	90	22	178	48
Total	1683	100	414	100	369	99
Percentage of total		58		14		13
Total in population	87,930		24,399		39,428	
Percentage of total population		41		11		18

	2nd German		1st German		2nd other		Black	
Position in the industry	N	%	N	%	N	%	N	%
Upper management	0	0	0	0	0	0	0	0
Lower management	0	0	5	5	9	6	0	0
White-collar	27	19	13	13	72	44	0	0
Conductor	27	19	6	6	18	11	0	0
Engineer	9	6	2	2	18	11	1	7
Fireman	0	0	1	1	27	17	0	0
Brakeman	27	19	11	11	0	0	0	0
Shopman	0	0	1	1	0	0	0	0
Laborer	54	38	59	60	18	11	14	93
Total	144	101	98	99	162	100	15	100
Percentage of total		5		3		6		1
Total in population	13,860		27,099		13,527		9,525	
Percentage of total population		6		13		6		4

KEY: 1st, 2nd = First, second generation; Other = Immigrants not from Germany or Ireland.

blacks are total figures and not samples). Weighting the NWAs in this analysis would have placed a weighted number of them at any given address, thereby greatly overestimating the density of that population.

Table G.4 lists the real property holdings of railwaymen in 1860 and 1870 in Philadelphia by position and ethnicity. Percent reporting real property holdings as well as value reported is given. Thirteen percent of all railwaymen in the city reported possessing real estate, which was average for the population at large. See Hershberg, p. 248. The correlation between position in the trade and property was much stronger than the association between ethnicity and real holdings. Using analysis of variance, in 1860 and 1870 Eta for position and real property was 0.67 and 0.58, and for ethnicity and real worth it was 0.24 and 0.34.

Table G.5 lists personal property holdings of railwaymen in 1860 and 1870 in Philadelphia by position and ethnicity. Percent reporting property holdings as well as value reported are given. Between 42 and 45 percent of all railwaymen reported having personal wealth, slightly above average for the population at large. See Theodore Hershberg and Robert Dockhorn, "Occupational Classification," *Historical Methods Newsletter* 9 (March/June 1976):76. The correlation between position in the trade and personal wealth was stronger than the association for ethnicity and personal holdings (Eta was 0.34 and 0.24 in 1860 and 1870 for the latter relationship and 0.02 and 0.11 for the former).

Table G.3. Residential Patterns of Philadelphia Railwaymen, 1860, 1870, 1880

Occupational/ ethnic categories	No.	No. of grid spaces occupied	No. of railwaymen per grid space
1860			
All railwaymen	123	76	1.6
NWA	48	42	1.1
Irish	71	36	1.9
German	4	*	*
Black	0	—	—
Management**	22	18	1.2
White-collar	4	*	*
Conductor	24	20	1.2
Locomotive engineer	13	*	*
Fireman	2	*	*
Brakeman	27	16	1.7
Shopman	4	*	*
Laborer	27	6	4.5
1870			
All railwaymen	578	307	1.9
NWA	184	150	1.2
Irish	314	159	1.9
German	63	54	1.2
Black	17	14	1.2
Management**	34	33	1.0
White-collar	97	86	1.1
Conductor	106	79	1.3
Locomotive engineer	74	59	1.3
Fireman	27	19	1.4
Brakeman	48	41	1.2
Shopman	15	8	1.9
Laborer	177	109	1.6
1880			
All railwaymen	755	388	1.9
NWA***	211	151	1.4
Irish****	415	241	1.6
German****	114	92	1.2
Black	15	13	1.1
Management**	41	40	1.0
White-collar	170	138	1.2
Conductor	57	49	1.2
Locomotive engineer	56	41	1.4
Fireman	27	22	1.2
Brakeman	88	68	1.3
Shopman	10	10	1.0
Laborer	306	201	1.5

Table G.3. Continued

Occupational ethnic categories	% living in grid spaces with stated no. of other railwaymen			
	1–2	3–4	5–6	7+
1860				
All railwaymen	61	17	4	18
NWA	92	8	0	0
Irish	49	19	0	31
German	*	*	*	*
Black	–	–	–	–
Management**	73	27	0	0
White-collar	*	*	*	*
Conductor	100	0	0	0
Locomotive engineer	*	*	*	*
Fireman	*	*	*	*
Brakeman	44	37	19	0
Shopman	*	*	*	*
Laborer	19	–	–	81
1870				
All railwaymen	53	23	9	15
NWA	91	9	0	0
Irish	53	14	6	27
German	91	9	0	0
Black	77	23	0	0
Management**	100	0	0	0
White-collar	91	9	0	0
Conductor	83	6	4	7
Locomotive engineer	87	13	0	0
Fireman	63	37	0	0
Brakeman	85	15	0	0
Shopman	53	0	0	47
Laborer	63	22	9	6
1880				
All railwaymen	52	26	9	13
NWA***	78	14	5	3
Irish****	60	21	11	8
German****	87	13	0	0
Black	80	20	0	0
Management**	100	0	0	0
White-collar	95	5	0	0
Conductor	90	10		
Locomotive engineer	73	18	9	0
Fireman	89	11	0	0
Brakeman	78	22	0	0
Shopman	100	0	0	0
Laborer	72	18	5	5

* Figures too small to warrant analysis.
** Includes upper and lower management positions.
*** Excludes second-generation Irish and Germans.
**** Includes second-generation Irish and Germans.

Table G.4. Real Personal Property Holdings of Philadelphia Railwaymen, 1860, 1870

Position in industry	Total	NWA	Irish	German	Black
	% reporting real personal property				
1860					
Upper management	37	33	100	–	–
Lower management	10	10	12	–	–
White-collar	5	0	100	–	–
Conductor	12	13	0		
Locomotive engineer	29	33	20	–	–
Fireman	14	0	100	–	–
Brakeman	2	0	6	0	–
Shopman	37	33	100	–	–
Laborer	5	0	8	–	–
Average	13	13	14	0	–
1870					
Upper management	38	36	67	–	–
Lower management	28	30	0	0	–
White-collar	11	10	20	67	–
Conductor	7	6	100	9	–
Locomotive engineer	9	5	29	0	0
Fireman	25	20	42	0	–
Brakeman	8	6	19	17	0
Shopman	8	0	25	–	–
Laborer	13	5	22	35	8
Average	13	10	23	24	6

Position in industry	Total	NWA	Irish	German	Black
	Mean value reported (in rounded dollars)				
1860					
Upper management	18571	20000	10000	–	–
Lower management	2286	1500	7000		
White-collar	4500	0	4500		
Conductor	17750	17750	0	–	–
Locomotive engineer	2463	3000	850	–	–
Fireman	3000	0	3000	–	–
Brakeman	1200	0	1200	0	–
Shopman	829	700	1600	–	–
Laborer	550	0	550	–	–
Average	8572	1265	424	0	–
1870					
Upper management	15460	16675	4525	–	–
Lower management	11000	11000	0	0	–
White-collar	6370	6640	5938	4200	–
Conductor	7212	6967	9820	800	–
Locomotive engineer	2014	900	2785	0	0
Fireman	1971	1600	2388	–	–
Brakeman	2764	3500	1425	1500	–
Shopman	1800	0	1800	0	–
Laborer	1982	2800	1910	1317	2500
Average	6696	8578	3250	2063	2500

Table G.5. Personal Property Holdings of Philadelphia Railwaymen,
1860, 1870

Position in industry	Percent reporting personal property				
	Total	NWA	Irish	German	Black
1860					
Upper management	100	100	100	–	–
Lower management	34	30	63	–	–
White-collar	68	67	100	–	–
Conductor	67	69	50	–	–
Locomotive engineer	75	100	30	–	–
Fireman	0	0	0	–	–
Brakeman	8	0	31	0	–
Shopman	37	33	100	–	–
Laborer	35	100	4	–	–
Average	47	52	30	0	–
1870					
Upper management	64	64	67	–	–
Lower management	68	70	40	50	–
White-collar	35	33	42	100	–
Conductor	42	41	41	45	–
Locomotive engineer	37	35	43	66	0
Fireman	36	20	68	67	–
Brakeman	30	29	33	50	25
Shopman	46	33	75	–	–
Laborer	49	48	45	81	33
Average	42	40	46	68	29

Position in industry	Mean value reported (in rounded dollars)				
	Total	NWA	Irish	German	Black
1860					
Upper management	5000	3833	26000	–	–
Lower management	515	567	330	–	–
White-collar	346	390	300	–	–
Conductor	1694	1784	200	–	–
Locomotive engineer	1981	2283	168	–	–
Fireman	0	0	0	–	–
Brakeman	100	0	100	0	–
Shopman	543	600	200	–	–
Laborer	327	350	50	–	–
Average	1638	1667	1429	0	–
1870					
Upper management	7263	7664	938	–	–
Lower management	3668	3829	350	200	–
White-collar	1632	1635	971	3433	–
Conductor	3767	4261	390	380	–
Locomotive engineer	276	264	310	300	0
Fireman	367	500	300	200	–
Brakeman	592	670	243	333	300
Shopman	175	100	250	–	–
Laborer	438	525	367	271	275
Average	2211	2706	430	728	280

BIBLIOGRAPHY

≡

Primary Sources

RAILROAD COMPANY PAPERS

The memoranda, letterbooks, rule books, organizational studies, printed circulars, payroll accounts, etc. found in railroad corporate archives are sources of valuable information on nineteenth-century railroad work, though labor-related materials generally constitute only a small, often scattered portion of most collections. For the early period of American railroading, the following collections were most useful:

Atlantic & St. Lawrence Railroad Company Papers, Bowdoin College Library, Brunswick, Maine.

Baltimore & Ohio Railroad Company Papers, Maryland Historical Society, Baltimore, Maryland.

Boston & Lowell and Boston & Nashua Railroad Papers, Baker Library, Harvard University, Cambridge, Massachusetts.

Boston & Worcester Railroad Company Papers, Baker Library, Harvard University, Cambridge, Massachusetts.

Chicago, Burlington & Quincy Railroad Company Archives, Newberry Library, Chicago, Illinois.

Delaware, Lackawanna & Western Railroad Company Papers, Syracuse University Library, Syracuse, New York.

Erie Railway Company Papers, Syracuse University Library, Syracuse, New York.

Illinois Central Railroad Company Archives, Newberry Library, Chicago, Illinois.

Lackawanna & Wyoming Valley Railroad Corporate Papers, Syracuse University Library, Syracuse, New York.

Newcastle & Frenchtown Railroad Company Papers, Historical Society of Delaware, Wilmington, Delaware.

New York Central & Hudson River Railroad Company Papers, New York Public Library, Manuscript Division, New York, New York.

New York Central System Archives, Syracuse University Library, Syracuse, New York.

New York, New Haven & Hartford Railroad Company Papers, Baker Library, Harvard University, Cambridge, Massachusetts.

New York, Ontario & Western Railway Company Papers, Cornell University Library, Ithaca, New York.

Reading Railroad Company Papers, Eleutherian Mills Historical Library, Wilmington, Delaware.

Syracuse & Utica Railroad Company Papers, New York Public Library, Manuscript Division, New York, New York.

Western Railroad Company Papers, Baker Library, Harvard University, Cambridge, Massachusetts.

OTHER MANUSCRIPT COLLECTIONS

Baldwin Locomotive Papers, Historical Society of Pennsylvania, Philadelphia, Pennsylvania.

Bliss Family Diaries, State Historical Society of Wisconsin, Madison, Wisconsin.

Elijah Cleveland Business Records, University of Vermont Library, Burlington, Vermont.

George Clinton Gardner Letters, Eleutherian Mills Historical Library, Wilmington, Delaware.

Hammond Family Business Records, Cornell University Library, Ithaca, New York.

Michael Harrington Papers, State Historical Society of Wisconsin, Madison, Wisconsin.

Herman Haupt Letterbook, Historical Society of Pennsylvania, Philadelphia, Pennsylvania.

Roy Martin Papers, State Historical Society of Wisconsin, Madison, Wisconsin.

John Wilson Diaries, Historical Society of Pennsylvania, Philadelphia, Pennsylvania.

PRINTED CORPORATE RECORDS

Printed rule books and special investigatory and annual stockholders reports contain valuable information for the student of nineteenth-century railroad work. The Boston & Maine Railroad, for instance, between 1849 and 1868 listed names of employees and wages in annual reports to shareholders. Fairly complete series of early printed corporate records can be found in Baker Library, Harvard University, Cambridge, Massachusetts; the American Antiquarian Society, Worcester, Massachusetts; and the Pliny Fisk Collection of Firestone Library, Princeton University, Princeton, New Jersey. The printed reports of the following railroads in the specific years noted contained useful information for this study:

Baltimore & Ohio Railroad, annual stockholders reports, 1832–1880; organizational study, 1848; payroll lists, 1842, 1852, 1855.

Baltimore & Susquehanna Railroad, annual stockholders report, 1836.

Boston & Albany Railroad, library catalog, 1868.

Boston & Maine Railroad, annual stockholders reports, 1849–1876.

Boston & Providence Railroad, annual stockholders reports, 1840–1859; investigatory reports, 1840, 1849.

Boston & Worcester Railroad, annual stockholders reports, 1841–1853.

Boston, Concord & Montreal Railroad, annual stockholders reports, 1850–1860; investigatory report, 1857.

Cape Cod Railroad, annual stockholders report, 1858.

Central Ohio Rail Road, regulations, 1852.

Central Pacific Railroad, annual stockholders report, 1873.

Charlotte & South Carolina Railroad, annual stockholders report, 1856.

Chesapeake & Ohio Railroad, annual stockholders report, 1868.

Chesire Railroad, annual stockholders reports, 1850–1852.

Chicago & Alton Railroad Company, annual stockholders report, 1865.

Concord Railroad, annual stockholders reports, 1850–1873, investigatory report, 1857.

Eastern Railroad, annual stockholders report, 1848.

Fall River Railroad, annual stockholders reports, 1850–1851.

Fitchburg Railroad, annual stockholders reports, 1849–1857.

Long Island Railroad, investigatory report, 1865.

Louisville & Nashville Railroad, annual stockholders reports, 1877–1878.

Michigan Central Railroad, annual stockholders reports, 1867–1870.

Mine Hill & Schuylkill Haven Railroad, annual stockholders report, 1864.

New Hampshire Central Rail Road, annual stockholders report, 1850.

New York & Erie Railroad, annual stockholders reports, 1852–1877; organizational reports, 1852–1855.

New York & New Haven Railroad, annual stockholders report, 1860.

New York Central Railroad, annual stockholders report, 1855.

Norfolk Railroad Company, annual stockholders report, 1853.
North Carolina Rail Road, annual stockholders reports, 1857–1871.
Northern Railroad, investigatory report, 1850.
North Pennsylvania Railroad, regulations, 1875.
Old Colony Railroad, annual stockholders reports, 1849–1875.
Philadelphia & Reading Railroad, investigatory report, 1846; annual stockholders report, 1850.
Philadelphia, Wilmington & Baltimore Railroad, annual stockholders reports, 1842–1879.
Providence & Worcester Railroad, annual stockholders reports, 1849–1880.
Rutland & Burlington Railroad, regulations, 1855.
Sandusky, Dayton & Cincinnati Railroad, annual stockholders report, 1858.
South Carolina Canal & Rail-Road, annual stockholders report, 1834.
South Shore Rail Road, annual stockholders report, 1854.
Vermont & Canada Railroad, annual stockholders report, 1860.
Virginia & Tennessee Railroad, annual stockholders report, 1860.
Virginia Central Railroad, annual stockholders report, 1852.
Western Railroad, annual stockholders reports, 1838–1860; investigatory reports, 1843, 1844.
Worcester & Nashua Railroad, annual stockholders report, 1856.

STATE RAILROAD COMMISSION REPORTS
Information on strikes, managerial attitudes, working conditions, and accidental injuries and deaths and other safety-related matters can be found in state railroad commission reports. The following were useful for this study:

Connecticut General Railroad Commissioners, annual reports, 1856–1880.
Illinois Railroad and Warehouse Commission, annual reports, 1872–1879.
Iowa Board of Railroad Commissioners, annual reports, 1878–1880.
Maine Railroad Commissioners, annual reports, 1870–1880.
Massachusetts Board of Railroad Commissioners, annual reports, 1870–1880. Before 1870 reports of individual Massachusetts corporations can be found in bound volumes entitled *Annual Reports of the Railroad Corporations in the State of Massachusetts to the State Legislature*.
Michigan Commission of Railroads, annual reports, 1872–1880.
Minnesota Railroad Commission, annual reports, 1872–1880.

New Jersey, *Annual Reports of Railroad and Canal Companies*, 1852–
1880.
New York State Engineer and Surveyor, annual reports, 1852–1880.
New York State Railroad Commissioners, annual reports, 1856–1880.

RAILROAD TRADE JOURNALS AND UNION PUBLICATIONS
American Engineer, 1857.
American Railroad Journal, 1832–1862.
American Railway Review, 1859–1861.
American Railway Times, 1851–1871.
Colburn's Railroad Advocate, 1855–1856.
Holley's Railroad Advocate, 1856–1857.
Locomotive Engineer's Journal, 1867–1900.
Railroad Clerk, 1929.
Railroad Gazette, 1870–1880.
Railroad Record, 1853–1859.
Railway Age, 1932.
Rock Island Magazine, 1922.

Secondary Sources

Abbott, Edith. "The Wages of Unskilled Labor in the United States,
1850–1900." *Journal of Political Economy* 13 (June 1905): 321–
367.
Adams, B. B., Jr. "The Every-Day Life of Railroad Men." In T. C.
Clarke et al., *The American Railway*, pp. 383–424. New York, 1889.
Adams, Charles F., Jr. *Railroads: Their Origin and Problems.* New
York, 1878.
Adams, Charles F., Jr. "The Prevention of Railway Strikes." In T. C.
Clarke et al., *The American Railway*, pp. 370–382. New York, 1889.
Baker, George P. *The Formation of the New England Railroad Systems:
A Study of Railroad Combination in the Nineteenth Century.* Cam-
bridge, Mass., 1937.
Barnard, W. T. *Service Report on Technical Education.* Baltimore, 1877.
Bendix, Reinhard. *Work and Authority in Industry: Ideologies of Man-
agement in the Course of Industrialization.* Berkeley, Calif., 1974.
Black, Paul. "Robert Harris and the Problem of Railway Labor Man-
agement: 1867–1870." Unpublished paper in possession of author.
——. "The Development of Management Personnel Policies on the Bur-
lington Railroad, 1860–1900." Ph.D. diss., Univ. of Wisconsin, 1972.

——. "Experiment in Bureaucratic Centralization: Employee Blacklisting on the Burlington Railroad, 1877–1892." *Business History Review* 51 (Winter 1977): 444–459.

——. "Employee Alcoholism on the Burlington Railroad, 1876–1902." *Journal of the West* 17 (October 1978): 5–11.

Black, Robert C. III. *The Railroads of the Confederacy*. Chapel Hill, N.C., 1952.

Bogen, Jules. *The Anthracite Railroads: A Study in American Enterprise*. New York, 1927.

Bonney, Charles C. *Rules of Law for the Carriage and Delivery of Persons and Property by Railway*. Chicago, 1864.

Botkin, B. A. and Harlow, Alvin, eds. *A Treasury of Railroad Folklore*. New York, 1953.

Bowman, Hank. *Pioneer Railroads*. New York, 1954.

Bradlee, Francis. *The Boston and Lowell Railroad, the Nashua and Lowell Railroad, and the Salem and Lowell Railroad*. Salem, Mass., 1918.

——. *The Eastern Railroad*. Salem, Mass., 1922.

Brailsford, Brazeal. *The Brotherhood of Sleeping Car Porters: Its Origins and Development*. New York, 1946.

Brissenden, Paul and Frankel, Emil. *Labor Turnover in Industry: A Statistical Analysis*. New York, 1922.

Bruce, Robert. *1877: Year of Violence*. New York, 1959.

Bryant, Keith, Jr. *History of the Atchison, Topeka and Santa Fe Railway*. New York, 1974.

Burawoy, Michael. *Manufacturing Consent: Changes in the Labor Process Under Monopoly Capitalism*. Chicago, 1979.

Burgess, George and Kennedy, Miles. *Centennial History of the Pennsylvania Railroad Company*. Philadelphia, 1949.

Burt, Jesse C., Jr. "The Savor of Old-Time Southern Railroading," *Railway and Locomotive Historical Society Bulletin*, no. 84 (October 1951), pp. 36–45.

Buttrick, John. "The Inside Contract System." *Journal of Economic History* 12 (Spring 1952): 205–221.

Carter, Charles F. *When Railroads Were New*. New York, 1926.

Chadbourne, James. "Recollections," *Railway and Locomotive Historical Society Bulletin*, no. 4 (1923), pp. 14–18.

Chandler, Alfred D., Jr. *Henry Varnum Poor: Business Editor, Analyst and Reformer*. Cambridge, Mass., 1956.

——. "Management Decentralization: An Historical Analysis." *Business History Review* 30 (June 1956): 111–174.

Chandler, Alfred D., Jr. "The Beginnings of 'Big Business' in American Industry." *Business History Review* 33 (Spring 1959): 1–31.

——. *Strategy and Structure: Chapters in the History of American Enterprise.* Cambridge, Mass., 1962.

——. "The Railroads: Pioneers in Modern Corporate Management," *Business History Review* 39 (Spring 1965): 16–40.

——. *The Visible Hand: The Managerial Revolution in American Business.* Cambridge, Mass., 1977.

Chandler, Alfred D., Jr., ed. *The Railroads: The Nation's First Big Business.* New York, 1965.

Chandler, Alfred D., Jr. and Redlich, Fritz. "Recent Developments in American Business Administration and Conceptualization." *Business History Review* 35 (Spring 1961): 1–27.

Chandler, Alfred D., Jr. and Salsbury, Stephen. "The Railroads: Innovators in Modern Business Administration." In *The Railroad and the Space Program: An Exploration in Historical Analogy,* edited by Bruce Mazlish, pp. 127–162. Cambridge, Mass., 1965.

Clark, Charles. "The Railroad Safety Movement in the United States: Origins and Development, 1869–1893." Ph.D. diss. Univ. of Illinois at Urbana, 1966.

Cochran, Thomas. *Railroad Leaders, 1845–1890: The Business Mind in Action.* Cambridge, Mass., 1953.

Colburn, Zerah and Holley, Alexander. *The Permanent Way.* New York, 1858.

Coleman, Terry. *The Railway Navvies: A History of the Men Who Made the Railways.* London, 1965.

Corliss, Carlton. *Main Line of Mid-America: The Story of the Illinois Central.* New York, 1920.

Cottrell, William. *The Railroader.* Stanford, Calif., 1940.

David, Paul. *Technical Choice, Innovation and Economic Growth: Essays on American and British Experience in the Nineteenth Century.* London, 1975.

Denton, Nixson. *History of the Brotherhood of Railway and Steamship Clerks, Freight Handlers, Express and Station Employees.* Cincinnati, Ohio, 1965.

Derrick, Samuel. *Centennial History of the South Carolina Railroad.* Columbia, S.C., 1930.

Dew, Charles. "Disciplining Slave Ironworkers in the Antebellum South: Coercion, Conciliation, and Accommodation." *American Historical Review* 79 (April 1974): 393–418.

Dewhurst, H. S. *The Railroad Police.* Springfield, Illinois, 1955.

Dimmick, L. F. *Discourse on the Moral Influence of Rail-Roads*. Boston, 1841.

Doherty, Lawrence. "The Wheeler Station." *Railway and Locomotive Historical Society Bulletin*, no. 49 (May 1939), pp. 91–94.

Dorsey, Edward B. *English and American Railroads Compared*. New York, 1887.

Dozier, Howard. *A History of the Atlantic Coast Line*. Boston, 1920.

Ducker, James. "Men of the Steel Rails: Workers on the Atchison, Topeka, and Santa Fe." Ph.D. diss., Univ. of Illinois at Champaign-Urbana, 1980.

Dunham, A. L. *The Pioneer Period of Railroads in England, France and the United States*. Cambridge, Mass., 1946.

Edwards, Richard. *Contested Terrain: The Transformation of the Workplace in the Twentieth Century*. New York, 1979.

Eggert, Gerald. *Railroad Labor Disputes: The Beginning of Federal Strike Policy*. Ann Arbor, Mich. 1967.

Fall, Charles. *Employer's Liability for Personal Injuries to the Employee*. Boston, 1889.

Fels, Rendig. *Wages, Earnings and Employment, Nashville, Chattanooga and St. Louis Railway, 1866–1896*. Nashville, Tenn., 1953.

Fishlow, Albert. *American Railroads and the Transformation of the Ante-Bellum Economy*. Cambridge, Mass., 1965.

——. "Productivity and Technological Change in the Railroad Sector, 1840–1910." In *Output, Employment, and Productivity in the United States after 1800*. National Bureau of Economic Research, Inc., Studies in Income and Wealth, vol. 30, pp. 581–646. New York, 1965.

Fogel, Robert. *Railroads and American Economic Growth: Essays in Econometric History*. Baltimore, 1964.

Foner, Philip. *History of the Labor Movement in the United States, Volume II: From the Founding of the American Federation of Labor to the Emergence of American Imperialism*. New York, 1955.

——. *The Great Labor Uprising of 1877*. New York, 1977.

French, Chauncey Del. *Railroadman*. New York, 1938.

Genovese, Eugene. *The World the Slaveholders Made: Two Essays in Interpretation*. New York, 1969.

——. *Roll, Jordan, Roll: The World the Slaves Made*. New York, 1974.

George, Charles. *Forty Years on the Rail: Reminiscences of a Veteran Conductor*. Chicago, 1887.

Glover, J. E. *The Click of the Rails*. Jackson, Tenn., 1929.

Graves, Carl. "Scientific Management and the Santa Fe Railway Shopmen of Topeka, Kansas, 1900–1925." Ph.D. diss., Harvard Univ., 1980.

Green, James. *The World of the Worker: Labor in Twentieth-Century America*. New York, 1980.

Greenwald, Maurine. "Women Workers and World War I: The American Railroad Industry, a Case Study." *Journal of Social History* 9 (Winter 1975): 154–177.

Griffen, Clyde and Griffen, Sally. *Natives and Newcomers: The Ordering of Opportunity in Mid-Nineteenth-Century Poughkeepsie*. Cambridge, Mass., 1978.

Gutman, Herbert. "Trouble on the Railroads in 1873–1874: Prelude to the 1877 Crisis?" *Labor History* 2 (Spring 1961): 215–235.

——. "Workers' Search for Power: Labor in the Gilded Age." In *The Gilded Age: A Reappraisal*, edited by H. Wayne Morgan, pp. 215–235. Syracuse, 1963.

Habakkuk, H. J. *American and British Technology in the Nineteenth Century: The Search for Labour-Saving Inventions*. Cambridge, England, 1967.

Hamblen, Herbert. *The General Manager's Story*. New York, 1898.

Hammett, Hugh. "Labor and Race: The Georgia Railroad Strike of 1909." *Labor History* 16 (Fall 1975): 470–484.

Hampton, Taylor. *The Nickel Plate Road: The History of a Great Railroad*. Cleveland, 1947.

Haney, Lewis. *A Congressional History of Railways in the United States to 1850*. Madison, Wisc., 1908.

——. *A Congressional History of Railways in the United States from 1850 to 1887*. Madison, Wisc. 1910.

Hargrave, Frank. *A Pioneer Indiana Railroad*. Indianapolis, 1932.

Harlow, Alvin. *The Road of the Century: The Story of the New York Central*. New York, 1947.

Hershberg, Theodore. "The Philadelphia Social History Project: A Methodological History." Ph.D. diss., Stanford Univ., 1973.

Hershberg, Theodore and Dockham, Robert. "Occupational Classification." *Historical Methods Newsletter* 9 (March/June 1976): 59–98.

Hertel, Willard. *History of the Brotherhood of Maintenance of Way Employees: Its Birth and Growth, 1877–1955*. Washington, D.C., 1955.

Holbrook, Stewart. *The Story of American Railroads*. New York, 1947.

Horowitz, Morris. *Manpower Utilization in the Railroad Industry: An Analysis of Working Rules and Practices*. Boston, 1960.

Hungerford, Edward. *The Story of the Baltimore and Ohio Railroad, 1827–1927*. 2 vols. New York, 1928.
——. *Men of the Erie: A Story of Human Effort*. New York, 1946.
Hunt, Robert. *Law and Locomotives*. Madison, Wisc., 1958.
Illinois Central Railroad. *History of the Illinois Central Railroad and Representative Employees*. Chicago, 1900.
Jacobs, Warren. "The Fall River Line Boat Train." *Railway and Locomotive Society Bulletin*, no. 2 (1921), pp. 4–18.
——. "Early Rules and the Standard Code." *Railway and Locomotive Society Bulletin*, no. 50. (October 1939), pp. 29–55.
Jacqmin, F. *Railroad Employes in France*. New York, 1877.
Jenks, Leland. "Railroads as an Economic Force in American Development." *Journal of Economic History* 4 (May 1944): 1-20.
——. "Early History of Railway Organization." *Business History Review* 35 (Summer 1961): 153–179.
——. "Multiple-Level Organization of a Great Railroad." *Business History Review* 35 (Autumn 1961): 336–343.
Johnson, Arthur M. and Supple, Barry E. *Boston Capitalists and Western Railroads: A Study in the Nineteenth Century Investment Process*. Cambridge, Mass., 1967.
Johnson, Emory. "Railway Departments for the Relief and Insurance of Employes." *Annals of the American Academy of Political and Social Science* 6 (November 1895): 64–108.
Johnston, Angus James II. *Virginia Railroads in the Civil War*. Chapel Hill, N.C., 1961.
Jones, Harry. *Railroad Wages and Labor Relations, 1900–1952*. New York, 1953.
Kendall, John. "The Connecticut and Passumpsic Rivers R.R." *Railway and Locomotive Historical Society Bulletin*, no. 49 (May 1939), pp. 23–32.
Kelly, Ralph. *Boston in the 1830's and the "William Penn."* New York, 1947.
Kennedy, Charles. "The Early Business History of Four Massachusetts Railroads." *Bulletin of the Business Historical Society* 25 (March, June, September, December 1951): 52–72, 84–98, 188–203, 207–229.
——. "The Eastern Rail-Road Company to 1855." *Business History Review* 31 (Spring, Summer 1957): 92–123, 179–108.
Kingsford, Peter. *Victorian Railwaymen: The Emergence and Growth of Railway Labour, 1830–1870*. London, 1970.

Kirkland, Edward. *Men, Cities and Transportation: A Study in New England History, 1820–1900.* 2 vols. Cambridge, Mass., 1948.

Kirkman, Marshall. *Railway Expenditures.* Chicago, 1880.

——. *Railway Train and Station Service.* Chicago, 1884.

Kirkpatrick, O. H. *Working on the Railroad.* Philadelphia, 1949.

Klein, Maury. *History of the Louisville & Nashville Railroad.* New York, 1972.

Knight, Jonathan and Latrobe, Benjamin. *Report upon the Locomotive Engines and the Police and Management of Several of the Principal Rail Roads in the Northern and Middle States.* Baltimore, 1838.

Lardner, Dionysus. *Investigation of the Causes of the Explosion of the Locomotive Engine, 'Richmond', near Reading, Pa. on the 2nd Sept. 1844.* N.p., 1844.

——. *Railway Economy.* London, 1850.

Lathrop, Gilbert. *Little Engines and Big Men.* Caldwell, Idaho, 1954.

Layer, Robert. *Earnings of Cotton Mill Operatives, 1825–1914.* Cambridge, Mass., 1952.

Lebergott, Stanley. *Manpower in Economic Growth: The American Record since 1800.* New York, 1964.

——. "Labor Force Employment, 1800–1960." In *Output, Employment, and Productivity in the United State after 1800.* National Bureau of Economic Research, Inc., Studies in Income and Wealth, vol. 30, pp. 117–210. New York, 1965.

Lecht, Leonard. *Experience Under Railway Labor Legislation.* New York, 1955.

Licht, Walter. "The Railwaymen of Philadelphia, 1860–1880: A Socio-Demographic Portrait." Paper read at the convention of the Social Science History Association, November 1979, Cambridge, Massachusetts.

Lightner, David. "Labor on the Illinois Central Railroad, 1852–1900." Ph.D. diss., Cornell Univ., 1969.

Lindsay, Almont. *The Pullman Strike.* Chicago, 1942.

Lindsay, Samuel McCune. "Report on Railway Labor in the United States." In United States Industrial Commission, *Reports of the Industrial Commission on Labor Organizations, Labor Disputes, and Arbitration and on Railway Labor,* vol 17. Washington, D.C., 1901.

Link, Arthur. *Woodrow Wilson and the Progressive Era, 1910–1917.* New York, 1954.

Loring, Louis. "Early Railroads in Boston." *Bostonian* 1 (December 1894): 299–309.

Lucas, Walter Arndt. *From the Hills to the Hudson: A History of the Paterson and Hudson River Rail Road.* New York, 1944.

McMurray, Donald. *The Great Burlington Strike of 1888: A Case History in Labor Relations.* Cambridge, Mass., 1956.

Mater, Dan. "The Development and Operation of the Railroad Seniority System." *Journal of Business of the Univ. of Chicago* 13 (October 1940): 387–419.

——. "The Railroad Seniority System: History, Description and Evaluation." Ph.D. diss., Univ. of Chicago, 1942.

Monds, Jean. "Workers' Control and the Historians: A New Economism." *New Left Review,* 97 (May–June 1976): 81–104.

Monroe, Joseph E. *Railroad Men and Wages.* Washington, D.C., 1947.

Montgomery, David. "The Working Class of Pre-Industrial American Cities, 1780–1830." *Labor History* 9 (Winter 1968): 3–22.

——. *Workers' Control in America.* New York, 1979.

Moore, John. *The Story of the Railroad "Y".* New York, 1930.

Morris, Ray. *Railroad Administration.* New York, 1910.

Morris, Stuart. "Stalled Professionalism: The Recruitment of Railway Officials in the United States, 1885–1940." *Business History Review* 47 (Autumn 1973): 317–334.

Mott, Edward. *Between the Ocean and the Lakes: The Story of the Erie.* New York, 1899.

Nelson, Daniel. *Managers and Workers: Origins of the New Factory System in the United States, 1880–1920.* Madison, Wisc., 1975.

New England Association of Railroad Superintendents. *Reports and Other Papers.* Boston, 1850.

Overton, R. C. *The First Ninety Years: An Historical Sketch of the Burlington Railroad, 1850–1940.* Chicago, 1940.

Overton, Richard. *Burlington Route: A History of the Burlington Lines,* New York, 1965.

Pelling, Henry. *American Labor.* Chicago, 1960.

Pinkerton, Allan. *Report of the Trial of Frederick P. Hill, Late Conductor on the Philadelphia & Reading Railroad on a Charge of Embezzling the Funds of that Company in his Capacity as Conductor.* Chicago, 1864.

——. *Tests on Passenger Conductors: Report of the Trial of Jan Van Daniker, on a Charge of Embezzlement in his Capacity as Conductor on the Philadelphia & Erie Railroad.* Philadelphia, 1867.

——. *Tests on Passenger Conductors Made by the National Detective Agency.* Chicago, 1870.

318   BIBLIOGRAPHY

Pollard, Sidney. "Factory Discipline in the Industrial Revolution." *Economic History Review* 16 (December 1963): 254–271.
Prescott, D. C. *Early Day Railroading from Chicago*. Chicago, 1910.
Ray, Clarence. *The Railroad Spotter*. St. Paul, Minn., 1916.
Reed, J. Harvey. *Forty Years a Locomotive Engineer*. Prescott, Washington, 1915.
Reinhardt, Richard, ed. *Workin' on the Railroad: Reminiscences from the Age of Steam*. Palo Alto, Calif., 1970.
Reizenstein, Milton. *The Economic History of the Baltimore and Ohio Railroad, 1827–1853*. New York, 1973.
Reminiscences in the Life of a Locomotive Engineer. Columbus, Ohio, 1861.
"Report of the Committee on Cars to the Directors of the South Carolina Canal & Railroad Company, 1833." *The Railway and Locomotive Historical Society Bulletin*, no. 7 (1924), pp. 7–25.
Richardson, Reed. *The Locomotive Engineer: 1863–1963; A Century of Railway Labor Relations and Work Rules*. Ann Arbor, Mich., 1963.
Riegel, Robert. *The Story of Western Railroads: From 1852 through the Reign of the Giants*. New York, 1926.
Ringwalt, John. *Development of Transportation Systems in the United States*. Philadelphia, 1888.
Ripley, W. Z. "Railway Schedules and Agreements." In U.S. Eight Hour Commission, *Report of the Eight Hour Commission*, app. 6. Washington, D.C., 1918.
Risher, Howard W., Jr. *The Negro in the Railroad Industry*. Philadelphia, 1971.
Robbins, Clyde Edwin. "Railway Conductors: A Study in Organized Labor." *Studies in History, Economics and Public Law* 61 (1914): 1–185.
Rostow, Walt Whitman. *The Stages of Economic Growth*. Cambridge, England, 1960.
Rubin, Julius. "Canal or Railroad? Imitation and Innovation in the Response to the Erie Canal in Philadelphia, Baltimore, and Boston." *Transactions of the American Philosophical Society* 51 (November 1961): 5–106.
Salmons, C. H. *The Burlington Strike*. Aurora, Ill., 1889.
Salsbury, Stephen. *The State, the Investor and the Railroad: The Boston & Albany, 1825–1867*. Cambridge, Mass., 1967.
Salvatore, Nick. "Railroad Workers and the Great Strike of 1877: The

View From A Small Midwest City." *Labor History* 21 (Fall 1980): 522–545.

Schneirov, Richard. "The 1877 Great Upheaval in Chicago: 'Life by Labor or Death by Fight.' " Unpublished paper in author's possession.

Seidman, Joel. *The Brotherhood of Railway Trainmen: The Internal Political Life of a National Union.* New York, 1962.

Shephard, Allen. "Federal Railway Labor Policy, 1913–1926." Ph.D. diss., Univ. of Nebraska, 1971.

Sigmund, Elwin Wilbur. "Federal Laws Concerning Railroad Labor Disputes: A Legislative and Legal History, 1877–1934." Ph.D. diss., Univ. of Illinois at Urbana, 1961.

Sillcox, L. K. *Safety in Early American Railway Operations, 1853–1871.* New York, 1936.

Sipes, William. *Pennsylvania Railroad: Its Origin, Construction, Condition, and Connections.* Philadelphia, 1875.

Smith, J. Victor. *Trial of Oscar T. Caldwell, Late A Conductor on the Chicago and Burlington Railroad Line, for Embezzlement.* Chicago, 1855.

State of New Hampshire, *Hearings in the Matter of Concord Railroad Corporation vs. George Clough and Trustees.* Concord, N.H., 1869.

Stevens, Frank. *The Beginnings of the New York Central: A History.* New York, 1926.

Stevenson, James. "The Brotherhood of Locomotive Engineers and Its Leaders, 1863–1920." Ph.D. diss., Vanderbilt Univ., 1954.

Stott, Clive. "Robert Harris and the Strike of 1877." Master's thesis, Univ. of Western Ontario, 1967.

Stover, John. *The Railroads of the South, 1865–1900: A Study in Finance and Control.* Chapel Hill, N.C., 1955.

———. *American Railroads.* Chicago, 1961.

———. *The Life and Decline of the American Railroad.* New York, 1970.

Stromquist, Shelton. "Community Structure and Industrial Conflict in Nineteenth Century Railroad Towns." Unpublished paper read at the convention of the Organization of American Historians, April 1978, New York, New York.

Stuart, Inglis. "George Althouse." *Railway and Locomotive Historical Society Bulletin,* no. 11 (1926), pp. 11–22.

Taylor, George Rogers. *The Transportation Revolution, 1815–1860.* New York, 1968.

Taylor, George, and Neu, Irene. *The American Railroad Network, 1861–1890.* Cambridge, Mass., 1956.

Temin, Peter. "Labor Scarcity and the Problems of American Industrial

Efficiency." *Journal of Economic History* 26 (September 1966): 277–298.

Thernstrom, Stephen. *Poverty and Progress: Social Mobility in a Nineteenth Century City.* New York, 1971.

——. *The Other Bostonians: Poverty and Progress in the American Metropolis, 1880–1970.* Cambridge, Mass., 1973.

——. "Urbanization, Migration, and Social Mobility in Late Nineteenth-Century America," In *Towards a New Past: Dissenting Essays in American History,* edited by Barton Bernstein, pp. 158–175. New York, 1969.

Thompson, E. P. "Time, Work-Discipline, and Industrial Capitalism." *Past and Present* 38 (December 1967): 56–97.

Turner, Charles. "The Richmond, Fredericksburg and Potomac, 1861–1865." *Civil War History* 7 (September 1961): 255–263.

Turner, Charles W. *Chessie's Road.* Richmond, Va., 1956.

U.S. Department of Commerce, Bureau of the Census. *Historical Statistics of the United States, Colonial Times to 1957.* Washington, D.C., 1960.

U.S. Department of Labor, Bureau of Statistics. *Bulletin No. 64: History of Wages in the United States from Colonial Times to 1928.* Washington, D.C., 1934.

U.S. Eight Hour Commission. *Report of the Eight Hour Commission.* Washington, D.C., 1918.

U.S. Interstate Commerce Commission. *Annual Report,* 1888–1890.

Vaughan, B. C. "Early Recollections." *Railway and Locomotive Historical Society Bulletin,* no. 7 (1924), pp. 67–74.

Wallock, Leonard. "The B & O 'Monopoly' and the Baltimore Crowd: Patterns of Crowd Participation in the Riots of 1877." Master's thesis, Columbia Univ., 1974.

Weber, Max. *The Theory of Social and Economic Organization.* New York, 1966.

Weber, Thomas. *The Northern Railroads in the Civil War, 1861–1865.* New York, 1952.

Whiton, James. *Railroads and Their Management.* Concord, N.H., 1856.

Wilson, William. *History of the Pennsylvania Railroad.* 2 vols. Philadelphia, 1899.

Yungmeyer, D. W. "Selected Items from the Minute Book of the Galena and Chicago Union Railroad Company." *Railway and Locomotive Historical Society Bulletin,* no. 65 (October 1944), pp. 27–42.

INDEX

≡

326

INDEX

Philadelphia, Wilmington & Baltimore Railroad, 22–23, 55
Pinkerton, Allen, 96, 122–123
Pittsburgh, Fort Wayne & Chicago Railroad, 255
Pomeroy, Samuel, 121
Poor, Henry Varnum, 20, 133
promotions. See fringe benefits of railway work: promotions
Pullman, George, 224
Pullman Company, 250, 252
Pullman porters, xvii, 224

railroad strikes. See strikes on the railroads
Railroad Young Men's Christian Association, 239, 262
railroads, American: impact of, 1–3; formation of, 7–8; incorporation of, 6, 8; capitalization of, 9; construction of, 9–10, 60–61; track mileage, 10; revenues, 10; management of, 11–19, 25–30, 74, 76, 116, 151–152, 167, 254–255, 257–264; paternalistic practices in industry, 28–29, 143, 145–147, 201–212; government intervention into, 9, 255–257, 262; law and, 120–122, 197–201, 217, 262; figures for employment in industry, 31–36; employment patterns in industry, 73–78, 164–174, 196, 275–282; labor costs of, 25n; labor supply problems of, 58–73, 114–115; southern railroads, 35, 42, 43, 65–69, 70–73, 88–89, 123–124, 129–130, 224–226; women in the industry, 214–216. See also accidents and railway employees; compensation of railway employees; disciplinary problems on the railroads; fringe benefits of railway work; trade unionism on American railroads; recruitment of railway workers; also individual companies

railroads, English, 20, 118, 120, 121, 129, 271
railroads, European, general, 147, 207, 212. See also railroads, English; railroads, French
railroads, French, 147
Railway Labor Act of 1926, 256
railwaymen, American: numbers of, 31–36; recruitment of, 36–73; age profile of, 216–218, 220; ethnic profile of, 221–225, 295, 297–300; social backgrounds of, 157–158, 221–225; education and training of, 45, 46n, 157, 219–220, 225; literacy rates of, 154, 225; health of, 46; in old age, 145, 212–213, 220–221, 263; hours of work of, 174–180; employment patterns of, 164–174; marital status of, 154, 157–158, 172, 226; family lives of, 226–228; residential patterns and lives of, 87–88, 142–145, 228–230, 301–305; personal behavior of, 84–89, 100–103, 225–239; social lives of, 232–239; community lives of, 230; community support for, 253–354; political activity of, 230–231; geographical mobility of, 58–59, 76–77, 144, 168–169; young railwaymen, 217–221; southern railwaymen, 65–69, 129–130, 224–226; black railwaymen, 21, 42, 67–69, 71, 88–89, 201, 215, 223–225; Irish railwaymen, 148, 222–223; Civil War service, 69–73, 145, 173. See also accidents and railway employees; apprenticeship programs in railway industry; compensation of railway employees; disciplinary problems on the railroads; fringe benefits of railway work; seniority; trade unionism on American railroads; also individual railroad occupations
railwaymen, English, 129

Library of Congress Cataloging in Publication Data

Licht, Walter, 1946-
Working for the railroad.
Bibliography: p.
Includes index.
1. Railroads—United States—Employees—History. 2. Railroads—
United States—Personnel management—History. I. Title.
HD8039.R12U648   1983   331.7'61385'0973   82-61372
ISBN 0-691-04700-6